Praise for *Programs and Interventions for Maltreated Children and Families at Risk*

"A useful handbook for new and experienced practitioners who work with child welfare clients and for those who refer child welfare clients to therapists. It is simultaneously practical and thought-provoking."

—Sherrill Clark, Ph.D.
Program Evaluation Specialist
California Social Work Education Center
University of California School of Social Welfare

"At long last, a welcome and timely resource is available that identifies effective evidence-based intervention programs for at-risk and abusing and neglecting families. It is well written and organized to inform child welfare practitioners, therapists, and mental health professionals about prevention and intervention programs specific to problems and needs of individuals, families, and communities. This book should become a standard reference and resource for students, agency administrators, and practicing professionals."

—Alberta J. Ellett, Ph.D.
Director & Principal Investigator
Child Welfare Education Program
University of Georgia School of Social Work

"This volume represents an important step in the diffusion of evidence-based practices and programs to child welfare stakeholders. Although child maltreatment has serious deleterious consequences for children, families, and society, the child welfare system has been slow to embrace evidence-based practices. Dr. Rubin is commended for compiling a comprehensive collection, with chapters authored by many leading treatment developers and researchers, of those interventions and programs that have demonstrated effectiveness or are among the most promising in the field."

—Scott Henggeler, Ph.D.
Director, Family Services Research Center
Department of Psychiatry and Behavioral Sciences
Medical University of South Carolina

"Allen Rubin has edited an impressive collection of original chapters authored by experts in the field of child maltreatment into a comprehensive summary of empirically supported interventions. Topics are exceptionally diverse, ranging from directly treating abused children, family work, therapy with children exposed to parental domestic violence and substance abuse, and parent training programs. All the structured programs with high levels of empirical support are included, making this an invaluable resource for all providers of services in the area of child maltreatment. This would also make an excellent primary textbook for courses focused on child maltreatment."

—Bruce A. Thyer, Ph.D., LCSW, BCBA
Editor, *Research on Social Work Practice*
College of Social Work
Florida State University

Programs and Interventions for Maltreated Children and Families at Risk

Clinician's Guide to Evidence-Based Practice Series

Treatment of Traumatized Adults and Children
Allen Rubin and David W. Springer, Editors

Substance Abuse Treatment for Youth and Adults
David W. Springer and Allen Rubin, Editors

Psychosocial Treatment of Schizophrenia
Allen Rubin, David W. Springer, and Kathi Trawver, Editors

Treatment of Depression in Adolescents and Adults
David W. Springer, Allen Rubin, and Christopher G. Beevers, Editors

Programs and Interventions for Maltreated Children and Families at Risk
Allen Rubin, Editor

The Clinician's Guide to
Evidence-Based Practice Series

Programs and Interventions for Maltreated Children and Families at Risk

ALLEN RUBIN, EDITOR

WILEY

John Wiley & Sons, Inc.

Library of Congress Cataloging-in-Publication Data:

Programs and interventions for maltreated children and families at risk/Allen Rubin, editor.
      p.; cm.—(Clinician's guide to evidence-based practice series)
  Includes bibliographical references and indexes.
  ISBN 978-0-470-89063-9 (pbk.: alk. Paper); 978-1-118-12280-8 (eMobi); 978-1-118-12278-5 (ePub); 978-1-118-121504 (ePDF)
  1. Child abuse—Prevention. 2. Child health services. 3. Child welfare. 4. Children—Health risk assessment. I. Rubin, Allen.
II. Series: Clinician's guide to evidence-based practice series.
  [DNLM: 1. Child Abuse—prevention & control. 2. Child Health Services. 3. Child Welfare. 4. Risk Factors. WA 325]
  RC569.5.C55P76 2012
  362.76—dc23   2011012869

Printed in the United States of America

10 9 8 7 6 5 4 3 2 1

To Chris, who is my tennis coach, best friend, and beloved wife.

Contents

Series Introduction

One of the most daunting challenges to the evidence-based practice (EBP) movement is the fact that busy clinicians who learn of evidence-based interventions are often unable to implement them because they lack expertise in the intervention and lack the time and resources to obtain the needed expertise. This is the fifth in a series of edited volumes that attempt to alleviate that problem and thus make learning how to provide evidence-based interventions more feasible for such clinicians.

Each volume will be a how-to guide for practitioners—not a research-focused review. Each will contain chapters detailing how to provide interventions whose effectiveness is being supported by the best scientific evidence. Instead of emphasizing the research support in the chapters, that support will be summarized in an Appendix. Each chapter will focus on helping practitioners learn how to begin providing an evidence-based intervention that they are being urged by managed care companies (and others) to provide, but with which they may be inexperienced. The chapters will also identify resources for gaining more advanced expertise in the interventions.

We believe that this series will be unique in its focus on the needs of practitioners and in making empirically supported interventions more feasible for them to learn about and provide. We hope that you will agree and that you will find this volume and this series to be of value in guiding your practice and in maximizing your effectiveness as an evidence-based practitioner.

Allen Rubin, Ph.D.
David W. Springer, Ph.D.

Preface

Allen Rubin

Social workers and other human service practitioners are under increasing pressure to provide programs and services that are evidence-based. This pressure is occurring across all fields of practice, and the field of child welfare certainly is no exception. Nor should it be. Child maltreatment is a heartbreaking problem, and practitioners should not need the pressure of third-party payers to spur them to seek to provide the most effective services possible. Compassion for the current and future victims of child maltreatment should be motivation enough. Moreover, seeking to provide the most effective services to clients is a hallmark of professional ethics across all of the helping professions.

It is understandable, however, that some practitioners resent the pressure for evidence-based practice (EBP), in that they misperceive it as demanding that they mechanistically implement interventions that have been given a "seal of approval" by some funding body or prestigious panel without regard to their professional expertise and knowledge about the idiosyncratic attributes, values, and preferences of their clients. I used the term *misperceive* because in its original conception, and as it has been described by its most expert and avid proponents (Gibbs & Gambrill, 2002; Sackett, Straus, Richardson, Rosenberg, & Haynes, 2000; Thyer, 2004), EBP is a process that gives practitioners flexibility in deciding how to intervene in light of the evidence base for alternative approaches. Thus, if in light of their professional expertise and knowledge about their client they think that an intervention with less empirical support is a better fit for that client than an intervention with more empirical support, the EBP process encourages them to choose the former intervention.

The chapters in this book provide child welfare practitioners, including those working at both the macro level and the micro level, an assortment of empirically supported programs and interventions for preventing child maltreatment, alleviating the damage it inflicts on its victims, and intervening with its perpetrators. Although all of the programs and interventions described in this book have some degree of empirical support, they vary in their degree of such support, as readers can see in Appendix A, which summarizes the best research providing the empirical support for the programs and interventions covered in each chapter. Readers can decide whether to implement any particular program or intervention in light of its degree of empirical support as well as other factors, such as whether the program or intervention will be feasible for them to implement and whether it is a good fit for their client or practice context.

The programs and interventions described in this book are divided into eight parts. In the first part, I provide an overview of child welfare services and elaborate on the issue of empirical support. Part II contains three chapters describing programs for treating parents, as well as their children, who have been referred for child maltreatment to Child Protective Services (CPS) systems. Part III contains four chapters that describe interventions for alleviating the impact of maltreatment on children—interventions that treat the parents as well as the children in families that may or may not be in a CPS system. Part IV also deals with alleviating the impact of maltreatment on children that may or may not be in the CPS system, but its two chapters describe interventions that focus primarily on processing the traumatic events. Part V contains two chapters that describe interventions for parents or children with intimate partner violence involvement. Part VI describes two interventions for treating substance-abusing parents. Part VII contains five chapters that describe additional programs for CPS or other parents at high-risk for child maltreatment. Part VIII departs from the preceding sections by describing an evidence-based public health approach for preventing child maltreatment.

I hope you will find this book to be useful. I would appreciate any feedback you can provide as to the ways it has been helpful to you or any suggestions you might have for improving it. You can email your feedback to me at arubin@mail.utexas.edu.

References

Gibbs, L., & Gambrill, E. (2002). Evidence-based practice: Counterarguments to objections. *Research on Social Work Practice, 12*(3), 452–476.

Sackett, D. L., Straus, S. E., Richardson, W. S., Rosenberg, W.M.C., & Haynes, R. B. (2000). *Evidence-based medicine: How to practice and teach EBM* (2nd ed.). New York, NY: Churchill Livingstone.

Thyer, B. A. (2004). What is evidence-based practice? *Brief Treatment and Crisis Intervention, 4*(2), 167–176.

Acknowledgements

Special thanks go to four Wiley staff members who helped make this volume possible. In alphabetical order they are: Peggy Alexander, vice president and publisher; Rachel Livsey; senior editor; Kim Nir, senior production editor; and Amanda Orenstein, editorial assistant. Thanks also go to this volume's chapter authors for their fine work and timely submissions.

About the Editor

Allen Rubin, PhD, is the Bert Kruger Smith Centennial Professor in the School of Social Work at The University of Texas at Austin, where he has been a faculty member since 1979. While there, he worked as a therapist in a child guidance center and he developed and taught a course on the assessment and treatment of traumatized populations. Earlier in his career he worked in a community mental health program providing services to adolescents and their families. He is internationally known for his many publications pertaining to research and evidence-based practice. In 1997 he was a co-recipient of the Society for Social Work and Research Award for Outstanding Examples of Published Research for a study on the treatment of male batterers and their spouses. His most recent studies have been on the effectiveness of EMDR and on practitioners' views of evidence-based practice. Among his 12 books, his most recent is *Practitioner's Guide to Using Research for Evidence-Based Practice.* He has served as a consulting editor for seven professional journals. He was a founding member of the Society for Social Work and Research and served as its president from 1998 to 2000. In 1993 he received the University of Pittsburgh, School of Social Work's Distinguished Alumnus Award. In 2007 he received the Council on Social Work Education's Significant Lifetime Achievement in Social Work Education Award. In 2010 he was inducted as a Fellow in the American Academy of Social Work and Social Welfare.

About the Contributors

Robbie Adler-Tapia, PhD, has worked as a psychologist, educator, researcher, and writer for 25 years regarding the treatment of trauma in young children and their families. She has extensive experience in child welfare, in the forensic arena, and as a mental health consultant for the National Fallen Firefighters' Foundation. Dr. Adler-Tapia is co-author of *EMDR and the Art of Psychotherapy With Children*, has presented internationally on EMDR including using EMDR for attachment and dissociation, and has taught graduate level course work. Her volunteer work includes promoting EMDR HAPKIDS, while working internationally to train therapists working with children orphaned by AIDS.

Rachel E. Baden, MA, is a doctoral student in clinical psychology at the University of Alabama. She has worked as an interventionist for the Coping Power program, in which she has delivered an empirically supported, cognitive behavioral intervention to youth at risk for aggression. She has special interests in the transmission of conflict from the marital relationship to the parent-child relationship, the mechanisms that might explain this transmission of conflict, and how family systems variables influence children's behavioral outcomes.

Stephen J. Bavolek, PhD, is the president of Family Development Resources, Inc. and the executive director of the Family Nurturing Centers, International. He is also the principal author of the Nurturing Parenting Programs and the Adult Adolescent Parenting Inventory. During the past 40 years, Dr. Bavolek has conducted hundreds of workshops and won numerous international, national, state, and local awards for his work in the prevention and treatment of child abuse and neglect.

Charlotte L. Booth, MSW, is the executive director of the Institute for Family Development. Along with two colleagues, Charlotte founded the institute in 1982 to form a base for the development, evaluation, and dissemination of in-home service models for high-risk families. She is a founding board member of the National Family Preservation Network. She is co-author of *Keeping Families Together: The Homebuilders Model*, and co-editor of *Reaching High Risk Families: Intensive Family Preservation in Human Services*.

Phyllis B. Booth, MA, is clinical director emeritus of the Theraplay Institute in Chicago. She collaborated with Ann Jernberg in developing the Theraplay method for helping children and families with attachment and relationship problems. She is the primary author of the third edition of *Theraplay: Helping Parents and Children Build Better Relationships Through Attachment-Based Play*, Jossey-Bass, 2010. She has conducted workshops and training in the Theraplay method throughout the United States, Canada, England, Denmark, Finland, Sweden, and South Korea.

Caroline L. Boxmeyer, PhD, is a research scientist in the Center for the Prevention of Youth Behavior Problems and the Department of Psychology at the University of Alabama. She studies prevention and early intervention of children's disruptive behavior problems and implementation and dissemination of evidence-based programs. Dr. Boxmeyer is an expert trainer in the Coping Power program, a cognitive behavioral intervention for at-risk aggressive children and their parents.

Rhea M. Chase, PhD, is a clinical associate faculty member in Psychiatry & Behavioral Sciences at Duke University Medical Center. She has extensive experience in the implementation of parent-child interaction therapy (PCIT) and is a master trainer endorsed by PCIT International. She currently serves as lead clinical faculty for *PCIT of the Carolinas*, the nation's first Learning Collaborative focused on the spread of PCIT. Her research interests are in effective psychosocial treatments for children and the translation of evidence-based practices to community settings. She has published numerous articles and chapters related to the treatment of child disruptive behavior and anxiety disorders.

Miriam Hernandez Dimmler, PhD, is a licensed clinical psychologist at the Child Trauma Research Program (CTRP) at the University of California, San Francisco. She coordinates and evaluates a partnership between CTRP and Tipping Point Community (TPC) as part of the TPC mental health initiative. The overarching goal of this initiative is to increase access to evidence-based interventions to low-income families at community-based agencies while building capacity in the area of mental health among the staff within these organizations.

Anna Edwards-Guara, PhD, is clinical assistant professor and associate director at the National SafeCare® Training and Research Center at Georgia State University. Her clinical and research interests center on prevention of and intervention for child maltreatment, including the dissemination and implementation of evidence-based parenting programs. She has published multiple articles related to the implementation of evidence-based parenting programs and prevention of child maltreatment and its negative effects on children. She currently participates in a number of ongoing grant activities and coordinates efforts with partners around the United States to implement the evidence-based SafeCare parenting program.

Sheila Eyberg, PhD, is Distinguished Professor of Clinical and Health Psychology at the University of Florida. She developed Parent-Child Interaction Therapy (PCIT) and its related assessment instruments, the Dyadic Parent-Child Interaction Coding System, Eyberg Child Behavior Inventory, and Therapy Attitude Inventory, and has published over 150 related research articles and papers. She is past president of three American Psychological Association divisions and was recipient of APA's Distinguished Contributions to Education and Training Award in 2007.

Rena Gold, MSW, is the vice president of Implementations, a consultant at TFC Consultants Inc., and has 16 years of experience working with children and families in child welfare, mental health, and juvenile justice. She currently provides administrative support to Multidimensional Treatment Foster Care (MTFC) implementation agencies, supervises MTFC consultants, and is the clinical consultant for a number of developing MTFC programs. Prior to her current positions she worked as a clinician in MTFC for seven years and a manager for two years at OSLC Community programs. She has experience in each clinical role in MTFC and has developed numerous manuals and training programs in the model.

Donald A. Gordon, PhD, is currently employed by Family Works Inc. as its president, and is executive director of the Center for Divorce Education. He is an emeritus professor of psychology from Ohio University where he was employed for 23 years training doctoral students in family interventions and conducting research evaluating family and parenting interventions that he refined or developed. The programs Dr. Gordon refined were Functional Family Therapy, and he developed the Children in the Middle program (with Dr. Jack Arbuthnot) and the Parenting Wisely interactive CD-ROM parent-training program.

Therese Grant, PhD, is associate professor of psychiatry and behavioral sciences and director of the Fetal Alcohol and Drug Unit at the University of Washington School of Medicine. She is the Ann Streissguth Endowed Professor in Fetal Alcohol Spectrum Disorders and directs the Parent-Child Assistance Program (PCAP), a multisite, evidence-based intervention working with mothers who abuse alcohol and drugs during pregnancy. Dr. Grant has published and spoken widely on intervention with high-risk mothers and their children, effects of prenatal alcohol/drug exposure, and fetal alcohol spectrum disorders.

Cynthia V. Healey, PhD, is an early career scientist at the Oregon Social Learning Center where she is collaborating with the Stress Neurobiology and Prevention lab to develop, implement, and disseminate evidence-based interventions for high-risk children and their caregivers. She has worked as a clinician and trainer in the Multidimensional Treatment Foster Care programs for 10 years. Her current work is focused on the development of self-regulation and stress reactivity in early childhood, attention and its role in development, mechanisms of resilience, parenting practices for caregivers of infants and children with intensive needs, and clinical applications of mindfulness practices.

Rhenda Hotard Hodnett, PhD, is the program director of prevention and child protection services for Louisiana's Department of Children and Family Services. Over the past 22 years she has worked in all program areas of the state child welfare agency. She is also an adjunct faculty member of the Louisiana State University School of Social Work where she teaches the child welfare courses required of master-level IV-E stipend students, among others.

Melinda Hohman, PhD, is professor at the School of Social Work, San Diego State University, San Diego. Dr. Hohman teaches courses in substance abuse treatment, research, motivational interviewing (MI), and social work practice. Dr. Hohman's research interests include substance abuse assessment and treatment services and the overlap of substance abuse treatment and child welfare services. She has been a trainer in motivational interviewing since 1999, training community social workers, child welfare workers, probation officers, and addiction counselors across Southern California. She is the author of the upcoming book, *Motivational Interviewing in Social Work Practice.*

Shannon E. Hourigan, MS, is a clinical psychology doctoral student at Virginia Commonwealth University (VCU). Shannon is a chief therapist at VCU's Anxiety Clinic where she supervises other students in the delivery of cognitive behavioral treatments for anxiety. Her research interests include dissemination and implementation of evidence-based treatments in community and pediatric medical settings.

Bill James, LCSW, is a protective services supervisor for the County of San Diego and has worked in child welfare since 1993. Since 2001, his focus has been on foster youth with mental health challenges and their families. He started working to integrate motivational interviewing into child welfare practice in 2006.

Ernest N. Jouriles, PhD, is professor and chair of the Department of Psychology at Southern Methodist University in Dallas, Texas, and co-director of the SMU Family Research Center. He also serves as an associate editor for the *Journal of Family Psychology.* His research focuses on family violence and child functioning, and together with Renee McDonald has conducted pioneering research on interventions for children in families characterized by frequent and severe intimate partner violence. More recently, he has begun a research program on violence in adolescent romantic relationships.

Philip C. Kendall, PhD, ABPP, distinguished university professor and Laura H. Carnell Professor of Psychology at Temple University, has more than 450 publications. His treatment programs have been translated into dozens of languages, and he has had more than 25 years of grant support. Dr. Kendall was a fellow at the Center for Advanced Study in the Behavioral Sciences and recipient of the Research Recognition award from the Anxiety Disorders Association of America. He won a Great Teacher Award and an award for his Outstanding Contribution by an Individual for Educational/Training Activities.

Shelley E. Leavitt, PhD, is associate director of the Institute for Family Development (IFD), where she directs IFD's Training and Dissemination Division and in-home family-counseling programs throughout Washington State. Prior to joining IFD, she designed and evaluated training and dissemination materials for children and families at Father Flanagan's Boys Home (Boys Town, Nebraska). She is the author of *Active Parenting* and coauthor of *Helping Kids Make Friends*, and numerous articles on intensive family-preservation services and parenting. She has provided training and consultation on developing, managing, and evaluating programs for children, youth, and families throughout the United States and in Australia, Belgium, Canada, Lithuania, the Netherlands, Portugal, Romania, Taiwan, and the United Kingdom.

Dafna Lender, LCSW, is the training director at the Theraplay Institute and has worked in the field of children's mental health for 16 years. Dafna is a certified theraplay therapist, supervisor, and trainer. She also is a certified Dyadic Developmental Psychotherapist®. In her previous professional roles, Dafna worked in a range of settings in the child welfare system. She co-authored two chapters, working with traumatized children and working with adoptive/foster children, in the third edition of *Theraplay: Helping Children and Parents Build Better Relationships Through Attachment-Based Play*. She also wrote "Therapeutic Use of Self in Dyadic Developmental Psychotherapy" in *Creating Capacity for Attachment*.

Ericka Lewis, MSW, is a senior training specialist for National SafeCare Training and Research Center at Georgia State University.

Alicia F. Lieberman, PhD, is Irving B. Harris Endowed Chair of Infant Mental Health, professor and vice chair for academic affairs at the University of California, San Francisco (UCSF) Department of Psychiatry, and director of the Child Trauma Research Program. She is the developer of Child-Parent Psychotherapy, an evidence-based treatment for children ages birth to 5 exposed to trauma or multiple adversities. She is the author of numerous books, articles, and chapters about infancy and therapeutic interventions in the early years, including *Psychotherapy With Infants and Young Children: Repairing the Effect of Stress and Trauma on Early Attachment*.

Sandra Lindaman, MSW, LCSW, MA, LSLP, is the senior training advisor for the Theraplay Institute in Wilmette, Illinois. She has been with the Theraplay Institute since 1990. She co-authored three chapters in the 2010 third edition of *Theraplay: Helping Parents and Children Build Better Relationships Through Attachment-Based Play*. Sandra's primary responsibility is the training and supervision of mental health professionals in the Theraplay model internationally.

John E. Lochman, PhD, ABPP, is professor and Doddridge Saxon Chairholder in Clinical Psychology, directs the Center for Prevention of Youth Behavior Problems, and has received the Blackmon-Moody Outstanding Professor and Burnum Distinguished Faculty awards at the University of Alabama. He received the International Collaborative Prevention award from the Society for Prevention Research in 2009, and will receive the 2011 Distinguished Career award from Division 53 of the American Psychological Association. He was awarded an honorary doctorate by the University of Utrecht for his prevention research and has more than 290 publications on risk factors and intervention research with aggressive children.

John R. Lutzker, PhD, is director of the Center for Healthy Development and professor of public health at Georgia State University. He has published 147 professional articles and chapters, six books, and has made 410 professional presentations, nationally and internationally. He is a fellow in five divisions of the American Psychological Association. He received the Outstanding Research Career award from the American Professional Society on the Abuse of Children. He is on the editorial boards of seven professional journals. His media appearances include *Morning Edition* of National Public Radio and *Good Morning America.* He served as a consultant for *60 Minutes.*

Renee McDonald, PhD, is an associate professor in the Department of Psychology at Southern Methodist University, where she is also co-founder and co-director of SMU's Family Research Center. She has spearheaded efforts to document the prevalence of children's exposure to intimate partner violence, to understand short- and long-term outcomes of violence exposure, and to develop and evaluate treatments for children exposed to violence. Her research has been funded by NIMH, NIJ, NIAA, the CDC, and the DOJ.

Jessica A. Minney, BA, is a graduate student in clinical child psychology at the University of Alabama and serves as an interventionist for the Coping Power program.

Laura Minze, MA, MSEd, is a doctoral candidate in clinical psychology at Southern Methodist University. Her research interests include understanding the consequences of exposure to intimate partner violence to young children as well as the development and evaluation of interventions for young children in violent families. She has served as a therapist and clinical supervisor for clinicians delivering project support, an in-home parenting intervention for children exposed to intimate partner violence, and as director of children's outreach services for an agency serving families affected by domestic violence.

Larissa N. Niec, PhD, is a Professor of Clinical Psychology and the Director of the Parent-Child Interaction Therapy Clinic and Research Center at Central Michigan University. She is a Master Trainer of PCIT, disseminating the intervention nationally and internationally, and also serves on the Board of Directors of PCIT International. She has numerous publications in the areas of child maltreatment and childhood conduct problems. She is co-editor of the book *Play in Clinical Practice: Evidence-based Approaches.*

Thomas W. Phelan, PhD, registered clinical psychologist, has worked with children, adults, and families for more than 30 years. He is a member of the American Psychological Association and the Illinois Psychological Association. He has authored numerous books, DVDs, and audios and maintains an active schedule of international lectures. His articles appear in numerous regional and national publications. He is a frequent guest on radio and television. He has also served on the boards of directors for national organizations for the parents of children with ADD. He was inducted into the CHADD Hall of Fame in 1997.

Nicole P. Powell, PhD, MPH, is a research psychologist at the Center for the Prevention of Youth Behavior Problems at the University of Alabama. She also serves as a consulting psychologist for the Brewer-Porch Children's Center and as an adjunct faculty member in the University of Alabama's Department of Psychology.

Ronald J. Prinz, PhD, ABPP, is a Carolina Distinguished Professor and the director of the Parenting and Family Research Center at the University of South Carolina. He serves as editor (with T. Ollendick) of the journal *Clinical Child and Family Psychology Review* and also directs the USC Research Consortium on Children and Families. He is an honorary professor at the University of Queensland. Prinz conducts parenting and family research on population-based prevention of child maltreatment and children's mental health problems. He also co-directs an NIH-sponsored research-training program interfacing biomedical and behavioral dimensions of prevention science.

Robert E. Pushak, MTS, is a child and youth mental health clinician who specializes in treating children and their families with disruptive disorders. He developed the group parent–training programs for the young child, adolescent, and foster parent/residential versions of the Parenting Wisely program. He received the British Columbia 2006–2007 Premiers' Innovation and Special Achievement Award for achieving a fundamental shift in the way business is conducted that produces substantial benefits for civil servants and society.

M. Jamila Reid, PhD, is the co-director of the parenting clinic at the University of Washington, where she has worked for the past 13 years. Dr. Reid's research and clinical interests are in preventing and early treatment of children's conduct disorders. She also serves as a trainer and therapist for the Incredible Years programs, working directly with parents, teachers, and children and training other professionals to deliver these interventions.

Matthew R. Sanders, PhD, is a professor of clinical psychology and director of the Parenting and Family Support Centre at the University of Queensland. He is also a visiting professor at Oxford University, Manchester University, University of South Carolina, Glasgow Caledonian University, and the University of Auckland. As the founder of the Triple P-Positive Parenting program, Professor Sanders is considered a world leader in the development, implementation, evaluation, and dissemination of population-based approaches to parenting and family interventions. Triple P is currently in use across 22 countries worldwide, translated into 16 languages, with 58,000 practitioners having delivered the intervention to more than 7 million children.

Cindy M. Schaeffer, PhD, is an associate professor at the Family Services Research Center in the Department of Psychiatry and Behavioral Sciences of the Medical University of South Carolina. She is a co-developer of Multisystemic Therapy—Building Stronger Families, an intensive family-based intervention for families involved in the child protective service system due to co-occurring problems of child maltreatment and parental substance abuse. She is an author of numerous journal articles and a book on behavioral treatment for adult substance abuse. Currently she is developing an ecologically based peer intervention for juvenile offending.

Shannon Self-Brown, PhD, is a clinical psychologist who has served on projects testing technology-based parenting programs targeting child maltreatment prevention. She is currently the associate director of research for the National SafeCare Training and Research Center at Georgia State University. She has more than 25 peer-reviewed publications focusing on the impact of youth violence and disaster exposure, as well as the evaluation of child maltreatment prevention programs.

Cara A. Settipani, MA, is a graduate student in clinical psychology at Temple University, where she received her MA in psychology in 2010. Cara's research interests involve the role of social and emotional competencies in the development and maintenance of anxiety in youth, and implications for personalizing anxiety treatment for youth with interpersonal difficulties. Her clinical interests include the assessment and treatment of children and adolescents with anxiety disorders using cognitive-behavioral therapy.

Cheri Shapiro, PhD, is a research associate professor with the Department of Psychology and a scientist with the Parenting and Family Research Center at the University of South Carolina. She is a licensed clinical psychologist with more than 20 years of experience in practice, administrative, and research settings. Her research focuses on implementing evidence-based parenting interventions for preventing behavioral problems and child maltreatment. She served as project director of the federally funded U.S. Triple P Population Trial and is principal investigator of the Family Networks Project, a federally funded research and demonstration project examining strategies for strengthening families and preventing child maltreatment.

Michael A. Southam-Gerow, PhD, is an associate professor of psychology and pediatrics at Virginia Commonwealth University (VCU) and is the co-director of the Anxiety Clinic at VCU. Dr. Southam-Gerow's research focuses on identifying factors associated with successful implementation and dissemination of evidence-based treatments for children and adolescents. He also studies measurement of treatment integrity and emotion regulation.

Sara L. Stromeyer, MA, is a doctoral student in clinical child psychology at the University of Alabama. She has worked as an interventionist for the Coping Power program, in which she has delivered an empirically supported, cognitive behavioral intervention to youth at risk for aggression. She is particularly interested in the contextual factors that relate to children's aggression and disruptive behavior, especially the transactional role of maternal depression, the influence of parenting practices, and children's distorted perceptions of their peer relationships.

Cynthia Cupit Swenson, PhD, is professor and associate director at the Family Services Research Center in the Department of Psychiatry and Behavioral Sciences of the Medical University of South Carolina. She is developer of the Multisystemic Therapy for Child Abuse and Neglect. She has conducted research in the child abuse and neglect area nationally and internationally for 20 years. In addition, Dr. Swenson has authored many journal articles and recent books on treatment for physical abuse, youth substance abuse, and treating community violence and troubled neighborhoods. She is also involved in community development and health projects in Ghana, West Africa.

Patricia Van Horn, JD, PhD, is an associate clinical professor of psychiatry at the University of California, San Francisco. She is associate director of the UCSF Child Trauma Research Program and director of the San Francisco General Hospital Division of Infant, Child, and Adolescent Psychiatry. She is co-author of the books *Losing a Parent to Death in the Early Years: Guidelines for the Treatment of Traumatic Bereavement in Infancy and Early Childhood*; *Don't Hit My Mommy!: A Manual of Child-Parent Psychotherapy With Young Witnesses of Family Violence*; and *Psychotherapy With Infants and Young Children: Repairing the Effects of Stress and Trauma on Early Attachment*.

Lisa Gutiérrez Wang, PhD, is a licensed psychologist and postdoctoral fellow under the mentorship of Dr. Alicia F. Lieberman at the Child Trauma Research Program (CTRP) at the University of California, San Francisco (UCSF). Her current research focuses on evaluating the dissemination and implementation of Child-Parent Psychotherapy (CPP) in community-based agencies and clinics, and examining how family factors and exposure to cumulative traumas impact child functioning in families with a history of intimate partner violence.

Carolyn Webster-Stratton, PhD, is professor, licensed clinical psychologist, and director of the Parenting Clinic at the University of Washington. She is the developer of the Incredible Years Parents, Teachers and Children's programs and has done numerous randomized trials evaluating these prevention and treatment programs with high-risk populations and for children with conduct problems and ADHD. She is the author of several books for children, parents, and teachers about promoting children's social, emotional, and academic competence.

Daniel J. Whitaker, PhD, worked as a research scientist and team leader at the Centers for Disease Control and Prevention from 1997 to 2007. In 2008, he became a professor of public health at Georgia State University and the director of the National SafeCare Training and Research Center. Whitaker's research focuses on child maltreatment prevention and intimate partner violence. He has published more than 50 peer-reviewed articles and two books.

Introduction

The chapter in this section provides an overview of child welfare services and discusses the implications of the varying levels of empirical support for the programs and interventions to be described in the remaining sections of this book.

CHAPTER 1

Introduction

Overview of Child Welfare Services and Empirical Support

Allen Rubin

Introduction

Despite historical progress in protecting the rights of children and the evolution of various public and private agencies dedicated to protecting children from child abuse and neglect, child maltreatment remains a daunting and heartbreaking social problem in even the most advanced societies today (Crosson-Tower, 2010; McGowan, 2005). Recent governmental data, for example, indicate that in the United States in just one year (2008) as many as 772,000 children—about 1.3% of the population of children—were substantiated victims of child maltreatment. Approximately 72% of them experienced neglect, 16% were physically abused, 9% were sexually abused, and 7% were abused psychologically/emotionally. Nearly 56% of them were younger than 8 years old. During that year about 1,740 child fatalities were connected to abuse (U.S. Department of Health and Human Services, 2010).

Of course, not all incidents of child maltreatment are reported or substantiated. The Fourth National Incidence Study of Child Abuse and Neglect (NIS-4), for example, suggested that the actual prevalence rate of child maltreatment is much higher than the substantiated rate and that one in seven youths probably experience maltreatment at some point during childhood or adolescence (Finkelhor, Ormrod, Turner, & Hamby, 2005). Although the rates of child physical abuse and sexual abuse have decreased since the 1990s, the rate of neglect has remained about the same, accounting for 71% of the substantiated child maltreatment cases in 2008 (U.S. Department of Health and Human Services, 2010).

The act of child maltreatment is appalling in itself, but what makes matters worse is its probable long-term consequences, which can include various psychological disorders and cognitive limitations (Springer, Sheridan, Kuo, & Carnes, 2003); physical injuries, including impaired brain development (Glaser, 2000); and an increased likelihood of such difficulties as delinquency, academic problems, substance abuse, teen pregnancy, and so on (Silverman, Reinherz, & Giaconia, 1996). For example, more than 40% of children in the child welfare system have been diagnosed with oppositional defiant disorder, conduct disorder, developmental delays, or attention-deficit/hyperactivity disorder (Garland et al., 2001; National Survey of Child and Adolescent Well-Being [NSCAW] Research Group, 2002).

Child maltreatment not only takes a toll on emotional, psychological, physical, and psychosocial functioning; it also takes a toll financially. When combining the direct and indirect costs of child maltreatment, child abuse and neglect costs an estimated $103.8 billion annually. Hospitalization, mental health care for the victims, child welfare services, and law enforcement constitute the direct costs and account for approximately $33.1 billion. Special education, juvenile delinquency, mental health and health care, adult criminal justice system, and lost productivity to society constitute indirect costs comprising of approximately $70.65 billion (Wang & Holton, 2007).

In light of the serious ways that maltreatment can harm the child's psychosocial well-being, effective interventions for abused or neglected children are needed to ameliorate that damage. At the same time, effective interventions are needed for parents—not only in an effort to prevent child maltreatment, but also in recognition that approximately 90% of children remain living at home after investigations of abuse or neglect and that about half of those who are transferred from their biological home to foster care will be returned to their biological home within 18 months after removal (Wulczn, Barth, Yuan, Jones Harden, & Landsverk, 2005). Parents with substantiated cases of abuse or neglect are much more likely than parents in the general population to have problematic parenting skills, expectations that are unrealistic in light of their child's developmental stage, domestic violence, substance abuse, depression, family instability, and serious mental illness (Crosson-Tower, 2010). In addition to direct service provision, effective public health interventions are needed to disseminate information on positive parenting and to normalize and destigmatize the process of seeking or receiving support for parenting (as discussed by Sanders, Prinz, and Shapiro in Chapter 20 of this volume).

Child Welfare Services

Child welfare programs and interventions are diverse in terms of purpose, aims, philosophy, and setting. The first step in the process of intervening with families reported for child maltreatment is to investigate the degree of harm experienced by the child and determine whether the report is substantiated.

Child Protective Services (CPS) Reports of child maltreatment are investigated by state or county agencies that, although they have varied bureaucratic labels, are generally referred to by the child protective services (CPS) rubric. As discussed by Mallon and Hess (2005), the investigation phase is crucial. It can have life-and-death consequences for the child. It thus must be immediate and thorough and must determine whether the child will be safe if he or she remains living at home. If the abuse is substantiated, the investigation might recommend keeping the child at home, but with the provision of supportive services to the family. Alternatively, it might recommend out-of-home placement of the child. In either case, the CPS agency is responsible for ensuring that the children and families involved in substantiated cases receive a sufficient array of services.

In recent decades, the role of CPS has expanded to provide or contract for services for families and children and to make "reasonable efforts" to prevent out-of-home placements and keep families together or reunite them (Crosson-Tower, 2010). However, due in large part to insufficient funding, practitioners in CPS agencies typically have high levels of caseloads and experience role-conflict and other stresses related to bureaucratic rules and regulations and to discrepancies between those regulations and the practitioner's concern with the needs of clients. Consequently, burnout among these practitioners is common, and they therefore tend to have high turnover rates and limited ability to be effective in providing services for children and their families (Crosson-Tower, 2010; DePanfilis & Zlotnik, 2008; A. Ellett, C. Ellett, & Rugutt, 2003).

The number of in-home and out-of-home programs and interventions to which CPS can refer children and their families is extensive. Some have had their effectiveness supported by multiple replications of well-controlled, rigorous outcome studies and are therefore referred to by some as *evidence-based*. Others have had enough empirical support to be considered promising, but not enough yet to earn the label of *evidence-based* by groups that bestow such a "seal-of-approval." Still others have not yet had any scientifically credible degree of empirical support.

Although this book does not include chapters on the CPS investigation process, readers are reminded that that process is crucial and can have life-and-death consequences. To learn more about assessing risk in the investigation process, readers are referred to books by Crosson-Tower (2010) and Mallon and Hess (2005).

In-Home Services In-home services are provided when the child can remain safely at home provided that the family receives needed assistance to prevent further abuse or neglect and thus prevent the need for an out-of-home placement. These services might be voluntary, but in some cases they are legally mandated. They might include helping the family obtain resources needed to meet the child's (and family's) basic needs for food, clothing, adequate shelter, health care, and so on. Parents might additionally need employment training and help with child care. A critical component of in-home services involves training parents in the skills they will need to adequately care for and protect their children. Not all in-home services are geared to parents who already are involved with the child welfare system. Some are provided to prevent maltreatment among parents who are at high-risk for maltreatment but who have not yet had a substantiated incident of neglect or abuse. Until recently, few of the parent-training programs have had empirical support (Schoenwald & Hoagwood, 2001). Various chapters in this volume describe parent-training programs that have at least some promising empirical support.

Out-of-Home Services When it is legally decided that the child's safety requires removing the child from their home, out-of-home services provide 24-hour care of the child. As required by law, the out-of-home placement should be in the least restrictive setting possible—settings that most resemble the original family setting—such as with relatives. Other out-of-home placements include licensed family foster homes in which the family is not related to the child, therapeutic or medical foster homes in which the licensed foster parent has been trained to meet the child's special needs, short-term emergency shelters while awaiting an appropriate longer-term setting, licensed group homes housing 8 to 12 children, supervised independent living facilities for older adolescents who are near adulthood, and licensed residential treatment centers that provide on-site education as well as health, mental health, and social services (Mallon & Hess, 2005). For most children residing in out-of-home placements an important aspect is *family reunification as a permanency goal* (Mallon & Hess, 2005). This book's Chapter 14 describes the Homebuilders program, which has been empirically supported as effectively speeding the process of reunification. Some families, however, are so severely abusive or neglectful, or unable or unwilling to make the necessary changes to ensure the child's safety, that it is determined that family reunification cannot be achieved. In these cases, the permanency plan involves permanent placement, such as adoption by foster parents. This book's Chapter 3 describes an empirically supported program for treating children in foster care with behavior problems and for training and supporting their foster parents. Other empirically supported programs and interventions for treating maltreated children are described in Parts III and IV of this book.

Empirical Support

The chapters of this book describe programs and interventions that have had enough empirical support to be considered either promising or more conclusively evidence-based. The main distinction between these two categories of empirical support is that the more conclusively evidence-based programs or interventions have been supported by experimental evaluations that randomly assign clients to different treatment conditions, also known as randomized clinical trails (RCTs). The promising programs lack such support, but have been empirically supported by pretest/posttest studies that lack control groups or by quasi-experimental designs that did not employ random assignment to the treatment versus comparison group condition. The research supporting each chapter is summarized in this book's Appendix A.

Some may wonder why I say *more conclusively evidence-based* instead of more simply just saying *evidence-based*. The reason has to do with the scientific method and with the elusiveness of the term *evidence-based*. In science, all knowledge is provisional and subject to refutation. What we all might today deem to be the best evidence for intervening in child welfare might be refuted by new evidence that emerges tomorrow. Calling something *evidence-based* has a ring of finality to it. All of the programs and interventions described in this volume have a reasonable degree of empirical support. We could call them all *evidence-based*, and that would not be entirely incorrect since they all are based on some degree of scientific evidence, but I want to avoid connoting that sense of finality and instead prefer to connote a range of empirical support.

Likewise, readers might also wonder why the programs or interventions with only "promising" empirical support are included in this book. The rationale for their inclusion is based on the meaning of the term *evidence-based practice*. As that term has been defined in the previous volumes in this series, it refers to a *process* in which practitioners choose courses of action based not only on the best evidence, but also by integrating all of the evidence with their practice expertise and knowledge of the idiosyncratic circumstances and attributes of their clientele and practice setting. Sometimes the intervention with the best evidence is not a good fit for a particular client or group of clients. Sometimes a program is just not feasible to implement in a particular setting, perhaps due to costs. Sometimes a practitioner is more skillful providing an intervention with promising empirical support than providing one with a stronger evidence base, and therefore might be more effective when providing the former intervention. Consequently, the best fit might be a program or intervention that has promising evidence, only.

As you read the chapters in this book, it is important to keep in mind the lessons of implementation science. In particular, you should realize the importance of implementation fidelity. No matter how much research evidence might support the effectiveness of a program or intervention, its effectiveness when others implement it depends on the degree of implementation fidelity; that is, the extent to which they implement it in a way that matches the way it was implemented in the research on it. Thus, if you try to implement one of the programs or techniques described in the following chapters without understanding it completely, or without first obtaining the necessary training or developing the requisite skills in it, it will probably be less effective (and perhaps entirely ineffective) than it has been found to be in the existing research on it. This caveat applies not only to those programs or interventions with promising evidence, but also to those supported by the most conclusive evidence. As I alluded to above, you probably will have more success implementing with a high degree of fidelity an intervention or program with promising empirical support than you will have implementing with inadequate fidelity an intervention or program with more conclusive empirical support.

References

Crosson-Tower, C. (2010). *Understanding child abuse and neglect* (8th ed.). Boston, MA: Allyn & Bacon.

DePanfilis, D., & Zlotnik, J. L. (2008). Retention of front-line staff in child welfare: A systematic review of research. *Children and Youth Services Review, 30,* 9, 995–1008.

Ellett, A. J., Ellett, C. D., & Rugutt, J. K. (2003). *A study of personal and organizational factors contributing to employee retention and turnover in child welfare in Georgia: Final project report*. School of Social Work, University of Georgia.

Finkelhor, D., Ormrod, R., Turner, H., & Hamby, S. L. (2005). The victimization of children and youth: A comprehensive, national survey. *Child Maltreatment, 10*(1), 5–25.

Garland, A. F., Hough, R. L., McCabe, K. M., Yeh, M., Wood, P. A., & Aarons, G. A. (2001). Prevalence of psychiatric disorders in youths across five sectors of care. *Journal of the American Academy of Child and Adolescent Psychiatry, 40,* 409–418.

Glaser, D. (2000). Child abuse and neglect and the brain—A review. *The Journal of Child Psychology and Psychiatry, 41*(1), 97–116.

Mallon, G. P., & Hess, P. M. (Eds.). (2005). *Child welfare for the 21st century*. New York, NY: Columbia University Press.

McGowan, B. G. (2005). Historical evolution of child welfare services. In Mallon, G. P., & Hess, P. M. (Eds.), *Child welfare for the 21st century* (pp. 10–46). New York, NY: Columbia University Press.

National Survey of Child and Adolescent Well-Being (NSCAW) Research Group. (2002). Methodological lessons from the national survey of child and adolescent well-being: The first three years of the USA's first national probability study of children and families investigated for abuse and neglect. *Child Youth Services Review, 24*, 513–541.

Schoenwald, S. K., & Hoagwood, K. (2001). Effectiveness, transportability, and dissemination of interventions: What matters when? *Journal of Psychiatric Services, 52*(9), 1190–1197.

Silverman, A. B., Reinherz, H. Z., & Giaconia, R. M. (1996). The long-term sequelae of child and adolescent abuse: A longitudinal community study. *Child Abuse & Neglect, 20*(8), 709–723.

Springer, K., Sheridan, J., Kuo, D., & Carnes, M. (2003). The long-term health outcomes of childhood abuse. *Journal of General Internal Medicine, 18*(10), 864–870.

U.S. Department of Health and Human Services, Administration for Children and Families, Administration on Children, Youth and Families, & Children's Bureau. (2010). *Child maltreatment 2008*. Retrieved November 2010 from Child Welfare Information Gateway website: www.acf.hhs.gov/programs/cb/pubs/cm08/cm08.pdf

Wang, C.-T., & Holton, J. (2007, September). *Total estimated cost of child abuse and neglect in the United States*. Retrieved November 2010 from Prevent Child Abuse America website: www.prevent childabuse.org/about_us/media_releases/pcaa_pew_economic_impact_study_final.pdf

Wulczn, F., Barth, R., Yuan, Y., Jones Harden, B., & Landsverk, J. (2005). Altering the early life course of children in child welfare. In *Beyond common sense: Child welfare, child well-being, and the evidence for policy reform*. New Brunswick, NJ: Aldine Transaction.

II

Programs for Treating Parents and Children Referred to Child Protective Services (CPS)

In Chapter 2, Carolyn Webster-Stratton and M. Jamila Reid describe "The Incredible Years," which consists of two empirically supported programs: a parent program and a therapeutic child treatment group. Using such methods as cognitive restructuring, emotional regulation strategies, behavioral practice, and live modeling methods of learning the program addresses parenting training, family interpersonal and support needs, and children's problems with attachment, emotional regulation, social skills, and cognitive development.

In Chapter 3, Cynthia Cupit Swenson and Cindy M. Schaeffer describe an empirically supported family-based model for treating families referred for child physical abuse or neglect in which child removal is highly likely if needed changes do not occur. The model, called Multisystemic Therapy for Child Abuse and Neglect (MST-CAN), is a team approach that has been adapted from the standard multisystemic therapy model that was originally developed to meet the clinical needs of youth experiencing serious antisocial behavior and their families. The adaptations were developed to meet the needs of families who experience serious clinical issues due to physical abuse and/or neglect. These adaptations include the following: a reduced caseload; the addition of a crisis caseworker; dedicated psychiatrist time; a longer treatment period; and the provision of research-based treatments for family conflict/violence, trauma, and adult substance misuse. Although the emphasis of the model is on treating the parents, children and other pertinent family members are also treated as needed. Swenson and Schaeffer depict MST-CAN as a radical departure from how CPS caseworkers and therapists tend to have separate responsibilities in most communities. In their model the MST-CAN therapist fully shares responsibility for the child's safety with the CPS caseworker, and both explain the nature of their partnership to families at the beginning of treatment. MST-CAN does not accept referrals from families in which there is ongoing intimate partner violence (see Chapter 10, Project Support, for a program designed specifically for mothers of children who have been exposed to intimate partner violence).

In Chapter 4, Rena Gold and Cynthia Heywood describe an empirically supported program for treating children in foster care and their parents. The Multidimensional Treatment Foster Care (MTFC) program has separate components for adolescents, for children between the ages of 7 and 11, and for preschool children. The youths are treated in a family setting, not in a residential setting. Based primarily on social learning theory, the foster parents are key in executing the program and are viewed as integral members of the treatment team, which also includes an individual therapist for the adolescent, skills coaches, a recruiter, a consultant for foster parents (for the preschool component only), and a team leader. The preschool component also includes a therapeutic playgroup designed to increase school readiness.

2

The Incredible Years

Evidence–Based Parenting and Child Programs for Families Involved in the Child Welfare System

Carolyn Webster–Stratton and M. Jamila Reid

The Incredible Years (IY) Parent and Child Series are evidence-based programs relevant for use with maltreating families with young children (C. Webster-Stratton, 2005; C. Webster-Stratton, 2009; C. Webster-Stratton & Reid, 2003; C. Webster-Stratton & Reid, 2010). It is embedded in a comprehensive service plan that addresses parenting training, family interpersonal and support needs, and children's problems with attachment, emotional regulation, social skills and cognitive development.

The IY program has several distinctive aspects. Being a group-based program, it aims to be less costly than individual treatment, to build family-support networks, and to decrease the isolation and sense of alienation commonly found among parents in child welfare. In accordance with modeling and self-efficacy theories of learning, IY makes extensive use of video modeling methods, showing vignettes of families from different cultural and socioeconomic backgrounds with a variety of parenting styles and child temperaments, so that participants will perceive at least some of the models as similar to themselves and will therefore accept the vignettes as relevant.

The program is delivered in a collaborative and interactive discussion format. Families are helped to focus on their personal goals and strengths rather than their deficits, and an emphasis is placed on group members' self-management. We believe that this approach empowers these parents in that it gives back dignity, respect, and self-control to parents who

Author note: Carolyn Webster-Stratton has disclosed a potential financial conflict of interest because she disseminates these treatments and stands to gain from favorable reports. Because of this, she has voluntarily agreed to distance herself from certain critical research activities, including recruitment, consenting, primary data handling, and data analysis. The University of Washington has approved these arrangements. Correspondence concerning this chapter should be addressed to Carolyn Webster-Stratton, Professor, University of Washington, 1411 8th Avenue West, Seattle, WA 98119. Email: cwebsterstratton@comcast.net.

are often seeking help at a time of low self-confidence and intense feelings of guilt and self-blame (C. Webster-Stratton, 1996b). This collaborative approach aims to enhance parent participation, motivation, and attendance. The program's group process and methods focus on cognitive restructuring, emotional regulation strategies, behavioral practice, and live modeling methods of learning rather than didactic lectures. The goals of this approach are to provide a variety of learning methods: visual, verbal, and performance; to be low-cost because of the group format; and easily disseminated because of the extensive videos and manuals.

The IY program is comprised of a parent program and a therapeutic child treatment group. The child treatment group will be described later in this chapter, after we discuss the parent program. The IY Parent Program offers both a basic component (focus on parenting strategies) and an advanced component (focusing on parental mood, coping with stress, and interpersonal problem solving). Because families involved with child welfare services often experience multiple stressors that go beyond parenting issues, it is highly recommended that they are offered both the basic and the advanced programs. (The IY program also serves families that are not involved in the child welfare system, and those families may be less likely to need the advanced program.) In keeping with the purpose of this book, this chapter will pertain to the IY program for child welfare involved families, only. However, to avoid confusion, especially for readers who might be familiar with IY services for families that are not involved in the child welfare system, Table 2.1 is provided to show how the Core IY Program is adapted for the child welfare population.

Table 2.1 Adapting the IY Program for the Child Welfare Population

Core IY Components	IY Adaptations for Child Welfare
Standard Topics and Protocols for each of four Basic Parenting Programs according to age group targeted (2008 versions)	Cover standard topics and protocols; increase focus in key areas: parent-child attachment, emotion and social coaching, parental attributions and positive self-talk, proactive discipline, monitoring, self-care.
Vignette Protocols	Use all core vignettes and add additional vignettes if parents in the group are not mastering material or if baseline knowledge level is low.
Program Dosage (18–20 sessions)	May need more sessions to cover core program if groups take longer to understand and master material.
Key Group Teaching/Learning Methods (behavioral practice, principle building, values exercises, tailoring to meet cultural and developmental issues, home activities)	Increased parent practice and role-plays in sessions, develop scripts for language skills and cognitions, more explicit teaching about developmentally appropriate parenting practices, adapt home activities for families without children in the home, and plan for visitations with children.
Alliance building techniques (collaborative learning, buddy calls, weekly leader support calls, praise to parents, incentives for parents)	All standard alliance building techniques apply to this population; may need increased efforts to engage families (more praise, more incentives, and spending longer to build a trusting relationship between parents and leaders).
Food, transportation, daycare	No adaptations needed, but essential to offer these.
Core model does not offer home visits	Add a minimum of four home visits to coach parent-child interactions using coach home visit manuals.
Core model does not address collaboration with case workers or planning for visitation with children	Train and coordinate with case workers to plan for parent-child visitations. Case workers must understand the core IY topics and parenting strategies to coach families during these visits.
Core model suggests use of IY Advance and Child Programs for children with diagnoses or very high risk families	Use additional IY programs: • Advance Program to teach anger and depression management and problem-solving steps. • Child Social, Emotional and Problem-Solving Skills Small Group Therapy Program (Dinosaur School) offered with parent program.

The Basic Parent Program

The Basic Parent Program has four separate versions, each of which is geared to parents of children in the following different age groups:

- Infants (0–1 year)
- Toddlers (1–3 years)
- Preschoolers (3–5 years)
- School age (6–8 and 9–12 years)

Since the Basic Parenting programs focus on helping parents adapt their parenting practices to the developmental level and temperament of their child, it is recommended that groups are comprised of parents who have children in roughly the same developmental stage/age groups. It is difficult for parents with histories of abuse and neglect to generalize parenting skills and behavior management principles for one age group to another age group.

The baby and young preschool children programs are especially important for the child welfare populations because the rate of maltreatment from birth to 1 year is approximately double the rate for children aged 4 to 7 years. Furthermore, more than three-quarters of all children who die due to abuse and neglect are younger than 4 years (U.S. Department of Health and Social Services Administration on Children Youth and Families, 2006). Ideally, high-risk parents would be offered the baby program as soon as their babies are born, followed by the toddler, preschool, and school age program as their children reach each age group. Disadvantaged families with histories of child welfare system involvement will need ongoing parent support and scaffolding for each stage of their children's developmental transition in order to be able to break the cycle of intergenerational transmission of abuse and neglect. A chronic condition is better treated with a repeated and ongoing dose of multifaceted intervention and is more likely to have sustainable outcomes and prevent future occurrence than a single dose model approach.

The core content components and topic objectives of the basic program for the child welfare population fall within two broad categories: (1) strengthening parent-child relationships and bonding; and (2) promoting predictable routines, effective limit setting, nonpunitive discipline, and problem solving. All these parenting topics are delivered within a framework that seeks to build parent competencies and increase their social support systems. The Basic program's specific aims within each of these two categories are listed in Figure 2.1.

Adaptations for Parents Referred by Child Welfare

The following section describes the rationale for providing enhanced parent focus and experiential practice for particular basic content areas as well as providing ongoing parent support at key child developmental stages when working with parents referred by child welfare.

Child-Directed Play and Coaching Skills—Strengthening Parent-Child Bonding and Building Children's Social and Emotional Competence The programs on child-directed

Figure 2.1 IY Parent Basic Program Objectives

Strengthen Parent-Child Relationships and Bonding
- Increase parents' empathy towards their children.
- Increase parent knowledge of normal child development and provide age appropriate expectations and sensitivity to individual differences in children.
- Promote consistent monitoring and predictable supervision to keep children safe.
- Increase parents' positive thoughts and decrease their negative attributions about their children.
- Encourage more effective praise and encouragement for targeted prosocial behaviors.
- Promote positive parent-child relationships and strengthen parent-child attachment.
- Increase child-directed play and parent enjoyment of parent-child interactions.
- Help parents to become social, emotion, persistence, and academic "coaches" for their children.

Promote Routines, Effective Limit Setting, Nonpunitive Discipline, and Problem Solving
- Promote understanding of the importance of predictable schedules, routines, and consistent responses, particularly in regard to separations and reunions with children.
- Teach anger management strategies and affect regulation so parents can stay calm, controlled, and patient when disciplining their children.
- Help parents set realistic goals for their children's social, emotional, and academic behavior.
- Help parents set up behavior plans and develop salient rewards for targeted prosocial behaviors.
- Reduce harsh and physical discipline and promote consistent, nonpunitive discipline.
- Promote children's self-regulation skills by using brief time-outs to calm down.
- Teach parents to help children manage anger through problem-solving and self-regulation strategies.
- Promote joyful experiences and memories and reduce exposure to adult arguments, violent TV, computer games, and an atmosphere of fear or depression.

play and academic, persistence, social, and emotion coaching are core components of the IY program and are an especially relevant topic for the child welfare population because of their focus on the parent-child relationship, bonding, and attachment. It is important not to move on to the discipline units until parents begin to understand the concept and language needed for child-directed play, coaching, praise, and incentives and have begun to form more positive relationships with their children. For this population it is recommended that most of the vignettes from the child-directed and coaching programs be shown (in groups with less challenging populations a subset of the total vignettes is suggested).

In addition, these parents are provided with many more intensive behavioral practice play experiences than a typical group. Parents take turns role-playing or practicing playing "parent" or "child." Leaders need to simplify skills and do repeated practices before moving on to more complex parenting. This not only provides practice with new parenting techniques but also gives parents an opportunity to see the world through the perspective of their children, which promotes feelings of empathy for their needs and developmental abilities. Parents also have daily home assignments to practice what they are learning. If children are in child care at the same location as the parenting group, it is ideal to allot some time at the end of each session for parents to practice the new play interaction and communication skills with their children, in the context of supportive coaching, support, and feedback from the group leader. Alternatively, parents can receive this coaching of their parenting skills during a home visit. A home visitor coach manual is available for use by home visitor coaches or case managers who will help parents practice the skills they are learning with their children.

Parents learn to provide consistent, positive attention for prosocial behaviors. They learn the value of child-directed play and having fun together for promoting their relationship, for teaching social skills, and improving school readiness skills. When viewing and discussing the video vignettes, parents also learn about children's normal developmental milestones and needs for contingent attention, predictable responses, and positive emotional experiences. They discover that this undivided, focused parental attention results in their children feeling valued and respected and leads to their increased self-esteem. They also learn about normal development differences in children's temperament, needs for attention, and social and emotional development. This helps them to be sensitive and responsive to the cues their children give that they are ready to learn or need extra support, teaching, and reassurance. Parents learn to watch, listen, observe, and enjoy their child's thinking process and to follow their child's lead in the play. They learn that children benefit from being in control of certain situations and may actually be more cooperative with their parents if they have the chance to explore their own ideas and wishes in play.

In addition to learning how to be an "appreciative audience" when interacting with their children, they learn how to communicate with them effectively by refraining from asking too many questions, giving commands, correcting or criticizing, or trying to teach the "right" way to play. Instead, as academic, persistence, and social coaches they learn to describe their children's activities, prosocial behaviors, and ability to stay focused on a difficult project. For many of these parents this is a foreign and difficult language to learn, which necessitates group leaders not only setting up a lot of practice exercises during group sessions, but also helping them write out their scripts, and encouraging their practice of this at home during daily play sessions.

Parents are encouraged to participate in pretend play during their play sessions in order to build their children's imaginary worlds. In addition to promoting fantasy play, parents are taught to be "emotion coaches" for their children. Emotion coaching involves naming the children's feelings and providing support for expression of positive emotions such as joy, love, happiness, curiosity, and calmness (e.g., "Wow! You look so proud that you built that dump truck." Or "I'm so pleased that you're staying calm while you build that difficult model. You've got great self-control").

Parents learn how to calmly label their children's negative emotions, while providing coping statements about these feelings (e.g., "I see that you're frustrated, but I think you're going to stay calm and try again," or, "That was really hard to share but that was so friendly and see how happy that made your friend feel"). This emotion coaching helps children recognize their own emotions and gives them words to express them and also helps them begin to recognize and understand others' emotions. Frequently parents referred to child welfare may have a limited emotion vocabulary themselves, so this training and practice serves the double purpose of helping the parents themselves learn about appropriate expression of feelings. The net result of this added emphasis on child-directed play and emotion coaching is the strengthening of a more secure attachment between parents and children as well as more sensitive and responsive parenting and more parental understanding when reacting to their children's behaviors. It also facilitates the strengthening of children's self-confidence; academic, social, and emotional competence; and language skills, which may have been delayed due to prior lack of adequate cognitive stimulation and parental language interactions.

Praise and Rewards—Increasing Positive Parenting Skills, Thoughts, and Communication With Others When parents are stressed and depressed, they are less likely to praise and encourage their children or even to notice positive behaviors when they occur. Moreover, they are more likely to be irritated, critical, or angry about minor annoying misbehaviors. At these times, parents need help to identify positive behaviors they want to encourage and to remember to praise these behaviors frequently. In the school age program sticker charts and incentive programs are used to encourage them to clearly identify, track, and reinforce positive behaviors. As with the play principle, parents are helped to understand the impact of praise and positive reinforcement on *all* relationships (partners, colleagues, family members, friendships, their children's teachers). Finally, in this program they begin to learn about the importance of positive self-talk or self-praise. They rehearse and record positive motivational statements they can use when they find themselves getting negative, such as: "I am a good parent; I'm doing my best; I can handle this; I will cope; I can stay calm; I can help her learn to control herself; I did a pretty good job talking to my case worker; No one is perfect—I can do this; I try hard." Learning to substitute these positive coping statements and self-praise for their negative self-defeating thoughts will be a recurring exercise for this population throughout all the parenting group sessions.

Positive Discipline—Increasing Children's Sense of Safety and Security Frequently, abusive parents have unrealistic expectations of their children's behavior. They do not understand that all toddlers are aggressive and noncompliant or that preschool children disobey about one-third of the time and all children whine, cry, tantrum, hit, and are defiant and oppositional at times. In this program, parents are helped to understand that these behaviors are normal and healthy expressions of self-confidence and a biological drive for independence and curiosity. They are also helped to identify the important rules for their family and to keep these to a minimum. They learn to reduce excessive and unnecessary commands and criticisms and to give necessary commands clearly, politely, and calmly without fear of their children's response. The message emphasized is the ability to state a command assertively and respectfully but without negative affect or hostility. Parents learn that yelling and excessive responses to child behaviors may inadvertently reinforce the child's misbehavior. This requires parents to use self-control strategies and regulate their own negative responses. Parents learn to identify the positive opposite behaviors that they want to see more of and to give praise, attention, and small incentives in order to increase those behaviors.

Parents also learn about the importance of predictable routines for their children at bedtime, in the morning, and during separations and reunions. They are given laminated schedules with picture cue cards and work to establish predictable routines at home.

Parents learn that having predictable household rules and routines results in children feeling safe and secure at home.

Handling Misbehavior—Strengthening Parents' and Children's Self-Regulation Skills Parents learn to ignore many of the annoying behaviors that children exhibit such as crying, tantruming, whining, arguing, and backtalk. The difference between briefly ignoring an inappropriate behavior and neglecting a child is emphasized. Developmental guidelines define what ignoring looks like and how to keep children safe while ignoring. The key to using ignoring successfully is that parents learn never to ignore the child, but instead, to briefly ignore an inappropriate behavior. Parents are taught to stay near the child during ignoring and that *the most important part of ignoring is to return positive attention to the child as soon as the inappropriate behavior stops.* Parents also discuss the fact that *planned ignoring* is only effective when the parent-child bond is strong. Thus, this topic comes in the last third of the program after 10 to 12 weeks spent building parent-child attachment and positive parenting and coaching strategies.

Parents are trained to use a *brief* time-out to calm down as a nonviolent and respectful consequence for aggressive behavior in children 3 to 8 years. Time-out is a brief (3 to 5 minutes) and well-monitored period where children learn to regulate their negative emotions. However, the group leader carefully considers parents' readiness to implement time-out. It is important that parents are engaged in regular play times and have successfully learned to coach and praise prosocial behaviors before starting time-out. It is also important that parents have learned some self-calming strategies before using time-out. This may mean that they practice numerous time-out scenarios in the group before initiating this at home. Next, parents discuss appropriate ways to monitor their child's safety during time-out. Finally, parents learn how to teach their children to calm down in time-out by practicing deep breathing and positive self-statements such as, "I can calm down; I can try again." They teach their children how time-out is used as a place to calm down and practice this strategy with their children when the children are calm and receptive. Time-out is not intended as a humiliation experience for the child, nor is it framed as a naughty place, rather it is a time for the child (and parent) to reflect and to calm themselves. This is followed immediately by a new opportunity for the child to be successful and to receive positive parental attention.

Many of the parents have used spanking or hitting in the past as their primary form of discipline and have experienced physical discipline as children. They usually are unaware of how to use time-out appropriately or why ignoring strategies work to reduce misbehavior. Therefore, it can be difficult for them to give up spanking or hitting, especially as it often seems to work to get their child to obey in the short run. A variety of practice, discussion, and brainstorming strategies help parents to think about both the short- and long-term advantages of spanking and time-out. The goal is to have parents discover that in the short term, spanking may help control their child, but its use leads to long-term difficulties for their child in terms of escalating aggression and fear of parent. In contrast, time-out delivered in a respectful and calm way is difficult for the parent in the short term because so much self-control is required, but in the long run results in more child self-regulation and healthier parent-child relationships. Discussions about spanking in the context of a group of parents who have been referred to the child welfare system will involve the reality that many of these parents are being carefully monitored. It is likely that spanking their children may result in additional consequences from the system. This provides an additional incentive to use other methods of discipline, but also may add to parents' resentment about being monitored and their helpless feelings if they feel they do not have other discipline strategies to manage misbehavior.

Providing parents with a chance to explore feelings of guilt, anger, inadequacy, fear of losing their children, and other emotions that occur during the use of physical discipline can help parents be more receptive to learning new coping strategies. In addition to learning nonviolent discipline approaches, parents learn ways to manage their own anger. These include: (a) recognizing early that anger is building up; (b) deep breathing and muscle relaxation exercises; (c) challenging negative self-talk and rewriting positive self-talk; (d) positive imagery, and (e) taking brief time-outs themselves. As part of this process, parents develop an "emergency" plan for times when they feel that they cannot handle a situation on their own without losing control. This may involve calling a buddy from the group or a friend, calling the group leader, or some other way of getting support to defuse a situation.

Teaching Children to Problem Solve   The final program in the series is helping parents learn how to teach their children to problem solve in conflict situations. Parents help children learn solutions to try when feeling angry, sad, hurt, or disappointed. They are given books to read to their children about problems they can solve using puppets and make believe games (C. Webster-Stratton, 1998a, 1998b, 1998c, 1998d). Parents often find it difficult to teach their children problem-solving skills because they have their own difficulties with problem solving. For this reason, supplementing with the Advance Program (see description below) on adult problem solving is recommended before the program on teaching children to problem solve.

Monitoring, Safety, and Home Child-Proofing   In order to parent in positive and consistent ways, parents must be monitoring their children. Particularly in the case of neglecting parents, monitoring is a key theme that is discussed in most sessions. Parents are given information about why they cannot leave children unattended and brainstorm what to do when they feel they have to leave their child. Options for appropriate and safe babysitters and child care are discussed, and problem solving occurs around barriers. Developmental expectations for monitoring different age children are also discussed. Parents discuss the value of appropriate continual monitoring for promoting their children's social and emotional development and sense of security. Parents are helped to see the potential negative outcomes of not monitoring, both for their children and themselves. Other safety issues are covered, with an emphasis on how these issues change for children of different ages and developmental levels. Lastly, the baby and toddler programs place a particular emphasis on home childproofing their environment.

They are asked to complete checklists of things to check in their home, and these are reviewed in detail in the sessions.

IY Group Process and Methods of Engaging Families

Earlier we discussed ways to tailor the program content to families involved in the child welfare system. In addition to the need for content adaptation or increased focus, other barriers often arise with this population. We now outline some of the group processes and methods that are used to overcome these barriers and are well suited to working with this population.

Collaborative Process The collaborative process is a core tenet of the IY program. In a collaborative relationship, the therapist (or group leader) works *with* parents by actively soliciting their ideas and feelings, understanding their cultural context, and involving them in the therapeutic process by inviting them to share their experiences, discuss their ideas, and engage in problem-solving. The therapist does not set him- or herself up as the "expert" dispensing advice or lectures to parents about how they *should* parent more effectively; rather, she or he invites parents to help write the "script" for the intervention program. The therapist's role as collaborator, then, is to understand the parents' perspectives, to clarify issues, to summarize important ideas and themes raised by the parents, to teach and interpret in a way that is culturally sensitive, and, finally, to teach and suggest possible alternative approaches or choices when parents request assistance and when misunderstandings occur. Eventually therapists help parents to incorporate a new cognitive and emotional framework of parenting. Collaboration implies a reciprocal relationship based on utilizing equally the therapist's knowledge and the parents' unique strengths and perspectives.

Parents involved in the child welfare system may be difficult to engage because they are angry about being required or mandated to participate in parent education. The IY parent program model, with its emphasis on collaboration rather than didactic prescriptions and its nonblaming focus on parent strengths instead of deficits, is designed to counteract parent resistance. Collaboration implies that parents are actively involved in setting their own goals for themselves and their children. Group leaders describe the group process as a partnership between the parents and themselves and emphasize that everyone in the group will be sharing ideas and learning from one another. Parents are assigned a buddy (another parent in the group) and are given specific assignments to contact the buddy between groups to share experiences. Group leaders also call parents each week to provide on-going support for their home practices. This approach builds a support system and diffuses parents' anger and sense of stigmatization. Making new friends and sharing mutual experiences is motivating and supportive for these parents, who often feel isolated and blamed (Coohey, 1996; Roditti, 2005).

Although the collaborative and supportive relationship between parents and therapists is the underlying structure for the IY process of intervention, within this relationship the program's incorporation of motivational concepts such as individual goal setting, self-monitoring, reinforcing motivational self-talk, examination of personal belief systems via benefit and barriers exercises, peer buddy calls, and group leader coaching helps to empower parents and promote demoralized parents' active engagement with the program. Although space limits the discussion of all these methods, we describe a few that are particularly relevant for helping this population of parents to determine and accept responsibility for what they want to achieve within a supportive context.

Benefits and Barriers Brainstorms Each content area of the program is introduced with a benefits and barriers exercise. These brainstorms are used as a therapeutic technique to help parents articulate and examine their own beliefs about each new topic. This brainstorm also provides therapists with an overview about what parents know and believe. During the brainstorms, the therapist's role is to reflect, clarify, and extend the points that parents are making. For example, during a brainstorm on the benefits of playing with children a parent might say, "Play makes children happy." The therapist would respond: "That's a good observation: Parent play makes children happy. Why do you think children are so happy to have their parents play with them?" This discussion could continue to help parents in the group explore the idea that children value parental attention above all else; that to a child, the parent is the most important person in the world. This realization can be eye opening for parents who might have felt that their child's demands for attention were irritating and bothersome. Therapists might also ask parents to think about whether playing with children has any benefits for the parent. Frequently in the program, parents are encouraged to think about parent-child interactions from both points of view: the parent and the child. This increases empathy for the child as well as helping the parents to see the mutual benefits of a strong-parent child relationship.

After the group members have explored the benefits of a particular topic, they are encouraged to explore the barriers. During this brainstorm, the therapist listens to each barrier and acknowledges it. This is not a time to dispute the barrier or to try to convince parents that a strategy is worth trying, in spite of the barriers. For instance, a parent might say, "I just don't have the time to play, and when I do play, he just wants to play the same game over and over." The therapist might say, "So, you're mentioning two really common barriers here. First, it can be really hard to find the time to play when you have so many other things to do just to keep up with day to day life. And the second thing you mentioned is that sometimes children's play is a little boring for adults. It really can be hard to sit through 15 minutes of lining up the same cars in a row and then racing them around a track." By acknowledging and trying to understand the parents' barriers, the therapist can begin to address the resistance that often comes when a new strategy is introduced. In the barriers exercise, it is understood by the whole group that there are things within it or its environment that make the new strategies hard to implement. From here, the therapist moves the group on to the discussion of the content by summarizing the benefits and letting the group members know that they will work to find acceptable solutions to the barriers.

Self-Monitoring and Home Activities Incentives At the end of each session parents are given home activities to complete before the next session. For example, parents may be asked to play every day with their child for 10 minutes using the coaching strategies they have learned in the session, to read a chapter or listen to it on CD in the *Incredible Years* toddler or parent book(C Webster-Stratton, 2005; C. Webster-Stratton, 2011), and to call their buddy to share their favorite play activity with their child. Before leaving the group parents are asked to write down their commitment to whatever part of the assignment they feel is realistic for them to complete that week and what their goal will be for the week. This strategy helps parents to take ownership of the learning process and helps to reduce resistance to being told what they *must* do for homework. At the beginning of the following session, parents record whether they have achieved their goal. Therapists review these personal homework goals and achievements in each week, making encouraging comments and even putting stickers on them for goals completion. In addition, the group therapists ask the parents to share with their buddy or the whole group what home activities they have achieved and feel most proud of. This exercise helps them learn to praise themselves and each other. Therapists give out prizes to individuals for achieving particularly difficult goals, or even challenge the whole group to a particular reward (e.g., pizza party) if all group members manage to complete their home activities or make their buddy calls. During the week therapists phone (text or email if no one home) to see how parents are doing with their home activities and to support their progress.

Balancing Collaboration and Teaching Although therapists are collaborative, this does not mean that they passively let parents in the group take over the discussion or withdraw from involvement. A skilled therapist will alternate between providing parents with accurate information about child development, encouraging parents' efforts at home, gently challenging or confronting a parents' belief in a harsh or ineffective parenting strategy, and engaging and coaching them in practices of the new skills they are learning or to reenact difficulties they have encountered at home. Group leaders work to maintain fidelity to teaching the core behavior-management principles, while helping families reflect on how these principles are relevant for their own goals. The leader balances the need to present basic information that the parents might not know with acknowledging parental perspectives and knowledge level and helping parents to see that different parenting styles can be effective. In some child welfare parent groups, parents may need more basic teaching than in a group of parents with more baseline skills. However, because child welfare parents may be more resistant to the program, the group leader will also need considerable therapeutic skill to bond with parents, to highlight the skills that these parents do have, and to empower them to feel as if they can make changes that will benefit their children. In a sense, a group leader working with this population needs to be more directive, more collaborative, more culturally sensitive, and more therapeutically skilled. Thus, group leaders will need high levels of consultation and support when using this program.

Mediating Video Vignettes and Practices The video vignettes are a key part of the learning process in the group because they provide the group with a common visual experience to watch and discuss. Prior to showing a vignette, the therapist provides some information to the group about the vignette and may prompt the parents to watch for something specific: "In this next vignette, see what you think about the pace of this mother's play with her child. In particular, I'm curious to hear what you think about how the child might be feeling." Therapists pause the vignettes periodically to find out what parents thought about a particular part of the interaction: "Before we go on, what feeling do you see in the child's face right there?" "Why do you think the child felt that way?" "What would you do next?" Parents are encouraged to notice and discuss effective parenting interactions, as well as less effective interactions. Experienced therapists understand that any reaction that a parent has to the vignette is important and can be used in the discussion and learning process. If parents believe that the interaction is effective, then the therapist helps to pull out a general principle from the parents' observations about the vignettes. "You know, I think I hear a principle there. You said that the mother was playing at a faster speed than the child could keep up with—let's call that the Pacing Principle. Often a child needs much more time to explore during their play than we do as adults." If parents are uncomfortable with the style of the interaction of the parent in the vignette, then the therapist helps the group to tailor the strategy to fit individual parent's style. "So, it sounds like you think that parent's voice is too sugary and you wouldn't be comfortable saying that. You know, there are so many different ways of letting your child know that you are enjoying them, and it's important to do this in a way that feels comfortable to you. What would it look like if you were going to let your daughter know that you were having fun with her?" Always, after parents have built up a list of effective parenting strategies, the therapist rounds out the learning by having parents in the group practice these strategies in a series of role-plays. This takes the learning from the cognitive level into active learning.

Building Supportive Relationships Another form of support is for the therapist to establish positive expectations for change. Parents are often skeptical about their ability to change, especially if they see in their behavior a family pattern, for patterns often seem fixed and irreversible. For example, one parent said, "My mother beat me, now I beat my children." In such a case, the therapist must express his or her confidence in the parent's ability to break the family cycle. The therapist can point out each small step toward change—even the step of coming to therapy in the first place—as evidence that the problem is *not* fixed or irreversible. These parents need to be reinforced through positive feedback for each success, however small, and for each change in their behavior, whether it results in improvement in their child's behavior. It can be helpful to cite examples of other parents in similar situations who have been successful in teaching their children to behave more appropriately. For example, the therapist might say, "You are working really hard to make a change in your parenting while your child is still young. This will help both of you avoid getting into a permanent rut of negative interactions but instead a more enjoyable relationship. Good for you for tackling this now. You will have a different relationship with your child than you did with your mother."

Childcare and Transportation Another barrier to attendance is addressed by providing practical assistance by offering dinner, child care, and transportation for the groups.

These are offered in all of our community-based groups, not just to families involved in child welfare and are rated highly as a strong motivator for families' ongoing participation. Over and over, when families are asked to list reasons for not attending a group, child care and transportation are among the top reasons listed.

Parents Who Have Lost Custody of Their Children Some parents have had their children removed to foster care, so they do not have children at home to practice the new parenting skills. In some cases, it may be feasible for biological parents and the foster parents of their children to attend the same parenting group. This kind of collaboration provides unique therapeutic challenges, but also potentially tremendous benefits for children. Regardless, parents who do not have custody will need extra coaching and practice during the group sessions. This can be accomplished by more frequent role-plays during the group or on-site practice with children who are in day care during the group. Home assignments should be modified depending on the parents' access to their children. Visitation times are an ideal time to practice the new skills, and parents can be helped to plan activities to do with their child during visitation and to anticipate their child's response to seeing them after a separation. It is recommended that the visitation supervisors be trained in the IY program so that their support will be consistent with what parents learn in the group. The focus for these parents will also be geared to helping them address some of their personal needs for confidence building and enhanced support networks. This is done by broadening their understanding of how the many parenting skills can be extended to other relationships.

IY Home Visitor Coaching and Model In addition to the IY basic group meetings, we recommend that a home visitor work individually with parents and children for a minimum of four visits to practice the skills taught in the groups. Case managers who are already visiting these families might be trained in IY to do in-home rehearsal and reinforcement of skills. A home visitor–coaching manual with session protocols is available, as well as workbooks for parents (C. Webster-Stratton, 2008). If parents cannot attend the group at all, the manual offers protocols for leaders to offer the entire 20-session program at home.

The Advanced Parent Program

As mentioned earlier, an advanced parent program is offered and is particularly applicable to families involved with child welfare services (in addition to the basic parent program) because those families often experience multiple stressors that make it difficult for them to focus solely on parenting issues. For example, such parents often have mental health issues (Burns et al., 2004), elevated rates of depression (U.S. Department of Health and Social Services Administration on Children Youth and Families, 2006), anger control difficulties (Ateah & Durrant, 2005), and conflictual relationships with partners and other family members that frequently escalate to domestic violence (Hazen, Connelly, Kelleher, Landsverk, & Barth, 2004). The advanced parent program component addresses many of these issues as they relate to parenting and also to parents' functioning in their adult family environment. Group leaders are also responsible for referring parents to other, more specialized treatment programs for substance abuse, domestic violence, or clinical levels depression.

Typically, the advanced program is offered after the basic program and takes another 8 to 9 sessions, for a total of 22 to 24 sessions. In the advanced program, parents learn effective communication skills, more ways to cope with discouraging and depressive thoughts, more practice with anger-management strategies, ways to give and get support, and effective problem-solving strategies. However, as we have seen, some of these advanced program themes are woven throughout the basic program. For instance, in every unit in the basic program, there is an emphasis on how the behavior management principles parents are learning can help them cope with their own emotions and their other adult relationships as well as with their child's behavior and emotions. If this is done skillfully and consistently, parents will have some experience with many of these concepts even if the advanced program is not offered after the basic program.

The Therapeutic Child Treatment Group

In addition to the parent group, the therapeutic child treatment group is provided because research has indicated that children who have been neglected or abused have more behavior problems, self-regulation and emotional difficulties, and other developmental, learning, and social difficulties than typical children (Crick & Dodge, 1994; Fantuzzo et al., 1991; Jaffee, Caspi, Moffitt, & Taylor, 2004; Knutson, DeGarmo, Koeppl, & Reid, 2005). The therapeutic child treatment group, which in the IY program is called the Dinosaur Treatment Program, promotes children's social, emotional, and problem-solving skills. The curriculum consists of 18 to 22 weekly 2-hour lessons. The therapists for this program use comprehensive manuals that outline every session's content, objectives, video vignettes, and descriptions of small group activities. Figure 2.2 lists the goals for each of the program units.

Methods of Presenting the Small Group Dinosaur Program

Methods and processes for teaching social skills to young children must fit with the children's learning styles, temperaments, and cognitive abilities. Within the 4-to 8-year-old age range, there are vast differences in children's developmental abilities. The Dinosaur Program provides relevant content areas for the preschool to early elementary school age group. A skilled therapist will use developmentally appropriate practices to present the material to the child in any given group according to the goals for that child. Each lesson uses a combination of structured circle time learning (with games, puppets, video vignettes, role-plays), small group practice activities, coached play, and social snack time (C. Webster-Stratton & Reid, 2008). Home practice activities are provided each week, and therapists work with teachers and parents or caregivers to develop individual behaviors plans targeting specific goals for each child. See the book, *How to Promote Children's Social and Emotional Competence*, for more details.

Figure 2.2 Dinosaur Treatment Group Goals

Making Friends and Learning School Rules and How to Do Your Best in School
- Increase children's compliance to adult requests and ability to follow basic rules such as raising hand, listening to teacher, keeping hands to self.
- Increase children's school readiness skills (e.g., concentration and persistence).

Understanding and Detecting Feelings
- Increase children's emotion vocabulary for both positive and negative feeling words.
- Build awareness of ways to identify feelings in self and others by attending to body language, facial expression, vocal tone, and behaviors.
- Be able to express feelings using words.
- Learn to cope with and manage uncomfortable feelings in ways that are productive and acceptable (talk about feelings, ask for help, learn to self-regulate, think of coping thoughts).

Detective Wally Teaches Problem-Solving Steps
- Learn that negative or uncomfortable feelings are a signal that there may be a problem.
- Learn a series of problem solving steps (identify feeling, identify problem, brainstorm solutions, try a solution, evaluate consequences).
- Understand and practice using many different prosocial solutions to common problems (share, help, take turns, ignore and walk away, get help, find something else to do).
- Move from practicing these solutions in hypothetical situations to real-life problem solving.

Detective Wally Teaches Anger Management Steps
- Learn that angry feelings make it difficult to problem solve.
- Practice stopping your body when you feel angry or frustrated.
- Practice behavioral (going into turtle shell) and cognitive (self-talk) strategies to manage anger and help to self-regulate emotions.

Molly Manners Teaches How to Be Friendly and How to Talk With Friends
- Conversational skills (making a suggestion, apologizing, agreeing, giving compliments).
- Increase repertoire of specific prosocial situations for common peer situations (entering group of children, compromising during conflict, being a good sport when losing).

Clinical Adaptations of the IY Child Program Content for the Child Welfare Population

All topics above are relevant to children in the child welfare system. In addition, below are listed topics of enhanced focus that are particularly important for these children.

Enhanced Focus: Strengthen Children's Sense of Safety and Trust in Their Environment
- Help children learn to cope with adult anger and understand what to do to stay safe.
- Children learn how to get help and where to go if they feel unsafe.
- Promote appropriate touch with adults and peers.
- Children experience and learn about predictable routines.
- Children learn to trust adults and build healthy relationships.
- Children practice how to separate and reunite with their parents or child givers.

Enhanced Focus: Emotional Literacy
- Children learn to feel safe in expression of feelings of sadness, anxiety, or anger regarding traumatizing events.
- Promotion of cognitive and behavioral coping strategies to manage uncomfortable emotions.

Adaptations for Children in the Child Welfare System

An additional challenge for this population is that children who have experienced abandonment, neglect, trauma, or abuse during their childhood years often develop insecure, ambivalent, or avoidant attachment patterns with their parents or caregivers (Bakermans-Kranenburg, Van Ijzendoorn, & Juffer, 2003). The child groups provide children with a model of a secure and healthy adult-child relationships and also teach specific skills that will help the child to navigate other relationships in their lives.

Content for Children With Attachment Problems Children who have attachment problems may have experienced inconsistent rules and responses to their behaviors in different homes, so knowledge of rules and clear expectations for their behavior in Dinosaur School will help them to feel safe and more secure in their relationships. Children who have experienced negative and traumatizing events may experience anger, anxiety, depression, or sadness. In many cases, these feelings may have been ignored or invalidated by caregivers, and the children may be confused by these feelings. Consequently, children may not be able to label or discuss their feelings easily and may also believe that it is not safe to share these feelings with others. Such children often have difficulty managing emotions and frequently express sadness and fears by appearing angry and hostile towards others. For children with attachment problems, extra time is spent on labeling and identifying feeling words. It is important to help children understand that *any* feeling is okay to have, and to learn that it is how they react to that feeling that is important (e.g., it's okay to be very mad at someone, but it's not okay to hit). It is also important for the therapists to watch for times when children are having positive emotions and to label these emotions. Typically children's negative emotions receive much more attention from adults than the positive ones (e.g., "John, you look like you are feeling proud of your new backpack," or "Sally, I see a big smile on your face. I think you are happy to see Wally today"). As children begin to have a larger repertoire of feeling words, then they can begin to express emotion in new ways.

Children with attachment problems also need help to develop coping strategies for managing anger and sadness. Depending on the age of the child, these strategies will be a combination of behavioral and cognitive techniques. For example, specific behaviors that children learn to manage anger are taking three deep breaths, counting to 10, and practicing making their bodies tense and relaxed. Cognitive strategies they learn range from simple statements such as, "I can do it, I can calm down" to more complex cognitions such as, "I'm feeling mad because my sister took my truck, but I'm going to be strong and ignore her. Then I won't get in trouble and I'll prove I can control my anger." Behavioral strategies for managing sadness include telling a safe adult that you feel sad, or to finding a fun activity to do. Cognitive strategies involve thinking of happy thoughts or places, giving a compliment to yourself, or telling yourself that feelings can change and even though you are sad now, you will feel better later.

It is important to discuss ways for the child to stay safe and to cope with an adult's anger. Depending on the child's current living situation, these discussions may focus on helping children understand that even when adults are angry, they still love their children or, for a child who is still in a potentially abusive situation, the emphasis should be on identifying when the adults around them are not safe and to have a plan for what to do when this happens. A discussion about the fact that sometimes, even though parents love their children, they act in ways that will hurt them can help children talk about these fearful times. Children learn that it is not okay for their parents to do this, and that it means that their parents need some help learning how to calm down and how to take care of them.

Methods and Processes for Working With Children With Attachment Problems Since children with attachment difficulties may be mistrustful of adults, the puppets are a particularly important teaching method. Children will often open up to the puppets and talk about things that they would not talk about with an adult. The puppets are also useful tools for demonstrating appropriate touch. The puppets model that it is important to ask before touching someone (e.g., "Would you like a hug or a handshake?" "I'd rather not have a kiss on the lips, but I'd love it if you gave me a hug or a high-five"). Children who are suspicious and reluctant to receive adult hugs accept it from the puppet. Gradually the puppets will help the therapist to form a bond with a mistrustful child.

Children with attachment problems have difficulty with separations and reunions with their caregivers and other adults. These issues can be addressed by making sure that the puppets and therapists have routine greeting rituals and welcome each child in a personal and predictable way at each Dinosaur School session. Puppets and therapists say good-bye at the end of each session, and before the end of treatment, several weeks are spent talking about the fact that Dinosaur school will be ending. The children's feelings about this are explored, and the therapists, children, and puppets discuss ways to cope with feeling sad and keeping in touch. The repeated predictability of greetings and reunions can help to increase children's sense of security with adult relationships. The therapists also help to model these greetings and reunions for parents at the beginning and ending of each group session.

Children with attachment problems who have been blamed or abused by adults in the past may be suspicious of praise. They may respond by rejecting it, getting over-excited, or misbehaving. For example, a child tears up his art paper when his teacher praises him, or a child gets up and runs around the room the instant that the therapist gives her a token for sitting in her chair. It is important to be persistent and generous with praise and reinforcement for these children, even though sometimes children become more disruptive at first. These children are good at training adults to *stop* praising them, which only reinforces their idea that they are "bad" children. Therapists may experiment with the way in which praise is given. Instead of exuberant praise, the praise may be given in quiet, personal moments. The therapist may give it quickly, and then deflect attention from the child, so as not to put the child on the spot to accept the praise. Any rejection or arguments that result from the praise are ignored. Gradually children will learn to accept and internalize the praise if it is consistent and genuine.

Summary

We have discussed how to deliver IY parent and child care program principles and adapt the program with fidelity to meet the needs of intact families referred by child welfare as well as families where the children have been removed from the home. The IY interventions as well as other evidence-based parent programs (Chaffin et al., 2004; Lutzker, 1990; Lutzker & Bigelow, 2002) have demonstrated ability to improve parent-child relationships and to build parents' own sense of competence and self-control as well as strengthen their supportive family and community networks. Although it is common for child welfare agencies to seek briefer interventions than the Incredible Years, these families are complex and in the highest risk category for re-abuse and maltreatment if not adequately trained and supported. Data in the parenting literature support the notion that parenting curricula need to be substantial to produce sustainable effects with challenging populations (Kazdin & Mazurick, 1994). Data from the IY programs have shown that the dosage of the intervention received and fidelity with which it is delivered are directly linked to changes in parenting and child behaviors (Baydar, Reid, & Webster-Stratton, 2003; Eames et al., 2009). Our standard treatment recommendation for child welfare families referred because of abuse and neglect is a minimum of 18 two-hour parent and child group sessions delivered by accredited IY group leaders who have high levels of support and consultation.

Parent participation in the full IY program is expected to accomplish the following: improve the parent-child relationship; increase parents' sense of competence and self-control; increase the use of positive discipline strategies, predictable schedules, and monitoring; and reduce the rates of harsh and physical discipline. Child participation in the full IY child program is expected to improve children's emotional regulation, social skills, and to strengthen problem-solving skills as well as attachment and trust with parents. In the long term, we expect that these improvements in parenting and parent-child relationships will lead to lower rates of re-abuse, fewer re-reports to child welfare services and more academically, emotionally, and socially competent children. In order to break the intergenerational cycle of parent-child violence and neglect and child conduct problems, it is also necessary to provide enough training and support to therapists to assure program fidelity with the goal of these children getting the best parenting possible.

References

Ateah, C. A., & Durrant, J. E. (2005). Maternal use of physical punishment in response to child misbehavior: implications for child abuse prevention. *Child Abuse and Neglect, 29*(2), 169–185.

Bakermans-Kranenburg, M. J., Van Ijzendoorn, M. H., & Juffer, F. (2003). Less is more: Meta-analyses of sensitivity and attachment interventions in early childhood. *Psychological Bulletin, 129*, 195–215.

Baydar, N., Reid, M. J., & Webster-Stratton, C. (2003). The role of mental health factors and program engagement in the effectiveness of a preventive parenting program for Head Start mothers. *Child Development, 74*(5), 1433–1453.

Burns, B. J., Phillips, S. D., Wagner, H. R., Barth, R. P., Kolko, D. J., & Campbell, Y. (2004). Mental health need and access to mental health services by youths involved with child welfare: A national survey. *Journal of American Academy of Child and Adolescent Psychiatry, 443*(8), 960–970.

Chaffin, M., Silovsky, J. F., Funderburk, B., Valle, L. A., Brestan, E. V., Balachova, T., . . . Bonner, B. L. (2004). Parent-child interaction therapy with physically abusive parents: Efficacy for reducing future abuse reports. *Journal of Consulting and Clinical Psychology, 72*(3), 500–510.

Coohey, C. (1996). Child Maltreatment: Testing the social isolation hypothesis. *Child Abuse and Neglect, 20*(3), 241–254.

Crick, N. R., & Dodge, K. A. (1994). A review and reformulation of social information processing mechanisms in children's social adjustment. *Psychological Bulletin, 115*, 74–101.

Eames, C., Daley, D., Hutchings, J., Whitaker, C. J., Jones, K., Hughes, J. C., & Bywater, T. (2009). Treatment fidelity as a predictor of behaviour change in parents attending group-based parent training. *Child: care, health and development*, 1–10.

Fantuzzo, J. W., DePaola, L. M., Lambert, L., Martino, T., Anderson, G., & Sutton, S. (1991). Effects of interpersonal violence on the psychological adjustment and competencies of young children. *Journal of Consulting and Clinical Psychology, 59*, 258–265.

Hazen, A., Connelly, C. D., Kelleher, K., Landsverk, J., & Barth, R. P. (2004). Intimate partner violence among female caregivers of children reported for child maltreatment. *Child Abuse and Neglect, 28*, 301–319.

Jaffee, S. R., Caspi, A., Moffitt, T. E., & Taylor, A. (2004). Physical maltreatment victim to antisocial child: Evidence of environmentally mediated process. *Journal of Abnormal Psychology, 113*, 44–55.

Kazdin, A., & Mazurick, J. L. (1994). Dropping out of child psychotherapy: Distinguishing early and late dropouts over the course of treatment. *Journal of Consulting and Clinical Psychology, 62*, 1069–1074.

Knutson, J. F., DeGarmo, D., Koeppl, G., & Reid, J. B. (2005). Care neglect, supervisory neglect and harsh parenting in the development of children's aggression: A replication and extension. *Child Maltreatment, 10*, 92–107.

Lutzker, J. R. (1990). Behavioral treatment of child neglect. *Behavior Modification, 14*(3), 301–315.

Lutzker, J. R., & Bigelow, K. M. (2002). *Reducing child maltreatment: A guidebook for parent services*. New York, NY: Guilford Press.

Roditti, M. G. (2005). Understanding communities of neglectful parents: Child caring networks and child neglect. *Child Welfare, 84*(2), 277–298.

U.S. Department of Health and Social Services Administration on Children Youth and Families. (2006). Child Maltreatment 2004. Retrieved from http://acf.dhhs.gov/programs/cb/pubs/cm04/chapterhree.htm#age

Webster-Stratton, C. (1996a). Parenting a young child with conduct problems: New insights using grounded theory methods. In T. H. Ollendick & R. S. Prinz (Eds.), *Advances in clinical child psychology* (pp. 333–355). Hillsdale, NJ: Lawrence Erlbaum Associates.

Webster-Stratton, C. (1996b). Videotape modeling intervention programs for families of young children with oppositional defiant disorder or conduct disorder. In P. S. Jensen & E. D. Hibbs (Eds.), *Psychosocial treatments for child and adolescent disorders: Empirically based approaches*. Washington, D. C.: APA.

Webster-Stratton, C. (1998a). *Wally Learns a Lesson from Tiny Turtle*. Seattle, WA: Incredible Years.

Webster-Stratton, C. (1998b). *Wally Meets Dina Dinosaur*. Seattle, WA: Incredible Years.

Webster-Stratton, C. (1998c). *Wally's Detective Book for Solving Problems at Home*. Seattle, WA: Incredible Years.

Webster-Stratton, C. (1998d). *Wally's Detective Book for Solving Problems at School*. Seattle, WA: Incredible Years.

Webster-Stratton, C. (1999). *How to promote children's social and emotional competence*. London: Sage Publications.

Webster-Stratton, C. (2000). *How to promote social and academic competence in young children*. London, England: Sage Publications.

Webster-Stratton, C. (2005). *Dina Dinosaur's Social, Emotional, Academic and Problem-Solving Curriculum for Young Children*. Seattle, WA: Incredible Years.

Webster-Stratton, C. (2008). *Home Visit Coaching and Coaches Guidelines: Incredible Years Basic Parents and Children's Series*. Seattle, WA: Incredible Years.

Webster-Stratton, C. (2009). Affirming Diversity: Multi-Cultural Collaboration to Deliver the Incredible Years Parent Programs *The International Journal of Child Health and Human Development*, 2(1), 17–32.

Webster-Stratton, C. (2011). *The Incredible Toddlers*. Seattle, WA: Incredible Years.

Webster-Stratton, C., & Reid, M. J. (2003). Treating conduct problems and strengthening social emotional competence in young children (ages 4-8 years): The Dina Dinosaur treatment program. *Journal of Emotional and Behavioral Disorders*, 11(3), 130–143.

Webster-Stratton, C., & Reid, M. J. (2008). Adapting the Incredible Years Child Dinosaur Social, Emotional and Problem Solving intervention to address co-morbid diagnoses. *Journal of Children's Services*, 3(3), 17–30.

Webster-Stratton, C., & Reid, M. J. (2010). The Incredible Years Program for children from infancy to pre-adolescence: Prevention and treatment of behavior problems. In R. Murrihy, A. Kidman & T. Ollendick (Eds.), *Clinician's handbook for the assessment and treatment of conduct problems in youth* (pp. 117–138): Springer Press.

CHAPTER **3**

Multisystemic Therapy for Child Abuse and Neglect

Cynthia Cupit Swenson and Cindy M. Schaeffer

Child physical abuse and neglect are highly complex events that have been associated with multiple serious short-term mental health and health consequences for children (Cyr, Euser, Bakermans-Kranenburg, & Van Ijzendoorn, 2010; Kim, Cicchetti, Rogosch, & Manly, 2009). These difficulties continue into adulthood, often intensifying when other life stressors are experienced and may even be transmitted across generations through parenting and family conflict (Sidebotham & Heron, 2006; Springer, Sheridan, Kuo, & Carnes, 2007). Physical abuse and neglect pervade every society and are widely recognized as a global public health problem (U.S. Department of Health and Human Services [HHS], 2009). Interventions are needed that match the complexity of the problems families face and that can be transported to real-world community settings.

The purpose of this chapter is to describe a family-based model for treatment of child physical abuse and neglect. This model, Multisystemic Therapy for Child Abuse and Neglect (MST-CAN; Swenson, Schaeffer, Henggeler, Faldowski, & Mayhew, 2010), has been empirically supported in a randomized clinical trial in a community mental health setting and has shown feasibility for transport to U.S.-based and international settings. MST-CAN is based on a social ecological model.

Support for a Social Ecological Model

When determining interventions that might be successful for complicated, long-standing, and serious clinical problems, it is critical to not only treat the major behavioral symptoms of children and parents but also to address risk factors that when treated will sustain the overall treatment success and prevent re-abuse and placement of the child. For example, a behavioral symptom of disruptive behavior in school will need to be treated through behavioral interventions conducted jointly by the parent and school. In assessing risk factors it is determined that the parent is having challenges following through on behavioral parenting strategies due to low management of parental anger, which leads to physical force toward the child. In this case, school-based interventions

31

will not be successful in the long term unless the problem of low skills for managing anger is addressed. Thus, the intervention should address the child symptoms (school disruption) and parental risk factors (low anger management).

To gain a thorough understanding of the types of risk factors that may need to be the focus of interventions in each family, the scientific literature on etiology of abuse and neglect provides an initial guide. Factors that are predictive of an increased abuse or neglect risk occur across multiple systems including the child, parent, family, and social network (see Kolko & Swenson, 2002, for a review). Child factors that place children at risk of abuse include aggression, noncompliance, difficult temperament, and delayed development. Examples of parental factors that increase risk of abuse are depression, substance abuse, poor impulse control, poor knowledge of child development, a negative perception of the child, and a personal history of maltreatment as a child. Family factors that have been related to maltreatment risk are those such as single parenting, an unsatisfactory partner relationship, and partner abuse. Finally, social network factors that increase risk are social isolation, dissatisfaction with social supports, low involvement with community activities, and low use of community resources. When families are referred for treatment, risk factors such as those listed above in each system should be assessed to determine the initial targets of treatment.

The etiological literature for abuse and neglect is consistent with Bronfenbrenner's (1979) theory of social ecology, which espouses that youth are embedded in multiple systems (parent, family, social network) and each of the systems influence youth behavior and are in turn influenced by youth behavior. Bronfenbrenner's work forms the theoretical basis of Multisystemic Therapy and the MST-CAN model. Given that risk factors for physical abuse and neglect occur across multiple systems, interventions must target the child, parent, family, and social network. To assure that treatment follows a goal-oriented path and does not drift from a focus on the ecology, several structures are in place within the MST-CAN model.

Multisystemic Therapy for Child Abuse and Neglect

MST-CAN is a treatment model for families who have very serious and multiple clinical needs. The MST-CAN model is based on Standard MST. As such, agencies that decide to implement an MST-CAN program will follow an administrative and clinical structure that is consistent with Standard MST.

General Description

MST-CAN is an adaptation of Standard MST (Henggeler, Schoenwald, Borduin, Rowland, & Cunningham, 2009) that was originally developed to meet the clinical needs of youth experiencing serious antisocial behavior and their families. The core structure of MST (nine principles, analytic process, home-based service delivery, flexible hours, ecological focus, quality assurance system) forms the base of MST-CAN. The adaptations (reduced caseload, addition of crisis caseworker, dedicated psychiatrist time, longer treatment period, use of research-based treatments for family conflict/violence, trauma, adult substance misuse) were developed to meet the needs of families who experience serious clinical issues due to physical abuse and/or neglect.

The Administrative Structure

MST-CAN is a treatment model that should be delivered as it was conducted in research trials. Administrative requirements are established for delivery of the model with fidelity. Agencies that would like to operate an MST-CAN team must commit to following goals and guidelines of the program such as collaborative relationships, established referral criteria, established program clinical goals, a team structure, and an agreement to implement the program fidelity requirements. First, a working relationship should be established between Child Protective Services (CPS) and the provider agency. CPS is considered a stakeholder and should weigh in on the referral flow and commit to collaborative work between the caseworker and MST-CAN clinical team. Key stakeholders should be involved in the initial site assessment to set up an MST-CAN program and collaborate on development of the program design. The established inclusion or referral criteria are: physical abuse and/or neglect within the last 180 days verified by CPS; target child is between the ages of 6 and 17; and, child is either living with his or her family or there is a plan to reunite rapidly. Expected program goals are to prevent re-abuse and placement and to improve several indices of functioning for the parent and child.

MST-CAN is operated as a distinct clinical team that does not take cases outside those referred to the team (i.e., do not serve families referred to other programs in the agency). A full-time supervisor oversees the work of three to four master's-level therapists and a bachelor-level crisis caseworker. Approximately 20% of psychiatrist-protected time is reserved for youth and parents in the project. This administrative structure supports the provision of clinical services and program fidelity.

Service Provision

MST-CAN is primarily a home-based treatment program. Although sessions are generally conducted in the family's home, some work is carried out in the youth's school and elsewhere in the community. Each therapist carries a maximum caseload of four families and although each therapist is the primary therapist for four families, the crisis caseworker may conduct case management with all families if needed. A family is referred to MST-CAN because of parental behavior (abuse or neglect). To a large extent the focus of treatment is with the adults in the family but on the average five people per family are treated. For example, the parent may be treated for posttraumatic stress disorder, the grandmother for substance misuse, and the children for anxiety. The team works a flexible schedule seeing families at times that are convenient to the family. Sessions may be at night or on the weekend. Out-of-hours work is compensated during the week. The team operates a 24-hour per day, 7-days per week on-call rotation service to help families manage crises that arise outside of general working hours.

Clinical Treatment

MST-CAN is delivered in a context of ongoing family engagement. Consistent with Standard MST, MST-CAN follows nine treatment principles, and intervention prioritization and development follow an analytic process. The treatments delivered in MST-CAN are those that have research support.

Engagement One of the most critical aspects of clinical treatment is engagement with the family. When a family has had multiple experiences with child protection issues, they may fear losing their children and have low trust for professionals, leading to avoidance. In contrast, some families may have learned that highly negative and verbally aggressive behavior may lead providers to avoid the family. All of these experiences make engagement with the family challenging for an MST-CAN therapist. The therapist must always keep a strengths focus and take a one-down approach. Listening to the family's past experiences is important to showing understanding, even when the telling of those experiences involves anxiety and a loud tone of voice. Given that the problems associated with abuse and neglect are highly treatable and that families can resolve their conflict through strong evidence-based treatments, the MST-CAN therapist can be a "bringer of hope" to motivate the family toward change. For avoidant families, a therapist show of positive persistence can result in strong engagement. Although the families wait for the therapist to give up when they do not answer their door many times, they are often surprised to find that the therapist has enough confidence in the family to keep trying. Engagement is an ongoing process. In some cases families making strides in treatment experience a stressor or difficulty in some way and disengage from the team well after treatment has begun. In these times, the focus of treatment shifts back to engagement to help the family regain a sense of hope and get back on track. Regardless of the reason for disengagement, the MST-CAN therapist and team maintain a positive stance about the family and the progress made. MST is known for doing "whatever it takes" to help a family, and that description certainly applies to engagement because without engagement there is no treatment.

Treatment Principles MST is based on nine principles. When these are followed with fidelity, clinical outcomes are better for families (Schoenwald, Sheidow, Letourneau, & Liao, 2003). These principles, shown in Table 3.1, are also followed in the MST-CAN model (Swenson, Henggeler, Taylor, & Addison, 2009). They serve to keep the clinical team on track with regard to keeping a family and ecology focus, staying goal oriented, delivering evidence-based interventions in ways that meet the developmental needs of families, continuously assessing progress or barriers to progress, and keeping a focus on sustainability of outcomes.

Analytic Process The MST analytic process is a clinical road map for assessing, organizing, and prioritizing interventions and measuring outcomes. This process, often referred to as a *do loop*, begins with a thorough assessment of family history, development

Table 3.1 The Nine Principles of Multisystemic Therapy

Principle 1	The primary purpose of assessment is to understand the fit between the identified problems and their broader systemic context.
Principle 2	Therapeutic contacts emphasize the positive and use systemic strengths as levers for change.
Principle 3	Interventions are designed to promote responsible behavior and decrease irresponsible behavior among family members.
Principle 4	Interventions are present focused and action oriented, targeting specific and well-defined problems.
Principle 5	Interventions target sequences of behavior within and between multiple systems that maintain the identified problems.
Principle 6	Interventions are developmentally appropriate and fit the developmental needs of the youth.
Principle 7	Interventions are designed to require daily or weekly effort by family members.
Principle 8	Intervention effectiveness is evaluated continuously from multiple perspectives with providers assuming accountability for overcoming barriers to successful outcomes.
Principle 9	Interventions are designed to promote treatment generalization and long-term maintenance of therapeutic change by empowering caregivers to address family members' needs across multiple systemic contexts.

of an extensive genogram to understand family structure, and review of the target behaviors for which the family was referred to treatment. The strengths of the family and ecology across multiple systems are determined. For MST-CAN families, the initial contacts include an assessment of child and adult traumatic events and the current impact of these events. The next step in the process includes interviewing all key people in the family's ecology (e.g., parents, children, grandparents, teachers, CPS staff) to understand the desired outcomes of each. The desired outcomes are combined into the family's overarching goals for treatment. Generally, the desired outcomes expressed by all in the ecology are consistent and result in four to five goals.

Once the clinical team has an understanding of why the family was referred and its current functioning and the goals have been set, the do loop guides intervention development and implementation. To determine what interventions are key to helping the family realize its goals, the team must understand the "fit" of the target problems. That is, a determination must be made of what factors are driving the target problems. For example, the family was referred to MST-CAN for neglect defined as the children not being supervised, the house in disarray and unhygienic, and the children not attending school. On the face, the problem appears to be low parenting skills. An assessment of the "fit" of the neglect reveals that the parent is well aware of parenting strategies and has shown good skills in the past. At present the parent is engaging in substance misuse, which is a coping strategy for managing symptoms of posttraumatic stress from prior domestic violence. This understanding of fit leads the team to develop and implement (with the parent) research supported treatments for substance misuse and trauma symptoms. Each week, the MST-CAN therapist sets intermediary goals related to the treatments being implemented and reports to the supervisor, team, and consultant on the family's progress toward achieving these goals. If goals are not met, the team (including the parent) works together to understand barriers to progress and how the intervention might need to be altered to help the family achieve its goals. If an intervention continues to be largely unsuccessful, the team may not have understood the correct "fit factor," and further exploration of a new understanding of "fit" is taken.

Interventions As with Standard MST, MST-CAN interventions are tailored to the strengths of families and the "fit" of their target problems. However, there are a few interventions that are conducted with all families as these interventions are critical for safety and sustainability of progress. In the initial treatment sessions, each family completes a safety plan that is specific to the risks that are understood early in the case. Weekly safety assessments are conducted to enable the team and family to continue to understand safety risks so that the plan can be meaningful to the family and revised on a regular basis. Second, critical to a good relationship between the family and child protection, MST-CAN works closely with caseworkers, often including them in family sessions and considering them a valuable part of the team. Third, each family completes a clarification process (Lipovsky, Swenson, Ralston, & Saunders, 1998). Through this process the parent addresses cognitions about the abuse or neglect incident and shows acceptance of responsibility and apology through development of a letter to the family and the reading of this letter in a family meeting.

Other research-supported interventions are used with families depending on whether the family is experiencing a problem for which these interventions can be helpful. Functional analysis is used in cases of physical abuse or ongoing family conflict to understand the sequences of events and where the interactions take a turn toward physical or verbal aggression. Interventions can be put in place when triggers for aggression are occurring to de-escalate the child or parents. Other interventions that are behavioral or cognitive behavioral in nature are used when needed. For example, anger management treatments (e.g., Feindler, Ecton, Kingsley & Dubey, 1986) are used when low skills in managing anger is evident for the child or parent, and a behavioral family model is used when families have difficulty with communication and problem solving (Robin, Bedway, & Gilroy, 1994). For parents who are experiencing PTSD symptoms, Stress Innoculation Training (SIT: Kilpatrick, Veronen, & Resick, 1982) and Prolonged Exposure therapies (Foa & Rothbaum, 1998) are used. Finally, for adults experiencing substance misuse, Reinforcement-Based Therapy (Tuten, Jones, Schaeffer, Wong, & Stitzer, in press) is provided.

Other Clinical Considerations

Families who participate in MST-CAN typically have serious and complex issues they are dealing with such as being under the guidance of Child Protective Services. Special clinical considerations must receive attention to manage these complex issues. As such, Child Protection is a close working partner. Due to abuse or neglect risk at the beginning of the case, CPS, the family, and MST-CAN staff must work closely together to carefully define success and manage special clinical issues that come into play during treatment.

CPS Partnership The MST-CAN model is a radical departure from how CPS caseworkers and therapists tend to work together in most communities. Typically, caseworkers refer families to an array of services with the intention of meeting the family's needs and preventing re-abuse. It is not uncommon for each member of the family to get one or more referrals for treatment and supplemental services (e.g., three children and one parent in a family each get referred for individual psychiatric care and mental health counseling; both parents referred to parenting classes). In this scenario, each provider is only responsible for a small piece of the family puzzle, and responsibility for the family's collective progress is spread among different agencies. Similarly, reports about the family's progress in treatment are limited to specific domains (e.g., a parent-training course has been completed) rather than functional improvements in the home (e.g., aggressive exchanges with the child have diminished). This situation leaves the caseworker solely responsible for child safety and with little useful information on which to make child removal or placement recommendations.

In the MST-CAN model, addressing the drivers that affect child safety is the primary goal of treatment, and the MST-CAN therapist fully shares responsibility for safety with the caseworker. The MST-CAN therapist's frequent contact with families in their homes facilitates safety monitoring and helps to ensure that any concerns are immediately addressed. In addition, MST-CAN interventions empower the family's natural ecology members (e.g., grandparents, noncustodial parents) to assist in monitoring safety, which greatly decreases risk and helps ensure that safety will be sustained after treatment ends. The MST-CAN therapist reports the family's progress on safety to the caseworker on at least a weekly basis, and joint sessions are held with the family as needed to emphasize the importance of adhering to interventions targeting safety concerns. MST-CAN therapists are able to provide caseworkers with the types of specific information (e.g., mother has effectively implemented a safety plan to control her anger on four occasions) they need to determine whether children can remain in the home.

Together, therapists and caseworkers should explain the nature of their partnership to families at the beginning of treatment. A positive, strength-based tone from both the therapist and the caseworker (e.g., "You obviously care about your children very much, and we want the family to stay together") helps families view the partnership and MST-CAN interventions as helpful rather than adversarial. Family members also should understand that only clinical information directly related to child safety will be disclosed to the caseworker. For example, when dissociative symptoms are a driver of child neglect, the therapist reports to the caseworker that the parent is progressing in prolonged exposure therapy and experiencing anxiety reduction, but does not disclose details about traumatic events. Although at times a family may view the MST-CAN therapist as an agent of CPS (e.g., when a therapist reports to CPS that a safety plan was not implemented), minor problems in engagement are usually quickly resolved by refocusing the family on the shared responsibility for safety and the goal to keep children in the home. MST-CAN and CPS staff convey jointly to parents that a child's removal from the home will depend ultimately more on the parent's overall pattern of adherence to safety plans and utilization of treatment than on any one particular incident that occurs.

Special Clinical Issues MST-CAN is an intensive treatment, designed for families in which there is a high probability of child removal if changes do not occur. Accordingly,

MST-CAN is well suited for families who have complex clinical needs, such as those in which multiple caregivers are indicated in abuse allegations, caregivers abuse substances, and/or multiple family members have mental health needs. However, there are three particular concerns that have not been a focus of MST-CAN research, and thus are exclusionary factors for referrals to MST-CAN programs. First, MST-CAN does not accept referrals for families in which there is active domestic violence (i.e., where the person who is actively violent still lives in the home). Intimate partner violence poses serious safety concerns and requires specialized interventions that are not a part of the MST-CAN protocol (Stith, Rosen, & McCollumn, 2002). Second, MST-CAN excludes cases in which a child has been sexually abused and the abuser still lives in the home, in light of the limited research available on effective family-based interventions for this population (Corcoran, 2004). Finally, MST-CAN interventions are likely to be inappropriate for cases in which there is active parental psychosis.

Although MST-CAN programs exclude such cases when these issues are known at the time of referral, it is not uncommon for such problems to come to light after MST-CAN interventions begin. When this occurs, the MST-CAN team continues to treat the family until either alternative interventions can be arranged or the problem is effectively addressed by the family and ecology members. The MST-CAN analytic process is used to design the most appropriate interventions possible to address the drivers of these problems, and in many cases referral to an alternative treatment is not necessary. For example, some domestic violence cases involve joint partner abuse that can be effectively addressed through couples interventions designed to improve communication, problem-solving, and anger management skills.

Defining Treatment Success Ideally, after receiving MST-CAN interventions, families meet their overarching goals for the safety of children and effective parenting and make changes that are sustainable long after treatment ends. However, a successful outcome of treatment is not defined solely by whether or not parents retain custody of their children. Rather, MST-CAN defines success as child permanence in placement with caregivers in their natural environment (versus institutional care); at the end of treatment children are living with supportive and effective caregivers who are known to them and who are committed to their long-term well-being. In cases in which the risk for re-abuse by the parent remains high (e.g., a parent who continues to abuse substances), the most supportive and sustainable environment may be an alternative caregiver from the child's natural ecology, such as an aunt, adult sibling, or grandparent. Because MST-CAN works extensively with ecology members throughout treatment (e.g., as part of safety planning), the therapist (in partnership with CPS) can help to identify such individuals, facilitate the child's transition to this setting, and address other factors critical to the child's welfare (e.g., maintaining children's ties to their schools, peers, siblings, and, if appropriate, biological parents). Placements with natural ecology members are strongly preferred, and extensive efforts are made to prevent placements within the "formal" child welfare system (e.g., foster homes, treatment facilities, group homes).

Training and Quality Assurance

The MST-CAN quality assurance program follows that set by Standard MST, with the purpose of delivering MST-CAN with fidelity and preventing drift from the model protocols. The quality assurance program includes training and measures of model adherence.

Training When the clinical team is hired each individual completes a 5-day orientation to the Standard MST model to gain an understanding of how to conceptualize cases from a social ecological perspective and provide targeted interventions. Next, each team member completes 4 days of training in MST-CAN, with 2 of those days focusing on training in Reinforcement-Based Therapy for adult substance misuse. Quarterly booster trainings are held to address clinical issues and treatments that the team needs additional expertise on. The first booster is generally a 4-day training on treatment of trauma for adults and children.

Each team is assigned a consultant who is an expert in MST-CAN and whose role is to help the team maintain fidelity to the model. Weekly, the team completes a weekly goals and progress report that is sent to the consultant for review prior to telephone consultation. Two telephone consultations are conducted weekly. The first is between the consultant and the MST-CAN supervisor to review cases and problem solve particularly challenging issues. The second includes the clinical team and the consultant. Each case is reviewed to discuss progress and problem solving issues such as barriers to progress, prioritization of interventions, assessment of fit factors, and engagement. Prior to the consultation, group supervision is held to discuss case details, crises, success of current interventions, and goals. Each clinician may also participate in individual supervision with the MST-CAN supervisor on an as needed basis.

Measuring Adherence As with Standard MST, MST-CAN utilizes two measures of adherence. The MST-CAN Therapist Adherence Measure (CAN-TAM) is a Likert-format interview that is conducted with the parent by an interviewer who does not provide clinical services. The measure is scored to provide therapists feedback regarding whether the treatment is being delivered with fidelity. Therapists complete a Supervisor Adherence Measure (SAM) to rate the supervisor's adherence to the model. Adherence scores are discussed in consultation and during booster trainings.

Empirical Support and Dissemination

The research base for MST-CAN involves efficacy and effectiveness studies, including two randomized controlled trials that support MST-CAN as an evidence-based treatment for families where child abuse and neglect occurs and where families are experiencing multiple and serious clinical needs (Brunk et al., 1987; Swenson et al., 2010). Following the second successful trial, MST-CAN was disseminated to other communities, both domestically and internationally, and the data gathered so far from those communities suggest that the program is being transported successfully (See Appendix A for more details about the research base for MST-CAN.)

Summary

Child physical abuse and neglect are complex events that relate to factors within multiple systems in the life of a child (i.e., child, parent, family, social network). Treatment must match the complexity of the problems occurring and must be family-based to address the systems issues. MST-CAN is a treatment that has recently been found effective for reducing child and parent symptomatology, parent to child violence and neglectful parenting, and out-of-home placements for children. MST-CAN is currently being disseminated in the U.S. and internationally in a very careful manner to assure feasibility, acceptability, and clinical outcomes. Importantly, MST-CAN research has established that complex family-based treatments can be delivered in communities in ways that are in keeping with how they were delivered in research trials. As such, treatments that are truly evidence-based (i.e., have support through rigorous research trials) can be implemented with families in varying cultures (multiple U.S. and international) in places (e.g., home and community) and at times (flexible hours) that make it possible for them to engage and benefit clinically.

References

Bronfenbrenner, U. (1979). *The ecology of human development: Experiments by design and nature*. Cambridge, MA: Harvard University Press.

Brunk, M., Henggeler, S. W., & Whelan, J. P. (1987). Comparison of multisystemic therapy and parent training in the brief treatment of child abuse and neglect. *Journal of Consulting and Clinical Psychology*, *55*, 171–178. doi:10.1037/0022-006X.55.2.171

Corcoran, J. (2004). Treatment outcome research with the non-offending parents of sexually abused children: A critical review. *Journal of Child Sexual Abuse: Research, Treatment, & Program Innovations for Victims, Survivors, & Offenders*, *13*, 59–84. doi: 10.1300/J070v13n02_04

Cyr, C., Euser, E. M., Bakermans-Kranenburg, M. J., & Van Ijzendoorn, M. H. (2010). Attachment security and disorganization in maltreating and high-risk families: A series of meta-analyses. *Development and Psychopathology*, *22*, 87–108.

Feindler, E. L., Ecton, R. B., Kingsley, D., & Dubey, D. R. (1986). Group anger-control training for institutionalized psychiatric male adolescents. *Behavior Therapy*, *17*, 109–123. doi: 10.1016/S0005-7894(86)80079-X

Foa, E. B., & Rothbaum, B. O. (1998). *Treating the trauma of rape: Cognitive behavioral therapy for PTSD*. New York, NY: Guilford Press.

Henggeler, S. W., Schoenwald, S. K., Borduin, C. M., Rowland, M. D., & Cunningham, P. B. (2009). *Multisystemic therapy for antisocial behavior in children and Adolescents* (2nd ed.). New York, NY: Guilford Press.

Kilpatrick, D. G., Veronen, L. J., & Resick, P. A. (1982). Psychological sequelae to rape: Assessment and treatment strategies. In D. M. Dolays & R. L. Meredith (Eds.), *Behavioral medicine: Assessment and treatment strategies* (pp. 473–497). New York, NY: Plenum Press.

Kim, J., Cicchetti, D., Rogosch, F. A., & Manly, J. T. (2009). Child maltreatment and trajectories of personality and behavioral functioning: Implications for the development of personality disorder. *Development and Psychopathology*, *21*, 889–912.

Kolko, D. J., & Swenson, C. C. (2002). *Assessing and treating physically abused children and their families: A cognitive-behavioral approach*. Thousand Oaks, CA: Sage.

Lipovsky, J. A., Swenson, C. C., Ralston, M. E., & Saunders, B. E. (1998). The abuse clarification process in the treatment of intrafamilial child abuse. *Child Abuse & Neglect, 22*, 729–741. doi:10.1016/S0145-2134 (98)00051-9

Robin, A. L., Bedway, M., & Gilroy, M. (1994). Problem solving communication training. In C. W. LeCroy (Ed.), *Handbook of child and adolescent treatment manuals* (pp. 92–125). New York, NY: Lexington Books.

Schoenwald, S. K., Sheidow, A. J., Letourneau, E. J., & Liao, J. G. (2003). Transportability of multi-systemic therapy: Evidence for multilevel influences. *Mental Health Services Research, 5*, 223–239.

Sidebotham, P., & Heron, J. (2006). Child maltreatment in the children of the nineties: A cohort study of risk factors. *Child Abuse & Neglect, 30*, 497–522. doi:10.1016/j.chiabu.2005.1

Springer, K. W., Sheridan, J., Kuo, D., & Carnes, M. (2007). Long-term physical and mental health-consequences of childhood physical abuse: Results from a large population-based sample of men and women. *Child Abuse & Neglect, 31*, 517–530. doi:10.1016/j.chiabu.2007.01.003

Stith, S. M., Rosen, K. H., & McCollum, E. E. (2002). Domestic violence. In D. A. Sprenkle (Ed.) *Effectiveness research in marriage and family therapy* (pp. 223–254). Alexandria, VA: American Association for Marriage and Family Therapy.

Swenson, C. C., Henggeler, S. W., Taylor, I. S., & Addison, O. W. (2009). *Multisystemic therapy and neighborhood partnerships: Reducing adolescent violence and substance abuse*. New York, NY: Guilford Press.

Swenson, C. C., Schaeffer, C. M., Henggeler, S. W., Faldowski, R., & Mayhew, A. (2010). Multisystemic therapy for child abuse and neglect: A randomized effectiveness trial. *Journal of Family Psychology, 24*, 497–507.

Tuten, M., Jones, H. E., Schaeffer, C. M., Wong, C. J., & Stitzer, M. L. (in press). *Reinforcement-based treatment (RBT): A practical guide for the behavioral treatment of drug addiction*. Washington, DC: American Psychological Association.

U.S. Department of Health and Human Services. (2009). *Child maltreatment 2007*. Washington, DC: U.S. Government Printing Office.

4

Implementing Multidimensional Treatment Foster Care (MTFC)

Rena Gold and Cynthia V. Healey

Background

The lives of children in foster care are typified by risk. Almost a half-million children are currently living in foster care in the United States (U.S. Department of Health and Human Services, 2009). Prior to placement in out-of-home care they are likely to have experienced a host of adversities including neglect, abuse, substance exposure, transiency, and domestic violence. Consequently, their predicted outcomes fare no better. Compared to the general population, foster children are in much greater need of intervention due to significantly higher rates of mental health problems (Pilowsky, 1995). One study found that 72% of child welfare children in their sample were not statistically unique from children participating in intensive mental health treatment programs (Trupin et al., 1993). Landsverk and Garland (1999) estimate that between one-half and two-thirds of all children entering the foster care system demonstrate emotional or behavioral problems significant enough to warrant mental health treatment.

Foster children and victims of childhood maltreatment have disproportionate levels of risk when making the transition to school and in their overall school adjustment (Benbenishty & Oyserman, 1995; Fantuzzo & Perlman, 2007; Leve, Fisher, & DeGarmo, 2007). Deficits in school functioning and severe academic skill delays are disproportionately higher among foster children than their same-age peers (Brooks & Barth, 1998; Zima et al., 2000). Furthermore, adverse health-related effects as a result of maltreatment have also been reported. The young foster child often enters out-of-home care demonstrating a high level of neurobiological vulnerability because of previous adversity and stress. Specifically, cortisol levels associated with stress reactivity and regulation have been observed as having atypical patterns in young foster children

(Bruce, Fisher, Pears, & Levine, 2009; Fisher, Stoolmiller, Gunnar, & Burraston, 2007). Cortisol activated by the hypothalamic-pituitary-adrenal (HPA) axis in the brain helps the individual respond to stress by limiting the impact of competing biological stress responses and facilitating a return to a state comparable to that before the stressful event occurred (Fisher, Gunnar, Dozier, Bruce, & Pears, 2006). Dysregulation of these systems, as commonly evidenced in foster children, increases vulnerability to stress as their ability to adequately regulate their responses to stressors is compromised.

Extensive research has demonstrated the link between child maltreatment and an increased likelihood for later delinquency and criminality. For example, Widom and Maxfield (2001) found that childhood abuse and neglect increased the likelihood of arrest as a juvenile by 59%. They also found that maltreated children were likely to be younger at their first arrest, committed almost twice as many offenses, and had a higher rate of overall arrests than their nonmaltreated peers. Though many delinquent youth have experienced abuse and neglect, some may have no history with child welfare but still evidence similar needs for intervention. While juvenile arrest rates have declined overall during the last decade, there were still more than 1 million arrests of youth under 18 years of age during 2009; in 2008 approximately 80,000 juvenile offenders were held in residential facilities (U.S. Department of Justice, 2009). In addition to criminal behavior, these youth typically have a host of comorbid issues that necessitate intensive support. Researchers have found that nearly two-thirds of males and three-fourths of females in juvenile detention facilities meet criteria for one or more psychiatric disorders (Teplin, Abram, McClelland, Dulcan, & Mericle, 2002).

The multifaceted constellation of needs among children in the child welfare and juvenile justice systems fueled the development of the Multidimensional Treatment Foster Care (MTFC) program from researchers at the Oregon Social Learning Center (Chamberlain, 2003). Based on more than 30 years of research on the development and treatment of antisocial behavior, MTFC was introduced in the 1980s as a community-based treatment alternative to more restrictive treatment settings (e.g., institutional, residential, and group care) for children and adolescents with severe and chronic behavior problems. MTFC began as a treatment program for delinquent and adjudicated adolescents. Since its inception, the model has been adapted to include children ages 3 and up and their families.

In this chapter we discuss the theoretical underpinnings of the MTFC model, provide an overview of the staffing and treatment components, and provide implementation information for each of the three MTFC programs: MTFC-Adolescent (MTFC-A) serving youth ages 12 to 18; MTFC-Child (MTFC-C) serving children ages 7 to 11; and MTFC-Preschool (MTFC-P) serving children ages 3 to 6.

Conceptual Foundations

One of the principal goals of MTFC is for youth to demonstrate prosocial behaviors and function in the context of a normative family environment. The idea is that by treating the youth in a family as opposed to a residential setting, youth are more likely to generalize new skills learned in the "treatment" environment to the family environment to which they will eventually return. Instead of the traditional treatment approach of child-directed therapy in an office setting, the MTFC child is immersed in a therapeutic environment in which caregivers are trained to utilize theory-driven evidence-based parenting practices. The components of MTFC were influenced primarily by three theories and their corresponding research: social learning theory, resilience frameworks, and coercion theory.

Social learning theory (Bandura, 1977), which provides the primary basis for MTFC, posits that a person's internal experiences (e.g., thoughts and feelings) and behaviors are strongly influenced by the environment. As a result, individuals learn through observation of others (e.g., modeling) and are shaped by the consequences of the environment (e.g., reinforcement and punishment). Several conditions must be met to attain efficacy. The observer (in this case the child) must pay attention to the expectations or model. They must then retain that information and replicate it. Lastly, they must be motivated to replicate the behavior.

How does MTFC set the stage for these conditions to be met? Expectations for behavior are stated explicitly at the beginning of treatment from both the foster parents and clinical team staff. These are reiterated in developmentally appropriate ways throughout the day through the use of daily point cards and sticker charts, which is explained in more detail later. The model posits that by saturating the child's attention in this way, he or she is better able to retain expectations. Throughout treatment, the foster family and clinical team provide instruction embedded in daily activities regarding the desired prosocial behavior. Finally, the model is constructed to motivate the child through the use of a strategic balance of encouragement (e.g., reinforcement) and limit setting.

To buffer the impact of risks and adversity, the MTFC model heavily emphasizes the development of protective factors as a means of improving the child's overall adjustment. Within the individual, family system (foster parent and biological parent), and extrafamilial context (the service system), the MTFC model focuses on increasing the child's exposure to assets as well as addressing the mediating processes that increase resiliency in the child (Leve, Fisher, & Chamberlain, 2009). The intervention targets processes and factors that are consistent with resiliency frameworks (Masten & Coatsworth, 1998). Specifically, the development of effective parenting practices (from both foster and biological parents), prosocial behaviors in the child across settings (home, school and community), and coordinated service delivery facilitate resilience outcomes in the child such as social competence, school adjustment, and behavioral adjustment (Leve et al., 2009).

Additionally, Patterson's work on coercive family processes strongly influenced the development of MTFC (Patterson, 1982). Specifically, the conceptualization of coercion theory describes a parent-child dynamic in which children learn that inappropriate behavior and escalations result in attention from parents that inadvertently reinforces the behavior. These processes begin during infancy as both children and parents begin to practice responses that are predictable and contingent on the others' behavior and thereby set the stage for adaptive or maladaptive responsivity (Patterson, 2002). In a maladaptive context, for example, some parents learn to acquiesce to tantrums and aggression as a way to stop the inappropriate behavior. Once the tantrumming has become intolerable, the parent gives in to the demand and the child's escalation stops. The child learns that they can get their needs met by escalating their negative behavior and the parents inadvertently reinforce these escalations in their attempts to stop the behavior. These processes informed the development of the MTFC foster parenting approach by training foster parents to use praise and attention to reinforce appropriate behavior and to withdraw adult attention or set limits on inappropriate behavior using a calm and matter-of-fact approach. However, this can be extraordinarily challenging as children with a history of this parent-child dynamic have great fluency in the coercive processes. As such, acquiring a normative skill set in relating to parent figures can require extensive remediation. The clinical team goes to great lengths to provide the support necessary to minimize parenting stress so that foster parents can maintain this therapeutic approach.

Informed by these three theories, the MTFC model is a coordinated approach to: (1) create an effective learning environment, (2) develop competencies and assets in the child and the environment that facilitate resilience in the face of adversity and risk, and (3) utilize strategies that decrease ineffectual parenting practices and negative child behaviors.

Multidimensional Treatment Foster Care for Adolescents (MTFC–A)

MTFC for adolescents was developed to treat both girls and boys with chronic delinquency as well as severe emotional and behavioral disorders and has shown to be an effective and viable method of preventing youth placement in institutional or residential settings (Chamberlain & Reid, 1991; Chamberlain & Reid, 1998). MTFC-A began with a focus on boys and was later adapted for and tested with children and adolescents of both genders.

MTFC aims to create opportunities for youth to thrive in the community while living in a family setting and to simultaneously coach parents (or other long-term home) to provide effective parenting for sustainable success. MTFC targets five key areas which are thought to account for treatment effectiveness in the clinical trials. These include: (1) a consistent, reinforcing environment with mentoring and encouragement, (2) daily structure with clear expectations and reasonable consequences, (3) a high level of youth supervision, (4) limited access to deviant peer associations simultaneous to access to prosocial peers and assistance for developing peer relationships, and (5) an environment that supports daily school attendance and homework completion (Eddy & Chamberlain, 2000; Eddy, Whaley, & Chamberlain, 2004; Leve & Chamberlain, 2005; Leve & Chamberlain, 2006).

MTFC-A treats youths between ages 12 and 18 in placements with an MTFC-trained and supported treatment foster home lasting 6 to 9 months, on average. Services utilize intensive, well-coordinated interventions with the foster home, the family, and the youth.

A team leader, or program supervisor, oversees and coordinates all aspects of each youth's program across various environments including school and recreational activities.

Recognizing the long-term influence of parents on their children's behavior, the involvement of the family or other long-term placement resource is heavily emphasized from the beginning of treatment. Family participation assists in developing youth and family treatment goals, developing parenting skills, and preparing parents for the youth to return to the home.

While in the program, youth behaviors are closely monitored. This allows the program to respond to behaviors with specific interventions in a timely manner. Feedback about behavior is given to youths primarily through their daily point and level system. Prosocial behaviors result in earning points while problem behaviors result in point loss. A behavior tracking system is also utilized for time spent at school via a school card. Progress is monitored closely via daily phone calls with MTFC foster parents in which data are collected on youth behavior and the stress level of MTFC foster parents.

A skills deficit perspective in which problem behaviors are viewed as the lack of specific prosocial skills is also utilized in treatment. The clinical team, with the help of the foster home, identifies and targets prosocial skills specific to each youth and develops a detailed treatment plan utilizing the strengths and interests of the youth. New skills and behaviors are then heavily reinforced to encourage their continuation across settings. The program minimizes opportunities for problem behaviors while simultaneously fostering the growth of new prosocial behaviors, thus providing the youth with the teaching and support often lacking during their earlier years.

Youths in MTFC-A

Youths are commonly referred to MTFC-A from juvenile courts, probation officers, and/or mental health workers and are identified as needing an out-of-home placement due to serious behavioral and/or emotional problems. Some youths may be referred by child welfare caseworkers; however, it is less common in this age range. Referred youths have typically been involved in serious criminal offending behavior and may have comorbid mental health disorders. Referrals to MTFC are most appropriate for this level of care after in-home family programs have been attempted or when youths are returning from institutional or group care placements.

Youths exhibiting acutely suicidal, homicidal or psychotic behavior are usually not placed in any age version of MTFC until more stabilization has occurred. Given the intensive nature of MTFC, the program can provide for all treatment needs as a sole, comprehensive treatment service.

Families of MTFC-A youths participate in weekly family therapy and are engaged in services immediately after placement in the program if not beforehand. Although the program is designed to utilize the role of the youth's family, the program can also be applied to youths who will graduate to a relative's home, a long-term foster home, an adoptive home, or independent living. Identification of the discharge plan either before placement or early into MTFC services allows the program to maximize the likelihood of a positive placement outcome.

Staffing

The MTFC-A team includes the program supervisor who is responsible for coordinating all aspects of the treatment program. They serve as guides to the MTFC homes providing support and supervision on a daily basis. They also make decisions about youth treatment plans on a regular basis and interface with schools, caseworkers, probation officers, as well as community resources.

MTFC foster parents are key to the execution of the youth's program. Without the foster parents and their willingness to have a challenging child in their home, the program would not exist. As such, MTFC foster homes are viewed as integral members of the treatment team. Foster parents are screened, selected, and trained before a youth is placed in their home. Supervision and support is provided throughout the placement; however, much of the training occurs "on the job." Foster parents participate in a weekly meeting to receive supervision and support from the program supervisor and to provide information and support to one another. Foster parents also have access to the program 24 hours a day, 7 days a week to receive support and assistance with behaviors as they occur.

Involvement of the biological family or other long-term resource is emphasized throughout treatment. A family therapist meets with each family on a weekly basis to provide coaching and support in the use of specific parenting approaches. Parents practice the techniques during family therapy sessions and in frequent visits with their youth. Program staff provides support to families as needed in the moment and frequent updates of their youth's progress. In addition, families have access to the program supervisor 24 hours a day, 7 days a week.

On a weekly basis youth meet with an individual therapist on the MTFC team. This role builds a foundation of support with the youths to assist them in problem solving and navigating the program. The therapist learns about the youth's strengths and interests and provides opportunities for youths to develop new skills as alternatives to the antisocial behaviors that led to their placement in the program. The therapist is trained in a variety of techniques to engage youth and develop their skills, including interventions outside of the youth's awareness. Sessions are frequently activity-based and occur in the community.

Skills coaching sessions are also delivered to youth on a weekly basis and are held in a variety of community settings. Youths practice social skills and are exposed to new activities and potential interests. When youth demonstrate prosocial skills, they receive frequent, positive reinforcement. Skills coaches are typically part-time or hourly staff who exhibit good social skills themselves, enjoy working with youth, demonstrate warmth and compassion, are flexible and adaptable, have a sense of humor, and are good team players.

Given how valuable MTFC foster parents are to the program and the qualities it takes to be a good foster parent, the team includes a role dedicated specifically to the recruitment and training of MTFC foster parents. Like all other team members, the person in this role receives training in the model. Recruiters employ specific strategies to reach and attract prospective families suitable for the program. Prospective homes participate in MTFC training conducted by the recruiter as well as a multilayered review process. Although programs typically exhibit a reduction in foster home turnover over time, foster parent recruitment is a routine and perpetual need, and therefore the recruiter is a permanent position on the team.

Team members are employed directly by the implementation site and are directly supervised by the team leader. Each MTFC team member has a discrete role in the program which does not overlap with other roles. This protects those team members who are in supportive roles from directly setting limits on clients and allows for a high degree of advocacy on their behalf. This also allows team members to fully understand the youth's or parents' point of view and maintain a therapeutic relationship when addressing difficult behaviors.

Multidimensional Treatment Foster Care for Middle Childhood (MTFC-C)

The middle childhood version of MTFC treats children 7 to 11 years old who are typically referred by child welfare and mental health caseworkers. Treatment may include a modified point and level system similar to the MTFC-A version or may utilize reinforcement and routine charts along with concrete incentives depending on the child's age. The goal of either behavior contingency system is to provide a high degree of reinforcement while discouraging problem behaviors. Systems are frequently adjusted and varied based on children's interests and attention. The child's program additionally includes a school card in an effort to shape school behaviors. The card is individually designed based on the child's school day and cognitive abilities.

Children in MTFC-C

Referred children are identified as needing an out-of-home placement or a placement change due to serious emotional, behavioral, or mental health problems. Many children in MTFC-C have had prior foster care placements, have participated in other treatment services, and may have a variety of diagnoses. Referrals to MTFC-C programs are recommended after less restrictive interventions have been utilized.

Families of MTFC-C children are engaged early in or prior to program placement and are critical to the overall effectiveness of the treatment. Referred children may alternatively have a case plan to be placed with a relative, in an adoptive home, or with a long-term foster family upon completion of MTFC-C.

Staffing

Staffing in MTFC-C mirrors that of MTFC-A with one exception. The role of individual therapist is incorporated into the role of the skills coach. Children in this age range receive support and guidance in the development of prosocial skills from their skills coach with a heavy emphasis on opportunities for practice. Repetition and reinforcement are key to successful skills coaching. If and when a child initiates discussion of traumatic or emotional topics, the skills coach provides support and guidance using techniques to maintain a child-directed, strengths-based approach with an eye on the child's positive future.

Multidimensional Treatment Foster Care for Preschoolers (MTFC-P)

MTFC-P is a version of the MTFC model developed to treat foster children between the ages of 3 and 6 years (Fisher, Ellis, & Chamberlain, 1999). Placements in the MTFC-P program average approximately nine months; the time period varies depending on the case plan and treatment progress.

MTFC-P approaches intervention and behavior change through a developmental lens. When first working with this population, developers noted that the behaviors exhibited by the children were similar at times to those of delinquent youth. As understanding grew, it became apparent that these were more accurately defined as behaviors typical of much younger children. Due to extensive early adversity experienced by these young children, the development of more functional and prosocial behaviors had arrested. Inconsistent and harsh parenting, neglect, chronic stress, exposure to substances in utero, and lack of appropriate models had interfered with healthy development and the acquisition of age-appropriate skills. Many MTFC-P children demonstrate social and behavioral skill deficits as well as developmental delays across a number of domains. Consequently, intervention strategies for MTFC-P children fall within a continuum of developmental sophistication and are individualized to the child based on his or her ability. However, similar to both the MTFC-A and MTFC-C programs, MTFC-P families work with the team leader to identify problem behaviors, define prosocial alternatives to those behaviors, and set up encouragement systems to develop skills while implementing brief and therapeutic limit setting strategies for instances of continued problem behaviors. Foster parents also work to establish highly predictable and structured daily routines in the home that serve to decrease anxiety in the child and increase the likelihood of compliance and independence.

The team leader also works with day-care providers and teachers to establish similar practices in the classroom environment so as to increase consistency across settings for the child. Older children or more developmentally advanced children may also utilize a simplified school card to increase awareness of expectations and target prosocial behavior at school.

Children in MTFC-P

Children appropriate for the MTFC-P are identified as having significant behavioral and emotional challenges, and many have experienced previous placement failures. Developmental delays are common. While delays do not exclude children from the program, they are assessed for appropriateness. Children do not have to be attending preschool or kindergarten but will likely be enrolled while in the program.

Staffing in MTFC-P

Clinical staff roles in MTFC-P largely parallel the MTFC-A and MTFC-C programs, with a few notable exceptions due to developmental considerations. In MTFC-A and MTFC-C, the program supervisor (PS) provides direction to foster parents, team members, and interfaces with caseworkers on behalf of both the program and foster parents. In MTFC-P, the team leader role is augmented by the role of foster parent consultant (FPC). The FPC's role in the clinical team is two-fold: as a source of support and as an advocate to the foster family. The role was developed uniquely for MTFC-P because foster children of this age typically demonstrate problem behaviors at a higher rate than older children. In addition, they are far less independent and thus need constant supervision and support. This can require significantly more effort on the part of foster parents. This additional effort often translates to increased stress. Consequently, the role of FPC was developed to provide more intensive support to families and enhance role stratification with the PS. The PS introduces intervention strategies to the foster family, and the FPC works with the family to provide the necessary support to implement those interventions with fidelity and consistency. The utility of this role also becomes evident when taking into account the nature of the home-based interventions and encouragement systems.

Encouragement systems in MTFC-P homes vary constantly as do some systems in MTFC-C. However point systems suitable for older children prove too abstract to keep young children focused on working toward incentives and practicing target behaviors. Instead, MTFC-P foster families implement a wide variety of encouragement systems throughout the treatment period that match the child's developmental ability. This could mean a high rate of tangible rewards throughout the day to reinforce demonstrations of good behavior or more developmentally sophisticated systems such as sticker charts or simple token economies. The bottom line is that children will typically lose interest in these systems after a short while. As a result, foster parents are regularly required to start new systems under the direction of the PS to retain focus on targeting prosocial behaviors and to maintain positive momentum in establishing these new behavioral routines. The FPC provides the support needed to keep these systems intact and uses role stratification effectively by validating the foster family's stress levels while still encouraging intervention implementation.

As an advocate, the FPC functions as a thermometer for the clinical team and "takes the temperature" of the foster home. It is the FPC's job to get to know the families and understand their strengths and values. By spending time in the foster home, listening, and providing support, the FPC effectively advises the clinical team and PS regarding the family's willingness and abilities to implement the intervention.

Therapeutic Playgroup

The therapeutic playgroup (TPG) is unique to MTFC-P. All MTFC-P children attend the group together, which occurs in conjunction with the weekly foster parent meeting. The TPG is designed to increase school readiness by providing a structured and predictable setting much like a kindergarten classroom. During the TPG, children receive a combination of explicit instruction and activity-based intervention targeting the development of social competence, self-regulation, and emergent literacy skills. Children are encouraged to successfully learn and practice skills by receiving a high rate of positive reinforcement for their efforts while participating in highly engaging, age-appropriate, and structured activities.

The TPG is staffed by the MTFC-P skills coaches and includes one lead teacher and one or two assistant teachers (depending on the total number of children). During activities and across numerous transitions during the session, TPG staff members utilize evidence-based behavior management strategies and instructional techniques to encourage rule adherence and maintain a high level of engagement with the material. Further, extensive role stratification is used in order to maintain the therapeutic role of the skills coaches (e.g., PS is used as the limit setter and is available to TPG staff as needed).

Implementation Support for MTFC Programs

When a community or organization is interested in developing an MTFC program TFC Consultants (TFCC) initiates a program development process. Founded in 2002, TFCC is dedicated to the implementation of model-adherent MTFC programs. It provides direct consultation, training, and technical assistance for both developing and ongoing MTFC programs. TFCC also assists service providers, policy makers, and community leaders in resolving issues related to the implementation of MTFC. Through TFC Consultants, MTFC (across age versions) is currently implemented throughout the United States, Sweden, Norway, Denmark, The Netherlands, United Kingdom, Ireland, and New Zealand.

Readiness Process

Starting with a review of the feasibility of developing an MTFC program, a dialogue is initiated between TFCC and the prospective implementation agency. Questions for both parties examine how MTFC operates day-to-day and if the circumstances of funding, location, and community support exist to support the development of a model-adherent program.

Once feasibility is established, the implementation agency begins the program development phase. Although the feasibility phase is generally completed quickly, the readiness phase spans several months as the agency begins to develop the foundation of the program. Frequent meetings are held to assist the implementation site with program development needs and problem-solving issues as they arise. Topics discussed include funding, staffing, foster parent recruitment, geography, referrals, matching and placements, and interfacing with system partners. Two of the key components in the program development phase are hiring staff and recruitment of MTFC foster homes.

TFCC works with the site to develop a full plan for program development, including an individualized timeline. Typically, staffing of the program begins by hiring the program supervisor and recruiter. The program supervisor works to develop relationships with referral sources, develops internal systems and paperwork, and creates the atmosphere for the team. The program supervisor position is full-time. The recruiter advertises the program, meets and screens prospective foster parents and conducts their MTFC training. The recruiter position may be a three-quarter or full-time position depending on the whether their duties include conducting home studies and licensing MTFC homes. TFCC takes into account other factors influencing the staffing of these roles as well. Depending on the organization's readiness plan, the program supervisor, recruiter, and an administrator may attend MTFC training at this early stage.

MTFC homes are selected based on their interest in fostering as well as their ability to work with the program to create an MTFC treatment foster home. In the recruitment of foster homes, a variety of strategies are recommended. An individualized recruitment plan is developed that meets the needs of the site and fits within the scheme of recruitment in the area. Many MTFC foster homes report having read advertisements about the program on multiple occasions before calling for information. MTFC parents also report that they enjoy the work and the program and could not do it without the support. Based on this information, it is often suggested that implementation sites utilize frequent advertising that emphasizes specific components of the services while also encouraging current MTFC homes to share information about the program with people they know and meet. Guidance and support is provided by TFCC as implementation sites weave together the recruitment of MTFC foster homes with local mandates and processes.

Once prospective homes have completed the required background checks, clearances, and state mandated trainings, they participate in MTFC foster parent training. Foster parents may also be invited to attend foster parent meetings in addition to other orientation activities. The initial training of foster parents is conducted by a TFCC foster parent trainer onsite. Subsequent trainings are conducted by the recruiter/trainer. This team member also conducts the daily data collection calls, which creates a tight network of services and support for foster parents.

As prospective MTFC foster homes are identified and prepared, therapists and skills coaches are hired. Developing a relationship with a consulting psychiatrist is also recommended at this stage. By utilizing the same psychiatrist or psychiatric nurse practitioner to address the medication needs of all MTFC youths, the program integrates medication with the rest of their treatment. As the psychiatrist becomes familiar with the program, he or she can utilize data from the program's behavioral tracking systems and the most up to date information of functioning across settings provided by the program supervisor.

The final stage in the program readiness phase is training. All remaining team members attend the clinical training at this time. All training is provided by TFC

Consultants or a network partner organization approved as an MTFC training provider, with the exception of the skills coaches, who are trained by program supervisors. Next, the initial group of foster parents is trained by TFCC at the implementation agency. Lastly, the recruiter and the program supervisor are oriented to the web-based foster parent report system.

As the program supervisor develops the community's awareness of MTFC and interest in the types of youth appropriate for the program, referrals are sent for review and screening by the program supervisor. Once the team and foster parents are trained and initial referrals are received, the program development phase is completed and the program and is ready for consultation support services to begin.

Consultation Services

Implementation sites are supported through weekly consultation calls wherein a consultant in MTFC provides guidance and feedback on the program operation and treatment, using information provided by the PS and video recordings of program meetings. Providing feedback in a timely manner ensures that teams respond to behaviors quickly and effectively.

Within the first year, services also include three 2-day visits to the implementation site by the consultant. Site visits allow the consultant to provide support and guidance to the program supervisor and other team members in the moment. Feedback is also provided to MTFC programs via periodic written evaluations that include fidelity scoring of program meetings. At the end of the first year, a full fidelity evaluation is conducted which indicates the level of support and the services subsequently needed to reach model fidelity standards.

Certification in MTFC

Certification exists for each distinct MTFC version and is designated by the Center for Research to Practice (CR2P). This organization is a nonprofit research organization dedicated to building linkages between research and practice in the child welfare, juvenile justice, and mental health systems.

When an MTFC program meets the minimum requirements to apply for certification and believes it has achieved an adequate level of fidelity across the domains of the model, it submits a certification application to CR2P including program data and video of program meetings. Applications are evaluated and a written outcome is provided to the implementation agency. A copy of the application is available on the TFCC website at www.mtfc.com/certification.html.

Upon certification, the team operates with minimal oversight and guidance by TFC Consultants. Self-monitoring is highly recommended to assist the program with identifying and problem solving drift in model fidelity. Periodic evaluations are conducted by TFCC between certification points. Initial certification is designated for a period of 2 years, while recertification is designated to qualifying programs for a period of 3 years.

Setting Up for Success

The implementation of MTFC is somewhat nascent in comparison to some other evidence-based models, but replication has highlighted qualities of successful program development and program operation in the model. In the development of the program, one critical component is a realistic timeline for moving through the preservice phases. This includes adequate time for foster parent recruitment, which is key to a successful startup. In addition, timing the clinical training to occur within 2 or 3 months prior to the first placement allows team members to retain what they learn in training and quickly develop their clinical skills in the model as they apply that knowledge.

Also critical to a successful startup is the support of the community and system partners who fund the services or refer youth. When stakeholders have an understanding of MTFC and how collaboration is accomplished, the program is likely to avoid a situation where confusion leads to a lack of referrals.

Through a balance between referrals and recruitment of foster homes program capacity is steadily increased and sustained long term. With a full team serving 10 to 12 youth at a time, a change in the pace of program development can quickly affect the census as well as the overall sustainability a program.

Successful programs in MTFC also have a number of qualities exhibited by any strong treatment team. Team members who are best suited for the program enjoy working on a team, support humor in the midst of challenges, are flexible, and are creative. Unique to MTFC is the need for staff to support the stratification of the clinical roles, appreciate reinforcement of prosocial behavior, and have an interest in a behavioral approach to working with children and families.

References

Bandura, A. (1977). *Social learning theory*. Oxford, England: Prentice-Hall.

Benbenishty, R., & Oyserman, D. (1995). Children in foster care: Their present situation and plans for their future. *International Social Work, 38*(2), 117–131. doi:10.1177/002087289503800202

Brooks, D., & Barth, R. P. (1998). Characteristics and outcomes of drug-exposed and non drug-exposed children in kinship and non-relative foster care. *Children and Youth Services Review, 20*(6), 475–501.

Bruce, J., Fisher, P. A., Pears, K. C., & Levine, S. (2009). Morning cortisol Levels in preschool-aged foster children: Differential effects of maltreatment type. *Developmental Psychobiology, 51*(1), 14–23.

Chamberlain, P. (2003). The Oregon multidimensional treatment foster care model: Features, outcomes, and progress in dissemination. In S. Schoenwald & S. Henggeler (Series Eds.), Moving evidence-based treatments from the laboratory into clinical practice. *Cognitive and Behavioral Practice, 10*(4), 303–312.

Chamberlain, P., & Reid, J. B. (1991). Using a specialized foster care community treatment model for children and adolescents leaving a state mental hospital. *Journal of Community Psychology, 19*, 226–276.

Chamberlain, P., & Reid, J. B. (1998). Comparison of two community alternatives to incarceration for chronic juvenile offenders. *Journal of Consulting and Clinical Psychology, 66*(4), 624–633.

Eddy, J. M., Bridges Whaley, R., & Chamberlain, P. (2004). The prevention of violent behavior by chronic and serious male juvenile offenders: A 2-year follow-up of a randomized clinical trial. *Journal of Family Psychology, 12*(1), 2–8.

Eddy, J. M., & Chamberlain, P. (2000). Family management and deviant peer association as mediators of the impact of treatment condition on youth antisocial behavior. *Journal of Consulting and Clinical Psychology, 5*(68), 857–863.

Fantuzzo, J., & Perlman, S. (2007). The unique impact of out-of-home placement and the mediating effects of child maltreatment and homelessness on early school success. *Children and Youth Services Review, 29*(7), 941–960. doi:10.1016/j.childyouth.2006.11.003

Fisher, P. A., Ellis, B. H., & Chamberlain, P. (1999). Early intervention foster care: A model for preventing risk in young children who have been maltreated. *Children Services: Social Policy, Research, and Practice, 2*(3), 159–182.

Fisher, P. A., Gunnar, M. R., Dozier, M., Bruce, J., & Pears, K. C. (2006). Effects of a therapeutic intervention for foster children on behavior problems, caregiver attachment, and stress regulatory neural systems. *Annals of the New York Academy of Sciences, 1094*, 215–225.

Fisher, P. A., Stoolmiller, M., Gunnar, M. R., & Burraston, B. O. (2007). Effects of a therapeutic intervention for foster preschoolers on diurnal cortisol activity. *Psychoneuroendocrinology, 32*(8-10), 892–905.

Landsverk, J., & Garland, A. F. (1999). *Foster care and pathways to mental health services. The foster care crisis: Translating research into policy and practice* (pp. 193–210). Lincoln: University of Nebraska Press.

Leve, L. D., & Chamberlain, P. (2005). Association with delinquent peers: Intervention effects for youth in out-of-home care. *Journal of Abnormal Child Psychology, 33*(3), 339–347.

Leve, L. D., & Chamberlain, P. (2006, July). A randomized evaluation of multidimensional treatment foster care: Effects on school attendance and homework completion in juvenile justice girls. *Research on Social Work Practice, X*(X), 1–7.

Leve, L. D., Fisher, P., & Chamberlain, P. (2009, December). Multidimensional treatment foster care as a preventive intervention to promote resiliency among youth in the child welfare system. *Journal of Personality 77*, 6.

Leve, L. D., Fisher, P. A., & DeGarmo, D. S. (2007). Peer relations at school entry: Sex differences in the outcomes of foster care. *Journal of Developmental Psychology, 53*(4), 557–577.

Linares, L. O., Stovall-McClough, K. C., Li, M., Morin, N., Silva, R., Albert, A., & Cloitre, M. (2008). Salivary cortisol in foster children: A pilot study. *Child Abuse & Neglect, 32*(6), 665–670. doi:10.1016/j.chiabu.2007.06.012

Masten, A. S., & Coatsworth, J. D. (1998). The development of competence in favorable and unfavorable environments: Lessons from research on successful children. *American Psychologist, 53*(2), 205–220.

Patterson, G. R. (1982). *Coercive family process.* Eugene, OR: Castalia.

Patterson, G. R. (2002). *The early development of coercive family process antisocial behavior in children and adolescents: A developmental analysis and model for intervention* (pp. 25–44): Washington, DC: American Psychological Association.

Pilowsky, D. (1995). Psychopathology among children placed in family foster care. *Psychiatric Services, 46*(9), 906–910.

Teplin, L. A., Abram, K. M., McClelland, G. M., Dulcan, M. K., & Mericle, A. A. (2002). Psychiatric disorders in youth in juvenile detention. *Archives of General Psychiatry, 59*(12), 1133–1143.

Trupin, E. W., Tarico, V. S., Low, B. P., Jemelka, R., & McClellan, J. (1993). Children on child protective service caseloads: Prevalence and nature of serious emotional disturbance. *Child Abuse & Neglect, 17*(3), 345–355. doi:10.1016/0145-2134(93)90057-C

U.S. Department of Health and Human Services. (2009). The AFCARS report: Preliminary FY 2008 estimates as of October 2009 (16). Retrieved from www.acf.hhs.gov/programs/cb/stats_research/afcars/tar/report16.htm

U.S. Department of Justice. (2009). *Crime in the United States, 2009: Uniform crime reports.*

Widom, C. S., & Maxfield, M. G. (2001). *An update on the "Cycle of violence." Research in Brief.* Washington, D.C.: U.S. Department of Justice, National Institute of Justice, February 2001, NCJ 184894

Zima, B. T., Bussing, R., Freeman, S., Yang, X., Belin, T. R., & Forness, S. R. (2000). Behavior problems, academic skill delays and school failure among school-aged children in foster care: Their relationship to placement characteristics. *Journal of Child and Family Studies, 9*(1), 87–103. doi:10.1023/A:1009415800475

III

Interventions for Maltreated Children and Their Parents Who May Be In or Out of the CPS System

In Chapter 5, Larissa Niec, Sheila Eyberg, and Rhea Chase describe parent-child interaction therapy (PCIT). Originally developed to treat children with serious behavioral problems, PCIT has demonstrated efficacy in the treatment of families who are maltreating or who are at risk of maltreating their children. A distinctive feature of PCIT is the live, immediate coaching of parents while they interact with their children. Therapists watch the parents from behind a one-way mirror and use a bug-in-the-ear audio device to guide parental behavior and thus teach them more effective parenting techniques.

In Chapter 6, John Lochman and his associates discuss the Coping Power Program and its child welfare applications. The program contains both child and parent components and is designed for intervening with children exhibiting disruptive and aggressive behavior.

In Chapter 7, Shannon Hourigan and her associates describe the Coping Cat program, a cognitive-behavioral approach that emphasizes psychoeducation/skills training and exposure treatment to help traumatized children overcome anxiety related to generalized worry, separation from caregivers, and social situations. It has been adapted for use in different countries, and has been translated into Spanish and Norwegian. After providing relevant background information regarding anxiety disorders in youth and their epidemiology, the Coping Cat program is described in detail. Using a case example of an 11-year-old boy with a history of physical abuse, the authors illustrate how to implement the teaching and rehearsing of a set of anxiety coping skills as well as practicing those skills in real-life situations that provoke anxiety.

In Chapter 8, Dafna Lender, Phyllis Booth, and Sandra Lindaman describe Theraplay, a parent-child psychotherapy that focuses on attachment and relationship development that has been used for many years with foster and adoptive families.

5

Parent–Child Interaction Therapy

Implementing and Sustaining a Treatment Program for Families of Young Children With Disruptive Behavior Disorders

Larissa N. Niec, Sheila Eyberg, and Rhea M. Chase

Disruptive behavior disorders (DBDs) represent a serious, highly prevalent, and costly public health concern (Egger & Angold, 2006). As many as 10% of children meet diagnostic criteria for oppositional defiant disorder (ODD), and 2% to 9% for conduct disorder (CD) (Nock, Kazdin, Hiripi, & Kessler, 2007). For most children, DBDs have a chronic course, and without effective treatment, tend to increase in severity over time (Broidy et al., 2003). These disorders represent a significant risk factor for child maltreatment (Hinshaw & Lee, 2003).

In this chapter we discuss parent-child interaction therapy (PCIT), an evidence-based behavioral family intervention for the treatment of DBDs (Kazdin & De Los Reyes, 2008). We begin with an overview of the treatment process and discuss issues of training and implementation, including a promising new model for dissemination, the learning collaborative model. Finally, we describe the organizing and certifying body of PCIT, PCIT International, and consider current strategies to facilitate the continued development and dissemination of PCIT.

Treatment Overview

PCIT is an empirically supported treatment that enhances the parent-child relationship and increases parents' ability to manage child behavior through the use of behavioral principles (Eyberg & Funderburk, 2011; Niec, Gering, & Abbenante, 2011). Originally developed for children with severely disruptive behaviors, PCIT has also been used for the treatment of externalizing problems associated with children's medical, developmental, and neurological disorders (e.g., Bagner & Eyberg, 2007), for child internalizing disorders such as depression (Lenze, Pautsch, & Luby, 2011) and separation anxiety (Chase & Eyberg, 2008), and for parental physical abuse and neglect (Chaffin et al., 2004; Chaffin et al., 2009; Chaffin, Funderburk, Bard, Valle, & Gurwitch, 2010; Hakman, Chaffin, Funderburk, & Silovsky 2009).

PCIT begins with an assessment of child functioning and parent-child interactions prior to the two phases of treatment: child-directed interaction (CDI) and parent-directed interaction (PDI). Parents accomplish specific goals in each phase before progressing. The first session of each phase is a teaching session in which the therapist explains and demonstrates the new skills with the parents alone. Following the teaching session, the parents and child attend coaching sessions together. During most of each coaching session, the therapist watches from an observation room and actively coaches one parent in use of the skills via a bug-in-ear communication device while the parent plays with the child in the playroom. With two parents in treatment, parents take turns in each session being coached and observing with the therapist while their partner is being coached.

Assessment in PCIT

Assessment is a central feature of PCIT. Coaching is most effective when therapists have identified (a) the child's problem behaviors, (b) parent behaviors that maintain or escalate the child's misconduct, and (c) family strengths that can be enhanced. To assess these domains and screen for other pathology, the PCIT intake assessment begins with a clinical interview in which the therapist gathers information to understand the context of the presenting problems. The interview covers information related to the child's developmental, medical, social, and behavioral history and the parents' attitudes and behaviors regarding their child and their parenting role. Therapists obtain specific information about the salient child behavior problems and the parents' behavior management and discipline strategies. Therapists also discuss the parents' expectations for treatment, clarify any misperceptions, and reinforce the parent for seeking help for their child (or themselves) at this early stage in their child's life.

Following the interview, PCIT therapists conduct behavioral observations of parent-child interactions in standard analog situations using the *Dyadic Parent-Child Interaction Coding System* (Eyberg, Nelson, Ginn, Bhuiyan, & Boggs, 2011). Assessment of *actual* parent and child behavior (rather than only *reported* behavior) is a distinctive component of PCIT. To obtain parents' perception of their child's behaviors, parents complete standardized rating scales of child behavior such as the *Eyberg Child Behavior Inventory* (ECBI) (Eyberg & Pincus, 1999), a brief scale measuring the frequency of common behavior problems, and the *Child Behavior Checklist* (CBCL) (Achenbach & Rescorla, 2000), the *Behavior Assessment Scale for Children* (BASC-2) (Reynolds & Kamphaus, 2004) or other broad screening instruments. These broad assessment scales help clinicians identify potential problems of child functioning across the domains of child psychopathology (e.g., depression, anxiety, conduct disorder), which are particularly relevant to children who have experienced maltreatment.

Additional standardized rating scales may be used by PCIT therapists to evaluate other presenting concerns. When parents are referred through child welfare services for preventive intervention, for example, therapists may administer the *Child Abuse Potential Inventory* (CAP) (Milner, 1986). When children present with significant school behavior problems, therapists may give parents a teacher-rating scale, the *Sutter-Eyberg Student Behavior Inventory* (Eyberg & Pincus, 1999), for their child's teacher to complete.

With information from these intake assessment procedures, the therapist can develop relevant, focused treatment goals for the family. The procedures also provide baseline information to allow therapists to measure change over time. All pretreatment procedures (e.g., DPICS, ECBI, BASC-2) are repeated at the completion of treatment to document treatment outcome. The DPICS and the ECBI are also administered weekly throughout treatment to guide coaching and evaluate progress. The weekly DPICS observational data capture the actual behavior change in the parent-child interaction at each session. These 5-minute observations guide the therapist's decisions regarding specific parenting skills on which to focus during coaching, and they indicate objectively the family's readiness to move from one step in treatment to the next.

Child-Directed Interaction

During the Child-Directed Interaction (CDI), parents learn to follow their child's lead in play. They learn to use specific forms of positive attention that, for most children, function as positive reinforcement—describing and praising positive play behaviors and reflecting appropriate talk. Parents are also taught to avoid particular types of statements—commands, questions, and criticisms—that can be intrusive and often give attention to negative child behaviors. The therapist actively coaches parents to use *differential social attention* as they play with their child. That is, they teach parents to use strategic ignoring when a negative child behavior (such as whining, yelling, back-talking) occurs, and to switch back immediately to positive attention when a positive child behavior (any appropriate behavior) occurs.

The parent behaviors learned in CDI serve to teach children new skills (positive social interaction skills, cooperation) in a play interaction that both the parent and child enjoy. Throughout treatment, parents practice the CDI skills at home with their child during daily 5-minute sessions ("special time"). This treatment phase continues until parents demonstrate mastery of the CDI skills. The positive new parent-child interaction patterns learned in this first phase of PCIT provide the foundation for successful implementation of the discipline strategies introduced in the second phase of treatment. In fact, most children show substantial reductions in disruptive behavior during this initial CDI phase of treatment alone (Eisenstadt, Eyberg, McNeil, Newcomb, & Funderburk, 1993) as well as significant improvements in attachment security scores (Floyd & Eyberg, 2003).

Parent-Directed Interaction

During Parent-Directed Interaction (PDI), parents learn to lead and direct their child's behavior when needed. They are taught to use specific kinds of directions, or "commands," that are most effective with young children. Parents learn to give commands that are direct, age-appropriate, specific, positively stated, and stated one at a time. Parents also learn to explain the reason for a command before the command is given or after it is obeyed, but not between those times. This timing helps to assure that the child will "hear" the reason, and it helps parents avoid reinforcing noncompliance.

To learn consistency in discipline, parents are taught a specific parent-directed algorithm to implement within the context of the positive interaction established in the first phase of treatment. When the child obeys, the parent is taught to give very specific praise for obeying in order to reinforce child compliance. Conversely, if the child does not obey, the parent learns to initiate a time-out sequence. Children are not allowed to use time out as a way to escape compliance. A primary goal of the PDI phase of treatment is for parents to learn to use effective commands and consistent discipline across settings, including in public. To generalize parents' skills and children's compliance, parents are first coached in the clinic room, then in other clinic areas, and finally, *in vivo* in community settings.

PCIT is completed when parents demonstrate mastery of both CDI and PDI skills, report their child's behavior is within normal limits on the ECBI, and indicate confidence in their ability to manage their child's behavior on their own. PCIT is a "performance-based" rather than time-limited treatment, meaning that treatment completion is determined by the progress of the individual family. Therapists work actively to keep families in treatment until these goals are reached, which averages 13 to 16 sessions (Fernandez & Eyberg, 2009; Werba, Eyberg, Boggs, & Algina, 2006).

Implementing and Sustaining PCIT in the Community

PCIT was designed as an intervention for children with disruptive behavior disorders. Initially, graduate programs in clinical psychology served as the primary means for training PCIT therapists. Typically, students received classroom experience along with close, ongoing supervision for over a year to several years. The training model included a co-therapy approach, meaning that more advanced PCIT therapists were paired with less experienced therapists. However, training only within graduate programs was clearly too limited to address community need. As the evidence base for PCIT grew, professional workshops were developed to increase accessibility for other mental health professionals (e.g., master's level social workers) and psychologists working within the community. These workshops often involved intensive (e.g., 20–40 hour) didactic and experiential training experiences, during which trainees were taught the underlying theory of the intervention, practiced the child-centered skills required of parents, and began to develop basic coaching skills.

As dissemination efforts expanded, trainers identified barriers to implementation and maintenance of PCIT programs that occurred at therapist and system levels. Distance from the training site, training costs, and therapist and agency readiness for training are barriers commonly encountered in the dissemination of evidence-based approaches (Fixen, Blase, Duda, Naoom, & Van Dyke, 2010). Over the past decade, trainers have worked to develop models that reduce barriers to the implementation and maintenance of a PCIT program. For instance, to increase generalization of therapists' skills, regular phone consultation and discussion of videotaped sessions are implemented after the initial workshop in cases where distance prohibits live supervision. More recently, telemedicine technology has been used to allow trainers to consult with trainees from a distance and also provide live, immediate feedback to trainees during a PCIT session (Funderburk, Ware, Altshuler, & Chaffin, 2008).

In 2004, the Kauffman report identified PCIT as a best practice in the field of child abuse treatment (Chadwick Center on Children and Families, 2004). The report also noted that training and dissemination efforts had been limited and delineated a disturbing chasm between best and everyday practice in community settings. Recommendations subsequently included the exploration of new approaches to promote the implementation of evidence-based practices in the treatment of child abuse, including PCIT (Chadwick Center on Children and Families, 2004). The Institute for Healthcare Improvement (IHI) offered a promising model of training and implementation, referred to as the Breakthrough Series Collaborative (BSC). This innovative approach focuses on collaboration among sites interested in adopting new practices and addresses organizational barriers to implementation and sustainability. The National Center for Child Traumatic Stress (NCCTS) has pioneered the adaptation of the BSC methodology to best practices in mental health treatment. Preliminary results suggest the learning collaborative is a promising model of implementation, with community therapists who participate in the collaborative achieving comparable levels of fidelity and treatment outcome as reported in randomized clinical trials (Ebert, Amaya-Jackson, Markiewicz, & Fairbank, in press).

Overview of the Learning Collaborative Methodology and the Model for Improvement

The NCCTS Learning Collaborative on the Adoption and Implementation of Evidence-Based Treatments is designed to enhance fidelity and the diffusion of evidence-based treatments while overcoming implementation barriers. The learning collaborative achieves these goals by targeting three domains of implementation: (1) clinical competence; (2) family and client engagement; and (3) organizational support and readiness. Evidence suggests that full adoption and sustainability of an evidence-based treatment model requires changes within each of these domains. Thus, the Learning Collaborative (LC) includes three "tracks": clinicians (i.e., therapists), supervisors, and agency administrators or *senior leaders*. All three groups attend the face-to-face training sessions and participate in ongoing consultation calls throughout training. Therapists and senior leaders sometimes attend separate sessions to address content areas specific to their track. In a PCIT LC, for example, therapists may learn the DPICS coding system while senior leaders discuss and practice marketing strategies. However, the groups are often together, so that all participants understand the basic principles of the treatment program and everyone learns the *model for improvement*.

The *model for improvement* represents a platform of implementation, allowing trainees to address barriers to treatment fidelity and sustainability. Trainees learn to use data or *metrics* to monitor their progress and identify and address challenges specific to their agency using *small tests of change (STOC)*. A STOC involves the *Plan-Do-Study-Act (PDSA)* cycle, in which a trainee identifies an area of weakness or a barrier, tests a possible solution, evaluates the results, and determines next steps depending on the outcome. As an example, one therapist may notice that her PCIT families are having difficulty completing their homework. She decides to create a handout outlining the benefits of homework completion (*plan*). She provides one family with the handout (*do*), and evaluates its effectiveness at the next session (*study*). Depending on the results, the therapist and her agency team will take steps to improve and/or propagate the handout (*act*). A STOC is designed to be a simple and quick method used to address barriers to successful implementation that does not require full consensus at the administrative level.

The Structure of the Learning Collaborative

The LC methodology relies on active learning principles and recognizes that most learning occurs through live experience. Face-to-face trainings therefore occur in three *learning sessions* separated by *action periods*. Learning collaborative faculty-trainers provide ongoing consultation during each action period as trainees implement the skills learned during training. In a PCIT learning collaborative, *Learning Session 1* may be primarily dedicated to DPICS and the CDI. Therapists begin their cases soon afterwards in close consultation with a trainer. *Learning Session 2* occurs approximately eight weeks later, with a focus on advanced CDI topics and an introduction to PDI. During *Action Period 2*, consultation continues as therapists progress with their families into the PDI. *Learning Session 3* focuses on advanced clinical topics, with a strong focus on the achievements of the trainees. In *Action Period 3*, therapists continue to receive consultation, but the trainers increasingly ask therapists to rely on their own experiences to address challenges and barriers. Indeed, throughout the process, trainers recognize the wealth of expertise from all trainees. Trainees are frequently asked to share successes and failures throughout the training process, so that others may learn from their experience. The goal is to create a collaborative learning environment in which trainees rely on one another to maintain treatment fidelity as they move forward.

PCIT of the Carolinas

While other treatment protocols have been disseminated using the learning collaborative approach, these methods are only now being applied to PCIT. In 2009 The Duke Endowment approached the Center for Child and Family Health (CCFH) to develop dissemination strategies for PCIT. Through the combined expertise of faculty and staff from CCFH and the NCCTS, who work within the Duke Evidence Based Practice Implementation Center (EPIC), the *PCIT of the Carolinas* project was created to disseminate PCIT across North and South Carolina. The project aims to prevent child maltreatment and ameliorate associated risk factors through the widespread adoption and implementation of PCIT in communities across both states through the NCCTS LC approach. Results from this innovative project will inform future training efforts and provide much-needed data on optimal training efficiency to promote the spread while maintaining the fidelity of PCIT. The training requirements outlined by PCIT International, such as close consultation with a PCIT master trainer and live case experience, are mapped directly onto the structure of the learning collaborative. Additionally, the LC requires senior leaders to consider their agency's organizational capacity and readiness to implement PCIT. These implementation factors are increasingly recognized as necessary for the successful adoption of any evidence-based program, and may be even more important in the implementation of PCIT, given the intensity of the model and the space and equipment needs unique to PCIT. The LC seems a promising direction as the field works to increase the accessibility of evidence-based programs to children and families.

PCIT International

PCIT International is the organizing body that seeks to "promote fidelity in the practice of parent-child interaction therapy through well-conducted research, training, and continuing education of therapists and trainers" (http://pcit.org/). The organization was developed in response to rapid increases in national and international dissemination and the accompanying challenges to maintaining treatment fidelity and effectiveness.

Given the urgent need for effective interventions to reach a greater proportion of communities (e.g., Kazdin, 2008), empirically informed dissemination is a particular priority for PCIT International. The pressing call for effective mental health services for children may lead some to consider using only pieces of an evidence-based intervention such as PCIT, with the hope that some portion of the treatment or modified treatment might be less expensive to implement, and perhaps better than no treatment at all (Niec, Gehring, & Abbenante, 2011). However, without solid research to support modifications, children and families are likely to receive less effective or ineffective services. In the end, such changes are more costly to individuals, agencies, and society if children and families do not improve.

PCIT International's ongoing strategies to foster fidelity include the release of PCIT training guidelines (http://pcit.org/documents/PCIT_Training_Guidelines_2009.pdf), the development of certification requirements and continuing education for PCIT therapists, and the emphasis on collaboration between researchers and clinicians. The organization sponsors a biennial international PCIT conference and supports regional conferences as a means to reach community therapists and to connect trainers and researchers with those seeking support to develop or to sustain a PCIT program.

Summary

Parent-child interaction therapy is an evidence-based treatment for families with children with disruptive behavior disorders that teaches parents positive, child-centered interaction skills and healthy, developmentally appropriate behavior management strategies. PCIT has been identified as a best practice intervention for physically abusive families and has also demonstrated positive outcomes with neglectful families. As with other evidence-based interventions, dissemination efforts for PCIT still lag behind community need. However, training models are increasingly addressing prominent system and therapist barriers to facilitate the implementation and maintenance of PCIT programs within communities. The Learning Collaborative model is one promising means through which trainers, therapists, and senior leaders can work cooperatively to develop tailored strategies to reduce barriers within an individual agency. Telemedicine technology offers another innovative method of dissemination that may increase trainer-trainee contact and reduce distance and travel barriers.

As the dissemination of PCIT continues to expand, it will be increasingly important for PCIT International, the organizing and certifying body of PCIT, to maintain a strong link between PCIT researchers and clinicians. PCIT International helps to maintain the fidelity of the intervention in training and practice, facilitates the continued development of the protocol, and promotes empirically informed dissemination.

References

Achenbach, T., & Rescorla, L. (2000). *Manual for the ASEBA preschool forms and profiles*. Burlington, VT: ASEBA.

Bagner, D. M., & Eyberg, S. M. (2007). Parent-child interaction therapy for disruptive behavior in children with mental retardation: A randomized controlled trial. *Journal of Clinical Child & Adolescent Psychology, 36*, 418–429.

Broidy, L., Nagin, D. S., Tremblay, R. E., Bates, J. E., Brame, B., Dodge, K. A., et al. (2003). Developmental trajectories of childhood disruptive behaviors and adolescent delinquency: A six site, cross-national study. *Developmental Psychology, 39*, 222–245.

Chadwick Center on Children and Families. (2004). Closing the quality chasm in child abuse treatment: Identifying and disseminating best practices. San Diego, CA: Author.

Chaffin, M., Funderburk, B., Bard, D., Valle, L., & Gurwitch, R. (2010). A combined motivation and parent-child interaction therapy package reduces child welfare recidivism in a randomized dismantling field trial. *Journal of Consulting and Clinical Psychology, 79*(1), Feb 2011, 84–95

Chaffin, M., Silovsky, J. F., Funderburk, B., Valle, L. A., Brestan, E. V., Balachova, T. et al. (2004). Parent-child interaction therapy with physically abusive parents: Efficacy for reducing future abuse. *Journal of Consulting and Clinical Psychology, 72*, 500–510.

Chaffin, M., Valle, L., Funderburk, B., Gurwitch, R., Silovsky, J., Bard, D. et al. (2009). A motivational intervention can improve retention in PCIT for low-motivation child welfare clients. *Child Maltreatment, 14*(4), 356–368.

Chase, R., & Eyberg, S. (2008). Clinical presentation and treatment outcome for children with comorbid externalizing and internalizing symptoms. *Journal of Anxiety Disorders, 22*, 273–282.

Ebert, L., Amaya-Jackson, L., Markiewicz, J., & Fairbank, J.A. (in press). Development and application of the NCCTS Learning Collaborative Model for the implementation of evidence-based child trauma treatment. In D. Barlow and K. McHugh (Eds.), *Dissemination of evidence-based treatments*. New York, NY: Oxford University Press.

Egger, H., & Angold, A. (2006). Common etiological and behavioral disorders in preschool children: Presentation, nosology and epidemiology. *Journal of Child Psychology and Psychiatry, 47*, 313–337.

Eisenstadt, T. H., Eyberg, S. M., McNeil, C. B., Newcomb, K., & Funderburk, B. (1993). Parent-child interaction therapy with behavior problem children: Relative effectiveness of two stages and overall treatment outcome. *Journal of Clinical Child Psychology, 22*, 42–51.

Eyberg, S., & Funderburk, B. (2011). *Parent-child interaction therapy protocol*. Gainesville, FL: PCIT International, Inc.

Eyberg, S., Nelson, M., Ginn, N., Bhuiyan, N., & Boggs, S. (2011). *Dyadic Parent-Child Coding System Manual*. Gainesville, FL: PCIT International, Inc.

Eyberg, S. M., & Pincus, D. (1999). *Eyberg Child Behavior Inventory and Sutter-Eyberg Student Behavior Inventory: Professional manual*. Odessa, FL: Psychological Assessment Resources.

Fernandez, M., & Eyberg, S. (2009). Predicting treatment and follow-up attrition in parent-child interaction therapy. *Journal of Abnormal Child Psychology, 37*, 431–441.

Fixen, D., Blase, K., Duda, M., Naoom, S., & Van Dyke, M. (2010). Implementation of evidence-based treatments for children and adolescents: Research findings and their implications for the future. In J. Weisz & A. Kazdin (Eds.), *Evidence-based psychotherapies for children and adolescent* (pp. 435–450, 2nd ed. New York: Guilford.

Floyd, E. M., & Eyberg, S. M. (2003, August). *Testing the attachment theory of parent-child interaction therapy*. Poster session presented at the annual meeting of the American Psychological Association, Toronto, Canada.

Funderburk, B., Ware, L., Altshuler, E., & Chaffin, M. (2008). Use and feasibility of telemedicine technology in the dissemination of parent-child interaction therapy. *Child Maltreatment, 13*, 377–382.

Hakman, M., Chaffin, M., Funderburk, B., & Silovsky, J. F. (2009). Change trajectories for parent-child interaction sequences during parent-child interaction therapy for child physical abuse. *Child Abuse & Neglect, 33*, 461–470.

Hinshaw, S., & Lee, S. (2003). Conduct and oppositional defiant disorders. In E. Mash & R. Barkley (Eds.), *Child psychopathology* (pp. 144–198, 2nd ed. New York: Guilford.

Kazdin, A. E. (2008). Evidence-based treatments and delivery of psychological services: Shifting our emphases to increase impact. *Psychological Services, 5*, 201–215.

Kazdin, A. E., & De Los Reyes, A. (2008). Conduct disorder. In R.J. Morris & T.R. Kratochwill (Eds.), *The practice of child therapy* (pp. 207–247, 4th ed.). New York: Lawrence Erlbaum Associates.

Lenze, S. N., Pautsch, J., & Luby, J. L. (2011). Parent-child interaction therapy emotion development: A novel treatment for depression in preschool children. *Depression & Anxiety, 28*, 153–159.

Milner, J. S. (1986). *Child abuse potential inventory manual, Second Edition*. Lutz, FL: Psychological Assessment Resources.

Niec, L. N., Gering, C., & Abbenante, E. (2011). Parent-child interaction therapy: The role of play in the behavioral treatment of childhood conduct problems. In: S. Russ & L. Niec (Eds.), *Play in therapy: Evidence-based approaches to assessment and practice* (pp. 149–167). New York, NY: Guilford Press.

Nock, M. K., Kazdin, A. E., Hiripi, E., & Kessler, R. C. (2007). Lifetime prevalence, correlates, and persistence of oppositional defiant disorder: Results from the National Comorbidity Survey Replication. *Journal of Child Psychology and Psychiatry, 48*, 703–713.

Reynolds, C. R., & Kamphaus, R. W. (2004). *Behavioral assessment system for children, Second Edition*. Circle Pines, MN: American Guidance Service.

Werba, B., Eyberg, S. M., Boggs, S. R., & Algina, J. (2006). Predicting the outcome of parent-child interaction therapy: Success and Attrition. *Behavior Modification, 30*, 618–646.

CHAPTER **6**

The Coping Power Program
*Child Welfare Applications**

John E. Lochman, Caroline L. Boxmeyer,
Nicole P. Powell, Rachel E. Baden,
Sara L. Stromeyer, and Jessica A. Minney

Overview

The Coping Power program (Lochman, Wells, & Lenhart, 2008; Wells, Lochman, & Lenhart, 2008) was developed to specifically target anger and aggression in youth and has been researched extensively. Anger often precedes aggression, and angry children are also more likely to exhibit externalizing behaviors. Childhood aggression and behavior problems are especially important issues because they have been linked to adverse outcomes such as substance use, delinquency, academic issues, and poor adjustment (Loeber, 1990). Additionally, anger and aggression can have a large impact on peer and familial relationships, and may lead to mistreatment by others. Research has indicated that child externalizing behaviors and negative parenting are reciprocally related, such that negative parenting not only contributes to behavior problems, but is also exacerbated by them. This evidence suggests that concurrently treating aggressive children's behavior as well as addressing parenting deficits may reduce negative parenting practices, and therefore the potential for maltreatment.

Contextual Social–Cognitive Model

The Coping Power intervention was based on the contextual social-cognitive model of aggression, which reflects an ecological approach and posits that specific family and community factors both directly and indirectly affect children's externalizing behavior

* The preparation of this chapter was supported by a grant provided by the National Institute of Drug Abuse (DA23156–3). Correspondence can be sent to: John E. Lochman, Department of Psychology, Box 870348, The University of Alabama, Tuscaloosa, AL 35487.

(Lochman & Wells, 2002). Factors such as maternal depression, low socioeconomic status, and neighborhood violence may also exert influence through mediational processes, including parenting practices, peer relations, and social cognition and emotional regulation. Because these factors and processes are considered risk factors for the development and escalation of conduct problems, they may serve as targets of prevention and intervention efforts. Of note, all of these factors may interact reciprocally with children's externalizing behavior, such that children's behavior, social-cognitive factors, and ecological context influence and reinforce each other over time, likely leading to negative developmental outcomes.

In terms of contextual factors, many aspects of a child's environment can contribute to problems with anger and aggression. Family factors such as poverty, stressful events, mental illness, and criminality negatively affect children through their impact on parenting. Parents experiencing these issues are more likely to use harsh and inconsistent discipline, to use poor monitoring and supervision strategies, and are less likely to be warm and involved (e.g., Patterson, Reid, & Dishion, 1992). Consequently, these practices can lead to conduct problems in children. As discussed earlier, children with behavioral problems may also elicit these ineffective parenting strategies. Children's aggression may also contribute to peer rejection, which puts them at risk for developing more significant behavior problems. Additionally, rejection by prosocial peers may lead aggressive children to join deviant peer groups, which contributes to escalation of externalizing behavior and rule violation through modeling and social reinforcement. Furthermore, children who are exposed to aggression in their homes, neighborhoods, schools, or on television are more likely to exhibit aggression themselves. Notably, children who witness domestic violence or experience abuse are at increased risk for anger and aggression problems.

Aggressive children also display deficits in accurate encoding and appraisal of social information, as well as social problem solving. Crick and Dodge's (1994) social-information processing model entails six steps that describe how children respond to interpersonal interactions. During the first three steps, children encode internal and external cues, interpret these cues, and formulate a goal. Research has shown that aggressive children exhibit a hostile attribution bias, in that they excessively view others' intentions as hostile and recall more hostile cues. Aggressive children also tend to generate more interpersonal goals involving power and dominance than their peers. The last three steps of the model involve accessing possible responses, choosing a response, and enacting that response. Research has shown that compared to their peers, aggressive children tend to generate fewer solutions to social problems and view aggression as an acceptable and effective solution. Furthermore, they seem to have difficulty enacting solutions involving verbal assertion and compromise.

Finally, these social-cognitive processes may interact with children's emotional and physiological responses to contribute to further problem behavior. Perceptions of others' hostile intent can increase arousal and anger, which can lead to subsequent hostile attributions. Aggressive children's schemas involving the belief that others are hostile can negatively shade perceptions of current social interactions, which lead to arousal, anger, and aggressive behavior. Overall, angry and aggressive children are at risk for a variety of negative influences and outcomes. The Coping Power program addresses a number of these factors within the contextual social-cognitive model in order to ameliorate these children's developmental trajectories.

Coping Power Program: History and Goals

The Coping Power program was developed through adaptation of the Anger Coping program (Larson & Lochman, 2002) in order to enhance outcome effects and long-term maintenance of gains. Coping Power is a multicomponent, evidence-based intervention that is rooted in the contextual social-cognitive model and is indicated for children exhibiting disruptive and aggressive behavior. Although it was originally designed to be implemented with fourth- to sixth-grade children, Coping Power has also been successfully adapted for younger and older children. The program addresses individual child problems as well as malleable risk factors in the family, peer, neighborhood, and classroom contexts (for review, see Lochman, Wells, & Murray, 2007). Coping Power can be implemented as a targeted prevention or intervention in individual or group formats by mental health professionals in clinical practice settings or by school guidance counselors and related school personnel. Coping Power has also been successfully adapted for other languages (e.g., Dutch, Spanish) and cultures.

The Coping Power program is a manualized treatment that contains both child and parent components, which are normally delivered over a period of 16 to 18 months in group formats. The child component covers 34 sessions that use cognitive-behavioral strategies to encourage skill building in goal setting, emotion recognition and awareness, anger coping, relaxation techniques, perspective taking, social problem solving, handling peer pressure, and positive social skills. Children also identify goals and receive daily feedback on weekly goal sheets, which support skill generalization outside of the session.

The 16-session parent component is intended for concurrent use with the child component. Parents discuss how to reinforce positive behaviors, ignore minor misbehaviors, give effective instructions, establish appropriate rules and expectations, and give effective and appropriate consequences for child misbehavior. By learning complementary skills, parents can foster and reinforce their child's academic success and newly learned skills. Additionally, parents receive coaching in stress management, relationship building, and promotion of family communication. Finally, a teacher curriculum can be administered during in-service teacher workshops. Collaboration between leaders and teachers is encouraged, and recommendations are provided for working with teachers. Helping teachers participate in the goal-setting process and learn to reinforce student's positive behavior can also maximize child gains.

The efficacy and effectiveness of Coping Power have been well documented in several randomized controlled trials. Research indicates that children who received Coping Power exhibited fewer delinquent acts, less parent-reported substance abuse, and greater teacher-reported behavioral improvements after 1 year compared to children receiving care-as-usual (Lochman & Wells, 2004). The following sections detail specific intervention components.

Coping Power Child Component

Coping Power Child Component sessions follow a standard sequence, teaching skills that are often lacking in children with disruptive behavior problems. Students build awareness of their emotional experiences and learn strategies for managing anger and frustration. They also learn skills important for resolving interpersonal conflicts including perspective taking, accurate identification of social problems, and consideration of non-hostile reasons for another person's actions. A social problem-solving model is taught in which students consider an array of potential choices and their resulting consequences in determining how to respond in an interpersonal problem situation. Given that children with disruptive behavior may be particularly vulnerable to negative peer processes, the Coping Power program also addresses peer pressure resistance and strategies to increase involvement with nondeviant peers. The following section provides more detail about several of the Coping Power program's main areas of focus.

Emotion Awareness and Anger Management

The Coping Power child component includes a major focus on emotion awareness and anger management. This focus derives from clinical and empirical evidence suggesting that children with externalizing behavior problems often become angry prior to engaging in aggressive behavior. Sessions in line with this focus are intended to help children recognize when they are becoming angry so that they can short circuit their automatic, aggressive responses and manage their anger more adaptively. Sessions targeting emotion awareness and anger management involve the use of a variety of cognitive-behavioral techniques.

A number of Coping Power sessions focus on bolstering children's emotion awareness. In all of these sessions, Coping Power leaders normalize the experience of emotion and emphasize that all feelings are acceptable but that some behaviors are not. In the initial session, leaders guide children through a range of activities centered on emotion recognition and emotion labeling. For example, leaders might use cartoon sketches of faces, emotion cartoons, or pictures of real faces from a magazine and ask children to identify the emotion depicted. Leaders might also engage children in a miming activity, in which the leader and children take turns nonverbally expressing or acting out feeling states. Throughout this initial session, leaders might periodically identify how they are feeling, ask the children to do the same, and emphasize that monitoring feelings periodically can help people become more aware of them.

Sessions focused on emotion awareness also include a focus on the triggers for emotion and behavioral, physiological, and cognitive cues. Children are asked to identify situations that typically set off an emotion inside of them. They are also introduced to the notion of having specific behavioral, physiological, and cognitive cues for emotion. Leaders might use kid-friendly terms when introducing this concept, referring to cues as "what people can see," "what you feel inside of your body," and "the thoughts inside of your head." Leaders work through several different emotions (e.g., happy, scared, angry) with children and help them to identify the behavioral, physiological, and cognitive correlates for each. In addition to these discussion-based activities, children are engaged in role-plays, exposed to video clips, and asked to complete homework assignments—all targeting their awareness of feeling states and emotion cues.

Sessions focused on emotion awareness also emphasize that emotions exist on a continuum and are experienced at a range of intensity. These sessions may be particularly helpful for children who have trouble recognizing gradients in their emotional experience and who tend to perceive emotions as "all-or-nothing." The goal of these sessions is to help children recognize when they are experiencing low levels of anger arousal, so that they might intervene with coping strategies before their anger escalates and significantly taxes their coping resources. Leaders teach children about the range of emotional intensity using the analogy of a thermometer. Children receive a picture of an "emotion thermometer," and they are asked to label various levels within several specific emotions. Specific attention is given to anger and to labeling various levels of anger on the thermometer (e.g., "annoyed" at the bottom, "mad" in the middle, and "enraged" at the top). As homework, children are asked to record their daily experience of angry feelings on an anger thermometer. They are specifically asked to check off their anger intensity and to identify the trigger for their anger. The goal of these homework assignments is to help children generalize intervention lessons to the real world.

Sessions targeting emotion awareness lay the groundwork for sessions focused on anger management. In introducing the topic of anger management, leaders emphasize that individuals' ability to cope with emotions varies depending on the intensity of the emotion experienced. Leaders point out, for example, that coping with anger at low levels of intensity may be easier than coping with anger at high levels of intensity. Moreover, different coping strategies may be necessary to diffuse different levels of anger. Leaders and children might brainstorm possible strategies to use when coping with different levels of anger.

Additional sessions targeting anger management involve a process of gradually exposing children to progressively more emotionally arousing activities. Children are concurrently coached in additional anger management techniques. Children gain practice in managing low levels of anger by engaging in a memorization task (e.g., remembering the numbers in a stack of 10 playing cards) while the leader and/or group members make noise and tease the target child. Establishing ground rules for what types of teasing are off limits is essential prior to beginning this activity. An additional activity might involve asking the target child to build a tower of dominoes with one hand while the leader and/or group members tease and distract. It is important for leaders to debrief with children about these activities afterward, with an eye toward highlighting ways in which self-distraction techniques were used to keep anger low and performance high. Leaders should also help children draw parallels with real-life situations.

In the sessions that follow, progressively more anger-arousing activities are introduced. As these more challenging activities are introduced, children are coached in additional anger management techniques like the use of coping self-statements (e.g., "It's not worth it to get angry," "I won't be a fool, I'll keep cool"). Children are introduced to coping self-statements through video clips. They gain initial practice in using coping self-statements through role-plays with puppets, in which one puppet is being teased by other puppets. This activity is intended to prepare children for a more challenging activity, in which they are directly teased by the leader and/or other group members. Although it is important for leaders to identify some basic ground rules, this activity is designed to elicit mild to moderate levels of anger arousal to prepare the children for dealing with real-life situations they might encounter. Nonetheless, it is important for leaders to closely monitor this activity and intervene as necessary. In order to provide a visual illustration of the link between anger arousal and use of self-statements, leaders might ask children to indicate their anger arousal by walking up and down an over-size, floor thermometer while saying their coping self-statements out loud. As homework, children are asked to record their daily experience of angry feelings by checking off their anger intensity on their anger thermometer, identifying the trigger, and listing the coping statements they used.

The final anger management session involves coaching children in the use of additional coping strategies and brainstorming with them about how to overcome barriers to anger coping. In this session, children gain in-vivo practice in coping strategies like deep breathing and relaxation, and they are asked to brainstorm self-soothing strategies for managing anger after a conflict (e.g., talking to a friend, listening to music, going for a walk). Leaders also engage children in role-plays of difficult situations with barriers that must be overcome. Children gain experience in role-playing solutions for overcoming those barriers.

Perspective Taking, Problem Identification, and Attribution Retraining

Three perspective taking sessions introduce the first part of the problem-solving model, known as Problem Identification, Choices, and Consequences (PICC). These sessions focus on perspective taking by teaching group members to consider the various motivations and circumstances underlying social problems. Cognitive errors such as the hostile attribution bias, in which threat is perceived in others' neutral or even positive actions, are challenged in these sessions to improve the accuracy of participants' social problem identification. Like all of these units, children first are presented with a set of game-like tasks which are meant to be enjoyable and which permit the clinician to present the main points of the unit. For example, children view pictures which can be perceived in several different ways, including a picture that can be either seen as an old woman or a young woman depending on how one attends to the picture, and another picture that has a word hidden among some background figures. These game-like tasks allow the therapist to note that there can be several different interpretations of what we see, and that it is sometimes "hard to tell" what is the "right" interpretation. "Hard to tell" is the message for this task, and suggests that we sometimes need to slow down when we see ambiguous situations.

These initial tasks are followed by activities that are more challenging and are more related to the difficulties that the children experience. Role-playing and discussion are used to illustrate how hard it often is to accurately understand another person's intentions in a problem situation. Children engage in a brief role-play of an ambiguous social situation in which central characters may have had several different motivations for their behaviors. Children are "frozen" during the role-play and then interviewed by a "traveling reporter" about the causes for the behavior; the moral of the story is again that it is sometimes hard to tell why someone engaged in a certain behavior. These role-plays ultimately have a primary emphasis on retraining of the hostile attributional bias which many aggressive children have. If children can slow down their interpretations of others' intentions, they may conclude, in certain situations, that it is unclear if the other person definitely had aggressive intentions and that more information is necessary—it is "hard to tell."

Although the main focus of these activities is on peer situations, aggressive children also can be hypersensitive to whether adults such as teachers or foster parents are fair with them, and they often misperceive adults' intentions. Thus, a teacher interview has been designed to address children's perceived unfairness and harshness of teachers by permitting the teacher to provide alternate and more benign intentions for her or his teaching strategies and discipline efforts in the classroom. Children first ask teachers a series of questions about how school was for them when they were young, and then children ask about what teachers like about teaching and what their goals and intentions are in the classroom. These questions provide a teacher with the opportunity to state that their goal is to provide good education for all students in the classroom and to have a quiet classroom atmosphere so all children can learn. This interview can be readily adapted to be used with foster parents as well as teachers.

Social Problem–Solving Skills

The unit of the Coping Power child component with the largest number of sessions involves the steps and the use of the PICC problem-solving model. Children learn that PICC is an acronym for three basic problem-solving steps of Problem Identification—Choices—Consequences.

The Problem Identification step is first taught with concrete examples (e.g., a car that won't run; a video game that won't work) to illustrate how one has to "PICC apart" problem situations so that the problem is defined in a discrete observable way, and so that earlier antecedents to the identified problem can be seen. It is often easier to begin to use the PICC problem-solving process with a less-arousing earlier antecedent of a peer conflict, at a point when many solutions are still possible. As children learn to define the problems that they encounter in precise behavioral terms, they also indicate their degree of anger activation in the situation, using the anger thermometer that they have learned earlier. They also identify their goal in the situation. Clinicians shape the goal to be as positive as possible (e.g., what the child wants to achieve in the situation rather than wanting to get back in vengeful way at a presumed provocateur), and the brainstorming of solutions is directed towards this goal rather than the problem per se. Problem solving toward a goal, like problem solving with earlier antecedents of a problem, permits children to consider a range of more constructive solutions such as verbal assertion strategies and solutions that involve compromises.

Brainstorming discussions, as well as hands-on activities and use of PICC forms, are used to introduce the range of choices, or possible solutions, that children have in most social problem situations, and then to introduce the range of consequences which result from these various choices. Hypothetical problem situations are used first to help children consider a large number and range of solutions, in a game-like atmosphere. Children then begin to generate multiple solutions to problems that they have recently encountered. The therapist should insure that children are generating a range of both adaptive strategies (verbal assertion and compromise) and maladaptive (nonverbal direct action and aggressive strategies) for each problem, and if the children don't, the therapist can shape and insert types of strategies that have been missed. The idea of consequences is introduced with a game-like task called Trouble at Sea. On this task children must decide which of 10 items should be thrown overboard from a boat that has lost power at sea, discussing the consequences of throwing various items overboard.

A critical step in problem solving then involves brainstorming, in a nonevaluative way, similar to the brainstorming used in generating choices, of the numerous short and long term consequences of each solution. Thus, the range of consequences for aggressive responses should include positive consequences for the child (e.g., "It feels good") as well as negative, longer-term consequences (e.g., "I will be suspended from school. My foster parent will ground me"). It is also useful to shape children's statements about consequences into probabilistic rather than absolute terms (e.g., "The other child *might* move back permitting me to meet my goal of keeping my place in line" versus "The other child *will* move back"). These conditional predictions of consequences avoid creating an unrealistic likelihood of initial success, and readily lead to situational discussion of "Under what circumstances might this choice work?" The children then use the consequences they brainstormed to "PICC" a "winning" solution by rating each choice as being either a "++", "+", or "−" solution and then selecting the choice with the greatest likelihood of meeting their goal in the problem situation.

A series of activities also address how children's use of impulsive, automatic processing can impair their problem-solving skills. To illustrate how they can generate different, and potentially more successful, solutions to problems when they are able to use deliberate rather than automatic processing, children provide immediate solutions to a problem and then wait 20 seconds before providing solutions to a problem. Children examine how their solutions change if they can wait before responding, and how they may be more likely to be "winning" solutions. Through repeated practice of ideas about more adaptive solutions during therapeutic discussions and role-playing, the clinician ultimately assists children to have some of these better solutions retrieved during deliberate processing to become salient enough to emerge as their first choice when they automatically problem solve in real-life situations. Other structured activities are used to facilitate children's use of adaptive social goals and of more resilient problem-solving. It is not uncommon for some aggressive children to think first of an adaptive, verbally assertive response to a provocation from a peer, but if that should fail, to then respond with an aggressive response. To assist children in handling such frustration during their problem-solving efforts, children play a Solvers-Blockers game in which children alternate between solving, and then blocking the solution, of a hypothetical problem.

The PICC model is used on children's own problems during discussions and role-plays. A particularly useful way to generate children's active involvement in learning problem-solving is to have the children create a videotape of a problem situation with several possible "winning" solutions. Because they typically look forward to this task, the videotaping activity tends to maintain children's motivation in the program, even among these high-risk children. Later problem-solving sessions address how the PICC model could be used in common problem situations with teachers, siblings, and peers. The peer sessions focus on the difficulties many of these children experience with successfully joining ongoing activities of peers, and in negotiating with peers during disagreements.

Peer Pressure and Involvement With Nondeviant Peers

Later Coping Power sessions primarily address issues related to peer pressure, and children's involvement in deviant peer groups. These sessions focus on children's awareness of peer pressure to participate in drug use, and in various peer pressure coping strategies, using videotapes and role-plays. The dangers that can be evident in children's neighborhoods are addressed by having children complete neighborhood surveys, emphasizing dangers that can lead to peer pressure to engage in deviant behavior or that can lead to violence. These sessions also assist children in thinking about where they stand in existing peer groups at their schools and in their neighborhoods, and how they can become progressively more involved with less-deviant groups of peers.

Coping Power Parent Component

The Coping Power parent component has its origins in well-established social-learning theory-based parenting programs. The curriculum covers standard parenting skills including promoting the parent-child relationship, helping parents to identify problem behaviors and their prosocial opposites in specific operational terms, providing praise for desirable behaviors, giving effective instructions, establishing developmentally appropriate rules and expectations, managing inappropriate behaviors, and establishing a structure for communication among family members. In addition to covering standard parent training skills, the Coping Power parent component includes sessions focused on stress management, family problem-solving, and family cohesion building.

Although not designed to directly address the specific issues faced by families in which children have been maltreated or neglected, the Coping Power parent component can serve as a useful adjunctive intervention to assist parents in gaining and/or improving on basic parenting skills. The program can also be appropriate for assisting foster parents in managing children's challenging behaviors and for promoting positive family relationships. Again, other resources would likely be needed to help foster parents understand the emotional and behavioral effects of maltreatment and neglect, and to modify parenting strategies as needed. As described below, the program is designed to affect child behavior through positive parent-child relations and rewards for appropriate behavior. Corporal and harsh punishment strategies are devalued, and parents are given tools to safely and effectively manage their children's misbehavior.

Promoting the Parent–Child Relationship

An important initial goal of the Coping Power parent component is to help parents structure relationship-building interactions with their children. Leaders discuss the influential role of parents in their children's lives and emphasize the important protective effects of a close parent-child relationship against adolescent problems such as peer pressure and gang involvement. Time is spent within the session concretely identifying activities that will be enjoyable for the child, and establishing a structure and ground rules for parent-child "special time." Parents are encouraged to spend at least 10 to 15 minutes each day in positive activities with their children, during which they provide attention and praise, and refrain from criticizing or reprimanding.

Basic Social Learning Theory: Behaviors and Consequences

Parents are provided with a basic definition of social learning theory, as it applies to children's behavior. Leaders explain that behaviors are influenced by the events that come both before (antecedents) and after (consequences), and refer to this principle as the "A-B-C (Antecedent-Behavior-Consequence) Model." In this initial session, the focus is on behaviors and positive consequences. Antecedents are addressed in later sessions on delivering effective instructions and establishing rules and expectations. In regard to behaviors, parents are taught to identify their children's negative behaviors in specific, observable terms (e.g., "defies rules" or "curses" rather than "acts up"), then to identify the positive opposites of these behaviors (e.g., "follows instructions," "uses appropriate language"). The power of positive consequences for encouraging desirable behavior is then discussed. Rewards might include privileges or tangible items, though a particular emphasis is placed on praise. As a between-sessions homework assignment, parents are asked to track their children's negative and positive behaviors, to reward the "good" behaviors with praise, and to take note of how consistently rewarding desirable behaviors can lead them to increase in frequency with a decline in the corresponding negative behaviors.

Basic Social Learning Theory: Antecedents

Having established the role of consequences in promoting positive behaviors, the curriculum moves to a focus on behavioral antecedents. Noncompliance is presented as a negative behavior that concerns almost all parents involved in the program. Leaders explain how parents can increase the likelihood that children will comply if instructions are delivered in an effective manner. "Good instructions" start with the parent considering whether the instruction is important enough to warrant the parent expending energy following through and delivering a consequence if needed. In addition, parents should consider the timing of the instruction, realizing that a child is less likely to comply if interrupted from an enjoyable activity. Good instructions are defined as being given in a respectful tone of voice, given as a direct statement, given only once, and being followed by 10 seconds of silence. Parents are provided with examples of good instructions, as well as "bad instructions" that may increase the probability of noncompliance.

Parents are also assisted in establishing age-appropriate rules and expectations for their children. Clear communication about rules and expectations, along with pre-determined rewards for compliance and consequences for noncompliance, can set the stage for better cooperation from children. Rules are defined as behaviors that parents want their children to decrease (e.g., aggression, defiance), whereas expectations are behaviors that parents want their children to increase (e.g., complete chores, help others). Parents are instructed to familiarize their children with the family's rules and expectations over a 2-week period during which children receive reminders about the rules and expectations rather than consequences. Once the rules and expectations are established, however, parents are advised to provide an immediate consequence for violations. Immediate consequences are likely to result in the negative behavior decreasing more quickly, and also can assist the child in learning to control impulsive behaviors.

Management of Inappropriate Behaviors

Attention for positive behaviors is purposely placed prior to discipline strategies in the session sequence, and positive attention for desired behaviors often serves to decrease problem behaviors. However, positive attention does not always result in the elimination of problem behaviors, and limit-setting procedures may be required. Strategies for managing misbehavior taught in the program include selective ignoring of minor disruptive behaviors, time-out, privilege removal, and work chores.

Ignoring can be used to decrease the frequency of behaviors that are irritating, but not dangerous (e.g., taking back, cursing). Talking to a child after misbehavior, even when scolding or reprimanding, can serve to reinforce the behavior and increase its likelihood of recurrence. With this in mind, parents are taught to briefly ignore minor misbehavior by not talking to or looking at the child. They are also instructed to give positive attention to the child as soon as he or she engages in appropriate behavior. Role-plays highlight the difficulty of this simple-sounding procedure, and give parents the opportunity to practice the skill.

Prior to presenting punishment strategies, leaders discuss problems with using harsh and/or corporal punishment procedures. Leaders explain that coercive discipline is typically ineffective, fails to teach appropriate behavior and models aggression, can adversely affect children's self-esteem, and has the potential to result in abuse. As a more effective and less potentially harmful alternative, a structured model for time-out is presented, in which parents are taught to implement a specific sequence of events. The parent will deliver an instruction, wait 10 seconds, and if the child does not comply, the parent will give a warning that the child will earn a time-out if he or she does not follow the direction. If the child does not comply, the parent will ask the child to go to time-out, or accompany him or her there if needed. For children in the target age range (9 to 11 years), time-out will last 10 to 20 minutes. Importantly, the child will be required to comply with the initial instruction when the time-out has ended. If the child still does not comply, the sequence is repeated until the child eventually completes the initial task. Parents complete role-plays within the sessions, and discuss potential problems with the implementation of the procedure (e.g., child is destructive on the way to time-out).

Parents also learn to remove privileges and assign work chores as consequences for inappropriate behaviors. In removing privileges, parents are advised to choose natural consequences when possible (e.g., a child who does not clear his dishes from the table will not receive an evening snack) and to deliver the consequences immediately after the transgression. Leaders work with parents to establish reasonable periods of time during which privileges are revoked (e.g., no TV for 2 hours) and emphasize that the length should not be determined by the parents' level of irritation. Ideally, parents establish the privileges that will be removed and the length of the consequence for anticipated misbehaviors in advance of the transgression (e.g., children who do not put their belongings away will lose them for the rest of the day). This strategy prevents parents from delivering excessive consequences in the heat of the moment, and cuts down on children's arguing and attempts to bargain for a milder consequence.

Work chores are presented as another disciplinary alternative, with children being assigned a task outside of their regular chores as a consequence for misbehavior. Work chores should be within the child's abilities and should require about 10 to 15 minutes to complete. Children who refuse to complete an assigned work chore will be given a second work chore to complete. Should the child refuse to complete the second chore, "total reward shutdown" ensues. When a parent implements total reward shutdown, the child loses all privileges (e.g., TV, computer, phone) until both chores are completed. Importantly, the child can earn back all privileges as soon as the chores are completed, effectively transferring control of the situation back to the child and avoiding a common problem that occurs with grounding in which children lose motivation to improve their behavior because they perceive their punishment as long and unchangeable.

Family Communication

The importance of good communication among family members is emphasized in a session entirely devoted to this topic. Leaders discuss how communication is likely to become more challenging as children become adolescents, and parents are encouraged to develop flexible communication strategies that can be adjusted as children develop. Family meetings are presented as a structure for allowing parents and children to discuss issues and concerns in a calm and controlled manner, and to give children an opportunity to negotiate changing rules (e.g., about curfews, social activities). A main goal of this session is to emphasize the need for parents to remain closely involved in their children's lives through adolescence, and to monitor their children's activities.

Leaders present information about how high levels of parental involvement and supervision decrease children's and adolescents' involvement in risky activities. Toward this end, leaders assist parents in developing a standard list of questions to ask their children about potential peer activities (e.g., where the child is going and with whom, what he or she will be doing, when he or she will be home).

Parental Stress Management

Two sessions of the parent component are devoted to parental stress management. The first session focuses on helping parents identify how little time they take for themselves, and recognize the importance of self-care. The group leader guides the parents through a relaxation exercise, and provides a script for them to take home. The second stress management session emphasizes planning ahead to manage daily hassles, and introduces the cognitive model of stress and mood management.

During the first stress management session, parents list their different roles in life and use this list to create a pie chart of the time and energy devoted to each role. Many parents may realize how little time they devote to taking care of themselves; this realization can be directed into a discussion of the importance of self-care in effective parenting. For example, one father was surprised to realize that his personal stress had resulted in him having a shorter temper, and spending less quality time with his children (Boxmeyer, Lochman, Powell, Yaros, & Wojnaroski, 2007). Following the pie chart activity, the group leaders facilitate a discussion of setting boundaries to protect personal time, and have parents generate a list of ways they can care for themselves. The session is ended with one leader reading an active relaxation script while parents follow along, and then encouraging them to practice the script at home.

The second stress management session is focused on antecedent control; strategies are presented to help manage daily hassles, such as planning ahead, prioritizing tasks, and setting weekly goals. Concepts from the previous session about the importance of self-care are reinforced through encouraging parents to set aside time for themselves each day, as well as scheduling longer blocks of "time off" for doing enjoyed activities.

The other aspect of antecedent control presented in this session is based on the cognitive model of stress and mood management. The group leader explains how cognitions create feelings, which lead to behavior, and introduces the concept of *cognitive reframing*. Parents are then encouraged to identify any negative cognitions they may have about their children and consider the impact these thoughts have on their parenting practices. Some parents may find it fascinating to learn their children are also being taught cognitive reframing as a strategy for coping with frustration (Lochman, Boxmeyer, Powell, Wojnaroski, & Yaros, 2007). Parents are prompted to model positive reframing for their children, and discuss situations when it may be a useful strategy for coping with frustration. During this discussion, attention is also paid to the attributions made for an individual's actions and how these attributions impact cognitions. For example, one parent recalled a time when she had to wait a long time to see a doctor; she believed the nurse "had it out for poor families," but her group leader helped her make an attributional reframe, and she said "the physician might have been running late (. . .) and that the nurse had to wait until he arrived" (Lochman et al., 2007, p. 686). Leaders can help parents understand how the cognitive model of stress management extends beyond their parenting role and illustrate how reframing can reduce stress in all of their life roles.

Family Problem–Solving

As previously described in this chapter, the Coping Power child component focuses extensively on teaching children the PICC model to solve problems; likewise, parents are taught to apply this same model to solving problems at home. During this session leaders help parents identify sources of family conflict, such as between siblings, and to recognize the difference between punishing children for sibling conflicts and teaching them skills to manage disagreements. The material for this session can be taught in different ways, depending on the needs of the group. Leaders can guide parents through the PICC model using a common family problem, such as siblings arguing over which television program to watch, or have volunteers role-play the conflict, followed by a group discussion. Parents are also encouraged to model problem-solving for their children during parent-child and parent-parent conflicts. This discussion of the PICC model, particularly the consequences step, can be framed for parents in the social-learning (ABC) framework they previously learned about. Repetition of the ABC framework is designed to promote long-term maintenance and generalization of skills; research has shown that parents who understand the underlying principles of learned parenting skills are more likely to implement those skills at home over time (McMahon, Wells, & Kotler, 2006).

When possible, parents are shown the PICC video their children made. This not only provides an example of how their children might use the PICC model, but also provides a natural opportunity for parents to see what their children are learning and praise them for their work.

Family Cohesion Building

For the session on family cohesion parents are instructed to bring a spouse or significant other to the meeting. The session begins with a discussion of the parents' fears about their children growing up and their changing role as a parent. Group leaders raise the possibility of alcohol or drug use, and may present epidemiological data about the rates of substance abuse in middle school and high school. Leaders also address that many children will be exposed to, or involved in, violence and facilitate a discussion of how peer groups may influence a child's behavior. Some parents may assume that their children will want to spend less time with them as they get older, and these points are raised to help parents understand the continued importance of monitoring their children's whereabouts (Boxmeyer et al., 2007). In adolescence it is developmentally normal for peer relationships to become more important to the child, but parents should be reminded of their role in helping children choose appropriate friendships and gradually become more independent.

Family cohesion is presented as an investment that may prevent costly future problems when the child becomes an adolescent. Different strategies for building cohesion are discussed, such as having a "family night" at home spent playing games. Parents should also be encouraged to try to spend time alone with their children; this helps build a strong relationship that may foster more open communication as their children mature. When possible, group leaders should have a list of community resources and events available for parents to help them plan their own family cohesion-building activity.

These sessions on stress management, problem-solving, and family cohesion were designed to promote the generalization and maintenance of skills learned in the Coping Power Child Component, as well as address parental needs. Parents are able to model these skills at home, and reinforce their children for using these strategies to cope with frustration. Parent reinforcement and modeling of skills such as reframing and problem solving increases the likelihood children will use these strategies. These sessions are of particular importance since research has indicated that improvement in child behavior 1 year after participating in Coping Power is linked to children's attributions for behavior, and the belief that aggression will not be an effective strategy (Lochman & Wells, 2002).

Considerations for Implementing Coping Power in Child Welfare Settings

There are a number of considerations in deciding whether and how to implement the Coping Power program in child welfare settings. The most important consideration is whether the program is appropriate to use with specific child welfare clients. The Coping Power Program was designed primarily as a preventive intervention for children exhibiting moderate to severe levels of aggressive and disruptive behavior and for their primary caregivers. There are risk factors that can contribute to the development of aggressive and disruptive behavior problems in children, including challenges commonly faced by children in the welfare system such as maltreatment, trauma, and prenatal drug exposure, as well as instability in the living situation and in attachment relationships. While Coping Power was not specifically designed to address these welfare-related challenges, it does aim to teach children skills for managing emotional arousal and interpersonal conflict more effectively and to help parents improve the parent-child relationship, manage the stress of parenting, follow a system to increase positive child behaviors and decrease noncompliant behaviors, and provide children with consistent supervision and support. Because of the frequent need for these skills in the child welfare population, web-based resources such as the California Evidence-Based Clearinghouse for Child Welfare (www.cebc4cw.org) have identified Coping Power as one of the relevant programs for child welfare professionals working with children with disruptive behavior.

Although the simultaneous use of both the child and parent components of the Coping Power program has been shown to produce the most lasting and comprehensive effects on children's behavior in targeted prevention samples, there are scenarios in which it would be clinically indicated to use only one of these components, or to stagger their use. For example, if a child's residential placement is highly unstable, it might be preferable to implement the child component of the program first, with the possibility of initiating the parent/caregiver component later, once the child's living situation has become more stable. In contrast, it may be preferable to implement the parent/caregiver component first in cases in which the child's disruptive behavior seems driven primarily by caregiver needs or concerns. For cases in which the child's disruptive behavior appears to be largely the sequelae of trauma or maltreatment exposure, it would be important to provide intervention that is more directly focused on these concerns first and decide later whether an intervention specifically focused on anger management and social problem solving would also be warranted.

Specific Considerations for Use of the Coping Power Child Component in Child Welfare Settings

Once a decision has been made to utilize the child component of Coping Power, there are several additional issues to consider. One decision is whether to implement the child intervention in an individual or small group format. Coping Power has been used most often in a small group format; however, it has also been adapted for individual use. Group and individual work each offer advantages and disadvantages for children with disruptive behavior problems. In addition to offering greater efficiency by serving larger numbers of children at one time, group work offers important opportunities for children to practice new skills and gain peer reinforcement for behavioral improvements. In contrast, individual work allows for greater personalization of the program content and may provide a more comfortable forum for discussing sensitive topics (e.g., discussion of past traumas or family concerns). Aggregating youth with disruptive behavior problems carries the potential risk for deviancy training, where children receive peer reinforcement for counter norm talk or behavior. When deciding which implementation format to use with children in the welfare system, it may be important to weigh factors such as how much the child appears to be in need of social support from peers or opportunities to practice anger coping and social skills with peers versus the extent to which the child may need to process past traumas or significant family events in a private treatment setting.

Much of the content of the Coping Power child component can be used intact for children in the welfare system. However, there are a few aspects of the program that may need to be adapted or used more judiciously. In the child component, children set short-term and long-term personal behavior goals. It is common for children to identify family relational goals, such as "To get along better with my mom," or "To be able to see my dad more often." In such cases, it would be important for the clinician to help the child identify specific aspects of his or her behavior that could be changed to improve the parent-child relationship (e.g., "When I follow directions, my mom and I get along better;" "My mom seems to like it when my sister and I work things out without fighting") versus elements of the family relationship that are beyond the child's control (e.g., if the child's father is not currently allowed visitation, it would not be appropriate to set a goal of trying to see the father more often. However, it could be appropriate to have the child set a goal of practicing strategies for coping with his feelings of frustration and disappointment about not being allowed to see his dad).

The clinician will also need to determine the best way to provide the child with rewards for meeting his or her personal goals. For children whose parents have difficulty following through consistently, it would be preferable for the clinician to provide rewards directly in the therapy setting (e.g., use the last 10 minutes of the session to play a favorite computer or board game), rather than to rely on the parent to provide a reward at home. Children within the welfare system may also need to be given additional rationale for improving their own behavior, even if it won't help them reach a desired goal such as continuing to live with their biological parent or a favorite foster family. Clinicians can describe that the skills the children are learning in Coping Power will help them in other important areas of their life, such as doing well in school and making and keeping friends, as well as helping them cope with the challenges of their home life.

As described earlier, there are a series of exposure-based activities intended to provide children with opportunities to practice managing anger arousal in a safe therapy setting. Initial exposure activities are less personal (e.g., counting cards or stacking dominoes while other group members make noise and try to distract you). Later exposure activities are more personal and arousing (e.g., receiving direct teasing). Child welfare professionals are advised to use careful discretion in deciding whether and how to implement this portion of the program, particularly with maltreated or trauma-exposed youth. With such youth, it would be critical to ensure that the child has a clear understanding of the purpose of the activity (i.e., to learn to control his or her anger better), that the child sees this as an important goal for him or herself, and that the child is willing to give the clinician and/or group members permission to tease them in order to practice this skill. Prior to conducting the activity, it would also be important to identify specific topics that the child is ready to be teased about (e.g., "You stink at math;" "Your clothes are dirty and have holes in them") versus topics that he or she may wish to keep off limits for now (e.g., "Your whole family is crazy"; "Your parents must not love you or they would not have given you up"). It would also be useful to let the child indicate whether he or she would prefer to be teased by the group members, the clinician, or by one particular group member. For group-based work, it is very important that rule violations (e.g., teasing about a restricted topic, starting to argue with each other) during the anger exposure activities are immediately addressed and corrected.

In both the anger management and problem-solving sections of Coping Power, children are asked to share real life scenarios from their week in which they felt angry or faced a problem. With a child welfare population, clinicians may get concerning responses to such prompts (e.g., "I had a problem last night when my mom's boyfriend starting beating her. I am angry that the neighbors called the cops because they might take me away from my mom"). Prior to having children share real-life examples, it is important for the clinician to describe the limits of confidentiality and to set boundaries for what types of scenarios children will be encouraged or discouraged to share, particularly in the presence of other group members. When brainstorming possible solutions to problem scenarios, it is also important to generate and practice interpersonal solutions that will help children feel empowered (e.g., making an assertive request) rather than victimized (e.g., ignoring hurtful teasing) and to consider possible consequences in selecting the best choice (e.g., it may be preferable for a child to opt to seek help from a trusted adult rather than to try to address a contentious issue directly with a parent who could become abusive).

Specific Considerations for Use of the Coping Power Parent Component in Child Welfare Settings

There are also a number of considerations when planning to implement the Coping Power parent component in child welfare settings. A similar decision can be made about whether to implement the parent program individually or in a group format. For parent work, a group format may be preferable, as parents frequently indicate that receiving support from other parents and sharing stories with them is what that they liked best about the program and benefitted from the most. When forming a group, the clinician would want to avoid a situation in which one group member would be notably different from the rest (e.g., most of the potential group members are foster parents but one is a biological parent). In such cases, it would be best to work with the outlying parent individually, or to form a new group with more similar members.

Another important consideration is which parents or caregivers of a particular child to include in the program. For families involved in the child welfare system, there may be biological parents, foster parents, step- or noncustodial parents, grandparents, appointed guardians, and treatment providers who are all involved in the child's care. In general, it can be useful to have all of the caregivers who spend a significant amount of time with the child on the same page in terms of the behavioral management strategies and schedules being utilized. However, it may not be possible, or even advisable, to include all of a child's key caregivers in Coping Power parent sessions, either for practical reasons or because of conflicts between caregivers. Clinicians may opt to implement Coping Power with specific caregiver groups. For example, a clinician may run one group for parents at risk for having their child removed from the home and a separate group for foster parents who have taken in children with disruptive behavior problems. This would allow the clinician to adapt the Coping Power content to provide greater emphasis on topics and skills that are most relevant to the group's needs.

The focus on building a positive parent-child relationship and using positive reinforcement strategies to increase positive child behaviors is particularly central for caregivers in the child welfare system and should always precede the teaching of punitive parenting strategies such as the use of discipline and punishment. Teaching parents to respond to their child more consistently, and to use household routines and structures to foster positive child behavior and reduce the need for disciplinary actions, should also be central to clinicians' work with parents and caregivers in the child welfare system. In teaching caregivers to use specific behavior modification strategies such as ignoring, clinicians should emphasize that these strategies are meant to be used in a very time limited fashion (e.g., 10 to 15 seconds) and for very specific purposes (e.g., to allow the child time to stop fussing about having to put on a coat rather than nagging at the child further and risk having the interchange escalate into a heated argument).

Helping parents learn to manage their own anger arousal to prevent highly conflictual (and potentially abusive) interactions with their child would also be important to emphasize when implementing the Coping Power program with parents and caregivers in the child welfare system. In fact, child welfare professionals are advised to carefully evaluate each caregiver's ability to control his or her affect and to use an appropriate voice tone (i.e., authoritative rather than aggressive) when giving commands to their child and handling child noncompliance. If the caregiver demonstrates considerable difficulty in this area, the clinician is advised to spend additional time helping the parent practice these skills and obtaining needed supports and services (i.e., individual therapy, medication, or community services) before introducing later treatment components, such as the component on discipline and punishment.

It is important for the clinician to be aware of whether the caregiver has a history of abusive behavior toward the child prior to initiating this treatment component. Clinicians are encouraged to spend time identifying the types of discipline strategies the caregiver currently utilizes and to devalue any form of corporal punishment or potentially abusive behavior. Role-plays are particularly helpful in teaching parents the finer details of voice tone, style, and body language that can help them implement a specific system for fostering child compliance without engaging in harsh and conflictual interchanges. There is some potential for the clinician to learn information that could require additional mandated reporting in this section of the intervention, which should be anticipated and discussed with the caregiver in advance of initiating this treatment component.

A final consideration is the importance of helping caregivers anticipate and overcome common obstacles to implementing a behavior management system effectively. Role-plays can also be very useful in allowing caregivers to practice strategies such as remaining calm when a child escalates his or her disruptive behavior following the removal of a privilege, or to catch a child's anger when it is on the rise and to successfully redirect the child and diffuse the situation before it escalates. Discussion of a caregiver's own trigger points, or situations in which it tends to be more difficult to remain calm and interact positively with the child, may also be useful, followed by a problem-solving discussion of ways to minimize negative parent-child interactions at these times.

Summary

The Coping Power program has been designed to address children's aggression and other disruptive behaviors through intervention work with children and their parents. By addressing topics such as children's emotion awareness, ability to cope with anger and frustration, and social problem-solving skills, as well as parenting skills related to building positive family relationships and managing children's behavior, the program can be useful in work with a child welfare population. As noted, some special considerations may be warranted, and clinicians are encouraged to thoughtfully review client characteristics and histories prior to implementing the program. Information about intervention manuals, workbooks, and training is available at www.copingpower.com.

References

Boxmeyer, C., Lochman, J. E., Powell, N., Yaros, A., & Wojnaroski, M. (2007). A case study of the coping power program for angry and aggressive youth. *Journal of Contemporary Psychotherapy*, *37*(3), 165–174.

Crick, N. R., & Dodge, K. A. (1994). A review and reformulation of social information-processing mechanisms in children's social adjustment. *Psychological Bulletin*, *115*, 74–101.

Larson, J., & Lochman, J. E. (2002). *Helping schoolchildren cope with anger: A cognitive behavioral intervention*. New York, NY: Guildford Press.

Lochman, J. E., Boxmeyer, C., Powell, N., Wojnaroski, M., & Yaros, A. (2007). The use of the coping power program to treat a 10-year-old girl with disruptive behaviors. *Journal of Clinical Child and Adolescent Psychology*, *36*(4), 677–687.

Lochman, J. E., & Wells, K. C. (2002). Contextual social-cognitive mediators and child outcome: A test of the theoretical model in the coping power program. *Development and Psychopathology*, *14*(4), 945–967.

Lochman, J. E., & Wells, K. C. (2004). The coping power program for preadolescent aggressive boys and their parents: Outcome effects at the one-year follow-up. *Journal of Consulting and Clinical Psychology*, *72*, 571–578.

Lochman, J. E., Wells, K. C., & Lenhart, L. A. (2008). *Coping Power child group program facilitator guide*. New York, NY: Oxford University Press.

Lochman, J. E., Wells, K. C., & Murray, M. (2007). The coping power program: Preventive intervention at the middle school transition. In P. Tolan, J. Szapocznik, & S. Sambrano (Eds.), *Preventing substance abuse: 3 to 14* American Psychological Association: Washington, DC.

Loeber, R. (1990). Development and risk factors of juvenile antisocial behavior and delinquency. *Clinical Psychology Review*, *10*, 1–41.

McMahon, R. J., Wells, K. C., & Kotler, J. S. (2006). Conduct Problems. In E. J. Mash & R. A. Barkley (Eds.), *Treatment of childhood disorders* (3rd. ed.) (pp. 137–268). New York, NY: Guilford Press.

Patterson, G. R., Reid, J. B., & Dishion T. J. (1992). *Antisocial boys*. Eugene, OR: Castalia.

Wells, K. C., Lochman, J. E., & Lenhart, L. A. (2008). *Coping power parent group program facilitator guide*. New York, NY: Oxford University Press.

Coping Cat

A Cognitive–Behavioral Treatment for Childhood Anxiety Disorders*

Shannon E. Hourigan, Cara A. Settipani, Michael A. Southam–Gerow, and Philip C. Kendall

Introduction and Background

Anxiety disorders are one of the most prevalent problems experienced by children and adolescents and can be debilitating and long-lasting. Fortunately, there are some good treatment options for youths suffering from anxiety disorders. This chapter describes one such option, the Coping Cat program, a cognitive-behavioral treatment designed and tested for elementary- and middle-school-age youths with anxiety disorders. Specifically, the chapter provides some background information about anxiety disorders in youth, including epidemiological data, a description of the three *DSM-IV* anxiety disorders targeted by the Coping Cat, and a brief review of the primary etiological theories of anxiety disorders. We conclude the chapter with a detailed description of the Coping Cat program.

Epidemiology of Anxiety Disorders in Childhood

In situations involving real danger, anxiety is a brief and helpful emotion that readies the body to respond to the threat and dissipates when the danger has passed. In the case of anxiety disorders, children experience long-lasting worry or fear that is irrational or disproportionate to the actual threat (i.e., a *false alarm*) and causes significant distress or interference in their lives. Anxiety or fear in response to a real threat or danger is a normal, healthy, and adaptive emotion. However, 6% to 21% of children (i.e., youth under the age of 18 years) experience clinical levels of anxiety that interfere with their

*Support for some of the research reported was provided by NIMH research grants (MH080788 MH63747) awarded to Philip C. Kendall.

ability to function socially, at home, or in school. As a result of anxiety, these children may underperform at school, avoid after school sports or clubs, limit social contact with peers, experience frustration or tension at home, or become socially isolated. These children are at elevated risk for developing additional emotional or behavioral disorders; 65% to 84% of children with one anxiety disorder also experience an additional anxiety, behavior, or mood disorder, and maltreated children are at additionally elevated risk for a variety of emotional or behavioral problems. Further, most of these children are not referred to treatment, and anxiety and co-occurring disorders may last into adulthood. In terms of later co-occurring disorders, some studies indicate that youths with anxiety disorders in childhood are more likely to develop depressive and substance abuse disorders than are youths without anxiety disorders.

DSM-IV Anxiety Disorders

Although there are 13 anxiety disorders described in the *DSM*, three in particular have been studied extensively in children and adolescents and are the target of the Coping Cat treatment program: separation anxiety disorder, generalized anxiety disorder, and social phobia/social anxiety disorder. In this section, we provide a brief description of these three anxiety disorders.

Separation Anxiety Disorder Separation anxiety disorder (SAD) is the only anxiety disorder that must begin in childhood. Children with SAD experience an irrational fear that something will happen to cause separation from the attachment figure. Children may fear being kidnapped or lost and never reunited with their caregivers, or they may fear something happening to their caregivers, such as a lethal car accident. Children with SAD typically become very distressed when faced with a separation situation and exhibit a variety of behaviors to attempt to avoid the separation, such as crying, tantrums, and pleading with caregivers. These children also have difficulty being alone at home, may have difficulty sleeping alone, and may follow caregivers from room to room. Children with SAD are often referred for treatment for school refusal, and caregivers often report children experiencing head and stomach aches in anticipation of school after a period of being at home (i.e., at the end of vacations, Sunday evening, or in the morning before school).

The clinician working with a child suspected of having SAD must be careful to understand the source of the child's anxiety, as there are a number of reasons children may want to avoid school or separation that may not fit the criteria for SAD. For example, the child may worry for the safety of a caregiver who has been the victim of domestic violence or may reasonably fear the death of a caregiver who has had multiple hospitalizations. In this case, the child's fear may not be unreasonable, and treatment for SAD would not be appropriate. Alternatively, a teen may not want to go to school due to fear of giving a presentation in class, taking a test, or being bullied. SAD can be distinguished from social phobia, performance-based anxieties, or distress associated with trauma in that the primary focus of the worry or anxiety is harm befalling either child or caregiver causing a separation. This anxiety is out of proportion to the actual danger, and it interferes with the child's functioning.

Social Phobia Children who experience social phobia (SP; also called *social anxiety disorder*) fear social or performance situations in which they believe they might be negatively evaluated. Children may fear that others will think they are stupid, foolish, or "crazy," or they may fear that others will see symptoms of their anxiety, such as shaking hands or sweating, and perceive them as odd, inarticulate, or dumb. Children may fear a variety of situations, including eating, drinking, or speaking in front of others, meeting new people, participating in large social settings, writing on the board in class, or performing in front of others. Children with SP often overestimate the likelihood that they will be evaluated poorly or catastrophize the outcome of such an evaluation, and depending on age and cognitive sophistication, they may not recognize that this fear is excessive. For example, a child might fear that her teacher and all of her classmates will notice a tremble in her voice when she speaks in front of the class and interpret this shakiness as a sign of stupidity. When anxiety-provoking situations cannot be avoided, children with SP endure them with intense distress and often experience worries about the event for days or weeks preceding the situation. Distress in these situations must lead to clinical levels of impairment and must be distinguished from developmentally appropriate shyness or performance anxiety for a diagnosis of SP to be considered.

As with SAD, the clinician working with a child suspected of having SP must be careful to distinguish an irrational fear of being negatively evaluated from other anxieties that may occur in the context of a social situation. For example, a child who fears vomiting may avoid eating in the cafeteria because she believes doing so will likely induce vomiting, but because her fear is of vomiting, a diagnosis of SP is not appropriate.

Generalized Anxiety Disorder Children with generalized anxiety disorder (GAD) are often thought of as *worriers*. They experience uncontrollable worry about a variety of situations or activities in addition to at least one additional symptom (i.e., restlessness, being easily fatigued, difficulty concentrating). Children with GAD are often described as perfectionistic due to their worry about the quality of their schoolwork or their competence in athletics. They will repeat tasks or redo homework in an attempt to achieve perfection regardless of whether their work is being evaluated by others. Children may also be overly self-conscious and concerned with their appearance. Other common worries include catastrophic events such as tornados, terrorist attacks, or nuclear war and can be triggered by news reports. Children with GAD often repeatedly ask caregivers or teachers for reassurance about these concerns or for their approval.

GAD frequently co-occurs with other anxiety disorders, and the clinician must parse out whether the child's worries are better explained by SAD, SP, or obsessive-compulsive disorder (OCD), all of which have symptoms that can appear very similar to those of GAD. For a diagnosis of GAD to be warranted, the child's worries must not be better explained by another anxiety disorder and must interfere with a child's home, academic, or social functioning.

Treatment Approaches

There have been almost one hundred randomized controlled trial studies (RCTs) testing treatments for child anxiety since the 1970s. The most effective treatment type across these studies is cognitive-behavioral therapy, an approach that combines anxiety skills training with gradual exposure. More than 80% of all efficacious treatments for child/adolescent anxiety have included exposure as a primary element. An example of one specific treatment program that incorporates these strategies and has been widely supported across multiple studies is the Coping Cat. In the next section, we briefly review a case example of a young boy for whom the Coping Cat would be an appropriate treatment before we turn to a detailed description of this program.

Case Example

Evan is an 11-year-old boy with a history of physical abuse who was referred for treatment for his difficulty interacting with peers and participating in classroom activities. Evan's mother reports that he has always been a somewhat shy boy and "slow to warm up." He has no difficulty talking to family members, but he is extremely reluctant to talk to people he does not know and refuses to answer the phone or place orders at restaurants. Evan has never liked to talk in class; he reports fears that the teacher and his classmates will think he is stupid and has begun avoiding going to school when he has to give an oral presentation. He also dislikes having his picture taken, and he recently refused to attend the birthday parties of two friends due to the possibility that there may be other children there he did not know.

The Coping Cat Program

The Coping Cat program is an individual-focused cognitive-behavioral approach designed for youths with SAD, SP, and GAD. Coping Cat has been tested in several RCTs as an individual-focused approach; adaptations to the program to make it suitable for use in groups or with families have also been successfully tested. Coping Cat has also been adapted for use in different countries, such as Australia (Coping Koala) and Canada (Coping Bear), and has been translated into Spanish and Norwegian. In the next several sections, we provide a detailed description of the strategies used in Coping Cat. The program involves two distinct portions: (1) psychoeducation/skills training and (2) exposure. In the first portion, the goals include forming a relationship with the client, providing psychoeducational information about anxiety, and teaching and rehearsing the use of a variety of anxiety management skills. In the second portion of treatment, the focus shifts from skill-building to skill utilization in anxiety-provoking situations; in other words, the emphasis is exposure tasks. Copies of the Coping Cat therapist manual and workbook can be ordered online from workbookpublishing.com, which is a site dedicated to selling empirically supported therapy materials for mental health professionals. Next, we provide a detailed description of the program. The Coping Cat program is not gender-specific and can be successfully implemented by both male and female therapists; however, for clarity, we will refer to the therapist throughout with female pronouns. For illustrative purposes, we will describe various treatment elements using the case example of Evan, an 11-year-old boy with social phobia and a history of physical abuse.

Psychoeducation and Skills Training

The initial portion of the Coping Cat program provides the framework for later treatment. These early sessions present a treatment rationale and ensure the child has the necessary skills for successful exposures.

Overview The first phase of the Coping Cat program focuses on psychoeducation and skill building (typically Sessions 1 to 8). Strategies for managing anxiety are presented to the child as a "tool set" that he can draw from when faced with anxiety-provoking situations. Collaboratively, the therapist and child work on four main concepts, taught in order, allowing the child to build each new skill upon the previous one. First, the focus is on recognizing bodily reactions to anxiety. Next, the focus is on the child recognizing his own anxious self-talk and expectations about feared situations. Third, the child is introduced to and comes to understand how to cope in anxiety-provoking situations by using strategies such as coping thoughts and problem-solving. The last concept the child learns is rewarding himself for efforts made to approach and cope in feared situations. An acronym is used to help children remember these skills: the FEAR plan. FEAR is an acronym for **F**eeling Frightened? **E**xpecting bad things to happen? **A**ttitudes and Actions that can help, and **R**esults and Rewards.

In the next section, we review session goals sequentially through the program. Before doing so, though, we note a few commonalities that occur in most Coping Cat sessions. For example, each session begins with reviewing the homework (called a STIC—or Show That I Can—task) from the previous session. Accordingly, each session generally ends with the assignment of the STIC task. In addition, each session typically ends with a brief, fun activity, such as a game or a walk. This activity is included to support and bolster the client-therapist relationship. Another commonality across many sessions is a progression from modeling to role-playing, such that a child client learns each skill through multiple "channels": didactically, via a workbook, through modeling, and then through direct rehearsal (i.e., role-play). Most skills are taught using this progression.

Goal 1: Building Rapport The primary goal of the first session (or more) is to build rapport with the child. Rapport is especially important when working with anxious children—they tend to be shy and fearful of others and may be unaccustomed to discussing their thoughts or feelings. The Coping Cat program suggests the use of a child-nominated game or fun activity for part of the session. In addition, the program often involves the use of a Personal Facts game in which the therapist and child answer questions about themselves, such as, "What is your favorite activity for a summer afternoon?" and "Do you have any pets?" The key is to make the first session fun and engaging and not to push the child too quickly so that the child is willing to return for the second session.

Goal 2: Treatment Orientation The first session or two is also a chance to orient the child to the program by describing the structure and purpose of treatment and introduce the goals for treatment, such as learning how to identify anxious thoughts and using coping strategies. Often, the therapist can describe her role as similar to that of a coach who helps the child learn how to accomplish challenging tasks by teaching skills based on what has worked for other children and guiding the child to practice these skills. The therapist also introduces out-of-session activities or STIC tasks from the *Coping Cat Workbook,* which are assigned and reviewed at each session. The therapist tells the child that he receives 2 points for completing the STIC task, which go toward earning rewards. To illustrate, here is a sample therapist-client dialogue in which the therapist gives an overview of the program and describes her role to the child during the first session.

> Therapist: I want to give you an idea of what coming here will be like. Okay? We'll meet once a week and the two of us will be doing some team work together. Our program usually lasts about 16 weeks, or 4 months, but it could be shorter or longer depending on how things go. In the beginning, I'll learn about you—you are the expert on "you." Then we'll focus on giving you a chance to learn some tools that you can choose to use when you're feeling nervous or scared. I'm an expert of some of these strategies or tools.
>
> Evan: I'm scared when I have to read in front of class.
>
> Therapist: That's a great example. That's exactly the kind of situation we'll be working on to help you feel less scared. At first, we'll work on figuring out **when** you are nervous or scared, and later on we'll work on **what to do** when you are feeling scared. Later, in the second half of the program will be actually practicing how to cope in situations that make you nervous—we call them challenges. Sound okay?
>
> Evan: That sounds scary.
>
> Therapist: Yeah, I can see how that might seem scary right now—but we won't throw you into the situation without preparing first. We'll work together to get ready and we'll start with easy things before moving on to tougher challenges. We're also going to be playing games, and you'll get rewards for doing the challenges, so this could be fun. Do you have any questions about that?
>
> Evan: No, as long as I don't have to do the scary stuff today.
>
> Therapist: No, not today, we'll just get to know each other. Then we'll be like a team working on this—I know some things that have helped other kids feel less scared, but you are the expert on you, so your opinion is very important.

Goal 3: Psychoeducation on Anxiety and Emotion Education Sessions 2 and 3 focus on helping the child understand anxiety and emotions better, including a focus on distinguishing feelings of anxiety from other emotions and his physiological responses to anxiety. There are numerous activities to use in helping a client learn important emotion identification skills. For example, the therapist and child can take turns role-playing and guessing the physical expression of emotions by playing Feelings Charades. Alternatively, the child can create a Feelings Dictionary by cutting out magazine pictures that show different emotions, pasting them on construction or butcher paper, and labeling the corresponding emotions. The goal of these activities is to build a child's emotion vocabulary to introduce the concept that different feelings have different physical expressions.

The therapist also works to normalize the experience of anxiety by discussing how anxiety is a ubiquitous emotion and why it is necessary. A primary way that a therapist conveys this information is through the use of a technique called coping modeling. In coping modeling, the therapist shares a time that made her feel anxious and discusses how it initially felt uncomfortable yet how she was able to cope with the situation, which led to success.

> Therapist: What would you think if I told you that sometimes I feel nervous when I have to meet new people? In fact, I was nervous before I met you for the first time.
>
> Evan: Really? Why?
>
> Therapist: Well, I didn't know what you would be like, and I want to do a good job helping you, and I wanted you to like me. So before we met for the first time, I had some butterflies in my stomach.
>
> Evan: Wow.
>
> Therapist: Can I tell you how I coped with those nervous feelings?
>
> Evan: Sure.
>
> Therapist: Well, before you came in, I closed my eyes and took some deep breaths, and I reminded myself that I am good at my job and that most kids I work with like me. And when you came in, I was still a little bit nervous, but after we talked for a little while, those nervous feelings got smaller and smaller, and they eventually went away. And now we've met three times, and I don't have any more nervous feelings before you come in. In fact, I look forward to seeing you.

Another goal associated with psychoeducation and emotion education is a focus on the physiological symptoms commonly associated with anxiety (e.g., racing heart, butterflies in the stomach). The progression from "telling to showing to doing" is often useful. The therapist can start by explaining the idea that emotions are associated with specific body feelings, proceed to describe her own experience, and then solicit the client's own experiences. Younger children can take part in a "body drawing" activity in which the therapist and child draw an outline of a body on a large piece of butcher paper and draw in/label the physical symptoms of anxiety. An important teaching point here is that our bodily reactions to anxiety are a helpful signal that we are becoming anxious, thus serving as cue to begin using coping skills.

These psychoeducation and emotion education tasks culminate in the introduction of the first step of the four-step Coping Cat coping plan: the FEAR steps. Specifically, the therapist introduces the "F" step: Feeling Frightened? This step involves the child noting his somatic responses to anxiety and asking himself whether he is feeling frightened.

Goal 4: Fear Ladder An important goal that is integrated through many of the early sessions in Coping Cat is the creation and specification of the client's fear ladder, a hierarchy of feared stimuli that is used later as a guide for exposure tasks. The fear ladder is constructed over time with the client and the caregiver using a Feelings Thermometer/ Subjective Units of Distress Scale (SUDS) rating scale. The *Coping Cat Workbook* contains situation cards for the fear ladder that can be used to create and update the fear ladder over time. The development of the fear ladder is an ongoing process throughout treatment, with items moving down (or up) and new items being added. Below is some sample dialogue from a session with Evan. For this example, the therapist prepared ahead of time: a dry-erase board with a ladder drawn along one side, markers, and a pad of sticky notes.

Therapist: We've talked before about some of the things that make you feel nervous, things like getting together with kids your age, asking your teacher a question, or giving a book report in front of your class. The activity we're going to do now will be to write down all of those things that make you feel nervous on these sticky notes. Each fear gets its own note, and then after we have lots of things written down, we're going to put them on the white board. Do you see the ladder that I drew? [Evan nods.] Well, after we're done writing down these fears, we're going to put them in order on the ladder. We'll put the things that are the least scary on the bottom of the ladder, and the things that are the scariest at the top, and we'll fill the other things in between. Does that make sense?

Evan: Yeah, I think so.

Therapist: Okay, so one fear you've told me about is asking your teacher a question in class. Let's put that on a sticky note. Can you write that down here and put it on the board? [Evan writes "asking Miss Smith a question" on the note and places it on the board.] Thank you for doing that. What's another situation that makes you feel scared?

Evan: Giving a book report.

Therapist: That's a good example. Let's put that on a sticky note. How about another one?

Evan: Asking a friend to come over.

Therapist: Oh, that's a really good example. Do you feel the same amount of worry for all friends, or does asking some friends seem more scary than asking others?

Evan: Um, some are more scary, I guess.

Therapist: Who is a friend who is easier to invite over?

Evan: Well, Tim has been my friend forever, and he comes over a lot, so I guess it's not too hard to ask him.

Therapist: Is it a little bit hard to ask Tim? Or is it not at all hard to invite him over?

Evan: I guess it's still a little bit hard, but it's not really hard.

Therapist: Okay, let's put "invite Tim over" down on a sticky note since it's still something that's a little bit hard. And who is someone who is really hard to invite over?

Evan: If I tell you, am I going to have to do it?

Therapist: Do you remember when we talked before about doing exposure tasks or challenges, what they would be like? [Evan nods.] What did I say about doing things that are hard?

Evan: You said we'd start with easier things and work up to things that seem hard.

Therapist: That's right. Good memory. So let's put down lots of things that you're scared of, and we'll do the challenges when you're ready to do them. We won't jump right in to the hard challenges.

Evan: Okay [writes "invite Jeremy over" on a sticky note].

The process continues until there are enough items throughout the range of the fear hierarchy to begin exposure tasks. Throughout the process, the therapist elicits various anxiety-provoking events and identifies modifications that either increase or decrease the intensity. For example, in Evan's case, inviting Tim over to his house elicited less anxiety than inviting Jeremy over. After a range of situations had been identified, the therapist and client arrange the sticky notes or elements along the fear ladder so that the items lowest on the ladder are those that induce the least fear. The therapist also asks the client to identify current SUDS ratings for each item. This fear ladder can then be used as an assessment over time, with the client being asked to rate the SUDS for various items on the fear hierarchy throughout treatment.

When constructing a fear ladder, some therapists find it helpful to focus on one domain of anxiety. For example, a therapist might choose to construct a hierarchy that focuses on peer-related social situations and another focusing on academic situations (e.g., asking the teacher a question, giving a report in class). Having a more focused fear hierarchy may be particularly useful if the therapist plans to involve the teacher for more focused and intensive involvement.

Evan's Fear Ladder

SUDS	Item
8	Giving a book report in front of the class
8	Asking a teacher a question
7	Reading aloud in class
6	Inviting Jeremy over to my house
5	Having messed up hair in front of other people
5	Tripping in front of other people
4	Dropping something in front of someone
3	Ordering pizza on the phone
2	Inviting Tim over to my house
2	Getting my picture taken

Goal 5: Relaxation In Session 5, the child is taught how to use relaxation techniques to help reduce anxious distress. An important teaching point here is that the child be able to

distinguish tension and relaxation. Progressive muscle relaxation (PMR) exercises are used to provide a way to teach this skill. PMR typically involves consciously tensing and then relaxing muscle groups in a successive fashion, starting, for example, with the leg muscles and working up through the stomach, arm, shoulder, neck, and face muscles. With younger children, PMR often involves playful ways to do the exercises, such as pretending to squeeze lemons with one's hands or imitating a turtle by pulling one's neck into a shell. The therapist also introduces diaphragmatic breathing as a relaxation skill. These different relaxation skills are taught as coping strategies to use in anxiety-provoking situations. A recording of the therapist reading a PMR script can be provided to the client as a way to promote use of the skill outside of session. Further, caregivers should be involved to maximize the generalization of the skill to the home environment.

Goal 6: Identifying Anxious Self-Talk/Cognitive Restructuring Session 6 of the Coping Cat manual focuses on the development of cognitive skills. Specifically, the therapist helps the child begin to recognize his self-talk in anxiety-provoking situations, analyze the effects of particular types of thoughts, and generate thoughts that will promote coping and approach behaviors. The therapist can suggest to the child that there are some thoughts that probably occur when he feels anxious. The "thought bubbles" of cartoon characters can be a helpful way to explain this idea while providing a great opportunity to model and rehearse these cognitive skills. The introduction of cognitive skills is a lead-in to the "E" step of the FEAR plan: Expecting bad things to happen? For this step, the child is taught to notice the thoughts associated with anxiety, asking, "What do I expect to happen?" The child is then taught to (a) analyze the veracity of the thought (i.e., what is the evidence for the thought? How likely is the predicted outcome to occur?) and (b) identify thoughts that will promote coping and approach behaviors. As with all skills in Coping Cat, modeling and role-play are used extensively to teach and practice this difficult set of skills.

Goal 7: Problem-Solving The next skill is problem-solving. Here, the therapist introduces the idea that when confronted with anxiety provoking situations, there are things we can do and ways we can think to help ourselves feel less anxious *and* to do things that we are afraid to do. This teaching point leads to the introduction of the "A" step in the FEAR plan: Actions and Attitudes that help. The problem-solving process in Coping Cat is similar to that found in other programs and involves four steps: identifying the problem, brainstorming all possible solutions, evaluating the solutions, and selecting an option.

Goal 8: Self-Evaluation and Self-Reward The last of the FEAR steps is R: Results and Rewards. Here, the skills developed are twofold. First, the client is taught to evaluate how well he coped with the situation. That is, the focus is on the process of coping and *not* on the outcome of the situation. Many times, a great outcome is not possible, though we can cope well in many of those situations. Second, the client is taught to reward himself for coping effort (and not the production of a positive outcome). The use of coping modeling, role-plays, and other modalities are useful for this skill.

Goal 9: The Coping Plan After working on the R step, the client is then reintroduced to the entire FEAR plan and time is spent modeling and rehearsing the use of the plan as a four-step coping method. The focus here is preparation for the exposure tasks coming next.

Exposure

The purpose of exposure is to provide the child with opportunities to face feared, *nondangerous* situations and use coping strategies. In advance of starting exposure tasks, an important goal is to finalize the fear hierarchy to help guide ordering of the tasks in subsequent sessions. In addition, the therapist should review the guidelines and rationale for exposure tasks: the tasks will start off relatively easy and build to more challenging tasks; the child will experience some anxiety during the tasks; the child will need to stay in the situation for a certain period of time, generally until the anxiety subsides; the FEAR steps are designed to help in these situations; most important, the more you practice, the more quickly your anxiety will dissipate. Exposure tasks can be either imaginal or *in vivo* (i.e., exposure to actual feared stimuli, such as asking someone a question or approaching a feared object).

Imaginal exposure is often less anxiety-provoking and can be a useful way to start. Furthermore, exposure for some fears, particularly abstract worries (e.g., worrying that your caregivers will get sick or hurt) must be imaginal. For imaginal exposures, you can ask the child to role-play or write out the situation. The more detailed the imaginal scenario, the better. The idea is to evoke anxiety so that the client learns that (a) he can tolerate anxiety and (b) continued engagement with the feared situation will lead to a decrease in anxious feelings.

For example, Evan experienced a great deal of worry about dropping his full lunch tray in the cafeteria. However, this feared situation did not easily lend itself to repeated in vivo exposures. Instead of having Evan repeatedly drop a full lunch tray in the cafeteria, he and his therapist wrote a worst-case scenario story about Evan dropping his lunch tray. This story was told from a first-person perspective and included many vivid details about the elements Evan found most distressing (e.g., "I could feel the chocolate milk dripping off my T-shirt, and all of the other kids turned and started to laugh"). Evan and his therapist read the story repeatedly in session, and the therapist made sure to get SUDS ratings before and after each read through to gauge the changes in Evan's anxiety. In this way, Evan was able to gain exposure to situations he found distressing that could not be experienced repeatedly in real life.

In vivo exposures are the bread and butter of most Coping Cat exposure sessions. Here, the child faces a feared situation in person while coping with feelings of anxiety. Across sessions, the goal is to increase the difficulty level of the tasks, building toward a final graduation task. The first step on Evan's hierarchy was "getting my picture taken." For this exposure, the therapist identified ways to modify the exposure to elicit a variety of SUDS ratings. Evan generated SUDS ratings for having his picture taken with a silly pose (SUDS = 2), having his picture taken with a smiling pose (SUDS = 3), and having his picture taken with another therapist watching (SUDS = 5).

There are a few important tips to keep in mind. First, it is important to adequately prepare for the exposure task. Preparation can consist of clearly describing the task, specifying what the child will do in the task, and discussing how the child will cope with his anxiety. The therapist and child can collaboratively develop a FEAR plan for coping with the anxious feelings and negotiate a reward for completing the challenge.

> Therapist: Today we're going to start the challenges on your fear ladder. But before we begin, we're going to do the steps of the FEAR plan. So for this challenge, I brought in my camera, and I will take your picture, and I am going to ask you for your SUDS ratings both before and after I take your picture. And we'll do this over and over again.

Second, it is important during exposure tasks to take ratings so that you and the client can see if the exposures are producing the desired habituation to the stimuli. In other words, you need to know if exposure is leading to decreases in anxiety ratings. A good rule of thumb is that an exposure last until the anxiety is reduced by at least 50%. Although this may be difficult to judge in certain situations, the key is for the therapist to help the child stay in contact with the feared situation until he is able to feel substantially less discomfort.

Third, each exposure task should be practiced more than once. These repetitions are called trials and are an important way to increase the effectiveness of exposures. If the client practices the *same* exposure task multiple times, anxiety reduction tends to occur more rapidly with each successive task. The repetition is used to demonstrate that "the more we do it, the easier it gets."

Fourth, after each exposure task, the therapist and client discuss the results of exposure. For example, the therapist and child collaboratively evaluate the outcome and discuss what the child was thinking and feeling and how the child coped with the situation. The therapist praises the child and rewards him for his effort regardless of whether the outcome is perceived to be a total success. The overall process of exposures can be thought of like a football play: you huddle up to plan (prepare for the exposure), you run your play (engage in the exposure), and you huddle up again (discuss the outcome and plan for the next exposure).

> Therapist: Okay, Evan, we've done the FEAR plan and it's time to do the first challenge. What is your SUDS rating right now?
>
> Evan: Five.
>
> Therapist: [Notes Evan's SUDS rating.] Okay, now I'm going to take a picture. [Takes a picture.] What's your SUDS rating?
>
> Evan: Three.
>
> Therapist: We've done one already! How was it to get your picture taken?
>
> Evan: Um, okay.
>
> Therapist: Before I took your picture, what were you expecting to happen?
>
> Evan: I don't know. I guess I just don't like the way it feels to get my picture taken.

Therapist: Was it as bad as you expected?

Evan: No, it wasn't.

Therapist: Okay. Let's do it again. What's your SUDS rating now?

Evan: Three.

Finally, in addition to exposure tasks increasing with difficulty over time, it is also important to assign exposure tasks as homework to help generalize the effects of the strategy. Exposure tasks away from therapist meetings often involve caregivers, making this a good time to discuss caregiver involvement in Coping Cat.

Caregiver Involvement Although the Coping Cat program is an individual-based treatment with the therapist working mostly one-on-one with the child, it is important to involve and collaborate with caregivers for several reasons. First, caregivers are important sources of information about the child's symptoms and functioning at the start of treatment. Second, it is important to involve caregivers to monitor treatment progress during the course of therapy. Third, Coping Cat emphasizes involving caregivers to provide them with psychoeducational information about anxiety and knowledge about the anxiety management skills their children are learning in treatment.

In the Coping Cat manual, Session 4 is typically the first formal caregiver session after the intake. The purpose of this meeting is to provide additional information about the treatment program, encourage caregiver cooperation and participation, address any questions or concerns, and learn more about situations that are anxiety provoking for the child. In some cases, it may be necessary to teach the caregivers how to manage their child's anxiety or their own anxiety about the child. For example, the therapist can educate about the detrimental effects of accommodating the child's anxiety by allowing the child to avoid feared situations. Also, the topic of caregivers as models of both wanted and unwanted behavior can be addressed.

Therapist: Have you ever known anyone who has been really afraid of something and got over it? How did they do it? The way that has been shown to be the best for people to get over their fears is to face those fears. In Evan's case, he's afraid of doing things with other kids his age. He and I will be doing some practicing here, but for him to get the most out of our time together, it will be very important that you also help him keep up his practicing at home and even when we're done with therapy. However, I know that it can sometimes be hard for parents to watch their children experience something that is hard for them. It's natural for parents to want to protect their children and feel somewhat upset when their children are upset or afraid. However, in situations where Evan is afraid of something, it's important for you to help him to face that fear. The least helpful thing parents can do is to help their children get out of practicing.

Session 9 is set aside for a second meeting with the caregivers, which is similar to the first meeting; however, the focus of Session 9 is on the second half of treatment and the specific ways the caregivers can be involved in the exposure tasks.

End of Treatment

The end of the Coping Cat program involves completing a final "graduation" exposure task and producing a "commercial" that involves the child explaining what he has learned and accomplished in treatment. Ideally, the commercial is a fun experience for the child that also serves a consolidation function, emphasizing treatment gains and reviewing lessons learned. Another important component of the end of treatment is that the therapist summarizes the child's accomplishments over the course of the treatment program and encourages the caregivers to give feedback about the child's progress. An important goal of the final session is to help the caregivers and client understand that they have the tools and skills to handle future anxiety-related challenges.

Conclusion

Childhood anxiety disorders are among the most common childhood disorders; untreated, they can lead to a number of problems in later childhood, adolescence, and adulthood. Fortunately, highly effective programs exist to treat this common and potentially debilitating childhood problem. The Coping Cat is one such program, having repeatedly demonstrated success in helping children overcome anxiety related to generalized worry, separation from caregivers, and social situations. The Coping Cat program involves teaching and rehearsal of a set of anxiety coping skills along with ample opportunities to practice using those skills in real-life anxiety provoking situations.

8

The Theraplay Treatment Program

Description and Implementation of Attachment–Based Play for Children and Caregivers

Dafna Lender, Phyllis B. Booth, and Sandra Lindaman

Introduction

In this article we describe the Theraplay® method, a therapy that enhances the parent-child relationship and the child's functioning through attachment-based play. Theraplay therapy is unique in that the therapist works with the parent and child together, where the therapist sets up and guides the dyad in reciprocal, interpersonally oriented games. The therapist assists the parent right in the session to help fine-tune the interactions so as to make the dyad successful in connecting and enjoying each other.

Definition and Uses

Theraplay is a method of enhancing attachment, engagement, self-esteem, and trust in others. It is based on the natural patterns of healthy interaction between parent and child. It is personal, physical, engaging, and fun. Theraplay is a type of parent-child psychotherapy used in a variety of settings. Group Theraplay and Sunshine Groups are used by therapists and educators. The Theraplay attitude or philosophy can be taught and practiced in child intervention and prevention programs and parent education.

Background

Theraplay was developed in the late 1960s by Dr. Ann Jernberg, a clinical psychologist, to meet the mental health needs of young children in the Head Start program in Chicago. Since that time, Theraplay has been used successfully in early intervention and parenting programs, day care and preschools, special and regular education programs, and residential, community mental health and private mental health practice. The typical age range of clients is from birth to 12 years, although the method has been adapted for teens and even for the elderly. The Theraplay Institute trains and certifies professionals in this method. It is now being practiced throughout the United States and internationally.

Research demonstrates that early sensitive caregiving and joyful interaction nourish a child's brain; form the child's view of self, others, and the world; and have a lifelong impact on human behavior and feelings.

Parent-child relationships are the primary focus in Theraplay. We work to ensure that the positive connection between parents and children that is the basis of mental health is firmly established. If a family has experienced loss, trauma, or separation, we work on re-establishing the connection. Because of its focus on attachment and relationship development, Theraplay has been used successfully for many years with foster and adoptive families. Theraplay is a useful therapeutic program for children with a variety of social and emotional difficulties. It also serves as a preventive program to strengthen the parent-child relationship in the presence of risk factors or the stresses of everyday life.

Distinctive Characteristics of Theraplay

➤ Theraplay is modeled on "good enough" parenting, the kind that leads to secure attachment.

➤ Treatment involves emotionally attuned, interactive, physical play.

➤ Nurturing touch is an integral part of the interaction.

➤ The focus is on the here-and-now, not on what happened in the past, interpretation of symbolic meanings, or pretend games.

➤ Treatment is geared to the child's emotional level and therefore often includes activities that might otherwise seem more appropriate for a younger child.

➤ The Theraplay therapist takes charge, carefully planning and structuring the sessions to meet the child's needs.

➤ Parents are actively involved in the treatment to enable them to take home the new ways of interacting with their child.

➤ The therapist and parents work together to engage the child in a healthier relationship.

The goal is to enhance attachment, trust, self-esteem, and joyful engagement and to empower parents to continue on their own the health promoting interactions of the treatment sessions.

The Basic Assumptions of Theraplay

From the beginning, the Theraplay approach shared many assumptions with interactional theories of development, particularly those of Self Psychology (Kohut, 1971, 1977, 1984), Object Relations Theory (particularly the work of Winnicot, 1958, 1965, 1971), and Attachment Theory (Bowlby, 1969, 1988). Over the 40 years of its clinical practice, an increasing body of research into the nature of attachment, the importance of attunement and sensitivity, brain development and regulation (J. Schore & A. Schore, 2008, p. 9), the effects of trauma and the value of play has supported and refined our approach.

The basic assumptions that guide our work with all families are:

➤ The primary motivating force in human behavior is a drive toward relatedness. Personality development is essentially interpersonal. The early interaction between parent and child is the crucible in which the self and personality develop.

➤ The caregiver's playful, empathic, sensitive responses to the child's needs for comfort and a secure base are essential to healthy development and secure attachment.

➤ The adult capacity for emotional self-regulation as well as the capacity to understand and empathize with others depends on early experiences of empathy and co-regulation between caregiver and child.

➤ When things go well in the relationship, the child develops an inner representation of *himself* as lovable, special, competent, and able to make an impact on the world; of *others* as loving, caring, responsive, and trustworthy; and of *the world* as a safe, exciting place to explore. That is, within a secure attachment, he begins a process of learning about himself and the world that is positive and hopeful and that will have a powerful positive influence throughout his life.

➤ When given unresponsive, neglectful, or abusive care, or sometimes when the child is unable to receive and process loving care due to medical/neurological or developmental problems, the child develops an inner representation of *herself* as unlovable and incompetent; of *others* as uncaring and untrustworthy; of *the world* as unsafe and full of threat. That is, within an insecure or disorganized attachment, the process of learning about herself and the world becomes negative, hopeless and full of shame. Many behavior problems of children who are adopted or in foster care can be traced back to their beginnings in insecure or disorganized attachment and in the consequent dysregulation and negative views of themselves and the world.

Who Can Benefit From Theraplay?

Children with a wide variety of presenting problems have been successfully treated using the Theraplay model including withdrawn and depressed children and angry, noncompliant children, as well as children with regulatory problems and ADHD. Theraplay has become increasingly well known for its effective impact on children with attachment issues as a result of abuse and neglect, separation and loss, as well as autism spectrum disorder. Theraplay has been used in a variety of family constellations, both biologic and foster, high-risk and preventative cases, in domestic violence shelters, in homes, psychiatric hospitals, and even in residential centers where children have no parents available.

The Goals of Theraplay

The parent-child relationship is the primary focus in Theraplay. Our model for treatment is based on attachment research that demonstrates that early sensitive caregiving and joyful interaction nourish a child's brain, form the child's view of herself, of others and of how she expects them to respond to her (Internal Working Models), and have a lifelong impact on her behavior and feelings.

The goal of treatment is to create (or fine tune) a secure, attuned, joyful relationship between a child and her primary caregivers. When there is no parent available, for example a child in residential treatment or in a school setting, the goal is to establish such a relationship with one special staff person and establish an attuned, nurturing atmosphere. For children with autism and developmental problems, the goal is to address the social interaction problems associated with these challenges.

In order to do this we bring parents and child together in sessions to encourage and practice the playful, attuned, responsive interaction that characterize a healthy, secure relationship.

Preparing Parents for Their Active Role

In Theraplay we help parents understand and respond empathically and contingently to their child's signals and underlying needs in order to provide the regulatory experience the child needs. We help them understand and come to terms with those aspects of their own experiences and attitudes that might get in the way of their being able to change old patterns and respond to their child's needs.

The Results of Theraplay

As a result of experiencing a different kind of relationship—one that is noncongruent with what she has come to expect—the child's inner working model of herself, of her parents, and what she can expect in her relation with them changes from negative to positive (Bowlby, 1973, p. 203). The experience of having her caregivers attune to and modulate her arousal states leads to the capacity for self-regulation, reduces impulsive behavior, and so on (Schore, 1994, p. 33). The parent's inner working model of herself and her child will become more positive. The result of all these changes is a reduction of the behavior problems that led to the child's referral for treatment. But more importantly it leads to the full range of positive outcomes associated with secure attachment: better social skills, better school performance, and more competence and long-term mental health.

Basic Treatment Plan

Families come to the Theraplay Institute for a series of 18 to 25 weekly sessions with four follow-up sessions at quarterly intervals over the next year. The first session is an information-gathering interview with the parents. The second and third appointments are observation sessions using the Marschak Interaction Method (MIM), in which the child and one parent perform a series of interactive tasks together. The interactions are videotaped and later analyzed by institute staff in preparation for a fourth session with the parents. In that session the staff and parents discuss their observations of the interaction and together agree on a plan for treatment.

Sessions 5 through 20 involve direct Theraplay with the family, duplicating (regardless of age) the kind of playful behavior and fun games that parents and young children naturally engage in together. The interaction includes structuring, engaging, nurturing, and challenging activities in combinations geared to the specific needs and problems of the individual child and his or her family. After every three family sessions a session is scheduled for the therapist(s) and the parents to meet without the child to discuss progress and goals.

Parents observe all Theraplay sessions and eventually enter the room and join in Theraplay directly. We often have two therapists, one who interacts with the child and one who works with the parents. When two therapists are present, the parent therapist observes with the parents and discusses the rationale for the activities, for example, encouraging the development of trust and self-esteem, building a sense of self as lovable, developing confidence, permitting pleasurable experiences, encouraging intimacy, developing a positive body image, strengthening perceptual motor-coordination. This discussion includes ways in which the parents can implement these ideas at home. If one therapist is present, these discussions take place with the parents at the end of each session, by phone, or at a separately scheduled time.

The final session ends with a good-bye party. Four follow-up sessions are scheduled at quarterly intervals, with parents and child, over the next 12 months. A typical Theraplay program of 25 sessions (4 assessment, 21 treatment and discussion) is summarized below:

Typical Theraplay Session Sequence

Session	Program
1	Initial interview with mother and/or father.
2	One parent and child participate in Marschak Interaction Method (MIM), a structured technique for intensive observations of the ways parent and child typically interact with one another. Theraplay therapist observes and videotapes this interaction.
3	Same as 2, except that other parent participates.
4	Feedback session with mother and father.
5, 6, 7	The therapist interacts with child while parents watch. Explanations are given to parents ahead of time as to what will take place. Questions are answered after the session and parents are encouraged to try Theraplay techniques at home. Parents enter the session toward the middle or end of each session.
8	Meeting with parents only to go over videos of sessions/review progress/discuss issues with child at home.
9–11	Same as 5–7, with parents gradually becoming the focus of interaction with child with therapist's guidance.
12	Meeting with parents only to go over videos of sessions/review progress/discuss issues with child at home.
13–15	Same as 9–11, with parents gradually taking more of the lead role in interacting with child with therapist's guidance.
16	Meeting with parents only to go over videos of sessions/review progress regarding therapy goals/ discuss issues with child at home.

17–19	Same as 13–15, with parents gradually taking more of the lead role in interacting with child with therapist's guidance.
20	Meeting with parents to evaluate therapy goals/decide on end date/refer for additional treatment.
21–23	Theraplay session where parents are actively involved in planning and leading the sessions.
24	Final "good-bye Theraplay party" or additional sessions as needed.
25	Final meeting with parents to review goals achieved and areas for future work if necessary.

Treatment Plan for Families Created Through Foster Care or Adoption

Different types of psychotherapy may be helpful to the child and family across the life span to deal with adoption/foster concerns. At the time of the initial information gathering and assessment, the focus will be on the child's and family's immediate needs and determination of the most appropriate treatment plan. These needs may be met at the Theraplay Institute, or appropriate referrals will be made.

Theraplay may be an appropriate early treatment to work on strengthening relationships; this is especially true for children ages birth to 7, but also may apply to older children. In recognition of the typically greater needs of children who have experienced separation, loss, trauma, multiple caregivers, or institutional care, the treatment period is extended in length and intensity. Treatment may begin with the Theraplay plan as outlined above and gradually incorporate elements of processing the child's history and adaptation to the current family. Sessions may be extended to 1.5 hours or scheduled twice weekly to allow for this processing. A treatment period of 12 to 24 months is common. A significant aspect of the treatment is parent education/support in order to assist the parents in responding to the child and managing the child's environment in therapeutic ways.

Marschak Interaction Method

The Marschak Interaction Method (MIM) is a structured technique for observing and assessing the relationship between two individuals; for example, biological parent and child, foster or adoptive parent and child, teacher and child. It consists of a series of simple tasks designed to elicit a range of behaviors in four dimensions.

The MIM evaluates the parent's capacity: to set limits and to provide an appropriately ordered environment (Structure), to engage the child in interaction while being attuned to the child's state and reactions (Engagement), to meet the child's needs for attention, soothing and care (Nurture), and to support and encourage the child's efforts to achieve at a developmentally appropriate level (Challenge). At the same time it allows assessment of the child's ability to respond to the parent's efforts.

In addition to allowing a close look at problem areas in the relationship, the MIM provides a unique opportunity for observing the strengths of both adult and child and of their relationship. It is, therefore, a valuable tool in planning for treatment and in determining how to help families strengthen their relationships. The description of the relationship that results from this observation is a valuable aid in determining the appropriateness of custody arrangements, reunification, foster placement, and/or adoption. While the MIM provides useful information about the way two people interact, it is important that other sources such as case management data, interviews, and other types of assessments be taken into account when major decisions such as change of placement or permanent placement are being considered. The MIM is not a standardized instrument and is best used as a tool for describing parent-child interaction and planning treatment.

The MIM interaction takes from 30 to 60 minutes and is videotaped. Careful evaluation of the videotaped interaction precedes the preparation of the written report or feedback. Feedback includes showing parts of the videotape to demonstrate to the adult the most effective ways to engage and interact with the child. Individuals or agencies requesting this assessment may specify either a written report, personal feedback, or both.

Administration of the MIM The caregiver-child dyad is seated at a table or on floor with pillows, with a video camera set up to record the interaction. The examiner chooses the tasks beforehand from a list of recommended tasks provided by the Theraplay Institute. The tasks have instructions like "Play peek a boo with the child" or "Adult build a block structure and encourage child to copy it." Any task that has materials that go along with it has an envelope with the materials marked the same number as the task, and the envelopes and cards are placed by the adult's seat. The examiner gives instructions to the adult to go through the cards one at a time. The examiner then leaves room for MIM, reenters, asks questions at the end (see later section), gives brief supportive comments to parent, and confirms schedule for feedback session.

Videotaping

Videotaping the interaction is highly recommended as it allows careful analysis and the ability to show portions of the tape in the feedback and come to consensus about the events of the interaction.

We recommend that the examiner not be in the room during the MIM in order to achieve the most natural results.

Observing the MIM

The examiner usually observes the MIM through a one-way mirror or video hook-up if possible in order to be aware of the parent-child interaction and to be sure it is being recorded properly.

Do not allow one parent to observe the other's MIM, or a sibling to observe while the MIM is taking place.

The child will be aware of the videotaping; if the child is aware that the examiner also is observing from another room, he or she may be more anxious; we decide on whether to tell the child based on potential reaction.

Examiner Intervention

Because this is an assessment, the examiner should only intervene in the rare event that a danger occurs. Occasionally a parent needs a reminder in the first task that it is up to him or her to decide when to move on to the next task. If a dyad has completed only a few tasks and the available time is almost over, a reminder of the time is appropriate.

Questions After the MIM

After the therapist enters the room, he asks the following questions. The questions are directed to the parents of children under the age of 5 and to parent and child for school aged and adolescents:

What was your reaction to the session? (to parent all ages)

Did I get a picture of how things usually go when you're together?

If not, what did I miss?

Which task did you like the best?

What did you like about it?

Which did you like the least?

What did you not like about it?

Which task did (child) like the best?

Which did (child) like the least?

How can you tell?

(Child) is your parent right about that? What do you think?

Older children can predict what their parents liked the best and least as well.

After the MIM interaction is completed, the examiner reviews the MIM interaction a second time, observing the parent and child's verbal and nonverbal interactions, and formulates some clinical opinions about how the child responds to his parents' efforts to:

➤ Structure the environment and set clear, appropriate expectations and limits.

➤ Engage the child in interaction while being attuned to the child's state and reactions.

➤ Respond in a nurturing way to the child's needs, including being able to soothe and calm the child when needed.

➤ Provide appropriate challenge.

The examiner selects segments of the video where there is positive interaction to point out to the parent, with the message being that the therapy will find ways to increase the frequency of helpful, positive interactions. The difficult segments should be approached as a collaborative process where the examiner and parent think together about why the interaction is happening, and explore the parent-child thoughts and feelings. Both parents watch each other's feedback; therefore, we try to show different tasks for each parent to avoid direct comparisons. At the end of the feedback, we discuss treatment goals based on the four dimensions of Theraplay, developmental goals, and so on.

The Theraplay Dimensions

The Theraplay method is based on the concept that there are 4 dimensions necessary for good parenting and good corrective experience: Structure, Engagement, Nurture, and Challenge.

Structure

The key concepts of structure are safety, organization, and regulation. The fact that the adult is in charge is reassuring, teaching the child to be in control of self, and assuring the child of order in an environment that can be unruly or chaotic. Therefore, structure addresses inner and outer disorder and is especially relevant for children who are overactive, undirected, overstimulated, or who need to be in control. Structure is especially relevant for parents who are poorly regulated/disorganized, have difficulty setting limits and/or being a confident leader, rely on verbal/cognitive structuring, or are over- or understimulating.

An example of a structuring activity is making a stack of hands: The therapist puts a hand palm down in front of child, has the child put his hand on top; alternate hands to make a stack. Build the stack going up above the child's face and then back down, then make the hand stack go fast and slow.

Engagement

The key concepts for engagement are connection, attunement, acceptance, and expansion of positive affect. The child is focused on in an intensive, personal way in order to make an attuned connection. The goal is that the child feels "seen" and "felt." Engaging activities offer pleasant stimulation, variety, and a fresh view of life, allowing a child to understand that surprises can be fun and new experiences enjoyable. Engagement is especially appropriate for children who are withdrawn, avoidant of contact, or too rigidly structured. Very withdrawn or autistic children may experience engagement as uncomfortable. In response, the therapist slows the pace and monitors stimulation. Engagement is especially relevant for parents who are disengaged, preoccupied, inattentive, out-of-sync with the child, rely primarily on verbal engagement, or who do not enjoy the child.

An example of an engagement activity is the Beep and Honk game: The therapist makes a special noise when touching the child's body part, for example, a high "beep" sound for the nose and a low "honk" sound for the chin. The therapist tries to remember which noise goes with the part when doing a series of touches.

Nurture

The key concepts of nurture are regulation, secure base, and worthiness.

Nurturing activities are soothing, calming, quieting, caretaking activities that make the world feel safe, predictable, warm, and secure, and reassure the child that the adult provides comfort and stability. They meet the child's unfulfilled younger needs; help the child to be able to relax and allow herself to be taken care of; and build the inner representation that the child is lovable and valued. Nurturing activities are especially relevant for children who are overactive, aggressive, or pseudo-mature, and for parents who are dismissive, harsh, punitive, or have difficulty with touch and/or displaying affection.

An example of a nurturing activity is the Lotion or Powder Prints game: the therapist or parent applies lotion or powder to the child's hand or foot and makes a print on dark paper, floor mat or pillow. If made with a lotion print on dark paper, the therapist can shake powder on it and then blow or shake it off to enhance picture.

Challenge

The key concepts for challenge are competence, confidence, and supporting exploration.

The activities are fun and require a partnership, not done alone. They help the child take a mild, age appropriate risk, and promote feelings of competence and confidence. Challenging activities are especially useful for withdrawn, timid, or rigid children. They are also used to deal with resistance. They are especially useful for parents who have inappropriate developmental expectations, or are competitive.

An example of challenging activity is Balloon Tennis: The therapist, parent, and child keep the balloon in the air by using specified body parts; for example, heads, hands, no hands, shoulders.

All activities are conducted in an upbeat atmosphere of warmth, spontaneity, optimism, cheerfulness, and fun.

Phases of Treatment

Although the unique needs of each child guide the progression of treatment in Theraplay, it is also helpful to know that Theraplay therapy usually proceeds in roughly six or seven phases:

Introduction

➤ Therapist signals that Theraplay will be fun.
➤ Clearly structured as to time, space, and therapist roles.
➤ Begins in waiting room.

Exploration

➤ Therapist and child get to know each other.
➤ Check-ups—comparisons of differences.
➤ Child learns he is fun to be with.

Tentative Acceptance

➤ Beguiling because it seems so easy.
➤ Child is "playing along"—as in honeymoon phase of adoptions.
➤ Child's actual goal is to keep the therapist at bay.
➤ Therapist remains active, engaging, appealing, fun.

Negative Reaction

➤ Child puts up clear resistance against intimacy.
➤ Uses typical defensive patterns.
➤ Is passive, floppy, withdrawn—or actively resistant.

➤ Parents say— "finally someone sees what we go through all the time."

➤ Therapist remains calm and in control.

➤ Contains if necessary to keep things safe.

Growing Trust

➤ Longer periods of intimacy.

➤ Reciprocal play begins.

➤ Eye contact improves.

➤ A true partnership.

➤ Parents or caretakers are introduced to the session.

➤ Parents may come in earlier, even right from the beginning in case of new adoptions and very young children.

Termination

➤ Preparation—Time to consider conclusion of treatment when Theraplay sessions become pure fun and the child is able to transfer positive session behaviors into nonsession settings.

➤ Announcement—Child is told how many sessions are left.

➤ Emotional reactions to termination are acknowledged but not explored at length as in an individual, long-term therapy. The focus is on the transfer to the parent and on the improved parent-child relationship.

➤ Final party—Review fun activities, have favorite foods, look forward to good times to come.

Check Ups

➤ The parent and child come once a month for three months to refuel and reinstate the Theraplay attitude and principals between the dyad.

➤ After three months, sessions go on once every three months for a year if possible to maintain the gains made in treatment.

Sequence of a Theraplay Session

Preparation

➤ Plan session based on what you know about child, goals for treatment, and what happened at the last session.

➤ Gather all materials and place them in a container close at hand.

➤ Set up camera.

➤ Have a cozy place for the child to settle into, using pillows or beanbag chair against a wall to support child's back.

Typical Sequence

- ➤ Entrance
    - ➤ Active, playful way of coming into the room.
    - ➤ Help child settle into his special place.
- ➤ Check up
    - ➤ Noticing, attuning, caring for hurts.
- ➤ Goal-related activities (3 to 4 total)
    - ➤ Pattern of active-quiet-active.
- ➤ Parent/parents enter
    - ➤ Plan a special way for parents to come in—child hides, hide something on child for parents to find.
    - ➤ Repeat some of earlier activities.
    - ➤ New activities that meet relationship goals.
- ➤ Feeding
    - ➤ Aim for this to be as nurturing and calming as possible.
- ➤ Song
- ➤ Help child organize himself to leave.
    - ➤ Put shoes and socks on.
    - ➤ Put outer garments on.
    - ➤ Encourage parents to hold child's hand "all the way to the car, the elevator, etc."

A typical 30-minute session may consist of 9 to 10 activities including all of the components above. The order of the activities would be changed depending on the child's needs; for example, with a child who feels particularly anxious about being taken care of, we might leave the caring for hurts until the middle of the session when she feels more at ease. If a child is hungry at the beginning of the session, we will give her the snack at the beginning rather than saving it for the end. Attuning to the child's specific needs takes precedence over any predetermined list suggested in this manual.

Instruct the parent to respond to the child's later comments/questions about the session, but not to ask the child what they liked or thought about the session. The reason for this instruction is so that the child's experience of Theraplay does not become a cognitive, intellectual exercise. The purpose of the Theraplay interactions is fully discussed with the parents.

Working With Parents: Training Parents to Be Co-Therapists

One of the most important goals for working with parents in Theraplay is giving parents a more positive, empathic view of their child. The Theraplay therapist helps foster this more positive view in several ways. One is by affording the parent the opportunity to observe their child. By observing the Theraplay therapist with their child they see how much the therapist appreciates and values the child.

Furthermore, the therapist provides opportunities for guided observations. This helps increase empathy by helping parents understand how the child might be feeling. "How do you think she is feeling right now?" Finally, the therapist encourages more empathy in the parent by having them role-play the child's part. Parents learn what it feels like to be comforted or to have their out-of-control behavior stopped.

Steps Leading to Competence in Being Theraplay Therapists to Their Children

Theraplay therapy helps parents to feel more competent with their child. This begins during feedback when we explain our view of their child and her problem.

The therapist then models healthy interaction so parents can model their behavior on how we approach their child. The therapist then provides opportunity for guided practice. Parents are brought into session after four sessions. The therapist prepares the parent ahead of time about what activities she has planned and how she wants the parent to participate. The Theraplay therapist guides the parent's interaction in the session to make it successful.

The therapist assigns homework each week of playing several of the activities that were successful and fun in the session, and then follows up with the parent the following week about how it went.

Role-Playing

In preparation for parents' taking a more active role in leading the session, role-play serves two purposes: (1) practice in taking charge; (2) insight into how child feels.

Taking Charge

Parent plans and executes most of the session with support from therapists.

Teaching Parents About Developmental Issues and How to Handle Behavior Problems

In our once monthly parent sessions, we teach parents about appropriate developmental expectations for their child's specific circumstance. We are guided by the principles that children with attachment problems are emotionally immature and that attachment is fostered by attending to child's younger, baby needs. This is especially difficult but important with older adopted children.

Teaching the Concept of Inner Representations

We teach parents the idea of how their child learns what kind of person he is and how the early learning in unempathic settings colors the way the child behaves now.

Consulting About Behavior Management

Before each Theraplay session, we spend approximately 15 minutes meeting just with the parent and talk about how things went that week and make suggestions about how to handle problems—including principles of having a few clear rules, immediate follow through, and maintaining a calm attitude, and so on. We recommend a combination of nurture and structure plus understanding of the behavior as our general rule for handling misbehavior.

How Theraplay Can Be Adapted for Traumatized Children

Theraplay is very commonly used for children who have undergone complex trauma, or trauma that has occurred within the context of an attachment relationship over an extended period of time during the child's early years. These are the children who have been exposed to domestic violence situations, were themselves victims of abuse or neglect, and have undergone multiple losses due to foster care or death. Theraplay can be used to successfully heal the attachment problems inherent in these children's traumas. In order to do so, modifications need to be made to the treatment to accommodate the child's fears and coping mechanisms.

Adapting Theraplay for Traumatized Children

➤ While maintaining a comfortable, self-assured stance, increase your sensitivity to child's response. If the child seems uncomfortable, acknowledge his discomfort and try another approach.

➤ If the child is fearful, acknowledge that you see he is frightened and that you think this must be because he has been hurt in the past, but that his new caretakers and you are going to make sure that he is safe.

➤ Have trusted caretakers in the room. Have them make the initial physical contact with a particularly frightened child.

➤ Avoid a tentative, questioning approach that implies that the child might not be safe with you.

➤ Slow down, talk softly, and make sure the child is not overwhelmed.

➤ Use touch that is matter-of-fact, nonthreatening, soothing, and calming. Include safe touch in many activities.

➤ Empower the child to say no. Engage the child in activities that give her a chance to feel her strength, to use her body to push you away, to be assertive.

➤ If the child has been taught that people must ask permission to touch her, affirm that that is a very good rule to protect her from people who do not respect her. Her parents and her therapist respect her very much and will help her learn how to accept good touch from them.

➤ Above all, be playful and engaging. Convey the message that the child is a delightful, strong, interesting person and that you are a trustworthy, fun-loving, and caring adult.

References

Bowlby, J. (1969). *Attachment and loss, 1: Attachment*. New York, NY: Basic Books.

Bowlby, J. (1973). *Attachment and loss, Vol. 2: Separation anxiety and anger*. London: Hogarth Press.

Bowlby, J. (1988). *A secure base: Parent-child attachment and healthy human development*. New York, NY: Basic Books.

Kohut, H. (1971). *The analysis of the self*. New York, NY: International Universities Press.

Kohut, H. (1977). *The restoration of the self*. New York, NY: International Universities Press.

Kohut, H. (1984). *How does analysis cure?* A. Goldberg (ed.). Chicago, IL: University of Chicago Press.

Schore, A.N. (1994). *Affect regulation and the origin of the self: The neurobiology of emotional development*. Hillside, NJ: Erlbaum.

Schore, J. R., & Schore, A. N. (2008) Modern attachment theory: The central role of affect regulation in development and treatment. *Clinical Social Work Journal, 2001b*, 22(1-2), 201–269.

Winnicott, D.W. (1958). *Collected papers: Through paediatrics to psychoanalysis*. London: Tavistock

Winnicott, D.W. (1965). *The maturational processes and the facilitating nvironment: Studies in the theory of emotional development*. London: Hogarth Press.

Winnicott, D.W. (1971). *Playing and reality*. London: Tavistock.

PART IV

Trauma-Focused Interventions

Children who have been maltreated have all been traumatized to some degree. Thus, all of the interventions described so far in this volume for treating maltreated children pertain to treating the effects of trauma. What distinguishes the two chapters in this section, however, is the extent to which the interventions described focus on processing the traumatic events per se.

In Chapter 9, I describe how to provide trauma-focused cognitive behavioral therapy (TFCBT) for children (and their nonoffending caregivers) who have PTSD and related symptoms and behavioral problems stemming from having been physically or sexually abused or from witnessing domestic violence. In light of its strong empirical base of replicated RCTs (as specified in this volume's Appendix), TFCBT is considered to be the gold standard for treating traumatized children and their nonoffending caregivers.

In Chapter 10, Robbie Adler-Tapia summarizes the use of Eye Movement Desensitization and Reprocessing (EMDR) with traumatized children. EMDR is one of the two interventions with the most empirical support for treating adult posttraumatic stress disorder (PTSD; the other is prolonged exposure therapy). Its protocol for adults has to be translated to the appropriate developmental phase when treating children, and the evidence supporting its effectiveness with children is growing (as discussed in this book's appendix).

9

Trauma-Focused Cognitive Behavioral Therapy for Children

Allen Rubin

Based on the solid base of replicated experimental studies supporting its effectiveness (as summarized in the appendix of this volume), trauma-focused cognitive behavioral therapy (TFCBT) is the gold standard for the treatment of traumatized children and their nonoffending caregivers. Its developers—Judith Cohen, Esther Deblinger, and Anthony Manarino—authored an excellent book on TFCBT (2006). A lengthy, detailed chapter on how to provide TFCBT appeared in the first volume of this Clinician's Guide Series (Hoch, 2009). This chapter is derived from those two sources.

Much of the empirical support for TFCBT is in treating posttraumatic stress disorder (PTSD), depression, shame, and behavior problems related to sexual abuse. However, it has also been extended to treat symptoms of PTSD, depression, and anxiety connected to other forms of physical abuse and domestic violence. Cohen, Mannarino, and Deblinger (2006) caution that TFCBT "is not ideally suited for children whose *primary* difficulties reflect severe preexisting behavioral difficulties" (p. 32). However, it can alleviate some trauma-related behavioral problems. They suggest the acronym CRAFTS to summarize the core values of TFCBT, as follows:

➤ Components based
➤ Respectful of cultural values
➤ Adaptable and flexible
➤ Family focused
➤ Therapeutic relationship is central
➤ Self-efficacy is emphasized

Components based means that TFCBT emphasizes progressively building skills that are matched to the individual needs of the client and presented in a manner that builds on previously learned skills. TFCBT should be provided in a manner that respects cultural, religious, familial, and community values. To be successful, providers of TFCBT must be *adaptive and flexible* so that its components are implemented in a way that fits the idiosyncratic needs and circumstances of each child and family. However, the need to be adaptive and flexible in providing TFCBT does not mean that anything goes. Effectively providing TFCBT requires striking a balance between conforming to the protocol of the treatment model while simultaneously adapting it to each child and family. *Family involvement* is one of the most important components of TFCBT. The entire family is affected when a child is traumatized. Therefore, TFCBT involves caregivers in the treatment, and when clinically appropriate may also involve siblings and extended supports. Also central is the development and maintenance of a trusting, empathic, accepting, and validating *therapeutic relationship*. Although the efficacy of all empirically supported treatments requires that they be provided in the context of a strong therapeutic alliance, this component is especially important in treating clients whose trust, optimism and self-esteem have been shattered by traumatic events and need to be restored. *Self-efficacy* is a long-term goal of TF-CBT. Helping caregivers and children develop coping skills and safety skills can foster a feeling of mastery that last long after they finish treatment.

The TFCBT Model

A key component of TFCBT is built on adapting prolonged exposure therapy—originally developed for adults—for children and adolescents. Prolonged exposure therapy involves clients in gradually and incrementally recalling and narrating the traumatic event (imaginal exposure) or gradually and incrementally having contact with something feared in real life by clients that is associated with the trauma (in vivo exposure). The idea is to alleviate avoidance and other trauma-related symptoms through a process of habituation in which the client confronts feared memories and stimuli (in a gradual, hierarchical process starting with less feared memories and stimuli first and then gradually moving up to those that are more anxiety laden). The habituation occurs as fear-relevant information is elicited in a safe environment. Just as learned associations between two stimuli get extinguished when one stimulus repeatedly is presented in the absence of the other, repeatedly being exposed to trauma-related stimuli in a safe environment and in the context of a strong therapeutic/ supportive relationship helps clients learn that remembering the feared memory or confronting the feared stimuli is not dangerous. It helps them develop a greater sense of courage and mastery as they learn that they can face the feared memories or stimuli. Likewise, they learn to separate the trauma as a specific event that is in the past and to develop a more realistic appraisal of the world as a dangerous place, of the trustworthiness of other people, and of their own self-image or self-blame.[1]

Hoch (2009, p. 190) depicts the entire TFCBT process as gradually "encouraging the child to confront and discuss trauma related thoughts and other reminders. At the point

---

[1] For a fuller description of prolonged exposure therapy, see Thomas (2009) and/or Foa and Rothbaum (1998).

Figure 9.1   TFCBT Sessions Flow

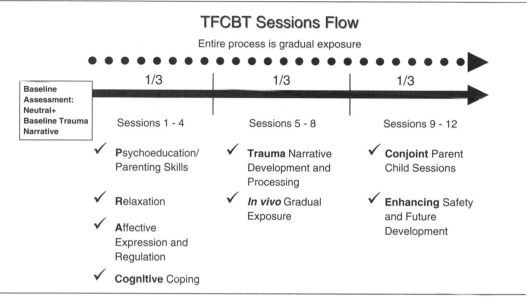

of intake or assessment, children and caregivers are asked questions about the trauma. Discussion related to the trauma becomes more specific and detailed as the sessions progress. At termination, ideally, the child and caregiver are able to talk more openly and with less discomfort about the trauma."

The TFCBT model is a directive approach to treatment that requires acknowledging the trauma within the first session. As illustrated in Figure 9.1, it consists of 12 weekly 90-minute sessions. The following PRACTICE acronym can be used to help remember the components of the TFCBT model:

Psychoeducation and Parenting Skills

Relaxation

Affective expression and regulation

Cognitive coping and processing

Trauma narrative development and processing

In vivo gradual exposure

Conjoint child-parent sessions

Enhancing safety and future development

In Figure 9.2, Hoch (2009) provides an illustration of what a mid-treatment session might look like. Hoch elaborates:

Forty-five minutes are spent with a non-offending caregiver and 45 minutes are spent with the child or adolescent. If unable to provide 90-minute sessions, sixteen to twenty 60-minute sessions are equivalent. With 60-minute sessions, 30 minutes are spent with the child and 30 minutes with the caregiver. In early sessions, children and caregivers are seen separately by the therapist. As sessions progress, joint sessions occur to enhance communication between child and caregiver(s).

Figure 9.2 Example of One 90-Minute Session from Midtreatment

	Goals	Activities	Time
Child–Individual Session	Review rationale for gradual exposure	Review child's gradual exposure work from prior sessions	30–40 minutes
	Reduce distress associated with the abusive experience	Continue to add additional "chapters" to child's book by providing choices of topics to focus on	
	Elicit abuse-related thoughts and feelings	Reinforce education about child sexual abuse when disputing dysfunctional beliefs	
	Process and dispute dysfunctional thoughts	Prepare for joint session with caregiver. Role play sharing the "chapter" from the child's book as well as praise for the caregiver	
Caregiver–Individual Session	Reduce distress associated with the child's abusive experience	Share the child's gradual exposure work	30–40 minutes
	Elicit abuse-related thoughts and feelings	Assist in applying cognitive coping skills to combat dysfunctional beliefs	
	Process and dispute dysfunctional thoughts	Prepare for joint session with child. Role play caregiver's comments to the selected "chapter" of the child's book as well as praise.	
	Assist caregiver in managing child's behavior at home		
Joint Session	Promote open communication about the child's experience of abuse	Child shares a "chapter" from gradual exposure book	
	Provide an opportunity for the caregiver to model comfort when discussing the abuse	Mutual exchange of praise	10–20 minutes
	Strengthen caregiver–child relationship		

Depending on the child's/caregiver's situation, other adaptations may need to be made. For example, if a caregiver has a difficult work schedule, the therapist might meet with the caregiver one week and the child the next. (pp. 188–189)

When providing TFCBT to children who are placed in foster care, both the foster parent and the nonoffending caregiver might be included in treatment. At first, it is best to hold separate sessions with each party to avoid conflicts. Typically, the foster parent will bring the child. The focus with the foster parent is on daily contact and behavior management issues. The focus with the caregiver typically is more on the trauma. Parenting skills should also be addressed to facilitate a successful reunification when the child returns home. Later in the treatment process joint sessions can be held with both the foster parent and the caregiver. However, the child may prefer having only the nonoffending caregiver present when talking directly about the trauma.

If the nonoffending parent cannot participate, another support person can be included, such as a foster parent, residential staff member, CPS worker, older sibling, or grandparent. With some cases it may not be feasible to engage a caregiver in the treatment process. In such cases TFCBT components can be provided to children alone, and can be effective in alleviating depression, shame, and PTSD. But for cases where the child exhibits serious behavior problems, it is especially important to try to engage the caregiver in treatment. Efforts to engage caregivers might involve addressing practical obstacles or dealing with motivation. Overcoming practical issues might involve such things as providing transportation vouchers or utilizing volunteers who can provide child care. It might also entail providing snacks or meals for families whose sessions conflict with meal times. If practitioners (or their agencies) do not have sufficient resources to offer those things, they should engage in brainstorming sessions with caregivers as to whether they can call on others to help them get to their sessions.

If lack of motivation is the obstacle to engagement, the practitioner should assess the basis for that lack and use psychoeducational techniques and perhaps motivational interviewing techniques to overcome that obstacle. Perhaps the caregivers have their own trauma history or are avoidant of the trauma for other reasons. Perhaps they don't understand their role in the process, and therefore believe that only the child should be involved. Similarly, foster parents might think that since they were not involved in the trauma they do not need to be included in the treatment. (As noted earlier and will be elaborated upon shortly, psychoeducation also is an essential component of the TFCBT treatment model.)

Assessment

Before TFCBT treatment commences, a comprehensive assessment should be completed. The assessment serves two purposes: (1) to inform treatment planning and (2) to evaluate treatment progress. The assessment should cover problems in cognitions, relationships, affect (including impulse control, difficulty with self-soothing, and dysregulated affective states), family difficulties (including attachment issues, parent-child conflict, and behavior management), trauma-related behaviors (such as risk taking, oppositional defiance, or sexualized behavior), and somatic symptoms. Assessment should also measure PTSD, depression, shame, and behavior problems in children and adolescents.

Cohen et al. (2006) and Hoch (2009) identify and describe a number of helpful instruments that can be used in the assessment process for both children and caregivers. For caregivers, assessment should examine depression, abuse-related distress (including their own PTSD symptoms related to the child's trauma), and parenting practices. Hoch (2009) adds:

> The pre-treatment assessment should be considered part of the gradual exposure process. During the assessment, children and caregivers are asked questions about the traumatic event(s). They are asked to think about the event and sit with thoughts, feelings, sensations, and reminders about the abuse. While formal

treatment has not yet begun, it is important to consider the total therapeutic experience as gradual exposure. Assessment is part of that therapeutic process. Feedback from the assessment to both caregivers and children is an important part of engaging families and orienting them to the TF-CBT model. (pp. 193–194)

Another important part of assessment, which takes place during the first TFCBT session, is to obtain two narratives from the child: (1) a neutral narrative and (2) a baseline trauma narrative. By comparing the two narratives, the therapist learns how difficult it is for the child to talk about or receive information about the trauma. Obtaining the trauma narrative also breaks the ice in discussing the trauma and conveys to the child that the therapist is comfortable talking about it.

In the neutral narrative the child describes thoughts, feelings, and body sensations connected to a recent event, such as a birthday, a holiday, a special outing, and so on. If no such events are recent, the child is asked to describe in detail their day from waking up through arriving for therapy. Immediately after obtaining the neutral narrative, and praising the child for providing so much information, the therapist elicits the baseline trauma narrative by asking the child asked to describe the traumatic event in as much detail as the child provided in the neutral narrative. (For a more detailed coverage of these two narratives, see Cohen et al., 2006, or Hoch, 2009.)

Psychoeducation and Parenting Skills

Psychoeducation involves informing clients about trauma and psychosocial issues related to it, such as PTSD. Psychoeducation also entails providing feedback about the assessment and educating children and caregivers about the TFCBT process and its rationale. It is important to provide psychoeducation in a manner that normalizes client reactions to having been traumatized, that validates their thoughts and feelings about the assessment process, and that builds rapport and trust. How to provide psychoeducation with children will depend on the developmental level of the child or adolescent, using simpler terms and briefer explanations with younger children than with older ones. (For a more detailed coverage of psychoducation with children, see Cohen et al., 2006, or Hoch, 2009.)

Psychoeducation takes place in the first session (as well as in later sessions). One goal is to help children and caregivers see that although talking about the abuse might involve some distress, it will be done in a way that is manageable, helpful, and necessary for a successful treatment outcome. Metaphors can be used such as cleaning out a wound or gradually getting used to cold swimming pool water. As alluded to earlier, skillfully providing psychoeducation can be key in obtaining commitment from caregivers to engage in the TFCBT treatment process. As Hoch (2009, p. 197) observes:

Of course, it is important to emphasize to caregivers that with their support and presence in the therapy process, their child will do better in treatment. Helping caregivers understand their role in therapy and their influence over their children's recovery gives them a sense of purpose and control. For many caregivers, this can counteract feelings of guilt, shame and helplessness around the abuse.

It is important to clarify for caregivers that they are participating in their child's treatment. Many caregivers have their own history of trauma for which they may not have received treatment. Emphasize to caregivers that TF-CBT may trigger thoughts and feelings about their own trauma history, but the treatment is for their child. The caregiver will learn skills and information that may indirectly impact how they manage their own trauma experience, but the therapist is not working with them on their own trauma. If needed, the therapist should make a referral to the caregiver for their own treatment.

Hoch (p. 198) adds:

An important goal of the first session with caregivers is to instill hope and confidence. Caregivers may be dealing with their own PTSD and depression symptoms related to their child's abuse. They may be struggling with thoughts such as *"My child's life is ruined," "I am a horrible parent for not protecting my child,"* and *"Life will never be the same."* With accurate information about abuse and confidence in effective treatment strategies, it is the therapist's job to help the caregiver see what he/she has already done to make the situation better. For example, telling a caregiver that they have already done the most important thing for their child, believing them, is a way to praise the caregiver and show them that there are protective responses in which they have engaged. Conveying to caregivers that PTSD and depression are treatable conditions and that most children who have been sexually abused lead productive, happy lives is also important psychoeducation that instills hope. Caregivers often walk into the first session feeling helpless, hopeless, and scared. The therapist must balance validation of these feelings with active questioning and problem solving as to how one can look at the situation in a different way.

When behavioral problems are an issue, psychoeducation should include conveying to caregivers that such problems are common in children who have been traumatized. Starting with the first session, psychoeducation also should introduce behavior management skills. After caregivers identify various behavioral problems, they can be asked to identify things that are going well. This enables the introduction of the concept of praise and how to give praise in a consistent and positive manner immediately after the positive behavior. The caregiver can then identify specific behaviors for which their child might deserve praise, followed by practicing how to give it. In a separate session with only the child, the therapist can help the child learn about praise and how to communicate it to the caregiver.

Parenting skills continue to be worked on throughout the TFCBT process. After working on praise, additional behavioral management skills can be taught, such as selective attention, using timeouts, and contingency reinforcement programs. (Because teaching these skills are covered in other chapters of this volume, they will not be elaborated upon here.)

Sexualized Behavior With children who have been sexually abused, an important part of psychoeducation is teaching caregivers how to distinguish developmentally appropriate behaviors (such as walking around in underwear, scratching one's own crotch, and so on) from problematic sexualized behaviors (such as imitating intercourse, masturbating with an object, and so on). Caregivers need to learn that not every sexual behavior is a sign that the child will become a perpetrator. They also need to learn how to manage their own emotional reactions to sexualized behaviors and learn when and how to respond to them. With problematic sexual behavior, safety will need to be addressed, along with the need for appropriate touch and physical affection. For more detail about safety and other issues pertaining to sexualized behavior, readers are referred to Cohen et al. (2006) and Hoch (2009).

Relaxation

After psychoeducation, the next component of TFCBT involves teaching children and caregivers relaxation techniques for handling stress and PTSD symptoms. These techniques may be needed later during the exposure parts of TFCBT. The techniques include focused breathing, visualization, mindfulness, meditation, progressive muscle relaxation, and aerobic exercises. More detail about these techniques can be found in Cohen et al. (2006) and Hoch (2009).

Affective Expression and Regulation

Beginning in the first session and continuing in subsequent sessions, the child's ability is assessed regarding identifying and expressing feelings and tolerating painful emotions connected to the trauma. With neutral prompts from the therapist as needed, a list of feelings about the trauma is created—one that includes not just negative feelings, but also positive ones, such as pride at being able to talk about the abuse, courage to say no to the perpetrator, and so on. The therapist then explains how many children have mixed feelings about their traumas and that there are no right or wrong feelings. Affect regulation skills are then taught in a manner befitting the child's developmental level and need.

Affective expression and regulation also are addressed in parallel sessions with caregivers. The therapist provides a comfortable atmosphere in which it is safe for caregivers to reveal less socially desirable feelings (such as anger at the child or loving feelings toward the sex offender). During early sessions the therapist validates the caregiver's feelings and acknowledges that there are no right or wrong ones. Caregivers are taught reflective listening skills so that they can support their children's efforts to verbalize their feelings.

Other skills taught to children and/or caregivers include thought interruption and positive imagery, positive self-talk, enhancing the child's sense of safety, problem solving, and social skills. More detail about these skills and about affective expression can be found in Cohen et al. (2006) and Hoch (2009).

Cognitive Coping and Processing

Like other forms of cognitive behavioral therapy, the cognitive coping component of TFCBT involves teaching clients about the connection between their thoughts, feelings, and actions, and how to use self-talk to change feelings. Cohen et al. (2006, p. 107) define cognitive coping as "a variety of interventions that encourage children and caregivers to explore their thoughts in order to ultimately challenge and correct cognitions that are either inaccurate or unhelpful."

Figure 9.3

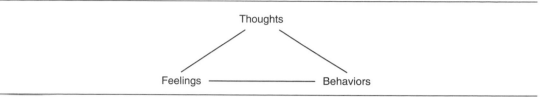

The first step in helping clients develop cognitive coping skills is to use exercises that encourage clients to express out loud some of the things they say internally to themselves when contemplating certain activities. Examples for might include saying such things as, "I'm tired" or "I don't want to school [or work]" before getting out of bed in the morning. The next step in teaching cognitive coping involves the therapist drawing the cognitive triangle, displayed in Figure 9.3, to help clients understand the difference and connection between thoughts and feelings and their connection to behaviors. The therapist then gives examples of these connections. For instance, they might discuss how the client might think a classmate hates the client because she never talks to the client. That thought might make clients feel very sad or angry. Then the therapist would ask the client how they would feel if they thought that the reason for the classmate not talking to them is that the classmate is very shy. Allowing the client to answer would probably elicit a different feeling, such as feeling sorry for the classmate instead of feeling so sad or angry.

Next, the therapist presents a variety of pleasant and unpleasant scenarios and asks the client to identify a thought and feeling connected to each scenario as well as the behaviors that might result from the thoughts. The scenarios would include common things that happen at school, at home, at work, in social situations and so on. After that, the client practices generating alternative thoughts about these scenarios that would help him or her to feel more positively about them. Eventually, this process should continue if possible—with scenarios from the client's real life.

Early in treatment, both the child and the caregiver learn cognitive coping. Children can use cognitive coping to reinforce or improve self-esteem, relaxation, safety, and hopefulness. Later in treatment, cognitive processing is used to address cognitive distortions associated with the trauma. Cognitive processing of the child's trauma involves talking through the trauma and developing a new perspective about it and making meaning of it. This cognitive processing step typically occurs after the child creates a trauma narrative, which is discussed as the next component of the TFCBT process.

Cognitive coping with caregivers should follow the same trajectory as with children, although their thoughts and feelings about the abuse can be processed earlier. Early in treatment, cognitive coping can help caregivers with related issues such as behavior management.

Trauma Narrative Development and Processing

The exposure component with children is implemented by engaging the child in developing a trauma narrative. In addition to using the narrative in exposure treatment with the child, it can be shared with caregivers to enhance processing of the abuse with them. This phase of treatment also begins with psychoeducation, this time about trauma and abuse. Helpful fact sheets are available (in English and Spanish) that can be provided to parents to facilitate the psychoeducation process with them. They can be found in the TF-CBT web training at www.musc.edu/tfcbt under the psychoeducation component.

Cohen et al. (2006) recommend that both psychoeducation and exposure components with children utilize books, games, and other child-oriented fun activities. They list specific suggestions as to which ones, as does Hoch (2009). An advantage of having children read a book about another child's traumas is that it will motivate children to write their own story (narrative) about their own traumatic experience. Hoch (p. 220), for example, suggests that the therapist introduce the idea of the child's narrative by saying, "Now that you've read a book about another child's experience, I think it would be a great idea to write your own book about the sexual abuse that happened to you." Hoch cautions, however, that, "the child may have anxiety about beginning to talk in a detailed way about their trauma but that is why the process remains *gradual* and safe in that the therapist will be coaching the child to use the coping skills he/she learned earlier in treatment."

Writing the narrative begins by developing a hierarchy of "chapters." Based on their knowledge of the trauma, the therapist should be prepared to suggest chapters for children—especially very young children—who need guidance regarding what chapters to include. Children can choose from the therapist's suggestions, and, with older children, the process is more collaborative. With all children, regardless of their age, children are given as much control as possible in selecting chapters. Figure 9.4 displays

Figure 9.4 Illustrative Examples of Possible Narrative Chapters

With an adolescent who was sexually abused over a period of years by her stepfather, a list of chapters might include:
> How people found out about the abuse
> The first incident of sexual abuse
> The last incident of sexual abuse
> The incident of abuse that is hardest to think about
> The relationship with the stepfather before the abuse started
> The medical exam
> Interview with child protective services or police
> Counseling
> Going to court

After writing these chapters, a final chapter that focuses on "advice to other kids," "how I feel now about the abuse," or "what strengths I've gained from this experience," can be written as a way to help the child put the experience in perspective.

With a young child who witnessed the homicide of her mother by her father, the chapter list might read:
> The time my Dad hurt my Mom
> Another time my Dad hurt my Mom
> A time my Mom had to go to the hospital
> A time the police came to the house
> When my Dad stabbed my Mom
> Talking to the Police
> Going into foster care

Source: Reproduced from Hoch (2009).

examples of chapters that might appear in an adolescent's narrative and in a young child's narrative.

The child chooses which chapter to begin with, and shows which part of the trauma is the easiest for the child to talk about. The therapist typically does the writing as the child narrates, especially with young children or older ones who have reading or writing difficulties. While writing, the therapist can prompt for many more details, such as regarding thoughts, feelings, and body sensations. When the chapter is completed, it is read aloud by the therapist and/or the child. This process adds another layer of exposure. After all the chapters are completed, the child can determine his or her order and pick a title for the narrative. Depending on the abilities and preferences of the child, narratives can vary in length and format. It could be a "book," short story, poem, song, puppet show, and so on—whatever will work in motivating the child to process the trauma.

The therapist should refrain from moving to the next stage—cognitive processing—while the narrative is being written. Instead, the therapist should simply listen to and accept the narrative as it is being told to validate the child's experience. After the narrative is completed, the final chapter—which covers what the children have learned in treatment, how they now have a different view of the trauma, the strengths they've developed, and how those strengths can be used in the future—can guide the cognitive processing. As Hoch (2009, p. 224) observes, "Sometimes the process of creating a narrative is all that is needed for a child to make meaning of his/her experience, and so a final chapter can be written rather quickly. For others, more intense cognitive processing of distorted or inaccurate thoughts may need to be done before a final chapter can be written."

Cognitive Processing Cognitive processing for caregivers does not involve writing a narrative. Instead, the caregivers tell their story about how they learned of the abuse. Common caregiver cognitions that may need to be processed include notions that their child's life has been ruined, self-blame for not preventing the abuse, not being able to trust anyone again, not being a competent parent, and so on. After normalizing caregiver negative thoughts and feelings as understandable reactions of any parent with similar circumstances, cognitive restructuring techniques are used. These may include asking them to think of and list evidence for and against the negative cognitions, Socratic questioning, and/or role-plays.

The foregoing cognitive restructuring techniques can also be used with children after the narrative has been completed and problematic feelings, thoughts, and body sensations have been identified in the narrative. The therapist chooses the issues to address with young children. The therapist asks all children (and adolescents) about their *current* thought, feeling, and body sensation in connection to the identified issue. If the event is described in the past tense in the children's narratives, the therapist asks what they think and feel *now* about it. For example, if the children report having felt scared and dirty after being sexually abused, the therapist would ask them if they *now* feel scared and dirty. Once the children respond in a manner indicating that they no longer have the negative thought or feeling, the new perspective is reinforced by having the children narrate a final chapter to the narrative that incorporates the new perspective. However, if the negative thought or feeling persists, the cognitive processing continues, using the same cognitive restructuring techniques. Hoch (2009) provides examples of these techniques in Figure 9.5.

Figure 9.5 Illustrative Examples of Cognitive Restructuring Techniques

Evidence Gathering: An experiment can be devised to show children how their thinking is altered. For example, after being sexually abused, a child may believe that ALL men sexually abuse kids. To SHOW the child the inaccuracy of their thinking, the therapist might ask the child to identify all the men/boys that they know. After identifying and writing down the names of all the men/boys the child knows, the therapist can have the child circle all of the men/boys that sexually abused him/her. The child can then SEE that most men/boys do not sexually abuse children. Having the child collect his/her own evidence about a distorted or inaccurate belief helps them to gain a new perspective and believe in it more strongly.

Socratic Questioning: This technique is the process of asking the child or caregiver questions to help them see the abuse from a new perspective. A child who was sexually abused may continue to believe that "sex is dirty" even after receiving psychoeducation on sexual abuse and talking about his/her own sexual abuse experience. To help the child gain a new perspective, the therapist might ask a series of questions that helps shake the foundation of the child's belief. The following exchange is an example of Socratic questioning:

Child: I never want to have sex with anyone. It's so dirty!

Therapist: What makes sex so dirty?

Child: Well, that's what my uncle did to me and that was gross.

Therapist: Was what happened to you sex or sexual abuse?

Child: Sexual abuse I guess.

Therapist: Well, what's the difference between sex and sexual abuse?

Child: Sex is when two people who love each other decide to have sex together. Sexual abuse is when an adult forces a child to touch them on their private parts.

Therapist: So, is sex dirty or is sexual abuse dirty?

Child: Sexual abuse.

Therapist: Why is it important to think about the difference?

Child: Because someday when I love someone I can decide to have sex with them.

Therapist: How will that experience be different?

Child: I will be older and the person won't force me to do anything I don't want to. We will love each other.

Therapist: Does that sound dirty?

Child: No.

Role Play: Having the child role play someone else, like their best friend or therapist, can have a therapeutic effect as well. The following dialogue is between the therapist and an 8-year old boy whose mother was killed in a car accident with him in the car. He is struggling with guilt and the thought that he should have died too.

Therapist: One of the things that you write in your narrative is that you feel guilty about not being able to save your mother from dying in the car accident. Do you still feel that way?

Child: Yes. Even though we've talked about it and I know accidents happen to people and it's not my fault. I still think that maybe if I had done something more she might have lived.

Therapist: OK, let's do a role play. I want you to play your best friend, Josh, and I'm going to be you. I'm going to come and talk to you about how I feel and I want you to be a good best friend, OK?

Child: OK

Therapist: Hi Josh! Can I talk to you?

Child: Sure.

Therapist: I've been thinking a lot about my mom and how she died. I feel really bad about it. I'm afraid to tell you what I did.

Child: You can tell me.

Therapist: I think you'll be mad at me. Maybe you won't even be my friend anymore.

Child: Listen, you can tell me and I won't be mad.

Therapist: OK . . . I think it's my fault that my mom died in that car accident.

Child: No way. Why?

Therapist: After we hit the truck and the car flipped over, I should have done something to help her get out of the car before it blew up.

Child: What could you have done?

Therapist: I don't know. Maybe undone her seatbelt and pulled her out.

Child: How could you do that when you were caught in the car too?

Therapist: I don't know.

Child: Well if you were stuck yourself, how could you get her out? Plus, how much did your mom weigh? Would you have been able to pull her out?

Therapist: I don't know. She was a lot bigger than me.

Child: What about the police people that came to the accident? They got you out. Why didn't they get your mom out?

Therapist: They tried but before they could get her out the car blew up. They took me first. I should have told them to get her out first.

Child: They made the decision, not you. Would they have listened to you?

Therapist: I don't know, but do you think it's my fault?

Child: No. You were trapped inside the car too and even if you got out of your seatbelt, your mom was too heavy to pull out. The police were in charge and they made the decision to pull you out, so it's not your fault.

Therapist: Are you sure?

Child: I'm sure. You were only 7 years old then. You weren't strong enough and you didn't make the decisions.

With a role play, the child must convince the therapist (playing him/her) that his/her thoughts are distorted or inaccurate. The very act of trying to convince the therapist and stating accurate/helpful information out loud helps the child solidify those statements in his/her own mind.

Source: Adapted from Hoch (2009, pp. 228–229).

In Vivo Gradual Exposure

Creating the trauma narrative can help children overcome their traumatic memories but may not be sufficient for helping them to stop avoiding inherently innocuous stimuli that remind them of the trauma. For some children, these avoidance behaviors can interfere with their overall functioning. For example, they may fear sleeping alone or sleeping in *any* bedrooms—even in a new house or in a friend's house—because they were sexually abused in their bedroom in their old home. If the trauma was a car accident, they may fear getting into any cars. If they witnessed their father battering their mother, they may not want to go to school, fearing that if their mother is left alone something bad may happen to her, even if the batterer is in prison.

The *in vivo* exposure component of TFCBT attempts to gradually overcome this type of avoidance and thus help traumatized children to improve their basic daily functioning. It does this by helping children gradually—little by little and starting with something that the children can tolerate—expose themselves to the innocuous objects, places or activities that they fear. It also involves encouraging the children to use the relaxation and coping skills that they learned earlier in the TFCBT process to help them tolerate each exposure.

The term *innocuous* here is vital. In vivo exposure should *not* encourage children to expose themselves to reminders of the trauma that remain unsafe. The child really does need to avoid those things. Thus, if children are still being abused when they visit a parent or other relative, the children really do need to stop visiting them, and it is both appropriate and healthy for children to fear such visits and want to avoid them. Likewise, if children really are unsafe in a certain part of the neighborhood, they really should fear and try to avoid passing through that area. In this connection, it bears noting that the first step in treating all traumatized individuals is to ensure their safety (Rubin, 2009). Desensitizing them to trauma cues that remain unsafe would endanger them, not protect them (Cohen et al., 2006).

The in vivo exposure component follows a desensitization plan that should be developed with the involvement of caregiver(s) or other support people (e.g., teachers, coaches) who are relevant to the avoidance. First, a hierarchy of feared but innocuous situations is developed, from the least anxiety provoking to the worst. Then, and beginning with the least anxiety provoking item on the hierarchy, the child is exposed to each item (while using their newly learned relaxation and coping skills), one step at a time, moving on to the next level only after mastering the previous one. For example, Hoch (2009, p. 232) reported the following hierarchy for a boy who did not want to be in or sleep in his bedroom after having been sexually abused by his uncle:

Playing in bedroom with parents for 5 minutes

Playing in bedroom with parents for 15 minutes

Playing in bedroom for 45 minutes

Sleeping in own bed with one parent until asleep

Sleeping alone in own bed

Before actually encountering each feared situation, the child can visualize encountering it while also practicing using coping skills to manage anxiety. Based on the above hierarchy, Hoch (2009, pp. 231–232) illustrates the process of in vivo exposure as follows:

> After disclosing that his uncle had been sexually abusing him in his bed over a period of months, Adam [not his real name] did not want to sleep alone. Instead, he wanted to sleep with his parents in their bed. After the disclosure, Adam's parents felt sad and upset for their son. They wanted to protect him and keep him safe, so they let Adam sleep with them for several months. Over those months, Adam became even more avoidant of his bedroom and complained of not wanting to enter his bedroom at all.

> Through a process of in vivo gradual exposure, Adam was gradually reintroduced to his bedroom. First, Adam's parents were directed to spend time with Adam in his bedroom playing with him, beginning with short intervals (5–15 minutes) and moving up to longer intervals (45 minutes to 1 hour). As Adam became more comfortable and was given praise for his efforts, he was required to start sleeping in his bed. At first, Adam's mother or father slept with Adam in his

own bed until he fell asleep. Adam's parent would then leave the room and return to their room. If Adam woke up in the middle of the night and came to his parents' bedroom, he was directed back to his bed by one of his parents who again lay down with him until he fell asleep. As time went on, Adam's parents put him to bed without staying with him. If he came in their room in the middle of the night, they again directed him to his own bed. Over time, they no longer had to stay with Adam in his room. He went to bed on his own and stayed in his bed the whole night.

Cohen et al. (2006) suggest that in addition to overcoming avoidance behaviors, in vivo exposure enhances other areas of functioning for children and the families. It helps the child "regain a sense of their own competence and mastery. Feeling (and being) at the mercy of overwhelming fears is a disempowering experience. By learning that they can overcome their terrifying memories and fears, children gain self-efficacy that can have far-reaching positive consequences in their lives" (p. 150).

Conjoint Child-Parent Sessions

After completing their cognitive processing in separate sessions, the child and parent are brought together in conjoint sessions. These sessions typically are conducted in three parts, beginning with separately meeting with the child for about one quarter of the session, then doing the same with the parent, and then spending about half of the session meeting with them together. The first two parts prepare the child and caregiver for the joint part.

During the first part, the therapist and child might review the information to be discussed in the joint session. In preparing for the first joint session, the child can read the whole trauma narrative again or just the parts that present the most difficulty, followed by a discussion of the child's worries or fears about the joint session and how to cope with them. This might include practicing coping skills in case they are needed in the joint session.

During the second part, an analogous process addresses the parent's worries or fears about the first joint session. The therapist reviews optimal ways of responding to prepare the parent for the narrative reading that will come in the joint session. For example, the parent should avoid excess emotion (such as sobbing) and instead be able to make supportive statements to the child. Optimal ways of asking the child questions and of responding to the child's questions are also reviewed. "For example, if a caregiver wants to ask the child why he/she didn't yell, scream, or fight back when the sexual assault occurred, the therapist should talk to the caregiver about why that question may be experienced as blaming to the child and provide more psychoeducation to the caregiver to help him/her understand why most kids don't fight back" (Hoch, 2009, p. 235). Hoch adds that the parent also should be oriented to the following goals of the first joint session:

➤ Creating a comfortable, fun atmosphere to counteract the child feeling sad, shame, or fear associated with the abuse.

➤ Enhancing open communication about the trauma.

➤ Showing the child that the parent can hear about and discuss the trauma comfortably.

During the first joint session, the parent listens as the child reads the trauma narrative and provides praise and other supportive statements about the narrative. Both the child and the parent ask questions of each other—questions that were developed earlier in individual sessions.

At least three joint sessions should be held. The first one, as discussed above, focuses on the specific trauma. To make it fun for the child, Hoch (2009) suggests using a game show in which the child and parent compete about answering questions about the trauma experienced by the child. Among the various games she suggests are: Breakaway and Survivor's Journey, both by Kidsrights; and Let's Talk About Touching (Cavanaugh-Johnson, 1992). "In other words, the therapist wants to create an experience in which the caregiver and child are having fun, feeling happy and laughing so that these emotions, rather than one's previously associated with the trauma (e.g. sadness, shame) become paired with talking about and thinking about the trauma" (pp. 233–234).

At the end of the first joint session, the parent, child, and therapist discuss and choose the focus of the next joint session. It might be similar to and build upon the first joint session, or it might involve activities in which other issues are discussed, such as sex education and safety skills, healthy relationships, anger resolution and/or conflict avoidance, avoiding risky activities, and so on. (For more information about these sessions, see Cohen et al., 2006, and Hoch, 2009.)

Enhancing Safety and Future Development

During the final component of the TFCBT model, the child and caregiver learn skills that will add to and help to maintain the treatment gains that they have already made. Education and training is provided in safety skills that pertain to the traumatic event that they experienced. For example, the child may be taught how to recognize both internal (their own body signals) and external cues regarding dangerous situations, assertively express their feelings and wants (such as how to say "no"), identify people and places that provide safety, distinguish between acceptable and unacceptable touching, ask for help, and so on. The joint sessions include information provision to both the child and caregiver as well as role-playing and practicing the skills.

Contraindications

The TFCBT model, as was illustrated in Figure 6.1, requires acknowledging the trauma within the first session. Consequently, it requires that prior substantiation of child maltreatment (physical abuse, sexual abuse, domestic violence) or other traumatic events (such as a natural disaster or the tragic death of a loved one). The therapist should not be involved in the substantiation process. Instead, it should come from Child Protective Services (CPS) or some other medical, mental health, or legal professional. Even if unsubstantiated abuse is suspected, including if the child is displaying sexualized behavior, TFCBT should not be used without prior substantiation. Before initiating TFCBT in cases of suspected abuse, the child should be referred to a professional who specializes in substantiating whether abuse has occurred. According to Hoch (2009, p. 187):

> If abuse is not substantiated, a more non-directive approach to treatment may be more appropriate. If a disclosure occurs in the context of more non-directive treatment, abuse-specific treatment can then begin. However, even with more non-directive treatment, components of TF-CBT can be used to provide education and safety skill training. In the case of sexualized behavior without any disclosure of abuse, various components of the TF-CBT model may be used to address the behavioral issues: parenting skills to help caregivers manage the sexualized behavior; relaxation, affective expression, and regulation and cognitive coping to help both caregivers and children understand the function of the sexualized behavior and how to redirect themselves; psychoeducation about sexual abuse and sexual behavior; and enhancing safety and future development to provide prevention education and safety skills. The trauma narrative and cognitive processing components of the model would not be used since there was no reported traumatic event. If, during the course of treatment, using some of the TF-CBT components, abuse is disclosed, a report to CPS should be made. Following the investigation by CPS, direct discussion about the child's abuse can then take place.

Even if abuse has been substantiated, TFCBT is contraindicated for clients who do not remember the trauma or whose memories of it are vague. The requirement that the trauma be remembered clearly is based on the exposure therapy component of TFCBT, which involves gradually and incrementally reducing anxiety and avoidance symptoms by having the client recall and narrate anxiety-provoking memories and material associated with the trauma. As Hoch notes:

> Without a clear memory of the trauma, narrative and cognitive processing work would be impossible and/or risky. Trauma-focused CBT is not about pulling for traumatic memories; it is about processing the ones that are distressing to the client. The therapist does not want to be in the position of possibly creating, changing or influencing memories, especially if the case is involved in litigation. (pp. 187–188)

Hoch adds that TFCBT does not solve *all* problems. With behaviors that are extremely risky or unsafe (such as suicidal ideation and attempts, psychosis, or substance abuse) more intensive services may be needed instead of or in conjunction with TFCBT.

Conclusion

Readers are reminded that this chapter does not convey the author's original thoughts. Everything in it was derived from Hoch (2009) and Cohen et al. (2006). In fact, it is for the most part an abridged version of a much lengthier chapter on this topic that Hoch wrote for a previous volume in this series. Because Hoch was unable to abridge her chapter herself for the purpose of this volume (which because of its different scope, required much shorter chapters), I abridged it, quoting her extensively. The material that is not in quotes simply reflects her ideas (or the ideas of Cohen et al.) rewritten with my wording. Because of the different scope and chapter page limitations of this volume, I was unable to include much of the useful additional details, case dialogues, handouts, and so on that readers can find in the Cohen et al. book or in the Hoch chapter. Readers who found this chapter useful are urged to examine both of those excellent sources.

References

Cavanaugh-Johnson, T. (1992). Let's talk about touching: A therapeutic game. Toni Cavanagh-Johnson, Ph.D., Pasadena, CA.

Cohen, J. A., Mannarino, A. P., & Deblinger, E. (2006). *Treating trauma and traumatic grief in children and adolescents*. New York, NY: Guilford Press.

Foa, E. B., & Rothbaum, B. O. (1998). *Treating the trauma of rape: Cognitive-behavioral therapy for PTSD*. New York, NY: Guilford Press.

Hoch, A. L. (2009). Trauma focused cognitive behavioral therapy for children. In A. Rubin & D. W. Springer (Eds.), *Treatment of traumatized adults and children* (pp. 179–253). Hoboken, NJ: John Wiley & Sons.

Rubin, A. (2009). Introduction:Evidence-based practice and empirically supported interventions for trauma. In A. Rubin & D. W. Springer (Eds.), *Treatment of traumatized adults and children* (pp. 3–28). Hoboken, NJ: John Wiley & Sons.

Thomas, G. (2009). Cognitive behavioral treatment of traumatized adults: Exposure therapy. In A. Rubin & D. W. Springer (Eds.), *Treatment of traumatized adults and children* (pp. 31–101). Hoboken, NJ: John Wiley & Sons.

10

EMDR for the Treatment of Children in the Child Welfare System Who Have Been Traumatized by Abuse and Neglect

Robbie Adler-Tapia

Children who have been abused or neglected commonly experience somatic, emotional and behavioral problems. Childhood distress and trauma contribute to increased adult mental health and medical issues (Felitti et al., 1998) and can impact neurodevelopment. And, the younger the child is when exposed to child abuse, the more likely the child is to evidence anxiety and depression in adulthood (Kaplow & Widom, 2007). Children involved in the child welfare system—who, in addition to having been abused or neglected, may be separated from siblings and placed in a new home, new family, new school, and a completely new environment—often display signs of regression in previously mastered developmental tasks, often resulting from instability in every aspect of their young lives.

The more severely traumatized children may manifest symptoms consistent with significant psychiatric disorders, including posttraumatic stress disorder (PTSD) and dissociation. Such trauma can change the actual neurobiology and neurodevelopment of the brain (Perry, 2004; Siegel, 2007; van der Kolk, 2005). Perry (2006), for example, suggests that traumatized children respond from brainstem-based behaviors when threatened, as the brain's alarm system interprets any stress as a threat to the individual, and that children who have experienced a chronic trauma history develop a neurological system that is in a persistent state of fear. Because these children are in this chronic state of alarm, their physical and mental health are impacted, which leads to maladaptively stored states and experiences.

Consequently, children who have experienced abuse and neglect can be challenging for even the seasoned child therapist. This chapter describes a promising, empirically supported treatment approach for such children: Eye Movement Desensitization and Reprocessing (EMDR), based on the EMDR psychotherapy treatment methodology created by Shapiro (1989a, 1989b). EMDR provides a treatment protocol that allows the therapist to work with developing resources in the child with attachment trauma while also reprocessing traumatic events that can lead to chronic and severe mental health and physical symptoms. Within the EMDR protocol there is the opportunity to provide reparative work even without a healthy attachment figure and to provide the child with a clinical intervention to address current symptoms while also creating a positive template for the future. When using EMDR with children, the therapist is in a unique role of having the opportunity to intervene at a time when neurodevelopment is most rapid and malleable and treatment can have its greatest impact. This chapter provides a brief overview of EMDR applied to the specific issues of children in the child welfare system. There are multiple publications that expand the discussion and application of EMDR with children (Adler-Tapia, Settle, & Shapiro, in press; Adler-Tapia & Settle, 2008; Greenwald, 1999; Lovett, 1999; Tinker & Wilson, 1999).

What Is EMDR?

EMDR is a comprehensive psychotherapy treatment approach based on an eight-phase model that was originally focused on treating trauma in adult clients (Shapiro, 1995, 2001). Since Shapiro created EMDR, the protocol has been expanded for use with child and adolescent clients (Adler-Tapia & Settle, 2008; Greenwald, 1999; Lovett, 1999; Tinker & Wilson, 1999). For a review of the literature on EMDR with children, see Adler-Tapia and Settle (2009). The EMDR treatment methodology is based on the Adaptive Information Processing theory (AIP) proposed by Shapiro as an explanation for why EMDR is an efficacious treatment (Shapiro, 1995, 1997, 2001, 2007). After discussing AIP theory, assessment, and diagnostic processes for children in the children welfare system, this chapter concludes with a proposal for a comprehensive and integrative treatment approach through the eight phases of the EMDR protocol for working with children in child welfare.

Adaptive Information Processing and EMDR in Child Psychotherapy

Shapiro (2001) developed the Adaptive Information Processing model (AIP) to explain the mechanisms by which EMDR assists clients in moving "disturbance to adaptive resolution." EMDR is a comprehensive treatment methodology while AIP is the comprehensive theoretical approach to psychotherapy. In the AIP model, Shapiro theorized that the human organism is hardwired to assimilate new information and to move to adaptive resolution when presented with experiences causing high arousal. In the event that the level of arousal is overwhelming and traumatic to the individual, the adaptive information processing progression is thwarted and healthy processing does not continue. Instead, the event is stored with all the sensations and perceptions that the individual experienced at the time of the event. When a traumatic event occurs, the individual continues through life with dysfunctionally encoded material manifesting in current symptomatology. The etiological event thus prevents the individual's natural healing process from functioning at full potential. With children, this traumatic event can also impact neurological development and all future experiences in the child's life. What experiences the child engages in or avoids is impacted by those previous life experiences.

The AIP model concludes that emotional, behavioral, and mental health symptoms originate from the maladaptive storage of previous life events. In the future, as those encoded experiences are activated, clients experience disturbances and dysfunction in their current lives. The AIP model also proposes that the brain processes trauma much like the body processes physical injury. The physiological processing of injury occurs when the body automatically searches for the mechanisms for healing. The body continues with this healing process unless there is interference to the healing process such as infection or foreign bodies preventing healing. Under these circumstances, the natural healing process is thwarted. The natural healing process then requires intervention in order to resume the process of healing.

With EMDR, the therapist guides the client through a series of procedural steps in order to access the maladaptively encoded information. By tapping into and then activating those memory networks, the EMDR protocol focuses on reprocessing the information so that the client can proceed with the healing process.

Because AIP theory postulates that the information must be accessed, stimulated, and then moved toward adaptive resolution (Shapiro, 2007), the client must be able to access and communicate this information, which is often difficult for children. Children may have more difficulty reporting the information to the therapist because children have not yet developed sufficient emotional literacy. Because children are at different stages of maturation, therapists must assess development in the client prior to proceeding with the EMDR protocol. The therapist can then adjust the EMDR protocol to meet the developmental needs of the client.

In addition, children often store memories in sensory/motor format; therefore, children may not have a coherent narrative to describe to the therapists; however, children can report sensations that arise when neural networks are probed. This is when the use of play therapy and art therapy techniques are indicated as the expressive tools children need to facilitate the treatment process.

AIP theory concludes that memories are a combination of sensory input, thoughts, emotions, physical sensations, and a belief system but may actually have metacognitions instead. Metacognitions are the ability to have cognitions about cognitions, or the ability to think about thinking. Children have not fully developed a belief system with which to understand and process an event or experience because children have not yet developed cognitively to the point where they are able to think about their own thought processes; therefore, accessing and processing of neural networks is different. In spite of the fact that children have not developed the same cognitive processes and do not have as expansive language skills as adolescents and adults, the AIP model still explains personality development as well as the development of dysfunction and pathology in children. (Chemtob, Nakashima, Carlson, 2002; Rubin, Bischofshausen, Conroy-Moore, Dennis, Hastie, Melnick, Smith, 2001).

If, according to AIP, the assimilation of events into the associative memory network and accommodations of the client's previous identity to encompass it can be considered the basis of personality development (Shapiro, 2007), the earlier the intervention the more positive the impact on the personality and the individual's overall health. AIP suggests that for individuals with extensive abuse and neglect histories, this learning and adaptive resolution cannot take place because they have insufficient internal resources and positive experiences to transform the initial dysfunction. When working with children in psychotherapy, the therapist also has a unique opportunity to provide opportunities for developing internal resources and positive experiences through resource development and mastery skills as part of the EMDR process.

The Phases of the EMDR Treatment Protocol

The eight phases of EMDR include Client History and Treatment Planning, Preparation, Assessment, Desensitization, Installation, Body Scan, Closure, and Re-evaluation (Shapiro, 1995, 2001). Each phase includes specific treatment goals and interventions to be accomplished before proceeding; however, this organization in no way suggests that the protocol is linear and sequential. On the contrary, the psychotherapy process with actual clients is often circular with the therapist needing to return to earlier phases of the protocol as more information arises during each phase of treatment. This is true of almost any treatment methodology in that as the therapist works with the client, the therapist learns more about the client's history, becomes attuned to the client, and gains new insights into the uniqueness of the client that impact the treatment goals in an ever-changing and dynamic process.

With child clients, the therapist is also noticing how the child's development impacts treatment from session to session. Theories and concepts of child development are integrated into the EMDR protocol. In addition, it is important to assimilate other techniques used in child psychotherapy along with the foundations and techniques from attachment therapy into case conceptualization throughout the eight phases of the EMDR protocol. Therapists need to use all their clinical skills and tools to create a therapist's toolbox that can be integrated into the EMDR eight phase treatment protocol. This is not to suggest that all other clinical skills or training be abandoned, but instead that therapists consider how organizing treatment and case conceptualization is a comprehensive process with the eight phases of EMDR. While reading the explanations of each phase of the EMDR protocol, the astute therapist will recognize clinical skills from attachment therapy, play therapy, and cognitive behavioral therapies that have been integrated into the comprehensive approach to psychotherapy.

Three-Pronged Approach

EMDR is a three-pronged approach that conceptualizes treatment based on past-present-future goals for treatment. Therapy begins with the identification of symptoms that are the manifestations of maladaptively encoded information that becomes triggered, as evidenced in symptom presentation. As therapy progresses those maladaptive encoded events from the past are reprocessed through to adaptive resolution, and then treatment focuses on present triggers that need to be targeted. Once past events and present triggers are cleared, the therapist guides the client to the future where the client processes a positive future template until the future event is anticipated absent of distress. Any distress for the future is conceptualized as anticipatory anxiety and/or missing skills that the client is taught. Anticipatory anxiety is reprocessed to adaptive resolution while missing skills are taught and practiced. This three-pronged approach guides the eight phases of the EMDR protocol.

Phase 1: Client History and Treatment Planning

Client History and Treatment Planning is the first phase of the EMDR protocol, which parallels most other types of treatment. Therapists in most treatment modalities are trained to collect a client history and identify treatment issues in order to aid in the treatment planning process. The purpose of this phase is to gather information about the client's history and symptoms that spurred the client to seek treatment and to create a treatment plan to guide the psychotherapeutic process. During this phase the therapist is establishing a relationship with the client and developing rapport and a clinical alliance within which the healing process occurs.

With EMDR, the unique addition to the client history taking process is that the therapist listens for the client's negative self-perceptions, beliefs, and cognitions as well as emotions and unique body sensations as the client describes his or her presenting issues. The therapist notes aspects of the client's presentation in each of these areas to be further explored in latter phases of the EMDR process. The themes would be considered in any psychotherapy intake process by clients and included in treatment planning; however, the significance of these issues are at the root of symptom manifestation from an AIP theoretical perspective. Eventually the therapist is considering diagnostic issues, including the etiology of the child's symptom presentation that may be rooted in distressing life events and even developmental trauma (American Psychiatric Association, 2000; van der Kolk, 2002). The EMDR protocol includes assessing for trauma and dissociation during this phase of treatment. For additional direction on the assessment of dissociation in children, therapists can review the guidelines for the assessment and treatment of children and adolescents from the International Society for the Study of Dissociation (ISST-D) Task Force on Children and Adolescents, (2004) along with assessment tools for evaluating trauma and dissociation (Armstrong, Carlson, & Putnam, 1997; Putnam, 1997).

During the assessment and treatment planning process with children, the therapist is listening to what the child says along with what the therapist observes from the child and between the child and child's caregivers. Not only is the therapist gathering data, but he or she is also observing the child's development, play, interactions with caregivers, and the meta-communications demonstrated in the therapist's office. Along with the therapist's previous intake protocol, the therapist is listening for what life events are possibly contributing to the child's symptom presentation. The therapist begins case conceptualization by considering the child's mastery of developmental tasks based on the child's chronological age and achievement of psychosocial, emotional, behavioral, cognitive, and developmental tasks of childhood and adolescence. As the therapist assesses the child's treatment goals, the therapist then needs to explain EMDR to the child and caregivers.

Explaining EMDR to Both Caregivers and Children It is important to explain EMDR to both parents or caregivers and children in terms that all family members can understand. With children in the child welfare system, the therapist may also need to explain EMDR to case managers, legal guardians for the child, and even in a court environment. Client understanding of the EMDR methodology is imperative in engaging the client in the therapeutic process. The explanation of EMDR needs to be provided in a language that meets the child and caregivers at their developmental level and level of psychological savvy. There are books (Adler-Tapia & Settle, 2008; Adler-Tapia & Tapia, 2009; Gomez, 2007) that can be used to explain EMDR to children and then guide children through the phases of EMDR. Therapists can incorporate play therapy techniques and drawing with children of all ages to develop rapport, engage the client, and assess the child's comprehension and expressive skills. Therapists have used creative and innovative techniques to explain EMDR to children and guide children through the stages of the EMDR protocol. The procedural steps of the protocol need to be adjusted to the unique presentation of the individual child based on accurate assessment of the child's development and therapist's attunement to the child. Once consent for treatment is obtained, the therapist then gathers information to aid in case conceptualization. It is beyond the scope of this chapter or book to cover all of the clinical implications and procedural considerations pertinent to case conceptualization. Additional details can be found in Adler-Tapia and Settle (2009). Such details include:

- ➤ Integrating both the parent input and child input in the process of collecting a client history and writing a treatment plan.
- ➤ The unusual ways that children may store the experience of a traumatic event.
- ➤ Developmental considerations.
- ➤ Dissociation.
- ➤ Assessing the child's readiness for therapy.
- ➤ Monitoring symptoms.
- ➤ Providing psychoeducational information.
- ➤ Creating a targeting sequencing plan.

Phase 2: Preparation

During the second phase of EMDR, the therapist's primary goal is to prepare the client for reprocessing during the remaining phases of EMDR. Assessing for affect management, affect tolerance, emotional regulation skills, self-soothing skills, and other needed skills are important processes to any type of therapy and are the focus of the Preparation Phase of EMDR. The final goal of the Preparation Phase is to teach client the mechanics of EMDR, which are described in detail in this section of the chapter.

The initial goal of the Preparation Phase is to teach children the ability to titrate the impact of intense emotions. The more the child feels capable of managing intense affect and self-soothing, the smoother and more effective the therapeutic process. Children especially need to feel powerful and competent in therapy in order to actively participate in the healing process. When children are feeling overwhelmed by their intense emotions, they are much more likely to be reluctant to participate in therapy.

During the Preparation Phase any previous skill-building activities that the therapist has typically used in psychotherapy can be implemented and taught to the client. Guided imagery, systematic desensitization, assertiveness training, dialectical behavior therapy (DBT), trauma-focused cognitive behavioral therapy (TFCBT), or any other interventions the therapist has found to be beneficial in working with children are equally important to consider teaching a child during the Preparation Phase or at any other time that you assess that the child needs particular skills to be successful in therapy. For example, children often benefit from learning how to take deep breaths for self-soothing and progressive muscle relaxation exercises. With EMDR, it is helpful to teach children resource skills and install mastery experiences in order to provide the scaffolding from which children can build healthy experiences and reprocess traumatic events. It is beyond the scope of this chapter or book to cover all of the clinical implications and procedural considerations pertinent to this process. Additional details can be found in Adler-Tapia and Settle (2009). Such details include:

➤ Teaching skills for dealing with strong emotions.
➤ Teaching calming and self-soothing skills.
➤ Installing mastery skills.
➤ Emotional literacy.
➤ Mindfulness and body awareness.
➤ Techniques for distancing and titrating intense affect.
➤ Techniques for discharging intense emotions.
➤ Skills for in between sessions.

During the Preparation Phase clients are also taught the mechanics of EMDR. These include the Train Metaphor, Stop Signal, Safe/Calm Place, and Bilateral Stimulation (BLS) in addition to skills for affect management, emotional literacy, and stabilization. These mechanics are part of the basic training (Shapiro, 2008) that therapists learn with adjustments to help children and adolescents understand EMDR. This begins by explaining the mechanics of EMDR in simple terms.

Train Metaphor The train metaphor is used in EMDR to teach the child to manage the information and intense affect that can potentially be activated during reprocessing. The child is taught to imagine being on a train looking out the window noticing their issues as just scenery going by. Old memories, body sensations, emotions, and symptoms are considered scenery that is just passing by as the individual participates in EMDR and reprocesses the maladaptively stored information to adaptive resolution. Since many children have not had the experience of a train, it is important to identify a metaphor that the child can understand.

Stop Signal The Stop Signal is used for the client to signal the therapist that the client needs to stop reprocessing and take a break because the client is feeling overwhelmed. The client and therapist have identified a specific signal that the therapist understands is about the client asking the therapist to stop reprocessing and have the client move to the client's Safe/Calm/Comfortable Place. Stop Signals with children are important and can be elicited from even very young children with adjustments to the directions the therapist uses. With children, teaching the Stop Signal can be as simple as having the child hold up his or her hand to signal that the therapist should stop.

Bilateral Stimulation (BLS) One of the nuances of using EMDR is learning how to implement the different types of bilateral stimulation. Bilateral stimulation includes eye movements (EM), tactile and auditory stimulation. In EMDR training, therapists are encouraged to use only eye movements because the research on EMDR is almost entirely based on eye movements as bilateral stimulation.

Eye movements can be elicited by the therapist by moving your fingers as taught in EMDR training. For children, the therapist can put stickers or draw figures on the therapist's fingers to assist the child to track. Therapists can also use penlights on the floor or wall for the client to follow or purchase specialized equipment for eliciting eye movements. Children will track with their eyes and enjoy the use of puppets or finger puppets, stuffed animals, or other toys selected by the child to increase the child's focus on the eye movements.

In addition to assessing the client's ability to track the type of BLS, the number of saccades also impact the client's ability to track the stimulus. It is important to determine the number of saccades that are necessary when working with a particular client. Eye movements should move as fast as the client can tolerate in order to activate processing rather than just tracking. The therapist can tell the client that, "I'm just guessing at the speed and number of passes, but you can tell me to stop or continue." By giving the client the power to continue or stop the saccades, the therapist becomes more attuned to the individual client's unique manner of processing.

Tactile Stimulation Therapists can also provide bilateral stimulation through tactile stimulation such as tapping on the client's hands, with the "Butterfly Hug" (Artigas &

Jarero, 2001) or using a device especially designed for therapist use during EMDR. The "Butterfly Hug" has the child cross his or her arms and then alternate tapping on the upper arms like butterfly wings. The *Neurotek©* device is a small machine that can be purchased by therapists to create artificial bilateral stimulation with tactile stimulation (children often call these buzzies because the machine buzzes as you contact them) or auditory stimulation with tones or by connecting the device to a CD player or MP3 player to create auditory stimulation discussed below. There are many different ways to use tactile forms of BLS with clients and some creative and fun ways to engage children with BLS including drumming, stomping, marching, or playing patty cake to list a few.

Auditory Stimulation Therapists can provide auditory stimulation by using technological equipment like the *Neurotek* that can either pulse in the client's ears or by attaching a CD player or iPod to the equipment in order for the client to use music as bilateral stimulation. When using the device that provides bilateral stimulation it is helpful to start by turning all controls including auditory and tactile volume and speed to the lowest level of the control. Proceed by slowly increasing the speed, intensity, or volume until the client chooses a setting that is most comfortable.

Some therapists use remote speakers that can be placed on either side of a play area or sand tray and then use a preprogrammed CD that provides alternating auditory stimulation. It is important to monitor whether actual bilateral stimulation is occurring because children are active and may not stay in between the two speakers.

Determining the Speed, Intensity, and Number of Saccades of BLS In addition to determining the most appropriate type of BLS, the therapist needs to determine what speed and number of saccades work most effectively with the client. When the therapist is installing resources, Safe/Calm Place, or mastery experiences, it is important to use short, slow sets. With children, two to four saccades are usually sufficient for installing something positive. The therapist needs to be ever aware of the goal of the BLS. If the therapist is trying to install something positive, then the therapist should not attempt to evoke maladaptively stored information for reprocessing when longer, faster sets of BLS are indicated. This issue is discussed further in the Desensitization Phase later in the chapter.

The process of instructing children about bilateral stimulation can be diagnostic and give information about the child's preference for processing and suggest sensory integration issues. For example, if the child is not able to process with eye movements, the therapist may try tactile or auditory saccades and find that the child processes more effectively in an auditory or tactile mode.

Safe/Calm Place As previously discussed, clients of all ages also need to have resources for titrating intense affect. The client needs to be able to metaphorically go to a Safe/Calm Place during reprocessing with EMDR if the affect becomes overwhelming and the client cannot continue. No matter what the age, all clients need to have identified a Safe/Calm Place and a Stop Signal with which to communicate with the therapist.

Finding a Safe/Calm Place with child clients is important and can be elicited from even very young children with adjustments to the directions the therapist uses. For example, young children may need to draw a picture or several pictures of a Safe/Calm Place that can be used in sessions. The protocol for teaching a Safe/Calm Place is part of basic training in EMDR. In addition to teaching the child a resource for self-soothing and distancing from intense affect, this protocol is also diagnostic.

As the therapist elicits a Safe/Calm Place from the child, the therapist can observe how the child processes and understands instructions. Installing a Safe/Calm Place can be difficult with severely and chronically traumatized children; therefore, the therapist may need to install mastery experiences and resources before the child is able to identify a real or imaginary Safe/Calm Place.

Assessing When the Child Is Sufficiently Prepared and Ready to Proceed Case conceptualization in EMDR with children is a circular process in which the therapist is assessing, teaching, modeling, reinforcing, and monitoring the child's responses to treatment. The early phases are critical during specific episodes of care, and the therapist may need to return to those phases if the child needs additional skills for coping and stabilization. Depending on the child's symptoms and needs, the therapist may need to spend a great deal of time front loading children's resources in order to continue with the Assessment Phase of EMDR. This is a decision point in treatment where therapists may be reinforced by the child's progress and abatement of symptoms and by noticing that the child may enjoy new skills in dealing with symptoms. Therapists need to use their clinical judgment as to how much time to spend in the Preparation Phase. Therapists who do not spend sufficient time in Preparation may find that the child will become overwhelmed during the trauma processing phases of EMDR, starting with the Assessment Phase. However, therapists who spend too much time in the Preparation Phase may never get to trauma reprocessing, and consequently maladaptively stored information will not get reprocessed. Thus, skipping later phases is not doing EMDR. Therapists need to resist the temptation to avoid children's pain and the consequent temptation to stick with the fun parts of treatment in which the child gets state changes but does not get the deeper trait change that is possible. If the maladaptively stored memory network is not reprocessed, the core of the symptomatology remains with the potential for significant developmental implications for child clients.

In order to approach this clinical issue, it is helpful to start with teaching Safe/Calm Place and if the child has one resource with which to self-soothe, the therapist can proceed with the Assessment Phase. At any point in the treatment process the therapist may assess that the child is in need of additional resources and return to the Preparation Phase to teach the child new skills.

Phase 3: Assessment

The Assessment Phase includes specific procedural steps therapists typically practice during the practicum component of EMDR basic training. Identifying targets for reprocessing is one of the significant goals of the Assessment Phase. Even though targets have been noted during the Client History and Treatment Planning Phase as part of the targeting sequence plan, it is during the Assessment Phase that the therapist identifies a specific target for reprocessing through the remaining phases of the protocol.

Selecting Targets There are many ways to identify targets with clients. When working with children, there are imaginative ways to identify targets that tap into a child's way of processing. After the target is identified, the client is asked to pinpoint the worst part of the memory. Children may identify the worst part of the memory by drawing pictures, working in the sand tray, using puppets, and employing many other types of art and play therapy techniques.

Tools for Target Identification With Children The targeting sequence plan organized during the Client History and Treatment Planning Phase of EMDR is revisited as the therapist and client select the first maladaptively stored event to reprocess. The therapist starts with exploring the validity of the touchstone event as the event the client wants to target with EMDR. Once the target is selected, the next procedural step of the EMDR Assessment Phase is to identify the image that represents the most distressing part of the target event.

Children can draw a picture of the target or create the target in the sand tray or with the toys in the therapist's office. Art therapy techniques such as painting the picture or creating the picture with clay are also some of the many creative techniques therapists can use with children.

The Image Once the target is identified, the client is asked to select the image. The target and the image are not the same thing. A target is an issue or incident or experience or memory from the client's life that is believed to be the maladaptively stored incident that is contributing to the child's current symptom presentation. The image is a picture that represents the worst part of the target. Again with children, the image can be painted or drawn or created in the sand tray. Some therapists have children create collages of the image or take digital pictures that represent the image.

Negative and Positive Cognitions (NC/PC) Distilling the negative and positive cognitions is the next step of the procedural steps of the Assessment Phase. This process requires patience, creativity, and attunement to the client. The negative cognition is a presently held, negative belief about one's self that is believed to have its origins in the maladaptively stored events most likely originating in the touchstone event. Once a negative cognition has been identified that is a presently held belief that is also irrational, self-referencing, and generalizable, the therapist has essentially connected to the client's memory network. Along with a negative cognition, the therapist then identifies the positive cognition. The positive cognition is what the client would like to believe about themselves instead of the negative cognition. The positive cognition needs to be realistic, self-referencing, and generalizable.

The therapist needs to invest time in identifying a negative cognition that resonates for the client. If the therapist was able to develop a targeting sequence plan during the Client History and Treatment Planning Phase of EMDR, the therapist and client have already identified the client's negative cognition as part of the targeting sequence plan.

If the client was unable to develop a targeting sequence plan during Client History and Treatment Planning, the therapist may need to return to the process of distilling a negative cognition for the target identified by the client. If this is true, the therapist then asks the client, "When you bring up that image of the worst part of the event, what is your negative belief about yourself now?"

Having the client identify what they want to believe is important because it's an educational process of having the client consider possibilities. What is it that the client wants to be able to believe about themselves instead?

It is important that the negative cognition and positive cognition "match." Typically they are polar opposites. For example, if the negative cognition is "I'm not good enough" and the positive cognition is "I'm safe now" the cognitions are significantly different and the therapist needs to ask the client which resonates more for the specific image. If the positive cognition resonates more, it is appropriate to then change the negative cognition to match the positive cognition.

Also, it is important to ensure that the negative cognition makes sense with the specific target. For example, if the client's target is the memory of a rape and the client's negative cognition is "I'm not good enough" the therapist may want to explore whether or not that negative cognition truly fits for the client or if the client is confused about the EMDR process.

If the child cannot follow this explanation of the negative cognition, the therapist can ask the child, "When you think about that picture of that bad thing that happened, what is your bad thought about yourself now?" The words *bad thought* and *good thought* replace the terms *negative and positive cognition* if the child is unable to understand the concept. The negative and positive cognitions for children may be trauma specific and presented in fantasy or metaphor or even in third person. For example, young children may describe a bad thought as a monster rather than a specific traumatic event.

Again, the child can draw a picture of the bad thought and good thought or even create these thoughts in the sand tray. It is possible to divide the sand tray in half and have the child create the bad thought on the left side of the tray and the good thought on the right side of the tray with a bridge between the bad thought and the good thought implying that the goal is to move from the bad thought to the good thought.

Validity of Cognition   Continuing in the EMDR process, the therapist next assesses the validity of the positive cognition (VoC). The VoC is measured on a 7-point scale from 1 (completely false) to 7 (completely true). Measuring the VoC is often confusing for adult clients as well as children because the measurement needs to be more concrete. Although measuring the VoC is somewhat challenging, it is possible and important to attempt to obtain a VoC from even the youngest clients. As was described above when the therapist uses the sand tray to develop a good thought and a bad thought, it is possible to ask the child to identify which step of the bridge with seven steps between the bad thought and good thought the client is at now. Once the therapist has asked the client how true the positive cognition feels to them now, the process has moved from a cognitive level to an emotional level. Using a VoC bridge with children makes this measurement very simple and easy for children to understand and follow.

Expressing the Emotion After the VoC the therapist asks the client for the emotion associated with the target. Whatever emotion the client reports, the therapist notes the emotion the client identified and continues with the procedural steps. With children, the therapist may have taught emotional literacy or the therapist may need to teach the child about identifying emotions at this point. The therapist may show the child the child's picture or the sand tray the child designed and then ask the child how the child feels about the bad thought. After identifying the emotion associated with the target and the bad thought, the therapist then needs to assess the level of disturbance.

Subjective Units of Disturbance (SUD) The SUD is a standard measurement of disturbance on a scale from 0 or no disturbance to 10 the most disturbing. Once the client has identified an emotion that is connected with the target, the therapist immediately asks the client to assess how disturbing the emotion feels to them now on the SUD scale.

If the child cannot understand this scale the therapist can demonstrate the amount of disturbance by asking the child, "Is it this big? This big? Or this big?" as the therapist moves his or her hands further and further apart. The therapist then notes the child's report of the level of disturbance and continues by assessing the location of the disturbance in the client's body.

Body Sensation As soon as the client chooses a SUD level the therapist asks the client for the body sensation. The body sensation is when the client is noting the location of the emotion in their body. The therapist asks the child, "Where do you feel that disturbing feeling in your body?" The therapist may need to remind the child of what the therapist taught the child about body sensations, or the therapist may need to teach the child about body sensations at this point in the protocol. The therapist then connects the image, negative cognition, emotion, and body sensation, and starts the bilateral stimulation, which signals the beginning of the Desensitization Phase of EMDR.

Children are often quite able to follow the steps of the Assessment Phase when the therapist can use age appropriate language and explain the process to the child. More in-depth and creative explanations for eliciting each step of the protocol with even young children are described in *EMDR and the Art of Psychotherapy With Children* (Adler-Tapia & Settle, 2008).

Phase 4: Desensitization

The goal of the Desensitization is to reprocess the maladaptively stored information that has been accessed and stimulated by the procedural steps of the previous phase.

The Desensitization Phase begins when the therapist starts bilateral stimulation (BLS) after asking the client to hold together the previously identified image or picture, the negative cognition, and to notice where the client feels the feelings in his or her body. The length of the Desensitization Phase can be only minutes within a single session or expand over several sessions that could take months depending on the experiences and memories associated with the chosen target. For example, if the client's negative cognition is "I'm not good enough" and the client first remembered thinking "I'm not good enough" at age 2 when the child was punished during potty training, and the client is now 40, the negative cognition or belief can have infiltrated 38 years of life experiences and memories for the client. The belief that I am not good enough can be a foundational belief for the client. The connections may be clear or may appear to be tangential and irrelevant. This is when the therapist's patience and attunement is vital. The therapist's ability to hang in there and stay out of the client's way is crucial to the desensitization process.

For children, the memory networks will most likely be shorter due to the age of the child. This is one of the many reasons why EMDR is not only effective with children, but profound in changing cognitive beliefs about self.

Evidence of Reprocessing Children evidence reprocessing in a variety of ways similar to adults, but also with nonverbal cues including yawning, by becoming more or less active, affective evidence like crying or sighing, and frequently by avoidance or becoming sleepy. This is where the therapist needs to be closely attuned to the child because reprocessing with children can be more subtle. Yawning or becoming sleepy may be evidence of mild dissociation because children may feel like they are being flooded by emotion and it is important for the therapist to have more training and skills in working with children.

While working with children, it is especially important for therapists to be actively involved and consider frequently changing the type of BLS and allowing the child to move. Children who can be active during reprocessing are more able to focus on reprocessing than children who are expected to sit still. Children may sit on a yoga ball and bounce during reprocessing in order to allow the child to move so the therapist may notice an increase or decrease in the child's bouncing. Or a child may need to take a break or get a drink or go to the restroom. Allowing children to be active as they reprocess traumatic events allows them to discharge energy and to be able to engage in the process for longer periods of time.

Clinical Implications One of the challenges of the Desensitization Phase is for therapists to follow the client's process and stay out of the way. Therapists may feel the need to provide reflective statements or link with insights; however, the EMDR protocol is that the response from the therapist should be to say to the client "just notice" and follow the BLS during the Desensitization Phase. Therapists may feel the need to ask questions or repeat the client's responses; however, no interpretation is necessary with EMDR.

Another clinical implication of EMDR desensitization is that as the desensitization process occurs, new memory networks are accessed, reprocessed, and moved to adaptive resolution. This process can involve the therapist and client moving through the previous phases in a circular rather than linear process. For example, the therapist may start desensitization and then realize the client needs additional preparation skills with which to process a particular memory network. The EMDR therapy process is often unpredictable and surprising as the therapist and client learn together how the client has experienced and stored the traumatic event. There is often a missing piece that arises which explains why the event has become encapsulated and not completed by the individual's natural healing process. At each phase of the EMDR protocol the therapist needs to be aware that each client processes in unique ways and it is the client's unique healing process that needs to be followed by the therapist using EMDR. This is where the previous tools you have learned as a therapist can be integrated into the phases of the EMDR protocol.

During the Desensitization Phase with children, it is also important to remember that children may not have stored the traumatic events in ways that make sense. Instead, children may express fears of monsters, sleeping in their own bed, or going to school; however, there is frequently no logic to the desensitization phase because it is the child's own perception of what occurred at the time that is encapsulated. Therefore, younger children may express traumas in fantasy or imagery or even in sensory-motor memories that are difficult to follow. It does not matter whether or not what the client reports makes sense to the therapist, but whether or not the child's symptoms improve.

It is beyond the scope of this chapter or book to cover all of the clinical implications and procedural considerations for the desensitization phase. Additional details can be found in Adler-Tapia and Settle (2009). Therapists will need to use clinical judgment when deciding that the client has completed the desensitization phase. When the therapist has had the client return to the original incident and the SUD is zero, the therapeutic process is moving from the Desensitization Phase to the Installation Phase.

Phase 5: Installation

The goal of the Installation Phase is to check the validity of the positive cognition (PC) and to strengthen the PC until it reaches a VoC of 7. The therapist begins the Installation Phase by combining the original incident and the PC and checking with the client to make sure that the original PC selected still applies. Once the client either stays with the original PC or chooses a more fitting PC, the therapist proceeds with BLS to strengthen the PC selected by the client. With each successive set of saccades, the therapist evaluates the VoC. Installation continues as long as the VoC strengthens. When the VoC reaches a 7 and holds, the process moves to the Body Scan Phase of EMDR.

Phase 6: Body Scan

After desensitizing the target to a SUD of zero and installing the positive cognition to a VoC of seven, the EMDR protocol continues with the Body Scan. During this phase, the client is asked to hold the original incident together with the positive cognition and to scan their body from head to toe for any remaining disturbance. If any disturbance is noted, the client is asked to focus on the disturbance and instructed to "go with that" as the therapist continues with bilateral stimulation at the same frequency and speed used throughout the desensitization phase.

Sometimes the client will quickly report feeling no disturbance in their body. The client may report that he or she is feeling fine or calm and then the process proceeds to closure. If the client reports some type of physiological disturbance, this disturbance is again desensitized using bilateral stimulation. The client is instructed to notice the disturbance and allow whatever comes up to come up and the therapist provides additional bilateral stimulation. This may be a link to another memory, or sometimes clients may just notice things in their body. A clear body scan is achieved when the child reports no discomfort in his or her body. At that point it is time to proceed to the next phase of the EMDR protocol.

Phase 7: Closure

The purpose of the Closure Phase is to end the session whether or not the client has completed a target. The goal is for the client to be grounded, stabilized, and prepared to cope with what happens between sessions. The progression of the Closure Phase of EMDR is dependent on the status of the EMDR session. If the client has completed all previous phases, closure continues with a future template, which is a positive template for the future related to the symptoms that initially brought the child into treatment. The symptoms with which the client presented at the initial intake guide the selection of the future template. For example, if the parents brought the child into therapy due to the child's refusal to go to school, the future template would focus on the child imaging getting ready and going to school tomorrow. The protocol for the future template would continue until the child can imagine going to school with positive outcomes. Future template is the opportunity to rehearse future desired behaviors and outcomes.

If the session is an incomplete session, closure continues with stabilization of the client with instructions for in-between sessions. For more details about closing a completed or incomplete session, see Adler-Tapia and Settle (2009).

Phase 8: Reevaluation

The final phase of EMDR is the Reevaluation Phase. There are actually three different times that the therapy protocol may necessitate reevaluation—at the end of a completed target, at the beginning of the next session, and when evaluating the treatment process in order to aid in discharge planning.

The first type of reevaluation is actually checking the target during a session. This occurs when the therapist has the client return to the original incident and asks the client, "When you bring up that original incident, what do you get now?" Whatever the client's answer, the therapist then instructs the client to "Go with that." This occurs during the Desensitization Phase as the therapist works with the client to reprocess the event in order to clear any disturbance.

The second type of reevaluation occurs at the beginning of the next session following a session in which a target has been desensitized. The therapist asks the client to return to the original incident and asks the client, "When you bring up that original incident, what do you get now?" Clinical judgment guides how this process unfolds and is described earlier in this chapter.

The final type of reevaluation occurs when the therapist and client review all targets in order to make sure that no additional disturbance exists and all targets have been reprocessed. Once the therapist and client have agreed that all targets have been reprocessed successfully and the symptoms identified at the beginning of treatment have been addressed, the therapist and client together can plan for treatment discharge following their successful treatment process. This is the goal for all clients.

With children, using drawings or pictures or other tangible ways of organizing the work in therapy will help children remember what they have accomplished and the child's successes in therapy. With children, the therapist monitors the child's progress in therapy not only based on the child's reports, but also based on parent reports and symptom monitoring.

The evidence of the adaptive resolution of trauma with EMDR is in symptom abatement. Discharge planning occurs when the symptoms that brought the child into treatment are no longer evident and the child is able to return to their individual course of normal development without the interference of trauma. This is the conclusion of the EMDR protocol that accompanies discharge planning; however, this comprehensive course of treatment may not be possible for all children. When comprehensive treatment with the full EMDR protocol is not possible, case conceptualization with EMDR allows for episodes of care.

The Impact of Child Welfare Involvement on EMDR With Children

The stability of the child's living situation is a complicated factor in treating children in the child welfare system. Because children in the child welfare system may experience multiple placements, changes in caregivers and school placements, legal proceedings including visitation with the parents who have not protected and/or abused the child, along with attachment fractures and the unknown future, psychotherapy is challenging. With instability of the child's placement often impacting the child's consistency of attendance for psychotherapy, the EMDR protocol needs to be titrated in episodes of care. These episodes of care often include case conceptualization in EMDR with each session considered as the one session and only session or the last session for the child. This type of realistic case conceptualization does not prevent the use of EMDR in psychotherapy, but just an adjustment in case conceptualization with consideration of the possibility of targets of opportunity with children and unique case conceptualization rotating between installation of mastery along with trauma reprocessing focused on those targets of opportunity.

Targets of Opportunity

Targets of opportunity are those with which the child presents in therapy. The therapist can reprocess the target identified by the child while also taking the adaptive resolution to present and future events in the child's life. Each target can be reprocessed through the three pronged approach of EMDR where one target is the focus of treatment—past, present, and future. The goal is one target at time through the three-pronged approach. This allows the therapist to conceptualize each session of therapy as a microcosm of the entire therapy process.

Session Case Conceptualization

The flow of a typical 50-minute session starts with review of progress and identification of successes the child has accomplished since the last session. Then installation of mastery for approximately 10 minutes followed by trauma reprocessing through phases 3 to 6 of the EMDR protocol through past, present, and future triggers fill the majority of the session. Sessions end with review of work accomplished and plans for between sessions.

Because of environmental instability, case conceptualization for children in the child welfare system is paced through episodes of care with EMDR. Each session has to be conceptualized as potentially the child's one and only session. The plan for each session must take into consideration the amount of psychotherapeutic work that can realistically be completed for the child's best interest. The session should start with a brief check-in with the child about the time since the last session and a review of any previous treatment. This is followed by probing for successes and mastery experiences that can be installed. This mastery installation provides a foundation to support the child in reprocessing a target of opportunity (the target that appears to be the most salient for the child), and then reprocessing through the three-pronged approach—past/present/future. The session ends with the therapist enacting closure skills for stabilization between sessions. This can be done in 50 minutes once you know the EMDR protocol.

When probing for successes and mastery experiences, the therapist may ask the child, "Tell me something that made you feel good or that you felt proud of that you did this week." The child may need assistance in identifying positive symptoms, and the therapist needs to listen closely for any positives that can be utilized to improve self-esteem, confidence, and feelings of competency for the child. Unfortunately, children in the child welfare system often feel unwanted and unimportant; therefore, the review of successes is even more important for this population. Once a specific event has been identified, the therapist can instruct the child, "Notice the positive or good feelings you get from being successful and where you feel those good feelings in your body." The therapist can instruct the child to do a butterfly hug or the therapist can implement two to three saccades of bilateral stimulation for installation of a positive experience for the child. After several sets of saccades, the therapist can then proceed with the trauma reprocessing phases of EMDR.

If the child has previously participated in EMDR and can recall any work from the previous sessions, the therapist can continue with the next phase of the EMDR protocol indicated in the child's process. If the child has not previously identified any targets, the therapist can ask the child to identify a target. Targets of opportunity are often most helpful to the child and engage the child in the EMDR process by providing the child with the feeling of power from treatment.

The therapy sessions continue for as much time as is available with the therapist allowing 5 to 10 minutes for closure at the end of each session. Ongoing therapy continues to focus on reprocessing as much trauma as is possible given the client's stability and time available for psychotherapy services.

Summary

As an integrative psychotherapy driven by AIP theory, EMDR is compatible with elements of other treatment interventions. However, as with any form of psychotherapy, one element alone does not suffice to represent the entirety of EMDR, nor substitute for any of the eight phases of this comprehensive psychotherapeutic process. Although some elements of the goals and objectives of the phases of EMDR may be evident in other treatment modalities such as MASTR, TFCBT, and so on, it is the aggregate of the theory, case conceptualization, and accurate implementation of this integrative psychotherapy that truly defines EMDR. Implementing a single session and labeling that session as an EMDR *treatment* misrepresents the therapy and cannot be assumed to have incorporated the appropriate assessment and implementation of the complete EMDR treatment process.

Case conceptualization using EMDR with children in the child welfare system offers a comprehensive and integrative treatment approach to address the trauma history to which most foster children are exposed while also laying the foundation for a positive future. With comprehensive treatment, the ongoing mental health issues manifested by children in the child welfare system can be reprocessed, alleviating the potential for issues in adulthood and replication of the legacy of the child welfare system, which often plays out generation after generation. With EMDR providing treatment to change the trajectory for children in the child welfare system, the future can be greatly improved.

References

Adler-Tapia, R. L., & Settle, C. S. (2008). *EMDR and the art of psychotherapy with children treatment manual*. New York, NY: Springer.

Adler-Tapia, R., & Settle, C. (2009). Evidence of the efficacy of EMDR with children and adolescents in individual psychotherapy: A review of the research published in peer-reviewed journals. *Journal of EMDR Practice and Research*, 3(4), 232–247.

Adler-Tapia, R., & Settle, C., & Shapiro, F. (in press). Eye movement desensitization and reprocessing (EMDR) psychotherapy with children who have experienced sexual abuse and trauma. In P. Goodyear-Brown (Ed.), *The handbook of child sexual abuse: Prevention, assessment and treatment*. Hoboken, NJ: John Wiley & Sons.

Adler-Tapia, R. L., & Tapia, M. (2008). *My EMDR workbook*. Author.

American Psychiatric Association (2000). *Diagnostic and statistical manual of mental disorders* (4th ed., text revised). Washington, DC: Author.

Armstrong, J., Carlson, E. B., & Putnam, F. (1997). Adolescent-dissociative experiences scale-II (A-DES). Retrieved December 31, 2010, from www.energyhealing.net/pdf_files/a-des.pdf

Artigas, L. & Jarero, I. (2001). *The butterfly hug*. Retrieved May 11, 2011, from www.amamecrisis.com.mx/proing_butterfly.htm

California Evidence Based Clearinghouse for Child Welfare. (2010). www.cebc4cw.org Retrieved, December 31, 2010.

Chemtob, C., Nakashima, J., & Carlson, J. (2002). Brief treatment for elementary school children with disaster-related posttraumatic stress disorder: A field study. *Journal of Clinical Psychology, 58*(1), 99–112.

Felitti, V. J., Anda, R. F., Nordernberg, D., Williamson, D. F., Spitz, A. M., Edwards, V., & Koss, M. P. (1998). Relationship of childhood abuse to many of the leading causes of death in adults: The adverse childhood experiences (ACE) study. *American Journal of Preventive Medicine, 14*(4), 245–258.

Gomez, A. (2008). *Dark bad day . . . go away*. Author.

Greenwald, R. (1999). *Eye movement desensitization and reprocessing (EMDR) in child and adolescent psychotherapy*. Lanham, MD: Jason Aronson Press.

International Society for the Study of Dissociation (ISST-D) Task Force on Children and Adolescents. (2004). Guidelines for the evaluation and treatment of dissociative symptoms in children and adolescents. *Journal of Trauma and Dissociation, 5*(3), 119–150.

Kaplow, J. B., & Widom, C. S. (2007, February). Age of onset of child maltreatment predicts long-term mental health outcomes. *Journal of Abnormal Psychology, 116*(1), 176–187.

Lovett, J. (1999). *Small wonders: Healing childhood trauma with EMDR*. New York, NY: Free Press.

Perry, B. (2006). Applying principles of neurodevelopment to clinical work with maltreated and traumatized children. In N. B. Webb (Ed.), *Working with traumatized youth in child welfare* (pp. 27–52). New York, NY: Guilford Press.

Putnam, F. (1997). *Child dissociative checklist, version 3*. Retrieved July 28, 2008, from www.energyhealing.net/pdf_files/cdc.pdf

Rubin, A., Bischofshausen, S., Conroy-Moore, K., Dennis, B., Hastie, M., Melnick, L., . . . Smith, T. (2001). The effectiveness of EMDR in a child guidance center. *Research on Social Work Practice, 11*(4), 435–457.

Shapiro, F. (1989a). Efficacy of the eye movement desensitization procedure in the treatment of traumatic memories. *Journal of Traumatic Stress, 2*(2), 199–223.

Shapiro, F. (1989b). Eye movement desensitization: A new treatment for post-traumatic stress disorder. *Journal of Behavior Therapy and Experimental Psychiatry, 20*, 211–217.

Shapiro, F. (1995). *Eye movement desensitization and reprocessing: Basic principles, protocols, and procedures*. New York, NY: Guilford Press.

Shapiro, F. (2001). *Eye movement desensitization and reprocessing: Basic principles, protocols, and procedures* (2nd ed.). New York, NY: Guilford Press.

Shapiro, F. (2007). EMDR, adaptive information processing, and case conceptualization. *Journal of EMDR Practice and Research, 1*, 68–87.

Siegel, D. (2007). *The mindful brain: Reflection and attunement in the cultivation of well-being*. New York, NY: W.W. Norton & Company.

Tinker, R. H., & Wilson, S. A. (1999). *Through the eyes of a child: EMDR with children*. New York, NY: Norton.

van der Kolk, B. A. (2005). Developmental trauma disorder. *Psychiatric Annals, 35*: 5, 401–408.

V

Interventions for Parents or Children With Intimate Partner Violence Involvement

In Chapter 11, Laura Minze, Renee McDonald, and Ernest Jouriles describe Project Support, an empirically supported home-based program for mothers who have sought shelter because of intimate partner violence as well as for parents in the child welfare system. In mostly weekly sessions over an average of 6 to 8 months, master's level therapists provide emotional support, assist with problem-solving skills, and help the mothers obtain material resources. The central component of Project Support, however, is training in child behavior management skills for handling externalizing behavior problems, which are commonly experienced by children who have been exposed to intimate partner violence. Consequently, the bulk of their chapter is devoted to discussing those parenting skills and how they are taught.

In Chapter 12 Miriam Hernandez Dimmler and her colleagues discuss the Child-Parent Psychotherapy (CPP) intervention, which was developed for families with young children, age birth to 5, who have been exposed to domestic violence. CPP integrates diverse treatment approaches based on psychodynamic, attachment, trauma, cognitive-behavioral, and social learning theories. Consequently, providing a comprehensively detailed guide for implementing CPP would require a manual and not be possible within a chapter. Instead, the chapter authors provide an overview of the treatment model and then describe ways to disseminate the model through practitioner training. After that, they discuss ways to disseminate and implement the model within community-based organizations.

11
Project Support

Reducing Conduct Problems of Children in Violent Families

Laura Minze, Renee McDonald, and Ernest N. Jouriles

Overview

An estimated 15.5 million children reside in homes in which intimate partner violence (IPV) has occurred within 12 months, and more than 7 million of those live in homes characterized by severe IPV (McDonald et al., 2006). Children exposed to severe IPV are at risk for considerable psychological and social problems. In fact, a large proportion (often reported to be at 50% or higher) of those who accompany their mothers to domestic violence shelters exhibit clinical levels of adjustment problems (Grych, Jouriles, Swank, McDonald, & Norwood, 2000; McDonald & Jouriles, 1991). Additionally, there is substantial overlap between families experiencing IPV and families referred for child maltreatment (Appel & Holden, 1998; Jouriles, McDonald, Slep, Heyman, & Garrido, 2008). Given the scope of children's exposure to IPV and the potentially serious outcomes resulting from such exposure, effective interventions designed to help these children are of critical importance.

Project Support is a theory-based intervention originally designed to address conduct problems among children, ages 2 to 9, who have been exposed to frequent and severe IPV. Two outcome studies support the effectiveness of Project Support in improving mother's parenting and reducing child problems in families departing from domestic violence shelters (Jouriles et al., 2009; Jouriles et al., 2001). Moreover, improvements have been maintained at assessments conducted approximately 2 years following treatment (McDonald, Jouriles, & Skopp, 2006). Because there is considerable overlap between children exposed to IPV and child maltreatment, a natural progression in this line of clinical research has been to evaluate Project Support for families referred for services because of child maltreatment, and it has also been shown to be effective in reducing problematic parenting and the risk for further maltreatment in such families (Jouriles et al., 2010).

This chapter is designed to introduce clinicians to the nuts and bolts of Project Support. Specifically, we describe the service-delivery format, and we provide a detailed description of the two key components of the intervention: (1) providing social and instrumental support, and (2) teaching of parenting skills, with an emphasis on how they are implemented.

Project Support Services

As an intervention designed to address a multifaceted issue, successful service delivery requires a somewhat novel approach. Although aspects of the services may differ across families, adherence to key principles and techniques ensures that each family receives an effective intervention.

Structure of the Services

Project Support services are typically offered in participants' homes. Providing in-home services increases the likelihood that those seeking services will attend sessions. For example, many of the families with which we have worked have to rely on public transportation. Traveling to and from sessions with children on public transportation can mean that a family spends a great deal of time and money simply to come to sessions. In addition, families in crisis (e.g., those seeking refuge at a domestic violence shelter, those referred for child protective services), almost by definition, are experiencing multiple stressors. Offering in-home sessions is designed to help reduce the burden on families receiving services.

In-home services also provide valuable insights for the clinician about the family and their living situation. The clinician sees the neighborhood and perhaps resources near the client. Too, the clinician may notice tangible needs that the client has overlooked. A common example is the failure of clients to note that they are in need of food. During a home visit the clinician is often able to note if food seems scarce and may ask in order to help a parent plan ahead. Additionally, the clinician sees firsthand the children's living environment and how they behave in it, information that can be useful in tailoring the parenting skills to meet the specific needs of the family. For example, finding a place for time-out can be difficult for parents. Practicing the time-out at home (as opposed to an office) allows the clinician to help the client figure out which place or places may be most conducive to producing the desired results.

Project Support sessions typically occur weekly; however, at times it is necessary to meet more or less frequently depending on the needs of the family. For example, when families first begin services, many have a number of needs that may need to be addressed immediately. This may necessitate more than one visit in a week in order to meet both the social and instrumental support needs as well as have time to focus on the child skills.

On the other hand, when a parent has started a new job and is learning to manage a new schedule, visits may need to happen less frequently for a few weeks.

In the evaluations of Project Support, the average client participated in 23 sessions over a 6- to 8-month period (McDonald, Jouriles, & Skopp, 2006). Master's level therapists provided the intervention, and because of the intensive nature of the services they maintained a small caseload (two to three cases) of Project Support cases and received intensive group supervision. Clinicians were paired with mentors who were typically undergraduates obtaining course credit and who were trained and supervised in the child behavior management skills that were taught to the parents. The mentors provided child care during the sessions, allowing the clinician uninterrupted time with the parent as needed, and allowing the children to be involved in the session when indicated. Additionally, because the mentors utilize the same skills that are taught to the parent, the child is gradually introduced to the new ways of interacting as the parent is learning them and the parent often overhears examples of how they may be used.

Social and Instrumental Support

The populations targeted by Project Support—women and children leaving domestic violence shelters and families involved with CPS—often are experiencing multiple stressors related to their immediate circumstances. For example, a family exiting a shelter often has to contend with moving, setting up a household, enrolling children in school or day care, searching for nearby employment, and/or government offices to obtain such services as WIC, food stamps, and so on. Although women's distress gradually decreases without intervention following shelter residence (Campbell, Sullivan, & Davidson, 1995; Sullivan & Bybee, 1999), facilitating or speeding its decrease, if possible, would clearly reduce suffering. The social and instrumental support component of Project Support is designed to alleviate some of this distress.

When parents face multiple stressors, they report very little time or emotional resources to deal with their children or their children's problems. Failing to address these issues limits the potential that the clinician is able to communicate the importance of parenting in helping to alleviate child behavior problems. Therefore, a portion of each session focuses on providing emotional support to the parent by addressing the issues she may be facing. Often, material resources are greatly needed. Connecting parents with other agencies to help them with such issues as housing, job training, or emergency food assistance is a major part of the instrumental support. Instrumental support is often most important in the early sessions. An important aspect of this component of the intervention is that it indicates to the client that we are interested in their family's welfare broadly, which fosters rapport and enhances client engagement.

The provision of social and instrumental support looks different for each client. For some clients, the social support is most important. They may be adept at finding and accessing available resources, but still find the process tedious and frustrating. Allowing the client time to feel heard, helping the client problem solve where possible, and providing encouragement does a lot to ease the distress clients feel. At other times it is necessary to make phone calls on clients' behalf or provide transportation to and from a social service agency or food bank. For example, a client with four children who generally uses public transportation may greatly benefit from a ride to an appointment at the social security office, along with the assistance that the clinician may provide with the children during the wait. During the sessions, clinicians help and encourage the parent to build their own social relationships so that they need this type of support less and less. Tangible goods and services that make up the instrumental support also vary according to resources. When possible and needed, we may help a client furnish an apartment, provide groceries or connect a client with a food bank, help the client obtain transportation, or day care. In addition to soliciting donations where appropriate, we keep a list of area service agencies that may assist clients. Maintaining this list means keeping current with agencies to ensure that they are able to assist clients, as many agencies themselves vary over time in their ability to provide assistance.

In addition, based on work suggesting the importance of problem solving in behavior change (D'Zurilla & Goldfried, 1971), the instrumental and social support component includes assistance with problem-solving skills. Many parents make quick decisions because of the crises they face, and these decisions may not always be the best in the long term. Clinicians help parents determine the relative merits of decisions (e.g., decisions about housing, budget and resource decisions, or evaluating a school or day care), weighing in potential costs and consequences of those decisions. The process of approaching practical issues from a problem-solving perspective serves the additional function of modeling the clinician's beliefs in the mothers' own agency to effect positive change in her life.

Parenting

Although the provision of social and instrumental support continues throughout the intervention, service providers also work intensively with families to improve parenting and the parent-child relationship. This aspect of the intervention is essential to enhancing family and child wellbeing.

Rationale for the Use of a Parenting Intervention   A considerable body of research has shown a link between IPV and three dimensions of parenting—aggression, inconsistent discipline, and supportiveness (see Appel & Holden, 1998, and Jouriles et al., 2008, for reviews). Specifically, IPV is positively associated with parental aggression toward children and with inconsistent discipline, and it is negatively associated with parental supportiveness. These dimensions of parenting seem to increase this risk of the development and maintenance of child behavior problems, in particular externalizing behavior problems, such as aggression, oppositional behavior, and rule-breaking or noncompliant behavior (Patterson, 1982). Because externalizing behavior problems are among the most common problems experienced by children exposed to IPV, Project Support was designed to address the components of parenting most likely to improve child outcomes. And, in fact, it appears that parenting is a key component in the effectiveness of interventions such as Project Support. A review of existing interventions for children exposed to IPV indicates that effective interventions with children exposed to

IPV share the following critical components: improving parenting skills and competence; enhancing the quality of the parent-child relationship; teaching parents to appreciate and reinforce their children for appropriate behavior; and teaching parents to discipline effectively and consistently, but without harshness or physical aggression (McDonald, Jouriles, & Minze, 2011).

Content of the Parenting Intervention: The Skills

The central component of the Project Support intervention is the training in child behavior management skills. It is similar to parenting interventions by other researchers (e.g., Dangel & Polster, 1988; Forehand & McMahon, 1981; Wolfe, 1991), with modifications designed to foster parents' success in learning and using the skills effectively (these modifications are described under "Teaching the Skills," below). The first skills focus on teaching parents how to use positive reinforcement effectively for encouraging good behavior. These are followed by skills for responding to misbehavior. Presented below are the 12 core parenting skills addressed in Project Support.

Attending Parents are taught not only to pay specific attention to the child's behavior, but also to communicate to the child that they are paying attention. The attending skill consists of a circumscribed playtime in which the child chooses an activity and the parent is instructed simply to describe or narrate the child's ongoing behavior. In its most basic form, this involves describing the child's actions concretely (e.g., "You are stacking that blue block on top of the yellow one"), but ideally also includes commentary on aspects of the child's behavior that the parent would like to encourage (e.g., "Now you are stacking the blocks carefully and keeping them all on the table!"), and is stated enthusiastically but realistically. Parents are instructed to describe the child's behavior in such a fashion that someone listening in another room would understand exactly what the child is doing at any given moment, and to overlook behaviors that are not significantly disruptive. Additionally, the parent is asked to refrain from teaching, criticizing, or questioning; they are asked instead to simply follow the child's lead. The skill is designed to provide positive attention to the child and to foster more positive parent-child interaction patterns. Learning to attend skillfully is also important because it forms the basis for all of the subsequent skills taught in the intervention. For example, to praise effectively, parents need to be adept at describing the particular behaviors that they see and would like to see more often.

Attending also plays a role in discipline. For example, intervening effectively on a problem behavior (e.g., temper tantrum, not taking turns) at the moment it is emerging can be easier than attempting to intervene once the child has lost emotional control. It also affords opportunities to teach the child prosocial ways of interacting and solving problems before the problems get out of hand. In practice, no mother attends closely to her child in an ongoing, moment-by-moment fashion, and we tell mothers that we do not expect them to do so. However, practicing attending in small bursts on a regular basis (e.g., 5 minutes each day) teaches them to be able to do it effectively and sensitizes them to the positive effects that simple positive attention can have on children. The positive results of attending are not limited to the child; mothers are often pleased and quite surprised at their child's positive response to attending, and begin to use it more deliberately and regularly as a consequence. This first success experience tends to lend credibility to the clinician and the intervention, and it can be helpful in keeping mothers engaged in the intervention.

Praise and Positive Attention Mothers are taught to provide praise in two forms. Verbal praise is simply the things that are said, "I like the way you put away your toys right when I asked," or "Thank you for helping your brother with his homework." Physical praise on the other hand are the things that are experienced, a parent's smile, a hug, a "high five," a parent's delighted tone of voice. Both are important and parents are taught to gauge their child's response and utilize the forms of praise to which their child is most responsive.

Teaching parents to praise early in the sessions is important in part because, like attending, praise is also used in each subsequent skill. Additionally, effective delivery of praise requires parents to focus on their child's positive behaviors, which, coupled with skillful attending, provides the child more frequent positive interactions with the parent. For parents who have been focused on their child's problem behaviors, this shift in the balance of positive versus negative interactions can be reinforcing for the parent as well as the child. Most of the parents we have worked with have praised their children, but they have not done so systematically or effectively (i.e., praise has not produced the desired response). We teach parents the importance of praising good behavior swiftly and to use praise systematically, identifying and focusing on specific behaviors they would like to encourage in their child and consistently praising those behaviors.

Listening and Comforting The goal of listening and comforting is for the child to express his or her feelings—fear, excitement, frustration, uncertainty, jealousy, sadness— and leave the conversation feeling that the parent understood and attended to the child's feelings. Parents often have difficulty listening for the purpose of listening, and may have any number of reactions from feeling guilty and choosing to ignore a feeling, to trying to fix a problem that the child expresses, to stifling a child's excitement. Parents are taught that there are times in which listening without action is appropriate. In order to do that, parents must focus their attention on the child, listen carefully to what the child is saying and the emotions the child is expressing, refrain from interrupting or questioning, learn how to give short responses that communicate interest without interrupting (e.g., "I see" or "Tell me more"), and reflect what the child is feeling (e.g., "You were really frustrated!"). Parents are reminded that listening and attending to what the child says does not necessarily mean agreeing with the behavior; instead, it is simply hearing a child out before using a different skill if it becomes necessary. Comforting is an extension of listening, used when a child is experiencing emotions such as sadness, fear, or frustration. Taking additional time, allowing the child to cry (if that is how they feel), using a soothing voice, reflecting feelings, and providing hugs are all ways that parents can show comfort.

Rewards and Privileges Rewards and privileges are another way to reinforce behaviors that the parent would like to see more often. Rewards do not necessarily need to cost any money and may be things the parent already does on occasion, such as allowing the child a few extra minutes of television viewing, reading, or playing a game with the child, or offering a special treat. These become rewards when they are provided in response to a specific positive behavior. Privileges can be as simple as giving the child a choice about something the child does not always control, for example, a choice at the grocery store. Rewards and privileges should never be used to stop a misbehavior (that would be a bribe). Instead, parents should be specific about the behavior that earns a reward, reward immediately and consistently after the behavior, and vary the rewards and privileges according to the difficulty of the behavior. Parents should be reminded that praise should accompany any reward or privilege.

Clear Instructions One way that parents influence their child's compliance is how they give a particular instruction. Clear, concise, age-appropriate instructions greatly increase the likelihood of compliance. Several things help ensure that parents are giving clear instructions. First, parents should make sure that they intend to follow up with consequences to the instructions that they give. Giving instructions with no intent to follow up with a consequence for noncompliance decreases the likelihood that a child will comply. Next parents need to make sure they have the child's attention (e.g., the child is not engaged in an activity such as watching television) and that they use a tone of voice that communicates seriousness without harshness. Instructions should be given as statements, not questions (e.g. "It is time to go," not "Are you ready to go?"), and parents should state what the child should do as opposed to what he or she should not do (e.g., "Sit on the chair," not, "Don't climb in the chair"). Reasons given should be simple and be given prior to the instruction. After giving the instruction, a parent should wait 5 seconds for compliance. If the child complies or begins to comply, the parent should immediately praise the child. If the child does not, the parent should be ready to repeat the instruction and follow up with a consequence if there is still no compliance.

Reprimands and Redirecting The initial step in correcting a child's undesirable or irritating behavior is by reprimanding and redirecting. The reprimand is a firm statement that the parent disapproves of a particular behavior. It should immediately be followed with a statement redirecting the child to an acceptable behavior. Using this skill strategically involves learning precisely when to use it. It is most effective when used before the child's behavior escalates to the undesired level. When behavior is out of control, parents are taught to shift to another skill for managing behavior. Additionally, strategic use of this skill involves targeting alternative behaviors that are acceptable to the parent, but that consider the needs of the child. For example, when the child's behavior is rambunctious, simply telling them to sit still is unlikely to be successful. Finding an acceptable place where they can take a quick "wiggle break" is more likely to be effective. Finally, strategic use of this skill means that parents must consistently reprimand and redirect the same and similar behaviors. For example, if it is not acceptable to jump on the sofa one day, it should not be acceptable to jump on the sofa on any other days, as well.

Time-Out Time-out can be used as a consequence for significant misbehaviors, such as aggression and defiance. It can be an effective technique for managing undesirable behaviors when used properly; however, it is unlikely to work when it is used to the point that it becomes routine. Time-out is time away from positive reinforcement— from the possibility of experiencing positive and enjoyable things. Therefore, the time-out spot should be dull and uninteresting to the child, but always safe. Hallways or a chair away from the room's activities are generally good options. Places like the child's room (too many toys) or the bathroom (not a safe place), generally are not. The length of time a child spends in time-out should be age appropriate. A rough guideline is one minute for every year of age. So if the child is 4 years old, the child should spend 4 minutes in a time out. Parents should be sure that they have followed all of the previous steps to giving clear instructions (e.g., making sure they have the child's attention and, using firm, specific, and concise directives). Next the parent should give a warning to let the child know that time out is the next consequence—"If you do not pick up your toys you will spend ___ minutes in time-out." If the child complies, the parent should use praise. However, if there is no compliance after waiting 5 seconds, the parent should implement the time-out by saying, "Since you did not pick up your toys, you will spend ___ minutes in time-out." If necessary, the parent should take the child by the hand and place him in time-out. The time-out begins when the child is in the time-out spot and is reasonably quiet. During this time, parents should not interact with the child. They should take action to make sure the child stays in time-out, but offer no additional rationale. At the end of the time-out period, the original directive should be repeated and the process started again.

Ignoring In many ways ignoring is the complimentary skill to attending. Simply put, ignoring is not paying attention to undesirable behaviors such as whining, nagging, interrupting, or temper tantrums. Many of these behaviors decrease in frequency when they do not receive attention, because the child realizes that they are no longer useful in getting what he or she wants. It should be noted that ignoring should not be used with aggressive, dangerous, or destructive behaviors. Effective ignoring is consistent and purposeful. The parent specifically targets behaviors she will ignore every time they occur. The parent instructs the child that she is not going to pay attention to that specific behavior and then actively turns her body away from the child, refraining from eye contact, physical contact, or any further verbal discussion of the behavior until the child ceases. Because many of the behaviors that the parent chooses to ignore are highly irritating (e.g., whining) the parent is taught to utilize self-talk when necessary to maintain her own focus. For example, the parent can remind herself that this is temporary, that it is important for her to follow through, that she should not give in at the risk of actually increasing the frequency or intensity of a behavior. Finally, the parent must effectively praise the child immediately when the misbehavior abates and good behavior begins (e.g., "It is so nice to hear your grown-up voice. I can understand you much better now!").

Withdrawal of Rewards and Privileges Certain misbehaviors can be addressed by strategically withdrawing rewards or privileges. For example, parents may reduce access to television, computers, or video games. As in providing rewards and privileges, similar guidelines apply to their removal. It should occur immediately after the misbehavior commences and should be commensurate with the level of misbehavior. We caution parents that in removing rewards and privileges, sometimes "less is more." For example, forbidding use of a video game or television for 15 to 30 minutes may be more effective than doing so for long periods of time—over longer periods of time children simply find other means of entertaining themselves, and the potency of the punishment is diminished. The period of removal should be no longer than that which causes the child to want to behave properly, rather than experience the loss of the privilege or reward. Finally, the parent should vary the reward or privilege that is withdrawn, corresponding to the nature of the infraction (e.g., not playing a game fairly could result in losing the privilege of playing the rest of the game) and should consistently follow through.

Rule Setting Lastly, the parent is taught the effective use of setting household rules. These rules are the things that are never acceptable and may lead to immediate time-out (or withdrawal of significant privileges) without warning. The rules should be few, selective, and absolute. They often include dangerous, aggressive, or destructive behaviors, such as hitting a sibling or leaving the house (or apartment) without permission. Parents are instructed to go over the rules, and the consequences of violating them, with the children before implementing the rules. Parents may also occasionally need to remind children of a rule and its consequence when temptations occur. And, parents should give frequent and specific praise when the child complies with the rule, especially when this occurs without a reminder.

A Note on Individualizing the Skills The treatment is manualized; however, flexibility within the intervention allows the clinician to address concerns specific to each family. For example, based on assessment of the child's behavior patterns and the parent's beliefs, knowledge, and abilities, the clinician may emphasize some skills and de-emphasize others. Parents differ with regard to which skills they find most challenging, but for most parents there is at least one skill that they have not been able to use effectively. When this happens, the clinician must attempt to understand the parent's perspective, assess how the skill has been used in the past, and respond accordingly, helping to correct the implementation problems or tailor the skill to the particular child or circumstance. Sometimes, parents have objections to particular skills on philosophical grounds. Understanding and respecting the parents' perspective is crucial, and will inform the clinician's response. Sometimes, correcting misinformation may be all that is needed; at other times, tailoring the skill to adapt to the parents' concerns may be sufficient. And in some cases, the clinician might simply ask if the mother would be willing to "give it a try" to see how a particular skill works, with plans to adjust accordingly if the desired results do not follow.

Sequencing of the Skills

The sequence of the parenting skills is structured in such a way so that the first cluster of skills—attending, praise and positive attention, listening and comforting, directives, rewards and privileges—focuses on increasing constructive and adaptive child behavior. The second cluster of skills—reprimands and redirecting, ignoring, rule setting, and time-out—then focuses on decreasing inappropriate child behavior. This sequence of the skills accomplishes several things. First, many parents can quickly identify behaviors that they do not want their children to be doing; however, often they have difficulty identifying specific and concrete behaviors that they would like them to do instead. In combination with assessing some of the behaviors that parents would like for their children to increase, teaching attending as the initial skill increases their ability to focus on specific aspects of the behavior. Second, when parents confront behavior problems frequently, they may begin to have difficulty focusing on the positive aspects of their child's behavior, increasing the strain on the parent-child relationship. Helping parents focus on children's positive behaviors can increase feelings of parental efficacy and warmth between parent and child. The positive skills may be sufficient to reduce some of the child's misbehavior. Finally, beginning with the attending skill, the skills begin to build upon one another. Parents first learn how to strategically pay attention to positive behavior. Subsequently, they use this skill in learning how to praise and reward, and thus shape, their child's behaviors.

Even when the positive, relationship-enhancing skills seem to mitigate the family's problems, the disciplinary skills are always taught in sequence following the mastery of the positive skills. Parents frequently find implementing the positive skills to be challenging; however, they find it extremely rewarding when done well. Teaching the disciplinary skills following the positive skills ensures that the disciplinary skills are employed in a less stressed environment. If the disciplinary skills are introduced too early, the clinician runs the risk of having the parents focus on their use in place of the positive skills.

Assessment

Ongoing assessment is imperative to the success of the skills training. There are multiple opportunities for assessment within the treatment. Initial formal assessments provide comprehensive information about the child's behavior (e.g., standardized measures of the child behavior problems, child's distress), parenting behaviors (e.g., harsh parenting practices as well as parenting strengths), the level and types of violence the family has experienced, and the needs of the family relevant to the instrumental and social support. After the formal assessment, the clinician continues to assess parental progress through discussion, a sequence of role-plays, mastery checks, and homework. The clinician should not progress to a later skill without determining that the parent understands *and can correctly implement* the current skill. Early on, ensuring a parent's competence often means that several sessions are spent on teaching one skill. However, the pace of learning often increases as the parents become more familiar with the new approach.

Teaching the Skills

Each skill is taught in a similar format. The clinician introduces the skill and makes an informal assessment of the parent's familiarity with the skill and her thoughts about how the skill is likely to affect her child. The instruction is partially didactic, but interactive, allowing the clinician to elicit from the parent ways that she may have used this skill in the past and how effective it has or has not been. Considerable time is spent explaining the rationale for the skill as well as specifics as to when and how it should be used. Common concerns that parents report include discomfort in implementing the skill and that similar things have failed in the past. Each concern is addressed and then the clinician demonstrates the skill in a role-play with the mother.

Role-plays provide an opportunity for the parent to practice the skill in a controlled situation and allow the clinician to assess the parent's mastery of the skill. Following instruction in the skill, the clinician devises a role-play to demonstrate proper use of the skill, using a situation in which the skill is likely to be useful for this particular family. In the role-play, the clinician plays the mother, and the client plays the child. Clients are instructed to act just as they think their child would in the role-play. (This often gives the clinician helpful insight into the mothers' perceptions of her child's behavior.) During the role-play, the client has an opportunity to observe the skill being used properly, gaining a head start in trying the skill herself. In addition, by playing the role of the child, clients often gain some sense of how the use of the skill will feel to her child. After the initial role-play, the clinician assesses the client's experience during the role-play and her thoughts about how her child would respond to the skill, and then she and the client switch roles. Switching roles and repeating the role-play allows the clinician to assess the mother's conceptual understanding of the new skill as well as her practical ability in applying it. Processing the role-play with the mother afterward can illuminate concerns of the mother (e.g., "this skill won't work because my child is stubborn!"), can allow the clinician to help the mother tailor the technique to challenging situations, and most importantly helps the clinician identify where improvements may be needed. Providing gentle, corrective feedback and repeating the role-play allows the mother to develop competence and confidence in her use of the skill.

The sequence of a role-play followed by discussion and additional role-playing is repeated until the clinician determines that the mother will be able to execute the skill successfully with her child. Depending on the particular skill being taught, the child is then brought into the session and an activity is devised that allows the mother to use the skill with the child for 5 minutes or so (e.g., the mother may play a game with the child, or ask the child to perform a task). Thus, the clinician can observe a somewhat naturalistic use of the skill and how the child responds to it, and can provide feedback to the mother accordingly. These "mastery checks" are conducted to enable Project Support clinicians to verify that the mother can implement the skill in a real scenario with the child and that the child is responding appropriately to the skill. For each skill, objective and observable behavioral criteria are used to determine mastery. If the parent has not mastered the skill, the clinician assesses which aspects of the skill need review, and continues working toward mastery with the mother.

The second aspect of the mastery check is monitoring the child's response to the mother's use of the skill. Most children respond enthusiastically to the positive skills, which constitute the first components of treatment. Parents typically feel encouraged to continue with the parenting work by these affirming responses. Occasionally, however, children respond with hesitation or uncertainty to the parent's use of the new skill. The parent may have executed the skill well, but the outcome is not what was expected. In such cases, the clinician's awareness of the child's response is important for tailoring the skills to maximize the potential for success.

The cyclical process of assessment in role-play and mastery check enables the clinician and client to modify and adapt each skill to the needs of the individual family. It should be noted that for disciplinary skills (e.g., time-out, withdrawal of privileges), mastery checks are not conducted in the same fashion. Instead, mothers are asked to explain to the child what will happen when the child engages in certain behaviors, and then step the child through the sequence of events that will follow if those behaviors occur (e.g., "If you aren't playing fairly, I will tell you only one time that you must play fairly or you can't play at all. If you don't play fairly right away, then you will not be allowed to play the rest of the game"). The clinician provides feedback and guidance as needed, to insure that the mother can implement the steps and that the child understands the expectation and the consequence for misbehavior.

Clinicians assign homework each week to encourage practice with the new skill once they are confident that the mother will be successful in its use. Homework helps the mother integrate new skills into her routine and to uncover errors in her understanding or implementation. Mothers typically experience a high degree of success due to our emphasis on over learning skills during session, and have frequently reported rapid improvements in their relationships with their children as they employ these more effective, positive parenting techniques.

Conclusion

Given the number of children exposed to IPV and child maltreatment, the development and dissemination of interventions such as Project Support is extremely important. Project Support has been shown to help parents make substantial and sustainable changes in their parenting practices, leading to improvements in child outcomes. The structure of the intervention—providing social and instrumental support while maintaining a focus on changing parenting skills—balances the needs of the parent with the needs of the child. The intensive nature of the services is a response to the intensive nature of the problem, and we believe that Project Support provides a model of how to flexibly and compassionately provide services that exert the maximum positive influence for the families we serve.

References

Appel, A. E., & Holden, G. W. (1998). The co-occurrence of spouse and physical child abuse: A review and appraisal. *Journal of Family Psychology, 12*, 578–599.

Campbell, R., Sullivan, C. M., & Davidson, W. S. (1995). Women who use domestic violence shelters: Changes in depression over time. *Psychology of Women, 19*, 237–255.

Dangel, R. F., & Polster, R. A. (1988). *Teaching child management skills.* New York, NY: Pergamon Press.

D'Zurilla, T. J., & Goldfried, M. R. (1971). Problem solving and behavior modification. *Journal of Abnormal Psychology, 78*, 107–126. doi:10.1037/h0031360

Forehand, R. L., & McMahon, R. J. (1981). *Helping the noncompliant child: A clinician's guide to parent training.* New York, NY: Guilford Press.

Grych, J. H., Jouriles, E. N., Swank, P., McDonald, R., & Norwood, W. D. (2000). Patterns of adjustment among children of battered women. *Journal of Consulting and Clinical Psychology, 68*, 84–94. doi:10.1037/0022-006X.68.1.84

Jouriles, E. N., McDonald, R., Rosenfield, D., Norwood, W. D., Spiller, L. C., Stephens, N., . . . Ehrensaft, M. (2010). Improving parenting in families referred for child maltreatment: A randomized controlled trial examining effects of Project Support. *Journal of Family Psychology, 24*, 328–338.

Jouriles, E. N., McDonald, R., Rosenfield, D., Stephens, N., Corbitt-Shindler, D., & Miller, P. C. (2009). Reducing conduct problems among children exposed to intimate partner violence: A randomized clinical trial examining effects of project support. *Journal of Consulting and Clinical Psychology, 77*, 705–17. doi:10.1037/a0015994

Jouriles, E., McDonald, R., Smith Slep, A. M., Heyman, R. E., & Garrido, E. (2008). Child abuse in the context of domestic violence: Prevalence, explanations, and practice implications. *Violence & Victims, 23*, 221–235. doi:10.1891/0886-6708. 23.2.221

Jouriles, E. N., McDonald, R., Spiller, L., Norwood, W. D., Swank, P. R., Stephens, N., . . . Buzy, W. (2001). Reducing conduct problems among children of battered women. *Journal of Consulting and Clinical Psychology, 69*, 774–785.

McDonald, R., & Jouriles, E. N. (1991). Marital aggression and child behavior problems: Research findings, mechanisms, and intervention strategies. *The Behavior Therapist, 14*, 189–192.

McDonald, R., Jouriles, E. N., & Minze, L. C. (2011). Interventions for young children exposed to IPV. In S. A. Graham-Bermann & A. A. Levendosky (Eds.), *How intimate partner violence affects children: Developmental research, case studies, and evidence-based treatment* (pp. 109–131). Washington, DC: American Psychological Association Books.

McDonald, R., Jouriles, E., Ramisetty-Mikler, S., Caetano, R., & Green, C. (2006). Estimating the number of American children living in partner-violent families. *Journal of Family Psychology, 20*, 137–142. doi:10.1037/0893-3200. 20.1.137

McDonald, R., Jouriles, E. N., & Skopp, N. A. (2006). Reducing conduct problems among children brought to women's shelters: Intervention effects 24 months following termination of services. *Journal of Family Psychology, 20*, 127–36. doi:10.1037/0893-3200. 20.1.27

Sullivan, C., & Bybee, D. (1999). Reducing violence using community-based advocacy for women with abusive partners. *Journal of Consulting and Clinical Psychology, 67*(1), 43–53.

Patterson, G. R. (1982). *Coercive family process.* Eugene, OR: Castalia.

Wolfe, D. A. (1991). *Preventing physical and emotional abuse of children.* New York, NY: Guilford Press.

12

Dissemination and Implementation of Child–Parent Psychotherapy

Collaboration With Community Programs

Miriam Hernandez Dimmler, Lisa Gutiérrez Wang, Patricia Van Horn, and Alicia F. Lieberman

Introduction

Childhood exposure to violence is an epidemic that violates the physical and emotional well-being of victims and increases the likelihood of future abusive patterns. Recent findings from the National Survey of Children's Exposure to Violence shows that more than 60% of children age 17 and younger in the United States were exposed to violence in the past year with nearly half of the children surveyed being direct victims of assaults. A staggering 87% of children reported multiple exposures to violence during their lifetime, which suggests that children may be at ongoing risk of victimization (Finkelhor, Turner, Ormrod, Hamby, & Kracke, 2009). Children under 5 are subject to higher rates of violence exposure in comparison to other age groups and suffer higher rates of injury and mortality after abuse and violence (Grossman, 2000), and it is not uncommon for family violence, especially violence between parents, to overlap significantly with child maltreatment (Edleson, 1999; Kitzmann, Gaylord, Holt, & Kenny, 2003). Children exposed to trauma such as domestic and community violence, physical and sexual abuse, neglect, and separation from caregivers are at increased risk of posttraumatic symptoms, depression, separation anxiety, aggression, and regressive behaviors, such as bedwetting and decreased verbalization (Osofsky, 1995; Zeanah & Scheeringa, 1997).

In light of the prevalence and detrimental effects of traumatic events in early childhood, there is an urgent need in the field of mental health to respond with early and effective intervention. One such intervention is Child-Parent Psychotherapy (CPP), a manualized relationship-based intervention for trauma-exposed families with young children, age birth to 5. Initially developed for families experiencing domestic violence, CPP also applies to other forms of adverse life stressors and interpersonal traumas that place children and caregivers at risk of traumatic stress disorder and other psychiatric symptoms (Lieberman, Van Horn, & Ghosh Ippen, 2005). Developed by clinical researchers at the Child Trauma Research Program (CTRP) at the University of California, San Francisco (UCSF), CPP integrates multiple theories including psychodynamic, attachment, trauma, cognitive-behavioral, and social learning theory.

The efficacy of CPP was established with high-risk, trauma-exposed groups of toddlers and preschool age children, including low-income, ethnically diverse families (see this book's appendix for a summary of this research). In recognition of its effectiveness, the National Child Traumatic Stress Network (NCTSN) classified CPP as a "well supported and efficacious" practice on its list of Empirically Supported Treatments and Promising Practices (NCTSN, 2005). The California Evidence-Based Clearinghouse for Child Welfare rated CPP a number 2 ("supported by the research evidence") on a scale of 1 to 5, with 1 being well-supported by the research evidence and 5 being a concerning practice. In addition, the California Evidence-Based Clearinghouse rated CPP a number 1 on a scale of 1 (high) to 3 (low), which indicates that this intervention is designed, or commonly used, to meet the needs of children and families receiving child welfare services. CPP has also been accepted as an approved evidence-based practice in jurisdictions such as Los Angeles County and the state of Oregon, both of which require clinicians seeking reimbursement from public funds to deliver evidence-based practices to their clients.

The dissemination of quality care like CPP to systems that reach underserved and underrepresented minority populations has the potential to reduce mental health service disparities for traumatized children and their families. When clinicians move evidence-based practices from academic institutions (where they were developed and evaluated) into community settings, they face the challenge of balancing fidelity to the model with flexibility in its application to the unique needs of the child and family within the context of their community. Efforts to transfer evidence-based practices into public health and clinical practice settings have been largely unsuccessful, and the Institute on Medicine (2001) has argued that the disconnect between research and practice is, "not just a gap, but a chasm" (p. 1). Since academic settings adhere to structured research guidelines that are not replicated easily in the community, it is imperative that dissemination and implementation efforts include systematic evaluation of treatment effectiveness. Consequently, in addition to describing CPP, this chapter describes training models used to disseminate CPP and explores community collaborations that serve as vehicles to bring CPP into systems of care that support underserved families.

Treatment Model

Child-parent interactions are the primary focus of CPP; therefore delivery of this treatment requires competency in dyadic interventions. There are recommended books on CPP for practitioners who seek to learn more about this dyadic treatment model. *Psychotherapy with Infants and Young Children: Repairing the Effects of Stress and Trauma on Early Attachment* (Lieberman & Van Horn, 2008) offers a comprehensive analysis of the theoretical background of CPP and delineates specific strategies of its implementation. This book can serve as a guide for mental health service providers and as a supplemental text in graduate-level courses. There are currently two treatment manuals that describe the application of CPP with young children and their caregivers. *Don't Hit My Mommy!: A Manual for Child-Parent Psychotherapy with Young Witnesses of Family Violence* (Lieberman & Van Horn, 2005) provides the domains and strategies to implement this model. *Losing a Parent to Death in the Early Years: Guidelines for the Treatment of Traumatic Bereavement in Infancy and Early Childhood* (Lieberman, Compton, Van Horn, & Ghosh Ippen, 2003) describes the treatment approach when young children experience the death of a parent or loved one. In sum, these books share a common objective—to assist practitioners in the treatment of child victims of trauma and violence by restoring attunement, safety, and security in the child-caregiver relationship.

Clinicians using the CPP model work with both the child and primary caregiver in dyadic sessions traditionally delivered over the course of a 12-month period. Sessions last approximately 1 hour and take place in an office playroom or in the family's home. Therapeutic strategies are aimed at restoring a sense of security and promoting congruence in the dyadic relationship. Caregivers and children exposed to traumatic events are at greater risk of misinterpreting each other's cues and engaging in mutually reinforced negative interactional patterns. CPP targets both parent's and child's inaccurate and maladaptive mental representations of each other so the dyad can more objectively understand and respect one another's internal world. These goals are achieved by promoting developmental progress through play, physical contact, and language; offering unstructured reflective developmental guidance; modeling appropriate protective behaviors; interpreting feelings and actions; providing emotional support and empathetic communication; and offering crisis intervention, case management, and concrete assistance with problems of living (Lieberman, Van Horn, & Ghosh Ippen, 2005). The child's primary attachment relationships serve as the mechanism by which CPP addresses each of these domains (Lieberman & Van Horn, 2008).

The intervention is flexible. Clinicians are encouraged to tailor engagement, assessment, and therapeutic strategies to meet each family's presenting needs. This may require customizing assessment protocols, including additional family members in the therapy (e.g., both parents, siblings), and scheduling individual sessions with the parent when specific issues arise that are best addressed privately. For these reasons, CPP treatment manuals provide descriptions of the stages of treatment and the domains of intervention (i.e., areas of focus that are unique to CPP). The manuals do not provide a session-by-session standardized format or a specified treatment course. Vignettes and narrative notes drawn from real-life cases are provided to illustrate how the model is applied by different clinicians working with diverse families.

Assessment

The use of psychological assessment protocols are encouraged for the collection of family information essential to guiding the intervention. Per Zero to Three (1994) recommendations, adequate assessment of young children and their families should incorporate several components, including: (a) an intake interview with the parent/primary caregiver to ascertain the family's current situation and presenting problems; (b) documentation of the child's developmental history and symptoms; (c) direct observation of the child in different contexts; (d) evaluation of the parent's history and psychological functioning; and (e) an assessment of the family's sociocultural background.

CPP clinicians administer assessment protocols both at intake and termination in order to have a basis for treatment planning and for gauging the success of intervention. Initial intake sessions are conducted with the parent alone; this is critical as it gives the clinician time to form an alliance with the parent, to assess whether the parent may have her own potentially overwhelming traumatic experiences, and to assess the parent's level of affect regulation. A structured intake interview is employed to gather relevant information about the child, parent, and family system. The clinician is encouraged to conduct the interview in a conversational fashion, attending to rapport building as a primary focus. During subsequent sessions, the parent completes standardized assessment instruments that measure current symptomatology. Child-focused assessment batteries consist of the Child Behavior Checklist (CBCL; Achenbach & Edelbrock 1983), Trauma Symptom Checklist for Young Children (TSCYC; Briere, 2005), the Traumatic Experiences Severity Index (TESI; Ippen et al., 2002), and may incorporate the Wechsler Preschool and Primary Scale of Intelligence (WPPSI; Wechsler, 1989). Parental measures include the Davidson Trauma Scale (DTS; Davidson, 1996), Beck Depression Inventory (BDI; Beck, Steer, Ball, & Ranieri, 1996), the Life Stressors Checklist (LSC; Wolfe, Kimmerling, & Brown 1993), and the Parenting Stress Index-Short Version (PSI-SV; Abidin, 1995), and Angels in the Nursery (Van Horn, unpublished). An instrument by Crowell (1985) is used to observe parent-child interactions. When families are in crisis and necessitate a prompt transition to the treatment phase, some assessment measures may be foregone. We consider it essential, however, to assess both parent's and child's experiences of traumatic events, current levels of symptomatology, and sources of strength and resilience. Once assessments have been completed, the clinician meets with the parent to review both the parent's and the clinician's impressions of the information that emerged during the assessment and develop a preliminary treatment agenda.

Assessment at the conclusion of treatment provides an opportunity to determine whether the goals of treatment have been met. Standardized instruments are re-administered to measure change in symptom level, and a feedback session is held with the parent to review progress. The collection of both initial and termination assessment measures at CTRP allows for continued evaluation of CPP as an intervention that effectively treats a broad range of traumatic events and populations. In clinical practice, the extent to which assessment is incorporated into treatment may vary. At minimum, it is recommended that families receiving CPP engage in an intake interview and are initially assessed for trauma exposure, posttraumatic stress, and depression. Parents should also be screened for co-occurring substance abuse. If a parent is identified as requiring individual therapy for a mental health and/or substance use disorder, referrals should be made and collaboration between practitioners should be pursued when clinically indicated. The assessment phase may also reveal practical concerns in a family's life that could potentially interfere with engagement to treatment (e.g., employment, transportation, or childcare), and clinicians often connect families to resources at this stage. Clinicians within community-based programs can partner with agency staff to identify appropriate resources as well as coordinate care so families can streamline multiple appointments.

Stages of Treatment

As a general rule, CPP is comprised of the three sequential stages. The first stage focuses on the *establishment of a collaborative process and formulation of the intervention.* This stage takes place during the first three months of treatment and is devoted to establishing a collaborative relationship with the family. It is expected that the clinician may often feel pulled in different directions as the family becomes accustomed to the dyadic sessions. Issues of safety and problems of living may present as critical during this stage, especially with resource-depleted families. The clinician may focus considerable attention on providing referrals and engaging in concrete safety planning. During this phase, both parent and child will turn to the clinician for guidance on how to integrate play and adult conversation. The clinician must attend to these processes and make every effort to divide attention in a thoughtful and therapeutic fashion. Time may be divided between the parent and child when individual claims for attention are "urgent and incompatible" (Lieberman & Van Horn, 2005, p. 33). When possible, the clinician should encourage joint activities and closely observe the child-parent interactions. These observations help the clinician further identify areas of strength and difficulty within the relationship and provide the basis for formulating specific interventions.

During this first stage, the clinician will also work with the family to name the trauma they have experienced. By naming the trauma in session, using age and culturally sensitive language, the child and parent are able to acknowledge the violence they survived in a safe, contained environment. Lieberman and Van Horn (2005) explain that, "The clinician acts as a safe mediator between the parent and the child, both of whom are often unable or reluctant to name the violence for fear that acknowledging it will trigger overwhelming feelings of guilt, shame, blame, and loss" (p. 15). Additionally, the clinician will begin helping the parent understand how trauma impacts typical child development and behavior. This guidance is often essential to helping the parent establish age-appropriate expectations of their child. The following is an example of a script delivered by a practitioner to a young child and caregiver during the first treatment session to clarify the purpose of their work together, "Your mommy tells me that it's hard for you to sleep and you cry when mommy leaves you at school. When children see their mommies and daddies fight like you did, sometimes they get big feelings inside.

Big feelings make it hard for children to sleep and be away from mommies. You and mommy are here because mommy wants to help make your scared and worried feelings smaller. We're all going to play together and talk about the big feelings you and mommy have after seeing mommy and daddy yell and hit. Your mommy wants you to feel safe, and I'm here to help your mommy with that."

The second stage, *clarification and targeting of the identified problem areas*, usually occurs between months 4 through 8. Transition into this stage occurs once the therapeutic relationship has developed and successful strategies of intervention have been established. During this stage, the family and clinician have set a fairly consistent pace for the sessions and have established how time is allocated. Through the use of play, themes have emerged and a joint trauma narrative begins to develop. The clinician facilitates this process by helping the parent understand the emotional meaning behind the child's behavior and linking it to relevant trauma reminders. In order to process the trauma through the creation of a joint narrative, the parent and child's capacity to cope with difficult emotions and to differentiate between reliving and remembering the trauma is expanded. Strategies for effectively increasing emotion regulation and reestablishing trust in bodily sensations are reinforced. Parents are supported in their efforts to self-soothe and are encouraged to reassure and guide their child in effective coping.

The third stage, *recapitulation and termination*, occurs during the last three months of treatment (months 9 through 12). The focus of treatment shifts from active intervention to reflection on growth and shared experience. Key to this stage is the acknowledgment of termination and the feelings associated with the end of treatment and the therapeutic relationship. For many families, termination is seen as a significant interpersonal loss. Feelings of sadness, anger, and apprehension may be expressed along with feelings of gratitude, pride, and hope for the future. The clinician works with the parent and child to recognize the complexity of such feelings and prepares them to move forward on their own as a family.

Dissemination of CPP Through Practitioner Training

The evidence base for CPP has given impetus to an increasing demand for structured channels to disseminate this model through individual practitioner training. The primary source of training in CPP recognized on a national level includes instruction along with consultation and/or supervision provided by the treatment developers at the UCSF's CTRP. The following are three different training channels offered by the developers of CPP: (1) clinical internship programs at CTRP; (2) the Child Trauma Training Institute (CTI); and (3) the National Child Traumatic Stress Network (NCTSN) Learning Collaboratives.

Child Trauma Research Program

The overarching training goal of CTRP is to provide culturally informed clinical and research training in trauma-focused infancy and early childhood mental health, particularly through training clinicians on how to implement CPP. This program is dedicated to the recruitment of multidisciplinary clinicians and clinical researchers who work with underserved and immigrant populations as a concerted effort to narrow the mental health service gap for underserved, low-income, and cultural minority groups. Psychology internships for pre- and postdoctoral level applicants are available through the California Psychology Internship Council (CAPIC) and UCSF's Clinical Psychology Training Program, which is a 2-year pre- and postdoctoral fellowship program accredited by the American Psychological Association (APA). There are also field placement positions for social workers, and psychiatry residents in the Department of Psychiatry at UCSF can apply for a rotation at CTRP. On a weekly basis, CTRP interns participate in an Infant-Early Childhood Mental Health and Trauma Seminar, Assessment Seminar, Clinical Case Review, and intensive individual clinical supervision. The theme of diversity in clinical work (e.g., client, trainee, and staff) is infused throughout didactic training, supervision, and grand round lectures at UCSF and San Francisco General Hospital. Participation in a 1- to 2-year, rigorous internship at CTRP is not a viable option for all clinicians who seek competency in CPP. This is especially true for those who have completed their graduate training and supervised clinical hours. This makes the Child Trauma Training Institute a desirable option for many established clinicians.

Child Trauma Training Institute

There is an increasing demand among mental health professionals and supervisors to obtain expertise in early childhood trauma treatment. The Child Trauma Training Institute (CTI) responds to this demand for local service providers in the public health and not-for-profit mental and behavioral health system in the San Francisco Bay Area. Approximately 60 clinicians across more than 25 agencies participate in the institute each year with the purpose of collaborating and learning CPP. The CTI is sponsored by Jewish Family and Children's Service in partnership with UCSF's CTRP with funding from Ingrid Tauber and the Lisa and John Pritzker Foundation. Participants in the CTI enroll in a 1- to 2-year program. The first year provides training in the foundations of Early Childhood Mental Health, trauma theory, and CPP, as well as training in how to screen children with special developmental needs. The second year of the CTI provides more in-depth training in CPP. Participation in the institute involves monthly didactics, biweekly group consultation, and commitment by the agencies to support the implementation of CPP. While the CTI provides local opportunities to learn CPP in the San Francisco Bay Area, and web-based opportunities for distance learners through the CTI Long Distance Program, there are also training opportunities on a national scale.

National Child Traumatic Stress Network (NCTSN) Learning Collaboratives

The National Child Traumatic Stress Network (NCTSN) has modified the Learning Collaborative methodology for use in training clinicians to implement evidence-based mental health interventions such as CPP. To date, NCTSN has sponsored three CPP learning collaboratives, which have trained clinicians from thirty community practice centers across the United States. The third NCTSN-sponsored learning collaborative also included a Train the Trainer track in order to broaden the pool of qualified CPP trainers. An NCTSN-sponsored learning collaborative includes seven essential features:

1. Meetings with a faculty or other group of experts to develop a change package that delineates the desired outcomes from the training.

2. A self-assessment and application process in which agencies that wish to send teams to the collaborative complete an application form that helps them assess their readiness to implement the practice.

3. A requirement that teams composed of line clinicians, supervisors, and senior leaders who can make policy changes in the agency participate in the training in order to maximize the likelihood that implementation will be sustained.

4. A prework phase that allows participants to gain basic familiarity with the practice so that they can begin to implement it immediately after the first learning session.

5. A series of three or four learning sessions spaced several months apart with case-based telephone consultation held twice monthly between the learning sessions.

6. A small-tests-of-change model for assessing the progress toward implementation.

7. Collection of metrics to assess progress toward implementation and the degree to which participants are implementing the practice with fidelity.

Our experience has been that participants in these intensive trainings have continued to implement the practice long after the learning collaborative is completed.

In addition to learning collaboratives sponsored by the NCTSN, CPP has been disseminated in grant-funded learning collaboratives in the state of Illinois and in the Gulf Coast region. Finally, the Zero to Three organization is supporting a learning collaborative to train clinicians who work with infants and toddlers in the dependency system in CPP in order to strengthen its Court Teams Initiative, which serves these vulnerable young children and their families.

Dissemination of CPP in Community Systems

Along with training individual mental health providers on how to implement CPP, UCSF's CTRP also employs models of dissemination that involve both direct service and systemic capacity building within community-based organizations. One such model is a university-foundation collaboration between UCSF's CTRP and Tipping Point Community, a foundation that funds poverty fighting nonprofit agencies in the San Francisco Bay Area.

Tipping Point Mental Health Initiative

A harsh reality that fuels the mental health service gap is that high-risk families do not access quality care at the same rate as their more affluent counterparts. The Tipping Point Mental Health Initiative is designed to reduce this disparity by strengthening community agencies that have already shown success in outreach to underserved families. Tipping Point Community and UCSF's CTRP have partnered in this initiative in efforts to increase access to treatment for traumatized, impoverished families with young children through (1) providing families direct services with CPP clinicians; (2) training staff on culturally informed detection of early trauma; and (3) assisting in systemic change in capacity building efforts to enhance mental health delivery systems within the agencies. The goals of this partnership have been carried out in a variety of distinct community programs that serve homeless and low-income families such as comprehensive social service agencies that provide case-management, a day care for children between the ages of 3 months to 5 years, elementary school, and a pediatric medical clinic.

Implementation of CPP in Community Programs

Through Tipping Point Community's Mental Health Initiative, CPP clinicians from CTRP's internship program are placed within community agencies in order to become a part of the milieu while receiving supervision and didactic training at UCSF. Interns provide CPP to clients on-site and consult with agency staff on issues pertaining to trauma and posttraumatic stress. A unique aspect of clinician placements within agencies is that clinicians and agency staff can more readily collaborate on practical assistance to families and case management to simultaneously enhance the delivery of mental health services and social service assistance. Interns are trained to navigate the complexity of implementing CPP to families within challenging circumstances endemic to community-based agencies. For example, agencies may struggle with staff turnover, budget cuts, high caseloads, limited time for reflection, and insufficient knowledge of mental health issues and stigmatization of mental health services. CPP clinicians overcome these obstacles by creating alliances with staff through informal rapport building, collaborating on shared clients, mental health consultation, and an openness to learn from staff expertise. The majority of CPP interns recruited for community placements through the Tipping Point Community Mental Health Initiative belong to underrepresented groups and have ambitions to continue working as mental health practitioners within community based programs.

Capacity Building Within Community Programs

Another important component of the Tipping Point Mental Health Initiative is training and dissemination in principles of infant and early childhood mental health and early trauma to a diverse array of staff at community-based agencies that interact with high-risk families—paraprofessionals, lawyers, peer advocates, day-care providers, community health workers, case managers, medical providers, and mental health practitioners. A goal of these community partnerships is to support frontline workers who have a variety of personal and professional experiences with trauma and mental health treatment so they can, in turn, more effectively identify and respond to families suffering from the effects of trauma exposure. Education of staff at agencies on CPP is imperative so they can identify families that could benefit from CPP and make appropriate referrals. These capacity-building efforts enhance the likelihood that sustainable infrastructures of mental health delivery systems are created at the agencies.

Implementation of CPP in Clinical Practice

Practitioners are ready to engage families in treatment once competency in CPP is achieved through appropriate training. Mental health service providers must then make decisions about which families would be appropriate for CPP and how to engage them in services. If practitioners are part of a larger organization, then support from the system is key to successful implementation. A pre-implementation assessment such as the Organizational Readiness and Capacity Assessment (Markiewicz, Ebert, Ling, Amaya-Jackson, & Kisiel, 2006) may be used to help agencies evaluate their readiness to implement an evidence-based practice like CPP.

Once families are identified for treatment, practitioners should have predetermined what intake or assessment measures, if any, would be adequate to measure family functioning and symptoms. The intervention should be delivered in a space large enough for children to play with their caregivers. The following is a list of some recommended toys to stock in a playroom or in a bag if the practitioner conducts sessions at the client's home or child's school: soft ball, baby doll (and at least one bottle), a doctor's kit, dishes, food toys, human doll figures, animal families, blocks, puppets, cars, a big dinosaur, emergency vehicles, books, play telephones, and a dollhouse. Consideration should be given to families' race, ethnicity, and culture—for example, include an array of human figures to represent a diversity of sex, age groups, and skin tones so children can construct families that reflect their experiences. Toys should be age-appropriate and encourage opportunities for children and parents to interact. The identified toys tend to elicit relational themes and may serve as catalysts for children to create trauma narratives through play, which is an integral component of CPP (Diaz & Lieberman, 2010).

Practitioners are encouraged to make frequent use of the CPP manual (Lieberman & Van Horn, 2005) as well as the aforementioned supporting literature throughout treatment as guides for CPP implementation. There are also measures designed to assess fidelity to the model. For example, "Evaluating Use of Core Elements of Child-Parent Psychotherapy" (Van Horn, 2008) is a nine-item form meant to be used with trainees of CPP. There is also a "Child-Parent (CPP) Knowledge Test" (Ghosh Ippen, 2008), which is a multiple choice and short answer questionnaire designed to test trainees of CPP in their knowledge of the model. Effective implementation of CPP requires a minimum of 1 year, supervised experience with multiple families. Supervisors of CPP are recommended to have at least 2 years of practice with the model.

Collaboration Between Practitioners and Community Programs

A quintessential ingredient to the success of CPP implementation in community-based settings is collaboration between mental health practitioners and agency staff. In order to maximize the likelihood that families who need services will be referred, staff should be able to recognize signs and symptoms of the effects of trauma on young children and the child-parent relationship. Such knowledge of the symptoms and risk factors is necessary to identify families that could benefit from CPP. In addition, staff members play a crucial role in reassuring anxious families when they can accurately describe services and, when appropriate, introduce clients to practitioners. Mental health practitioners can empower agency staff with this psychoeducation through one-on-one meetings, regularly scheduled consultation, literature materials, and training/workshop opportunities. Another outcome of such psychoeducation for agency staff may be increased empathy toward traumatized clients who are often categorized as difficult to engage, problematic, or resistant—behaviors that may be linked to complex trauma and posttraumatic stress symptoms.

Along with facilitating the referral process of families to CPP services, communication between CPP mental health practitioners and agency staff is important to enhance client engagement in therapy. Outreach to underserved populations may be particularly challenging; therefore, CPP practitioners could benefit from the assistance of agency staff. Families with multiple, complex stressors in their lives may find it difficult to engage in treatment that requires their active involvement, potentially over the course of a year. There are many reasons why underserved families exposed to violence and trauma may resist treatment, such as the following: worry about receiving a diagnosis; general distrust of mental health professionals and service providers; concern about child abuse reporting; concerns about confidentiality; or challenges with making it to appointments (e.g., due to transportation, conflicting appointments, health concerns, or child care). Agency staff can assist practitioners in the identification of relevant resources, including daycare or transportation vouchers. In addition, agency staff can provide clients opportunities to voice their concerns within a safe, supportive context and perhaps even help clients communicate their concerns to practitioners.

Conclusion

CPP is a treatment for trauma-exposed children and their families that improves both child and caregiver functioning when compared with controls in empirical studies (Lieberman & Van Horn, 2008). A unique advantage of CPP is that the intervention can be delivered in a clinic or in a setting that defines the family's life experience whether it is home, school, or other another context such as a community-based agency. This versatility of CPP is especially important when practitioners work with underserved, trauma exposed families who have historically been difficult to engage in mental health treatment. Community programs that serve low-income families with young children may benefit from having access to mental health practitioners trained in CPP because this population is particularly vulnerable to suffering from trauma exposure. Moreover, the dissemination and implementation of CPP to community settings where underserved groups receive other forms of support can potentially reduce disparities in access to quality mental health services.

References

Abidin, R. R. (1995). *Parenting stress index, third edition: Professional manual*. Odessa, FL: Psychological Assessment Resources.

Achenbach, T. M., & Edelbrock, C. (1983). *The child behavior checklist*. Burlington, VT: University Associates in Psychiatry.

Beck, A. T., Steer, R. A., Ball, R., & Ranieri, W. (December, 1996). Comparison of Beck Depression Inventories – I A and – II in psychiatric outpatients. *Journal of Personality Assessment, 67*(3): 588–597.

Beck, A. T., Steer, R. A., & Brown G. K. (1996). *Manual for Beck depression inventory II (BDI-II)*. San Antonio, TX: Psychology Corporation.

Briere, J. (2005). *Trauma symptom checklist for young children (TSCYC): Professional manual*. Odessa, FL: Psychological Assessment Resources.

Crowell, J. A. (1985). *Parent-child interaction and coding system for 2–5 year old children* (modified from Matas, Arend & Sroufe, 1978). Unpublished manuscript, Stanford University, Stanford, CA.

Davidson, J. (1996). *Davidson trauma scale [Manual]*. Toronto, Ontario, Canada: Multi-Health Systems.

Diaz, M. A., & Lieberman, A. F. (2010). Use of play in child-parent psychotherapy with preschoolers traumatized by domestic violence. In C. E. Schaefer (Ed.), *Play therapy for preschool children* (pp. 131–156). Washington, DC: American Psychological Association.

Edleson, J. L. (1999). The overlap between child maltreatment and woman battering. *Violence Against Women, 5*(2), 134–154.

Finkelhor, D., Turner, H., Ormrod, R., Hamby, S., & Kracke, K. (2009). Children's exposure to violence: A comprehensive national survey. *Juvenile Justice Bulletin*, 1–11.

Ghosh Ippen, C. (2008). *Child-parent psychotherapy (CPP) knowledge test*. San Francisco, CA. Unpublished instrument.

Grossman, D. C. (2000). The history of injury control and the epidemiology of child and adolescent injuries. *The Future of Children, 10*(1), 23–52.

Institute of Medicine. (2001). *Crossing the quality chasm: A new health system for the 21st century*. Washington, DC: National Academy Press.

Ippen, C. G., Ford, J., Racusin, R., Acker, M., Bosquet, M., Rogers, K., Edwards, J. (2002). Traumatic events screening inventory—Parent report revised. Unpublished instrument.

Kitzmann, K. M., Gaylord, N. K., Holt, A. R., & Kenny, E. D. (2003). Child witnesses to domestic violence: A meta-analytic review. *Journal of Consulting and Clinical Psychology, 71*, 339–352.

Lieberman, A. F., Compton, N. C., Van Horn, P., & Ghosh Ippen, C. (2003). *Losing a parent to death in the early years: Guidelines for the treatment of traumatic bereavement in infancy and early childhood*. Washington, DC: Zero to Three Press.

Lieberman, A. F., & Van Horn, P. (2005). *Don't hit my mommy!: A manual for child-parent psychotherapy with young witnesses of family violence*. Washington, DC: Zero to Three Press.

Lieberman, A. F., & Van Horn, P. (2008). *Psychotherapy with infants and young children: Repairing the effects of stress and trauma on early attachment*. New York, NY: Guilford Press.

Lieberman, A. F., Van Horn, P., & Ghosh Ippen, C. (2005). Toward evidence-based treatment: Child-parent psychotherapy with preschoolers exposed to marital violence. *Journal of the American Academy of Child & Adolescent Psychiatry, 44*(12), 1241–1248.

Markiewicz, J., Ebert, L., Ling, D., Amaya-Jackson, L., & Kisiel, C. (2006). *Learning collaborative toolkit*. Los Angeles, CA, and Durham, NC: National Center for Child Traumatic Stress.

National Child Trauma Stress Network. (2008). NCTSN empirically supported treatments and promising practices. Retrieved from www.NCTSN.org

Osofsky, J. D. (1995). The effects of exposure to violence on young children. *American Psychologist, 50*, 782–788.

Van Horn, P. (2008). Evaluating use of core elements of child-parent psychotherapy. Unpublished instrument.

Wechsler, D. (1989). *Wechsler preschool and primary scale of intelligence—Revised*. San Antonio, TX: Psychological Corporation.

Wolfe, J., Kimerling, R., & Brown, P. J. (1993). *The life stressor checklist*. Boston, MA: National Center for PTSD, Boston VA Medical Center.

Zeanah, C. H., & Scheeringa, M. S. (1997). The experience and effects of violence in infancy. In J. D. Osofsky (Ed.), *Children in a violent society* (pp. 97–123). New York, NY: Guilford Press.

Zero to Three. (Ed.). (1994). *Diagnostic classification: 0–3 diagnostic classification of mental health and developmental disorders of infancy and early childhood: 0–3*. Arlington, VA: Author.

PART VI

Interventions for Substance–Abusing Parents

In Chapter 13, Melinda Hohman and Bill James discuss the use of motivational interviewing (MI) with parents involved with CPS who misuse substances. After noting how using MI can be a paradigm shift for child welfare practitioners, the authors describe how to implement motivational interviewing and provide a sample dialogue with a parent who is unhappy about being sent to substance misuse treatment.

In Chapter 14, Therese Grant describes the Parent-Child Assistance Program (PCAP), an intensive home visitation case management program for mothers who used drugs or alcohol heavily during pregnancy. Most of the PCAP clients also reported psychiatric problems and are described by Grant as being part of a population of multiproblem mothers who are generally considered unmotivated and difficult to reach. Case managers with relatively small caseloads of 15 to 16 families offer support to the mothers over a 3-year period, teach them basic living and parenting skills, and link them with community service providers.

13

Global Goals and Specific Skills

*Integrating Motivational Interviewing Into Child Welfare Practice**

Melinda Hohman and Bill James

Substance misuse among parents involved with child protective service (CPS) agencies is more the norm than the exception. According to recent estimates, from 30% to 85% (Hohman, 1998) of all parents on active caseloads have some sort of an alcohol or other drug (AOD) problem. The relationship between substance misuse and child neglect, as compared to child abuse, is particularly strong (Chaffin, Kelleher, & Hollenberg, 1996). Parents with AOD problems who neglect their children often have a host of other psychosocial concerns, such as poverty, low education, few vocational skills, a history of their own abuse and trauma, and poor parenting skills (Donohue, 2004). Interventions for these parents must address all of these issues and do so in a timely manner due to legal time constraints that parents—and their social workers—face. Engaging parents in treatment programs and other interventions is crucial as the clock ticks down.

Parents involved with CPS often are not happy about the prospect of their lives being upended with a variety of demands: residential or out-patient drug treatment; parenting classes; mandatory drug testing; Alcoholics Anonymous attendance; drug abstinence requirements; participation in groups that requires talking to strangers; job searching and/or vocational training; and worst of all, the threat of or actual loss of custody of their children. Understandably, they are angry and resistant (Forrester, McCambridge, Waissbein, Emlyn-Jones, & Rollnick, 2007) toward their social worker and other professionals who are involved in this intervention plan. Living with all of these "losses" (loss of the use of the substance, loss of freedom to make autonomous decisions, loss of relationships

---

* This chapter is derived from Hohman, M. (forthcoming). *Motivational interviewing in social work practice.* New York, NY: Guilford Press

and custody) is painful, stressful, and humiliating. Parents may react by "pushing back" through argumentation, blaming, withdrawal, or superficial compliance (Miller & Rollnick, 2002). Social workers are faced with the double task of working through this resistance as well as facilitating engagement in the case plan so that parents can work toward real change.

Motivational interviewing (MI) is a communication method that was initially developed as an alternative to traditional confrontational methods to engage problem drinkers in treatment (Miller & Rollnick, 1991). It is defined as "a client-centered, directive method for enhancing intrinsic motivation to change by exploring and resolving ambivalence" (Miller & Rollnick, 2002, p. 25). Tested in more than 120 clinical trials across a variety of behavioral and health-related areas (Lundahl, Kunz, Brownell, Tollefson, & Burke, 2010), MI is particularly useful for working with resistant clients and for engaging them in further treatment services. Striving toward real change, MI practitioners target the intrinsic or internal motivators that clients have for themselves, not those that are imposed from an outside source (Miller & Rose, 2009). Those who use MI work to understand the losses that clients are experiencing as well as their anger, ambivalence, and hope about change. MI practitioners enhance client autonomy even though clients may be in an involuntary situation. The concepts and skills of MI are described below, with important concepts and specific skills underlined and with accompanying sample dialogue. However, first it is important to examine why social workers would even want to consider MI in the first place.

Why MI in CPS Work?

MI is useful in CPS work for several reasons. To begin, it is an evidence-based practice that reduces client resistance and can engage clients in treatment. (The research support for its effectiveness is summarized in Appendix A of this book.) Additional reasons are: (a) it is congruent with social work values and ethics and fits well with social work practice; (b) it enhances culturally competent practice; and (c) MI appears to fit well with Family Centered Practice proposed by the U.S. Department of Health and Human Services/Administration for Children and Families.

MI Is Congruent With Social Work Practice

MI consists of an approach to communication with clients as well as the use of specific skills. This overall approach is called the *spirit* of MI. It is comprised of *collaboration, evocation, and autonomy support* (Miller & Rollnick, 2002). What this means is that MI practitioners work in partnership with their clients and do not take an authoritative or expert approach. The expectation is that clients are experts on their lives and the social worker evokes or elicits their ideas, expectations, and goals, instead of "instilling" or telling clients what to do or how to change. Autonomy support involves honoring the knowledge that clients have about their lives and working with them to develop and implement plans that will succeed. The National Association of Social Workers Code of Ethics (NASW, 2008) stresses the importance of the dignity of and respect for clients, maximizing self-determination, enhancing the capacity for change and growth, all done in the context of a human relationship. All of these are congruent with and supported by MI.

MI Enhances Culturally Competent Practice

Social workers are called to work with diverse populations who are often at the margins of society. Social workers may encounter clients who are experiencing a variety of difficulties, socially, emotionally, and economically, and must be able to reach across potential barriers of race, ethnicity, class, age, ability, status, and the like. Because social workers who use MI suspend judgment and closely listen to clients, MI is inherently cross-cultural as practitioners enter the client's world from his or her perspective (Miller & Rollnick, 2002). A meta-analysis of MI research studies has found that MI was almost twice as effective with minority, as compared to white, clients (Hettema, Steele, & Miller, 2005). This may be also due to autonomy support that MI practitioners provide for their clients, which can be very different from interactions where goals and methods of change are imposed and are perhaps perceived as paternalistic. Treating clients as experts with the answers keeps the interaction embedded in clients' particular culture, context, and worldview (Anez, Silva, Paris, & Bedregal, 2008; Madsen, 2009). It should be noted that Miller and Rollnick's book on MI (2002) has been translated into over 38 languages (Miller & Rollnick, 2009), demonstrating the method's cross-cultural appeal.

MI Fits Well With Family Centered Practice

Family Centered Practice (FCP) is defined as, "a way of working with families across service systems to enhance their capacity to care for and protect their children . . . " by providing "services to engage, involve, strengthen, and support families as the most effective approach to ensuring children's safety, permanency, and well-being" (Administration for Children and Families, 2010). FCP is recommended by ACF to be implemented by all state and county CPS agencies. In this model, families are seen as competent and are actively involved the decision-making regarding their own needs as well as service goals and strategies. Social workers work collaboratively with families and strive to develop trusting relationships by providing support and encouragement (Madsen, 2009; Wells & Fuller, 2000). MI has been described as a *guiding* method of communication (Rollnick, Miller, & Butler, 2008) and is a framework for how social workers can achieve this aspect of FCP. All of these goals are included in the spirit of MI, with its emphasis on collaboration, evocation, and autonomy support. Furthermore, MI has been found to be effective as a pretreatment method for a variety of concerns and can be useful for social workers as they address family anger and resistance, with the goal of engaging families in services as well as their own contract planning (Madsen, 2009; Scott & Dadds, 2009).

The Spirit and Skills of MI

The spirit of MI is important as it sets the foundation for how clients (and humans in general) are approached. Using client-centered theory (Rogers, 1980), clients are seen as desiring to strive toward health (physical, mental, and social), given the right resources and support. Clients are assumed to be competent and able to make positive choices for themselves that best fit their needs. These assumptions can conflict with those who practice from a "deficit" worldview or model where clients are seen as lacking knowledge or information or at worst, being incompetent, in denial, lazy, or not caring. When this model is utilized, social workers are the "experts" whose job is to instill knowledge, skills, advice, deadlines, and use persuasion or possibly, threats (Forrester, McCambridge, Waissbein, & Rollnick, 2008; Miller & Moyers, 2006). The view is that these methods are seen as necessary and needed to motivate parents to change their behavior. Some clients do respond to court mandates or threats of loss of child custody, but this is not always the case and clients can become more resistant to change. As Corbett (2009) asks, how is it possible to feel valued—and motivated—when one is seen as deficient?

Using MI can be a paradigm shift in practice for many who work in child welfare. With the emphasis on FCS, there are social workers who do currently utilize the methods and the spirit of MI in their approach with clients. For others though, the responsibility for safety of children, accountability to judges, and the timeline deadlines prompts them to be wary of regarding parents as competent and resourceful. Given these concerns, social workers feel that if they do not advise, persuade, or provide a discussion of possible consequences that parents will not be motivated to comply. Clients do respond to external motivators such as these, and often social workers are successful using these approaches. The pressures social workers face can increase a sense of urgency and responsibility to make parents change, and these persuading behaviors become even more entrenched. Further, some social workers feel that if they are empathetic, they are colluding with parents around negative behaviors (Forrester et al., 2008). And yet studies have found the opposite, at least in work with heavy alcohol users (Miller & Baca, 1983).

If the spirit of MI involves supporting autonomy, working collaboratively, and evoking from clients their thoughts, ideas, and concerns, when do social workers use MI? MI is used when there needs to be a conversation about change, with the global goal of strengthening the client's own motivation and commitment to change. The first step for change for parents may involve attending drug treatment, parenting classes, individual or family therapy; social workers can use MI to help engage clients in the services that are mandated or that clients want. It goes beyond compliance; MI skills are used to tap into the client's own needs, goals, and motivators so that change is real. Social workers may have to explain casework decisions that the client does not, in fact, have any control over; using MI, a discussion could be facilitated regarding how parents may chose to respond to forced decisions, such as how to handle supervised visits.

Miller and Rollnick (1999) indicate that there are two phases to the MI interview: (1) building motivation for change and (2) strengthening commitment to change. Building motivation for change includes (a) entering into a relationship with the client and getting to know her or his thoughts and concerns, (b) deciding on a topic for the interview or agenda setting, and (c) eliciting change talk or a discussion with the focus on change. In Phase 2, the focus is on planning and securing a commitment to the change. Specific MI skills that are used in each phase are discussed here as well.

1. Building a Relationship

In the initial interview process, the social worker is focused on building a relationship with the client and listens closely to understand his or her concerns or dilemma. This can be difficult to do especially with clients who are angry about their involvement with CPS and are hostile with the social worker. Skills to begin to engage and learn about the client are those found in the acronym OARS: open-ended questions, affirmations, reflective listening statements, and summaries.

Open-ended questions typically are those that begin with words such as how, what, why, tell me about, when, and the like, are often broad, and provide the client with a lot of latitude to answer. Rosengren (2009) calls them the ''backbone of the MI information-gathering process'' (p. 59). Examples in the child welfare context could include, ''What is your understanding about what the judge has asked you to do?'' ''How do you keep your child safe?'' ''When you get disappointed in something your child has done, what do you do?'' ''Tell me what you like about being a parent.'' ''What is it you might need from me as your social worker in order to follow your case plan?'' These are compared to close-ended questions whereby clients simply answer yes or no without much room to elaborate.

Social workers often fall into what Miller and Rollnick (2002) call the *question-answer trap* where question after question is asked of clients, making them more passive and not actively involved in the conversation. To keep from falling into this trap, *reflective listening* is used to repeat, rephrase, or state in another way what clients have said. This allows clients to hear their own words, which can be powerful. In using reflective listening, the social worker is also signaling to clients that she is listening and really understands what they are trying to say. This does not mean that the social worker is agreeing with clients. As clients feel heard in a nonjudgmental and accepting manner, they are more likely to open up and engage with the social worker.

The following dialogue provides a sample of an open-ended question and follow-up reflective responses. In this vignette, the client, Luz, is a 28-year-old Latina who has come under supervision of CPS due to the neglect of her children. She was out partying with her friends when the police arrested her live-in boyfriend/father of her children for methamphetamine and marijuana possession with intent to sell. He had a large amount of the drugs in the home, which were in easy access of her children, ages 9 months and 2 years. Her children were placed in custody until she could be located, and she came to the local shelter looking for them under the influence of methamphetamine. Her children were placed with her mother and were later released to Luz at a court hearing where she was ordered to participate in drug counseling, parenting classes, drug testing, and vocational training. This is the second meeting with her social worker (SW) who has been assigned her case:

> SW: I am here to today to get to know you a little better. There's a lot I don't know about you. How are things going for you?
>
> C: What I don't know is why I have to comply with all of these rules. I just want you people out of my life! I don't need your help.

SW: Having to meet with me and do all the requirements from the judge seems like overkill in your situation.

C: Yes, we were doing just fine until now I have to do all this stuff. Who has time to go to parenting classes? What are they going to tell me anyway? I know what I'm doing.

SW: Going to the classes is not only a waste of your time, but a hardship as well.

C: Yes, we have to get on the bus—try doing that with a baby and a toddler—and carry all the stuff they need plus then leave them in child care while I sit through a class I don't need. Who knows what germs they'll pick up there? I don't need sick kids.

SW: So just the getting there will be a struggle and you are worried about the other kids in the child care.

C: Yes, my infant has a heart condition and I worry about him getting sick.

As the dialogue continues the social worker is learning more about the daily life and difficulties that the client experiences without asking her many questions. Issues and concerns may rise to the surface without the client even being asked about them. At some point the social worker may want to *affirm* the client or comment on a strength or characteristic about her:

SW: Being a parent is important to you and you are very concerned about your children.

Some who practice MI suggest that affirmations come at the beginning of the interview (Leffingwell, Neumann, Babitzke, & Leedy, 2007). Launching into a discussion of problems can put clients on the defensive. Clients can self-affirm by responding to such open-ended questions as, ''What do you like about being a parent?'' ''What things do you do well as a mom?'' ''What are some things I should know about your child?'' As clients tell their social workers positive things about themselves and/or their children, they are seeing themselves in a different light. When social workers *summarize* these qualities back to clients, they are hearing them again as well as know that the social worker sees them as people, not as a problem or a ''case.''

In the dialogue given above, the social worker reflected and then affirmed Luz's concern about her children getting sick. She then asked her what else she did to take good care of her children and summarized all of these things at the end of the discussion:

SW: You have your hands full with two little ones and are very dedicated to them. You work hard to make sure they aren't exposed to germs that might make them sick and you also make sure you take them to their doctor for their scheduled well-baby checks. You make sure they eat healthy foods. You play with them and read them books. You get them to bed at the same time each night. Being a mom is really important to you.

This is an affirmation as well as a summary of what she has discussed with the social worker. Some reading this might think, ''Oh for goodness sake! Quit beating around the bush with this woman. Just tell her what she needs to do!'' This is what Miller and

Rollnick (2002) call the *righting reflex* in that social workers and other counselors think that in the name of expedience or because the issue is so pressing, it is important to inform the client of the required changes or to advise them what to do. In MI, taking time to get to know clients a bit, and hear them out, is important in the engagement process. Using this time in this way can be efficient in that social workers are building a foundation for future positive behavior change.

2. Agenda Setting

Rollnick, Miller, and Butler (2008) introduced their concept of agenda setting, which is when the social worker helps or guides the client to find the focus or target of the discussion. The social worker may have some ideas of what needs to be discussed but also wants to hear about what is important to the individual client. In a continuation of the dialogue from above, the goal of the social worker was to review Luz's case plan and begin to get her engaged and willing to participate in drug treatment:

> SW: I was wondering how you would like to use this time with me today. We could discuss certain aspects of your case plan or we could talk about what you think you might need to do to get your case closed, or we could talk about whatever is important to you right now that you think I could assist you with.
>
> C: I guess I might as well discuss all these stupid requirements that the judge has said I need to do. I really would like to get these over with.
>
> SW: We could discuss the part about the parenting classes, as we have done a little bit already, or we could discuss the drug treatment part, or we could discuss the job part. Which part would you like to discuss?
>
> C: I don't have a drug problem so it would be a real waste of my time to go to a program and be with all those addicts. And what would I do with my kids while I was there? This just seems so stupid to me.
>
> SW: So while it feels like a real waste of your time to have to go to drug counseling, you would like to discuss what might be involved and how it will work with taking your kids and the childcare options.
>
> C: Yeah, I guess I need to know exactly what is going to happen when I go there, even though it will be obvious I don't belong.

Note that the social worker did not argue with Luz by telling her that she had a drug problem and that the judge ordered the drug treatment and testing for a reason. The social worker reflected Luz's concern as well as kept the direction on setting an agenda for their discussion. Miller and Rollnick (2002) call this *rolling with resistance* as exemplified by the social worker when she avoided an argument with the client by reflecting her concerns.

Sometimes clients need direction or information. Luz, in this instance, asked for information about drug treatment. A client may ask her social worker about what might be the best course of action or what in her opinion, she should do. In MI, the social worker can provide advice or opinions but only after permission to do so is given by the client. The

MI practitioner can also provide a *menu of options* for the client to choose from, thus supporting client autonomy as much as possible. This might not be feasible to do in all situations, such as when a judge has specified the type of treatment the client should have.

> C: Well, what do you think I need to do? How can I make sure that you won't take my kids away?
>
> SW: If it is okay with you, I can give you information about what other clients in your situation have done. What do you think?
>
> C: Okay.
>
> SW: Typically I discuss with clients their case plan, the orders made by the judge, and how they think they can best follow these orders. Some clients go to residential drug treatment where they can take their children with them; some go to an outpatient program that goes on for several hours a day; others go to see a counselor once a week. Mostly they all attend AA [Alcoholics Anonymous] or some other support group once or twice a week. They abstain from drug use and use the supports of these programs. They also have clean UA [urine analysis] tests. Often clients go to residential treatment as they are unsure of how they can stay clean and still live around all their using friends and family members. What do you think of these things?
>
> C: I don't know. I think they are all stupid for me. If I have to go to drug treatment, I would want to live here at home and just go from here. I don't want to go live some place where I don't know anyone. Plus I can tell my friends to leave me alone, that I have quit using. They would respect that.

3. Eliciting Change Talk

In this scenario, the social worker guided Luz regarding a discussion of drug treatment and provided information about different types available to her. Luz is still unhappy about going to any kind of counseling but has thought it through a bit how she might handle it. Eliciting from the client her thoughts and ideas helps the social worker learn about Luz's own intrinsic or internal motivators. What the social worker is listening for is *change talk*. Change talk is when the client discusses her desire, ability, reasons, need, and/or commitment to change (DARN-C in MI lingo). MI practitioners listen for this acutely and reflect and summarize it whenever they hear it. Clients hear themselves discuss these aspects of change as they are repeated or rephrased back to them. Sometimes clients provide change talk on their own; in the above dialogue Luz stated that she has the strength (ability change talk) to tell her partying friends to leave her alone. The main emphasis in this process is for the social worker to listen and reflect the client's own words about change. Other times clients don't provide change talk and the social worker uses strategic questions to elicit it from them:

> SW: You can tell your friends to leave you alone, that staying clean and keeping your kids is too important to mess up. What else do you think you can do to make sure your plan is working?

C: Well, I'll go to that stupid counseling [*commitment change talk*] but I am sure I won't fit in. I mean, I barely used drugs. I didn't party that much, it just happened on that one night, wouldn't you know. I told the kids' dad to not be bringing stuff into the house but he did and then the cops showed up. He's the one with a problem. I hope he gets some help in jail.

SW: You are thinking you won't fit in at the counseling and as you have said, getting there will be a hassle. What else might be the downside of going to the counseling?

C: I can think of a thousand other things that I'd rather be doing. What a waste. But I know I have to do it to keep the judge off my back [*reason change talk*].

SW: What might be some of the good things about going?

C: (silence) Well maybe I will learn something [*reason change talk*]. I do know I will have to be firm with my friends. I want to be a good mom [*desire*] and to keep my kids [*reason*]. Maybe other people there will know what it's like to say no and will give me some pointers. I'm usually pretty strong though [*ability*] when I put my mind to something.

SW: On the one hand, you feel it will be hard to go with your children being so little and you are not sure if you will fit in, and on the other hand, because your children are so important to you, you are willing to give it a try. And perhaps there might be some other clients there who are like you and can give you some pointers on how to stay away from drugs, even when friends come around. You know that you are strong and have the ability to follow through on a commitment once you make it.

The social worker evoked from Luz the "downside" of going to drug counseling and then the "good things" or "upside" of participating. Luz had some insight into what might helpful for her there and was able to articulate these things. The social worker then provided a *double-sided reflection* where she summarized both sides of Luz's ambivalence about participating. She reflected Luz's internal motivator—to be a good mom—as well as her picture of herself as being strong. The social worker could continue the conversation with a simple, "What else?" to evoke from Luz other DARN-C types of change talk. As the social worker hears different types of change talk, she could ask Luz to elaborate and then end with a summary of Luz's own words about change.

4. Consolidating Commitment

In MI, as clients listen to themselves express change talk and become more motivated to change, they are then more likely to move into Phase 2 of MI, which is planning the change and strengthening the commitment to it. In this process, the MI practitioner asks key questions about where the client stands and what she will do next. The social worker can also negotiate a change plan and ask for a commitment to it from the client. In the following dialogue, the social worker seeks to learn what Luz has decided to do:

SW: So Luz, given all that we have talked about, what are your next steps?

C: (sighs). I am going to call that program where they work with women and set up an appointment [*commitment change talk*]. I just hope they are friendly people and don't give me a hard time especially when they see that I don't belong there but I have to be there anyway.

SW: When will you do this?

C: I'll call them tomorrow and try to get in there next week. I'll have to see if my mom can watch the kids when I go. I can't promise you that I'll be happy about this but I will try to have a little bit of an open mind [*commitment change talk*].

SW: You'll make an appointment for next week. As long as you think they are nice people and treat you fairly, which I have seen them do with others like yourself, you will at least give it a try. It's not easy to go somewhere unfamiliar, especially when you don't want to. I am here to talk about it with you and provide you support. You are strong and can do something when you put your mind to it.

In this last sample of dialogue, the social worker asked Luz what her next steps were and asked her when she would do the things she promised. This is supportive of the client's autonomy for making decisions where and when she would follow through on what she was mandated to do. The social worker summarized her concerns, offered to provide her support, and affirmed her statement on her own strengths. All of these things are consistent with the spirit of MI of working collaboratively, evoking her thoughts and plans, and supporting her autonomy as much as was possible in this scenario.

Training and Learning MI

The above description and sample dialogue are only a brief introduction to MI. It has been said by Miller and Rollnick (2009) that MI is simple but not easy to learn. It is like learning to play the piano: it takes time, practice, and coaching to learn the skills. Studies of MI trainings have shown that participants may make an initial gain in skills after participating in 2-day workshops; however, it is difficult for them to maintain the skills as well as drop old habits (Forrester et al., 2007; Miller & Mount, 2001). The best way to learn MI is through direct observation, including coding of tapes of interactions with clients as well as personal feedback and coaching (Miller, Yahne, Moyers, Martinez, & Pirritano, 2004). This takes time and commitment. Sometimes those who are interested in doing this contact MI trainers (see www.motivationalinterview.org) and set up personal learning plans, as was the case of how we (the two authors) met. Of course, MI is then only learned on an individual-level basis.

Teaching and training MI systemwide in a CPS setting is challenging for several reasons. First, there is a general lack of awareness that the "micro" skills of the social workers could be the right place to focus training and supervision efforts. The child welfare system is largely constructed in the minds of legislators, who pass their vision down to administrators, who in turn write sweeping policies and procedures that they assume will achieve the outcome they are looking for. This process is predictable, even understandable, given the perspective of the individuals involved in the effort. Second, as mentioned earlier, in most of the cases that come through "the system," parents do make changes in behavior that leads to safer situations for their children. This leads the workforce to judge their current behavior to be appropriate and generally effective. Repeat cases of abuse or neglect are seen as a failure in the assessment of risk, not ascribed to actions taken by any single social worker. Third, there is a commonly recognized bifurcation in the social work field between the "clinical" field and child welfare. "I don't do clinical" or "We're not therapists" are both refrains heard in the offices of at least one child welfare office. The idea that one would carefully examine the interpersonal aspects of communication, as opposed to just "getting the job done," is culturally foreign to many in the child welfare workforce.

Some state administrators have recognized the value of learning MI as a communication method and have mandated all CPS staff to attend at least a one-day training (Hohman & Salsbury, 2009). Although this exposes many to the concepts of MI, it most likely has not produced much in the way of skill change (Forrester et al., 2007; Miller & Mount, 2001). To actually integrate MI into daily social work practice requires a culture/administration that is supportive and allows the time for quality supervision, learning, and coaching. Supervisors who are knowledgeable and skilled in MI can work with staff to find their own motivation and reasons for adopting and learning MI as well as tailor MI to the context of the setting. Teaching and coaching MI skills at this level may be one of the best ways to integrate it in to daily practice. The second author tape records role-plays of typical client-social worker interactions during group supervision and the social workers listen and discuss ways to utilize and improve their own individual use of MI skills. Staff initially was reluctant to be audiotaped but found this method enhanced their skills—and their conversations with clients—to a great extent.

Summary

MI has been shown to be linked to client behavior change, including engagement in treatment services, making it a strong practice method for CPS. Learning MI takes time, practice, feedback, and coaching. CPS systems, administrators, and supervisors can encourage the development of MI skills which can be useful in carrying out the mission and mandates such as for FCP. Having the agency support and accompanying culture to do this is important in integrating this evidence-based practice.

References

Administration for Children and Families. (2010). *Family centered programs.* Retrieved 7/21/2010 from www.childwelfare.gov/famcentered/overview/

Anez, L. M., Silva, M. A., Paris, M., & Bedregal, L. E. (2008). Engaging Latinos through the integration of cultural values and motivational interviewing principles. *Professional Psychology, 39,* 153–159.

California Evidence-Based Clearinghouse for Child Welfare. (2006–2007). Retrieved 7/20/2010, 2008, from www.cachildwelfareclearinghouse.org/

Chaffin, M., Kelleher, K., & Hollenberg, J. (1996). Onset of physical abuse and neglect: Psychiatric, substance abuse, and social risk factors from prospective community data. *Child Abuse & Neglect, 3,* 191–203.

Corbett, G. (2009). What the research says about the MI "spirit" and "competence worldview." *MINT Bulletin, 15,* 3–5.

Donohue, B. (2004). Coexisting child neglect and drug abuse in young mothers. *Behavior Modification, 28*(2), 206–233.

Forrester, D., McCambridge, J., Waissbein, C., Emlyn-Jones, R., & Rollnick, S. (2007). Child risk and parental resistance: Can motivational interviewing improve the practice of child and family social workers in working with parental alcohol misuse? *British Journal of Social Work, 37,* 1–18.

Forrester, D., McCambridge, J., Waissbein, C., & Rollnick, S. (2008). How do child and family social workers talk to parents about child welfare concerns? *Child Abuse Review, 17,* 23–35.

Hettema, J., Steele, J., & Miller, W. R. (2005). Motivational interviewing. *Annual Review of Clinical Psychology, 1,* 91–111.

Hohman, M. M. (1998). Motivational interviewing: An intervention tool for child welfare workers working with substance abusing parents. *Child Welfare, 77*(3), 275–289.

Hohman, M., & Salsbury, L. (2009). Motivational interviewing and child welfare: What have we learned? *APSAC Advisor, 21*(2), 2–6.

Leffingwell, T. R., Neumann, C. A., Babitzke, A. C., Leedy, M. J., & Walters, S. T. (2007). Social psychology and motivational interviewing: A review of relevant principles and recommendations for research and practice. *Behavioural and Cognitive Psychotherapy, 35,* 31–45.

Lundahl, B. W., Kunz, C., Brownell, C., Tollefson, D., & Burke, B. L. (2010). A meta-analysis of motivational interviewing: Twenty-five years of empirical studies. *Research on Social Work Practice, 20,* 137–160.

Madsen, W. C. (2009). Collaborative helping: A practice framework for family-centered services. *Family Process, 48,* 103–116.

Miller, W. R., & Baca, L. M. (1983). Two-year follow-up of bibliotherapy and therapist-directed controlled drinking training for problem drinkers. *Behavior Therapy, 14,* 441–448.

Miller, W. R., & Mount, K. A. (2001). A small study of training in motivational interviewing: Does one workshop change clinician and client behavior? *Behavioural and Cognitive Psychotherapy, 29,* 457–471.

Miller, W. R., & Moyers, T. B. (2006). Eight stages in learning motivational interviewing. *Journal of Teaching in the Addictions, 5,* 3–17.

Miller, W. R., & Rollnick, S. (1991). *Motivational interviewing: Preparing people to change addictive behavior.* New York, NY: Guilford Press.

Miller, W. R., & Rollnick, S. (2002). *Motivational interviewing: Preparing people for change* (2nd ed.). New York, NY: Guilford Press.

Miller, W. R., & Rollnick, S. (2009). Ten things that motivational interviewing is not. *Behavioural and Cognitive Psychotherapy, 37,* 129–140.

Miller, W. R., & Rose, G. S. (2009). Toward a theory of motivational interviewing. *American Psychologist, 64,* 527–537.

Miller, W. R., Yahne, C. E., Moyers, T. B., Martinez, J., & Pirritano, M. (2004). A randomized trial of methods to help clinicians learn motivational interviewing. *Journal of Consulting and Clinical Psychology, 72,* 1050–1062.

NASW (National Association of Social Workers). (2008). *Code of Ethics.* Retrieved 7/19/2010 from www.socialworkers.org/pubs/code/code.asp

Rogers, C. R. (1980). *A way of being.* Boston, MA: Houghton-Mifflin.

Rollnick, S., Miller, W. R., & Butler, C. C. (2008). *Motivational interviewing in health care*. New York, NY: Guilford Press.

Rosengren, D. (2009). *Building motivational interviewing skills*. New York, NY: Guilford Press.

Scott, S., & Dadds, M. R. (2009). Practitioner review: When parent training doesn't work: Theory-driven clinical strategies. *Journal of Child Psychology and Psychiatry*, *50*, 1441–1450.

Wells, S. J., & Fuller, T. (2000). *Elements of best practice in family centered services*. Retrieved 7/21/2010 from www.cfrc.illinois.edu/pubs/Pdf.files/fcsbest.pdf

14

Maternal Alcohol and Drug Abuse

Effective Case Management With High-Risk Mothers and Their Children

Therese Grant

Introduction

More than 20 years ago our research unit at the University of Washington conducted a study on the effects of prenatal cocaine exposure on infants and young children. As a research assistant my job entailed enrolling high-risk cocaine-using mothers, interviewing them, and bringing their babies into the lab for neuropsychological testing. I learned much from these women as they told their stories of severe family dysfunction that was just "life as usual" to them. Now these mothers were giving their babies the same kind of upbringing they had experienced as children because they did not know any other way. As the cocaine study came to an end, our research group decided that for us a more compelling challenge than studying effects of prenatal substance exposure would be to work in a meaningful way with the mothers who delivered these babies—to help them learn to take care of the children they already had, and avoid future births of exposed and affected children. Thus began the Parent-Child Assistance Program (PCAP), a 3-year home visitation/case management intervention.

PCAP began as a federally funded demonstration project with the aims of helping mothers obtain alcohol and drug treatment and stay in recovery; assuring that their children are in a safe, stable home environment; linking families with appropriate community resources; and preventing the births of future alcohol- and drug-affected children. The model demonstrated positive outcomes (Ernst, Grant, Streissguth, & Sampson, 1999; Grant, Ernst, & Pagalilauan, 2003; Grant, Ernst, Streissguth, & Stark, 2005), and the Washington State legislature subsequently funded PCAP sites in nine counties with a present capacity to serve 675 families statewide. The model has been replicated at numerous other sites in the United States and Canada.

A Profile of the Mothers

Women are eligible to enroll in PCAP who: (1) are pregnant or up to six months postpartum; (2) abused alcohol and/or drugs heavily during the pregnancy; and (3) are ineffectively engaged with community service providers. At enrollment, most PCAP clients' lives are characterized not only by substance abuse, but by problems associated with a dysfunctional upbringing and chaotic lifestyle. The typical PCAP client was born to substance-abusing parents. She was physically and/or sexually abused as a child, she did not complete high school, and began to use alcohol and drugs herself as a teenager. She is now in her late twenties, has been through drug treatment and relapsed, and has been in jail more than once. She does not use birth control or plan her pregnancies and now has three or more children, with at least one in the foster care system. She is abused by her current partner, her housing situation is unstable, and her main source of income is welfare.

Complicating this profile is the grim fact that most of our clients experience co-occurring substance-abuse and mental health problems. Among 458 recent PCAP graduates, at intake approximately 90% reported psychiatric problems in their lifetime. About 70% reported one or more psychiatric problems (usually depression, posttraumatic stress disorder [PTSD], or anxiety disorders) in the prior 30 days, higher than national estimates of 50% to 60% (Newmann & Sallman, 2004).

Women who fit this bleak description have been labeled unmotivated and difficult to reach, and many professionals have come to view them as a hopeless population. Yet these mothers *were themselves* the abused and neglected children of just a decade or two ago. They were born into troubled families and grew into young women who delivered babies born into the same circumstances as their mothers had been. Turning our backs on them because they are difficult to work with does not make their problems go away. It does ensure that these women will continue to experience a host of problems associated with intergenerational substance abuse, and continue to bear children who suffer in turn. PCAP's goal was to find a way to connect with this population.

PCAP Basics

PCAP is an intensive home visitation case management model that offers mothers support over 3 years, a period long enough for the process of gradual and realistic change to occur. The model incorporates fundamental and well-known characteristics of effective case management: it is individually tailored, promotes the competency of the client, and is family-centered, community-based, and multidisciplinary. PCAP is a paraprofessional model in the sense that case managers are not degreed in professions such as nursing or social work. Prior to hire, PCAP case managers must have at least a 2-year college degree and 4 years of community-based experience related to substance abuse or associated problems, or the equivalent combination of education and experience. Case managers receive extensive initial and ongoing training and regular supervision.

PCAP is not delivered according to a specific model of behavioral intervention. Instead, case managers develop a positive, empathic relationship with their clients, make regular home visits, and help the women address a wide range of environmental problems associated with their substance abuse. Working with a caseload of 15 to 16 families each, PCAP case managers spend an average of approximately two hours of face-to-face time in the home with each client every other week, and an additional 40 minutes per week working with the client's family members or service providers. PCAP case managers connect women and their families with existing community services and teach them how to access those services themselves. They coordinate services among this multidisciplinary network and assist clients in following through with provider recommendations.

For a substance-abusing mother, the process of becoming a whole person means far more than achieving sobriety. The following definition of *recovery* resonates with PCAP values: "Recovery from substance dependence is a voluntarily maintained lifestyle characterized by sobriety (abstinence from alcohol and nonprescribed drugs), personal health (improved quality of personal life), and citizenship (living with regard and respect for those around you)" (Betty Ford Institute Consensus Panel, 2007). PCAP creates an environment in which women can achieve recovery and offer their children the possibility of having a better life.

When we ask former clients what made the program work for them, we consistently hear "persistence": "My case manager never gave up on me. She kept believing in me until I finally started to believe in myself."

Theoretical Foundations

PCAP is based on three theoretical constructs that inform the intervention approach with clients, and that give shape to day-to-day case management practice.

Relational Theory

Relational theory emphasizes the importance of positive interpersonal relationships in women's growth, development, and definition of self (Miller, 1991), and in their addiction, treatment, and recovery (Finkelstein, 1993). This relationship aspect of intensive intervention—"having a person to talk to who really cared"—may be more critical to improvement than concrete services received (Pharis & Levin, 1991). Building on this concept, PCAP places value on hiring case managers who have successfully overcome difficult personal, family, or community life circumstances similar to those experienced by their clients (for example, substance abuse, poverty). Although not a requirement for employment, a shared history allows case managers to better understand, gain access to, and build rapport with clients who might otherwise be unapproachable. Case managers who have undergone challenging change processes and achieved significant goals are realistic role models who can inspire hope in their clients.

Stages of Change

The PCAP model incorporates stages of change theory, recognizing that people will be at different stages of readiness for change at different times, and that ambivalence about changing behavior is normal and should be expected (Prochaska & DiClemente, 1986). In practice, PCAP case managers use motivational interviewing (MI), a counseling style that helps clients examine their ambivalence about change and increase intrinsic motivation to change (Miller & Rollnick, 1991; Rollnick & Bell, 1991). The basic principles embodied in MI (expressing empathy, developing discrepancy, accommodating to resistance, and supporting self-efficacy) complement relational theory because they call for case managers to be empathetic and nonjudgmental, to listen respectfully to the client, and to trust in the client's perception and judgment about her own life. In PCAP, the most important way case managers affect their clients' self-efficacy is by helping them define explicit goals, accomplish them, and recognize the positive steps they have taken toward behavioral change.

Harm Reduction

The PCAP intervention is shaped by harm reduction theory. Harm reduction views alcohol and drug addiction and associated risks along a continuum, with the goal being to help a client move from excess to moderation, and ultimately to abstinence, in order to reduce the harmful consequences of the habit (Marlatt & Tapert, 1993). In this view, "any steps toward decreased risk are steps in the right direction" (Marlatt, Somers, & Tapert, 1993). In practice, case managers address all risk behaviors (not just substance abuse) in order to reduce harm to both the clients and their children. For example, an important PCAP goal is to reduce the incidence of future drug- and alcohol-exposed births. Although not every client will be able to become abstinent from alcohol and drugs, harm can be reduced by motivating a woman to use an effective family planning method if she is still using substances.

A Two-Pronged Intervention Approach: Working With Clients, Working With Community Service Providers

The PCAP intervention is a therapeutic process that develops over the course of the 3-year program, allowing for a client's gradual transition from initial dependence on the case manager's assistance and support, to interdependence as they work together to accomplish steps toward goals, to independence as the client begins to trust in herself as a worthwhile and capable person and learns the skills necessary to manage her life to the extent possible. The approach is two-pronged: Case managers work directly with clients and their families in the home and elsewhere, and at the same time they work closely with community service providers to identify appropriate services and assure that clients actually receive them.

Working With Clients: Establishing the Relationship

Case managers and clients begin by getting to know each other and establishing the trust that will enable them to work closely together for three years. This bonding process sometimes takes months for clients whose lifelong experiences of abuse and abandonment taught them not to trust anyone. At the first home visit, the case manager identifies and addresses immediate problems such as obtaining clothes and diapers for the newborn or locating temporary housing, activities that demonstrate from the beginning that the case manager cares and can be trusted to follow through. Within the first few weeks, the case manager sets the ground rules by defining the nature of this unique relationship. She may explain:

➢ "We'll have a three-year working relationship, not a three-year friendship."

➢ "My role is not to continually respond to your crises, but to help you move beyond crisis and toward achieving your goals."

➢ "You can trust that I will be with you through ups and downs. There will be times you don't like me; it's okay if you disagree with me, but we have to keep communication open."

➢ "I'll always be truthful with you. I won't lie to you, or for you."

➢ "If you take one step, I'll take two."

Successful case managers are persistent and find unique, sincere ways to build trust without being pushy. They tell their clients a little about themselves and why they chose to do this work. In addition to home visits, they make phone calls and send notes, letters, and text messages to their clients.

PCAP clients are not asked to leave the program because of noncompliance or relapse because, for any person, making fundamental changes in long established behavior patterns will naturally entail setbacks. Relapse should not be a surprise particularly among clients with a long history of drug or alcohol abuse. Beginning at PCAP intake we ask clients to contact their case manager quickly if they relapse so the case manager can help them resume recovery (or treatment), and repair damage done. Case managers do not shame or blame their clients, but instead approach the problem pragmatically and use relapse experiences to help clients examine events that triggered the setback, and to develop resiliency strategies. This practice reduces time clients spend in relapse and increases time between relapses. When a client is able to successfully rebound from a relapse event, she develops self-efficacy as she observes herself coping, overcoming a crisis, and moving on.

Working With Clients: A Family Context

Effective case management takes place within the context of a client's family. To whatever extent possible, PCAP case managers establish rapport with the older children, the husband or significant other, extended family members, and close acquaintances. Everyone in this network is involved in some way with the client's substance abuse and related problems, and they will be affected as well as she attempts to dismantle dysfunctional patterns and relationships. Family members may have a powerful influence over the woman. Gaining their trust (and hopefully their support for her recovery process) is a preliminary step that allows the case manager access and the opportunity to communicate with this important group throughout the intervention. It is important to remember that the family's support is not at all guaranteed; they may resent PCAP's "intrusion" and respond with resistance and triangulation.

The client will not be able to get well if her family members are not well, and case managers often provide referrals and service linkages for the client's family members. For example, for the older children they may obtain summer day camp scholarships or arrange for school psychologist services; for a partner or a sibling they may make referrals to treatment or job training; for the grandmother who cares for the client's children they may arrange for a neighborhood chore service.

Clients sometimes disappear for weeks or months at a time, leaving the children with family members. Having a close relationship with the family allows the case manager to continue to provide services on behalf of the children, as well as to learn the whereabouts of the missing client.

Working With Clients: Home Visitor Safety

As home visitors, PCAP case managers may find themselves in situations in which their personal safety is at risk. In our experience staff have never experienced assault, but they have had belongings stolen, have seen weapons openly displayed in homes, and have been offered drugs by client's acquaintances. PCAP has developed detailed safety guidelines to help staff avoid risky situations, prevent problems, and respond appropriately if they do arise. Topics in the guidelines include: safety policy, training recommendations, health risks and precautions, field safety (before leaving the office, at the home, when protective custody is anticipated, dogs, methamphetamine labs), office and building safety, domestic violence, threats against employees, emergency calls from clients to the PCAP office, and disaster response. PCAP shares these guidelines with other agencies, and we recommend that social service programs further tailor safety protocols under guidance and assistance from their own risk management or law enforcement agencies.

Working With Clients: Role Modeling, Teaching Basic Skills

As stated earlier, most of the mothers in PCAP were themselves abused, neglected, or very troubled as children. No one intervened then, and few of them now have a psychological template for what healthy adult life or parenting might look like. We believe most of our clients do want to be healthy adults and good mothers, but they need a great deal of help understanding what that means. They need to be taught, they need good role models, they need someone to demonstrate and help them practice, to give praise and offer constructive criticism. In practice, case managers find that the most effective teaching techniques are hands-on and experiential. PCAP case managers act as role models in all their activities with the client, including basic skills, telephone etiquette, social behavior, parenting skills, household management, and so on, and they provide explicit direction and instruction in the beginning.

Working With Clients: Identifying Goals and Steps to Achieve Them

The PCAP model is highly individualized and every client is closely involved in the direction the intervention will take for her. Case managers use concrete, explicit methods to help clients identify personal goals and the incremental steps that must be taken to meet those goals. We begin this process by using the Difference Game (Grant, Ernst, McAuliff, & Streissguth, 1997) at one of the first home visits. Adapted from a scale developed by Dunst, Trivette, and Deal (1988), the game is a card sort instrument consisting of 31 cards, each of which name a possible client need (e.g., housing, safe day care, drug or alcohol treatment). The client sorts the cards into two piles, items that would "make a difference," and those that "would not make a difference." Next, the client selects from the yes cards the five items that represent her most important needs, and then ranks these in order of her priorities. The case manager then engages the client in a conversation about each of the five cards selected ("Tell me about this . . . "). During this conversation the client's story emerges, and the case manager begins to learn what is important to her and how she thinks about her problems. Based on this discussion and using MI strategies, the case manager works with her client to identify a few specific, meaningful goals that she would like to work on during the next 2 to 4 months. Together they agree on realistic, incremental ("baby") steps they will *each* take toward meeting those goals, and who will be responsible for accomplishing different tasks. It is critical that some of the steps, no matter how small, be attainable by the client in the designated period, because it is as she observes herself accomplishing desired behavior that her sense of competency develops.

The case manager and the client evaluate and reestablish goals and steps every 4 months, but this doesn't mean goals are static once set. Instead the process is designed to be fluid, dynamic, and responsive to the client's activities and her real world. For example, when a client experiences a crisis (such as housing eviction), instead of allowing work on current goals to be derailed by the housing dilemma, the case manager helps the client turn the crisis into a new goal with logical, appropriate baby steps she must take to resolve the problem. We have learned that:

➤ First goals are often too lofty; they get more realistic over time.

➤ Clients may only be able to work on one or two main goals at a time.

➤ Clients can keep some of the same goals throughout the intervention. Good examples include: "Stay clean and sober" (baby steps: keep going to my AA meetings three times each week; stay away from my old drug-dealing friends; get involved with new friends at my church).

➤ The effectiveness of the Difference Game is that it requires the *client* to think about and choose her most meaningful priorities, instead of someone in a professional capacity determining those for her. The focus is on the woman's possibilities and desired outcomes as opposed to her weaknesses and negative attributes.

Working With Clients: Setting Boundaries

Healthy relationships between case managers and clients require that boundaries be articulated and maintained. Early in the development of the PCAP model we used a focus group process with case managers to identify essential home visitor boundaries, and we continue to refine these standards based on case managers' field experiences, both good and bad. At present, PCAP has 20 boundaries that case managers review and discuss annually. Some boundaries speak to the content of conversations, for example, "Case managers will role model/discuss aspects of their personal lives they believe are beneficial/relevant to a client's progress and well-being, but will not discuss other aspects of their own personal lives." Ask yourself "Whose needs are being met?" Others address realistic situations that arise in the course of the work; for example, "Case managers will not buy goods or services from clients."

Working With Clients: Addressing Health Issues Early in the Intervention Process

At PCAP intake, most of our substance-abusing clients report having mental health problems, and nearly half report having a chronic medical condition. Clients who have unresolved health problems are less likely to be able to take advantage of the services and support case managers offer. Consider these examples. When a client is struggling with an undiagnosed or untreated depressive disorder, it may render her not only incapable of working on self-improvement or court-ordered activities, but on a more basic level it may make it nearly impossible for her to get out of bed in the morning, or return phone calls. When a woman has a low-grade infection or chronic pain, her low energy level may make it difficult for her to accomplish rudimentary daily activities, much less take on the challenges of treatment or job training. When a woman has missing teeth or is suffering from tooth decay or other serious dental problems, she may be in pain and/or be embarrassed to talk or appear in public.

Clients are far more likely to have the energy and ability to work on their goals when their health problems are identified and treated, and when their mental conditions are regulated or stabilized. Working on these issues early in the intervention paves the way for a far more successful PCAP experience. Case managers take the following steps with clients during the first 6 weeks of enrollment in PCAP:

➤ Locate physical, dental, and mental health providers in the community who understand the kinds of clients we work with, and who are willing to work with them in a respectful, nonjudgmental manner.

➤ Obtain releases of information so they can verify important health information (e.g., immunization status, birth control status, recommended medications).

➤ Accompany clients to important appointments to help them communicate their symptoms and problems, and to help them understand what the provider says.

➤ Help clients learn to keep a notebook and write down what the physician tells them.

➤ Work with clients to develop a way to remember to take medications as prescribed and comply with recommendations for diet, activity, and so on.

Working With Clients: Considering Neurocognitive Functioning

Case managers should keep in mind the potential impact of a client's history (e.g., long-term substance abuse, possible fetal alcohol syndrome, possible traumatic head injury as a child or adult) on neurocognitive functioning, including impairments in attention and concentration, learning, impulsivity, abstraction, and executive functioning (Nordahl, Salo, & Leamon, 2003; Scott et al., 2007; Vocci, 2008). These problems may compromise the client's ability to participate in the goal-setting process, and they may impede everyday life functioning in areas such as planning, paying attention to and responding to one's children, and managing a household (Aharonovich et al., 2006; Dean et al., 2009; Henry, Minassian, & Perry, 2010; Sadek, Vigil, Grant, Heaton, & HIV Neurobehavioral Research Center Group, 2007).

For a client who may have such deficits, we suggest arranging for a neuropsychological examination to assess the individual's strengths and weaknesses. This should happen as early as possible in the intervention process in order to allow the time necessary to determine the woman's genuine functional capabilities, map out realistic expectations and evaluate her ability to parent. We recommend that providers working with these women present information in *concrete* rather than abstract ways: employing simple language; demonstrating concepts visually and asking the client to demonstrate her understanding of the information; specifying a limited number of viable alternatives for the client's consideration when a choice needs to be made; and role modeling and practicing specific behaviors.

For some of these mothers, particularly those who have indicators of co-occurring mental health and neurocognitive impairment, the question arises whether they will be able to make good decisions and provide adequate parenting over the long term, given that long-term case management is unlikely to be available through social services agencies. Ideally, a system of coordinated assistance can be achieved via the informal social relationships available within families and communities. In the course of stabilizing a family, a case manager can identify a network of committed community service providers, and work with these providers to identify healthy family members, friends, or neighbors who understand the mother's limitations and will continue to provide oversight and support after formal social services have ended.

Working With Community Service Providers

Research on parenting and substance abuse has long recognized that affected families have complex problems requiring comprehensive services and multidisciplinary intervention approaches (Marsh, Ryan, Choi, & Testa, 2006; Newmann & Sallmann, 2004; Suchman, Pajulo, DeCoste, & Mayes, 2006). Developing productive working relationships among case managers and community service providers is a critical component of the PCAP model, with the aim of facilitating linkages between clients and providers and assuring that families actually receive services intended. Professional and agency effectiveness are improved when the case manager tackles barriers (e.g., lack of transportation or child care, complicated agency paperwork) that could otherwise impede the provider's work with a client. Case managers offer individualized practical assistance and emotional support to clients in a manner not typically provided by service providers.

Working With Community Service Providers: Case Consultation

Beginning at enrollment, and after obtaining necessary releases of information from the client, the PCAP case manager contacts service providers who are already involved with her. In addition, based on PCAP intake assessments, the case manager identifies providers whose skills and services will be necessary to help the client meet her goals. The case manager organizes case consultations or conference calls among members of this group as often as necessary in order to develop a realistic and coordinated service plan that evolves in response to the client's progress and at the same time addresses court or child welfare mandates. Throughout the intervention the case manager functions as a liaison for communication within this network.

Clients should attend these meetings whenever possible for the obvious reason that it is their lives under discussion. Yet many clients have poor emotional regulation and interpersonal skills, and may respond to conflict and disappointments with angry outbursts, or by withdrawing. To prepare for these meetings the case manager helps the client identify her feelings and organize her thoughts, and works with her to practice articulating her views. Over time, the client can learn to speak up in a way that demonstrates respect for herself and others; with practice she can learn to develop and maintain relationships with providers in order to eventually be able to manage competently on her own.

In some situations a "strong arm" in the form of a written agreement with providers is beneficial. Case managers work with providers and clients to draw up agreements that define responsibilities and timelines, and the case manager refers to the document both in supporting the client and in upholding the position of an agency. Clients are more likely to adhere to goals when they participate in establishing the parameters of such a document, and individualized agreements heighten service providers' awareness of the possibilities of working successfully with this high-risk population.

Working With Community Service Providers: Interfacing With the Child Welfare System

The issue of child custody is a recurrent theme in PCAP clients' lives because most of the mothers have at some point had children removed from their care by the state. As regular home visitors, PCAP case managers are in a unique position to identify problems that may place children at risk. They are mandated to report child abuse and neglect, and they instigate removal of children from the home when necessary.

In general, PCAP and child welfare social workers work closely together. However, child welfare recommendations are sometimes based on biased attitudes or too little information. We note also that many of the mothers in PCAP have a limited understanding of the intricacies of the process (e.g., who actually has legal custody of their child, the meaning of terminology such as *third party custody*, *in-home dependency*, *voluntary placement*). This lack of knowledge contributes to a sense of powerlessness, may impede a parent's ability to advocate effectively for herself, and fosters an adversarial relationship with the child welfare system. In order to be responsible participants in the child welfare process, parents must truly understand the proceedings.

As advocates, PCAP case managers help clients comply with their individual contracts and act as liaisons between the agency and the client. At the same time they work closely with child welfare to assure that contract conditions and expectations are met. They keep careful documentation and maintain releases of information so they can communicate with all parties, verify client and agency compliance or noncompliance, and advocate accordingly.

In cases where PCAP workers believe it is necessary to make a report to child welfare, they make every attempt to involve the mother, and when possible support her in making the call to child welfare herself. Typically, when a client is reported to child welfare she feels victimized and blames the person reporting for being the bad guy. PCAP does not want to be in that position. Instead, our role is to help clients address the reality of their lives, and challenge them to take responsibility for their parenting. The turning point for successful resolution of child custody issues occurs when the mother realistically comes to terms with her ability to parent, and is willing to consider the best interests of the child. For some mothers this means deciding to relinquish custody to a foster family that has bonded with the child and would like to adopt. For others it means staying in recovery and doing whatever is necessary to resume or maintain custody of her child/ren.

Strategies for Preventing Future Alcohol- and Drug-Exposed Births

Future alcohol- and drug-exposed births can be prevented in one of two ways: by helping women avoid alcohol and drug use during pregnancy, or by helping them avoid becoming pregnant if they are using alcohol or drugs.

Strategies for Helping Mothers Enter and Complete Alcohol and Drug Treatment

Ideally, a client will acknowledge her own substance abuse problem and ask for help, but this does not always happen. Often the criminal or civil dependency court system will require the client to obtain treatment; sometimes PCAP case managers ask the court to mandate this. Once in a treatment setting clients can detoxify, begin to listen to other women like themselves, and start to examine their own lives.

Gender-specific women's residential treatment programs are usually the first choice of PCAP case managers for their clients, and we are fortunate to have these available in Washington State. A common reason why women are reluctant to enter and stay in treatment is concern about separation from their children. The most ideal inpatient or outpatient treatment programs are those where children may accompany their mothers in a safe environment, free of the chaos to which they are accustomed, and where mothers can learn and practice parenting skills under supervision.

Whether clients are in inpatient or outpatient treatment, PCAP case managers provide emotional support and help resolve problems that may jeopardize staying in treatment (e.g., child care, housing issues). If possible, case managers participate in treatment agency case staffing and discharge planning, and they help clients make posttreatment plans, particularly by exploring options for clean and sober social support and housing. A client is most likely to succeed if she is active in after-care programs; a case manager will introduce her to groups and sometimes attend 12-step meetings with her until the client is comfortable attending on her own. Through all of this, the message is that the client can succeed. If a relapse occurs it's considered a temporary setback, a time to reevaluate and get back on track.

Strategies for Helping Mothers Choose a Family-Planning Method

PCAP's family-planning objectives are to reduce the incidence of alcohol- and drug-exposed births and unintended pregnancies. Case managers help clients understand that "family planning" does not mean *never* having another baby; it does mean planning pregnancy to occur at an optimal time (for example, when the father is someone who will be a good partner and father; when she is in recovery from alcohol and drug addiction; when she has stable housing).

It is essential that case managers connect clients with family-planning clinics or health-care providers who will provide physical examinations, identify potential contraindications for various birth control methods, and determine the safest and most appropriate method for the woman. Case managers are most successful when they accompany their clients to clinic visits to help ask questions and review materials, and when they make sure clients understand how to use prescribed methods correctly.

Introducing family planning and motivating a client to obtain a birth control method is not necessarily a straightforward process for reasons ranging from personal, cultural, and familial, to those imposed by lawmakers or the insurance industry. The process takes time, and may involve setbacks, missed appointments, birth control side effects or failure, or subsequent unintended pregnancy. Anticipating this can reduce case manager frustration.

Administrative Components: Supporting the Case Managers

In a model that places strong emphasis on maintaining long-term, trusting relationships between case managers and clients, it is important that staff turnover be kept to a minimum. Transfer of a caseload to different staff can have psychological consequences for clients and can compromise their outcomes. Specific administrative components of the PCAP model contribute to the health of the organization, to job satisfaction and retention.

Individual Supervision PCAP supervisors are master's level or credentialed clinicians who meet individually with case managers for at least an hour, ideally every week and at a minimum twice each month, and are available for consultation throughout the week either in person or by phone. The supervisor knows every woman who is enrolled in PCAP because she screens incoming referrals, assigns new clients to case managers, administers project consent procedures, and conducts a thorough intake interview with each client (using the Addiction Severity Index). This personal familiarity is a strong asset as the supervisor guides and follows the case throughout the intervention. During supervision, as an administrator the supervisor discusses each client's status and reviews paperwork, case notes, and how the case manager allocates her time. As a teacher, she explores with the case manager how case activities are related to client goals, and helps the case manager differentiate between crises that need PCAP intervention versus those the client may be ready to handle herself. She works with the case manager to reflect on emotional reactions to the client and her child, and to examine and understand how these feelings relate to the choices the case manager makes about day-to-day activities with the client. As a mentor, the supervisor discusses areas of growth the case manager would like to see for herself and opportunities for additional training.

Weekly Staff Meetings Weekly group staff meetings are intended to be less about business matters and more about case discussions that provide case managers with insight, new ideas, and support from their colleagues. As she works with individual case managers during supervision sessions, the clinical supervisor listens for common problems or barriers that might be better addressed in the group, and she listens as well for success stories that illustrate effective strategies or breakthrough moments with clients. The supervisor asks case managers to discuss specific cases with the group and solicit ideas and feedback. Within two or three weeks, a case manager gives an update to the group, so others can know how their suggestions worked.

Periodically, the supervisor invites a local service provider (e.g., child welfare services, Planned Parenthood) to attend a staff meeting to talk about their agency services and dynamics, and discuss tips on how PCAP can work successfully with the agency. This familiarity builds positive relationships between PCAP and other providers that ultimately benefit the clients; it helps to prevent future service barriers; and it is invaluable in addressing and resolving service barriers and misunderstandings that may arise in the future.

Conclusion

Pregnant and parenting substance-abusing mothers can be a particularly challenging clientele. The PCAP experience has demonstrated that with the expertise of knowledgeable, dedicated staff and with the commitment of strong community partnerships, we have the potential to serve mothers and children affected by alcohol and drug abuse, improve their quality of life, and ultimately prevent the births of future alcohol-damaged children.

For more information about the Parent-Child Assistance Program (PCAP), including training opportunities and materials available, please contact the author at granttm@u .washington.edu.

References

Aharonovich, E., Hasin, D. S., Brooks, A. C., Liu, X., Bisaga, A., & Nunes, E. V. (2006). Cognitive deficits predict low treatment retention in cocaine dependent patients. *Drug and Alcohol Dependence, 81*(3), 313–322.

Betty Ford Institute Consensus Panel. (2007). What is recovery? A working definition from the Betty Ford institute. Betty Ford center and the treatment research institute. *Journal of Substance Abuse Treatment, 33*(3), 221–228.

Dean, A. C., London, E. D., Sugar, C. A., Kitchen, C. M., Swanson, A. N., Heinzerling, K. G., & Shoptaw, S. (2009). Predicting adherence to treatment for methamphetamine dependence from neuropsychological and drug use variables. *Drug and Alcohol Dependence, 105*(1-2), 48–55.

Dunst, C. J., Trivette, C. M., & Deal, A. G. (1988). *Enabling and empowering families: Principles and guidelines for practice.* Cambridge, MA: Brookline Books.

Ernst, C. C., Grant, T. M., Streissguth, A. P., & Sampson, P. D. (1999). Intervention with high-risk alcohol and drug-abusing mothers: II. 3-year findings from the Seattle model of paraprofessional advocacy. *Journal of Community Psychology, 27*(1), 19–38.

Finkelstein, N. (1993). Treatment programming for alcohol and drug-dependent pregnant women. *International Journal of the Addictions, 28*(13), 1275–1309.

Grant, T., Ernst, C. C., Pagalilauan G., & Streissguth, A. P. (2003). Post-program follow-up effects of paraprofessional intervention with high-risk women who abused alcohol and drugs during pregnancy. *Journal of Community Psychology, 31*(3), 211–222.

Grant, T., Ernst, C., Streissguth, A., & Stark, K. (2005). Preventing alcohol and drug exposed births in Washington state: Intervention findings from three parent-child assistance program sites. *American Journal of Drug and Alcohol Abuse, 31*(3), 471–490.

Grant T. M., Ernst C. C., McAuliff, S., & Streissguth, A. P. (1997). The difference game: Facilitating change in high-risk clients. *Families in Society: The Journal of Contemporary Human Services, 78*(4), 429–432.

Henry, B. L., Minassian, A., & Perry, W. (2010). Effect of methamphetamine dependence on everyday functional ability. *Addictive Behaviors, 35*(6), 593–598.

Marlatt, G. A., Somers, J. M., & Tapert, S. F. (1993). Harm reduction: Application to alcohol abuse problems. *NIDA Research Monograph, 137*, 147–166. Review.

Marlatt, G. A., & Tapert, S. F. (1993). Harm reduction: Reducing the risks of addictive behaviors. In J. S. Baer, G. A. Marlatt, & R. McMahon (Eds.), *Addictive behaviors across the lifespan* (pp. 243–273). Newbury Park, CA: Sage.

Marsh, J. C., Ryan, J., Choi, S., & Testa, M. (2006). Integrated service for families with multiple problems: Obstacles to family reunification. *Children and Youth Services Review, 28*, 1074–1087.

Miller, J. B. (1991). The development of women's sense of self. In J. D. Jordan, A. G. Kaplan, J. B. Miller, I. P. Stiver, & J. L. Surrey (Eds.), *Women's growth in connection* (pp. 11–26). New York, NY: Guilford Press.

Miller, W. R., & Rollnick, S. (1991). *Motivational interviewing: Preparing people to change addictive behavior.* New York, NY: Guilford Press.

Newmann, J. P., & Sallman, J. (2004) Women, trauma histories, and co-occurring disorders: Assessing the scope of the problem. *Social Service Review, 78*(3), 466–499.

Nordahl, T. E., Salo, R., & Leamon, M. (2003). Neuropsychological effects of chronic methamphetamine use on neurotransmitters and cognition: A review. *Journal of Neuropsychiatry and Clinical Neurosciences, 15*(3), 317–325. Review.

Pharis, M. E., & Levin, V. S. (1991). "A person to talk to who really cared": High-risk mothers' evaluations of services in an intensive intervention research program. *Child Welfare, 70*(3), 307–320.

Prochaska, J. O., & DiClemente, C. C. (1986). Toward a comprehensive model of change. In W. R. Miller & N. Heather (Eds.), *Treating addictive behaviors: Processes of change.* New York, NY: Plenum Press.

Rollnick, S., & Bell, A. (1991). Brief motivational interviewing for use by the nonspecialist. In W. R. Miller & S. Rollnick (Eds.), *Motivational interviewing: Preparing people to change addictive behavior.* New York, NY: Guilford Press.

Sadek, J. R., Vigil, O., Grant, I., Heaton, R. K., & Group, the HIV Neurobehavioral Research Center (2007). The impact of neuropsychological functioning and depressed mood on functional complaints in HIV-1 infection and methamphetamine dependence. *Journal of Clinical and Experimental Neuropsychology, 29*(3), 266–276.

Scott, J. C., Woods, S. P., Matt, G. E., Meyer, R. A., Heaton, R. K., Atkinson, J. H., & Grant, I. (2007). Neurocognitive effects of methamphetamine: A critical review and meta-analysis. *Neuropsychology Review, 17,* 275–297.

Suchman, N., Pajulo, M., Decoste, C., & Mayes, L. (2006). Parenting interventions for drug-dependent mothers and their young children: The case for an attachment-based approach. *Family Relations, 55*(2), 211–226.

Vocci, F. J. (2008). Cognitive remediation in the treatment of stimulant abuse disorders: A research agenda. *Experimental and Clinical Psychopharmacology, 16*(6), 484–497. Review.

PART VII
Other Programs for CPS and Other High-Risk Parents

In Chapter 15, Charlotte Booth and Shelley Leavitt discuss the Homebuilders program, which provides intensive, time-limited, home- and community-based family preservation services designed to prevent unnecessary out-of-home placements and to speed the return of children from placement. Therapists with small caseloads (serving only two to three families at a time) are available to clients on a 24/7 basis. They provide cognitive behavioral interventions to achieve clinical objectives as well as case management to help clients meet basic living needs and connect with community resources.

In Chapter 16, Thomas Phelan describes the 1–2–3 Magic Program, which is primarily a discipline instruction intervention that also attempts to improve parent-child attachment, children's oppositional and disruptive behavior, compliance with adult requests, and family relationships and emotional well being. In Chapter 17, Anna Edwards-Guara and her colleagues describe SafeCare, an in-home training program for parents who have been referred for child maltreatment and that attempts to improve parenting skills in child behavioral management, planned activities, home safety, and child health.

In Chapter 18, Robert Pushak and Donald Gordon describe Parenting Wisely, a video-based program that provides training in the use of positive parenting skills. After completing the computer portion of the program, parents are given a workbook to use in practicing the skills. In Chapter 19, Stephen Bavolek and Rhenda Hotard Hodnett summarize the Nurturing Parenting Programs, which are designed to build nurturing parenting skills among parents at risk for child abuse and neglect.

CHAPTER

15

The HOMEBUILDERS®
Model of Intensive
Family–Preservation Services

Charlotte L. Booth and Shelley E. Leavitt

Introduction

The term *family preservation* was coined in the early 1980s and is used generally to mean avoiding unnecessary removal of children from families, and specifically to refer to programs intended to strengthen families and increase child safety. Within a broad variety of family preservation programs, Intensive Family Preservation Services (IFPS) often refers to programs based on the HOMEBUILDERS® program, established in 1974 in Tacoma, Washington.

Homebuilders is an intensive in-home family treatment program designed to prevent unnecessary out-of-home placement in foster care, group care, psychiatric hospitals, or corrections institutions. The model is also widely used to speed the return of children from placement. The families served must have children in imminent danger of placement, or have children in placement who cannot be reunified without intensive services. The presenting problems may include child abuse and/or neglect, family conflict, juvenile delinquency, developmental disabilities, and mental health problems of children or parents.

Once accepted into the program, families are provided with time-limited intensive services. Therapists serve only two to three families at a time, and are available to clients 24 hours a day, 7 days a week. Therapists use cognitive behavioral interventions to increase life skills, enhance family relationships, and improve individual and family functioning. In addition to direct therapy, therapists provide families with a wide range of supports, including helping with basic needs such as food, shelter, and clothing, and connection with formal and informal community resources.

To help engage and motivate family members, the Homebuilders model attempts to minimize all known barriers to service. All of the work takes place in the family home and neighborhood. Sessions are offered at times that are convenient to the family. Concerns such as lack of adequate food or housing are immediately addressed. Therapists avoid use of labels and diagnoses, as these may offend clients. Clients are not asked to complete assessment tools or forms; intake paperwork is kept minimal.

The safety of family members, therapists, and other members of the community is the highest priority. Preventing placement or returning children home is not appropriate if it leaves children in danger.

Populations Served

The original funding for Homebuilders was from the U.S. National Institute of Mental Health, and the first population served was troubled adolescents and their families. Significant early funding also came from the U.S. Office of Juvenile Justice and Delinquency Prevention. In the United States today, IFPS programs operate primarily within the child welfare system. Referrals are usually made by public agency Child Protective Services staff.

Families referred to Homebuilders are typically experiencing multiple problems, some of which are chronic in nature. Homebuilders is not intended, nor is any service able, to help families resolve all of their problems. Rather, the model is designed to keep children safe while helping the family reach a level of functioning that allows their children to remain at home. To reach this limited objective, therapists focus specifically on addressing those issues most related to the threat of placement, and on helping families access other services and supports as needed.

Because it is one of the few treatment models researched in the field, rather than a university or other more controlled setting, Homebuilders has, from its inception, tested the effectiveness of the program across many ethnic and cultural groups. Two studies have specifically addressed the effectiveness of the model with families of color, and found it to be equally or slightly more effective with minority families than with Caucasian families (Fraser, Pecora, & Haapala, 1991; Kirk & Griffith, 2008). Dr. Vanessa Hodges has examined the values base and components of the model in terms of their appropriateness for use with families of color (Tracy, Haapala, Kinney, & Pecora, 1991).

Program Philosophy

The underlying philosophy of Homebuilders is that it is best to raise children in their own family whenever possible. Although it may be necessary, out-of-home placement is traumatic for children, and does not teach families how to keep their children safe. Immediate and extended families provide an important sense of belonging and cultural identity.

A major goal of Homebuilders is to teach family members new problem-solving and parenting skills, and help them learn how to access existing community support systems and other less intensive services and resources when needed. While Homebuilders offers short-term services, we know there will likely be future family crises or that families will need other services over time. We view the best approach to meeting a family's need for assistance as episodic, rather than continuous.

A "Whole Cloth" Model

Homebuilders has been described as a *whole cloth* model, in that it is based on an articulated set of values and beliefs, and includes structural components as well as clinical intervention components. Although no component analysis has been done to ascertain which of these is necessary for success, there is some speculation that it is the combination that accounts for the success of the model (Whittaker, Kinney, Tracy, & Booth, 1990). We do know from research that programs that do not demonstrate adherence to the structural and clinical components are less likely to show positive outcomes (Miller, 2006).

Program Values and Beliefs

Program values and beliefs drive service delivery design, and guide therapists' thinking about how to view the clients they serve and their role as a clinician. These values and beliefs are at the core of the model, and are directly tied to many of the model components. Our experience has been that therapists who share these values and beliefs are more successful implementing the model. Clearly delineating these thus provides a way for the program and prospective therapists to assess job fit.

We Cannot Predict Which Situations Are Most Amenable to Change

Even after numerous analyses of the relationship of success to various client characteristics, we have found few predictors of which families will not benefit from the program. Except where the potential for violence leaves family members at too much risk, all families deserve a chance to learn to resolve their problems together before children are removed.

A Crisis Is an Opportunity for Change

In times of high stress or crisis, people find their usual ways of managing their life are no longer working. This experience of the breakdown in usual coping methods creates an opportunity for change. By being available to families during those times, we can more effectively help them.

It Is Our Job to Motivate Clients and Instill Hope

Many clients served by Homebuilders have lost hope that their life can improve. Most have been through numerous programs and have experienced limited success. Therapists cannot expect families to be motivated at the beginning of service. We teach therapists, and they teach families that all people change constantly as a result of planned learning and life's experiences. Knowing that all people can and do change helps therapists and clients be optimistic.

Family Members Are Our Partners

The families we serve have the most complete information about themselves and their situations. They have more information than we, with all our professional insight, will ever have. They also have information about potential constraints and resources that can make our interventions either succeed or fail. We must work with them as partners to access this information.

We Can Make Life Worse for Families

Family relations are often fragile and susceptible to damage by poorly applied techniques. We can do harm as well as good. Manipulating, strategizing against, or tricking clients can reinforce their feelings of impotence and confusion. If therapists set expectations too high, clients feel overwhelmed. If we see clients as being resistant, they know this and it increases their feelings of anger and inadequacy. If we tell clients that they do not understand how to resolve their family problems, they feel less competent.

We Must Guard Against the Tendency to Want to Remake Clients Into Our Own Ideal Image of a Family

Our own image of the ideal family is shaped by our personal experiences and culture. The families we see often have experiences and cultural beliefs and customs that differ from ours. We need to be aware of our own beliefs about family and accepting of other ideas of family.

People Are Doing the Best They Can

Family members do not usually intend to harm one another. People attempt to manage their lives using the behaviors they know. With the information, energy, and resources any of us has at any point in time, most of us are doing the best we can. By taking this view of families, we are less likely to be caught up in the blaming that is common in families experiencing pain.

It Is Our Job to Empower Family Members

The model empowers families by actively involving them in assessment and service planning, providing psychoeducation, and teaching life skills. Even when helping clients meet their basic needs, our goal is to teach them to access what they need for themselves.

Structural Components

The Homebuilders model has ten structural components that define the parameters within which the clinical intervention is delivered. Components define the population to be served, where services are delivered, expected therapist availability to clients, program staffing, service intensity and duration, data collection requirements, and training and quality assurance activities. Adherence to these components is tracked and reported as part of ongoing program evaluation and monitoring of model fidelity.

Focus on a Specific Target Population

The program is an alternative to the unnecessary placement of children into out of home care. Supervisors carefully screen referrals to ensure serving only families whose children are in imminent danger of placement, or are in need of intensive services to achieve reunification.

Twenty-Four-Hour Availability for Intake

Therapists are available to receive referrals 24 hours a day, 7 days a week. Therapist openings are posted with the public agency referents 24 hours in advance.

Immediate Response to Referral

Once a referral is accepted, therapists meet with family members in their home as soon as possible; typically no more than 24 hours after referral. This rapid response allows high-risk families to be referred. Because families at imminent risk of having a child removed cannot safely wait for services, Homebuilders programs do not maintain waiting lists.

Services Provided in the Natural Environment

Services are delivered in clients' homes and other settings in their day-to-day life. It is possible to reach more seriously troubled clients by seeing them in their own homes. Many families are too disorganized or overwhelmed to schedule and transport themselves to office visits. Some have no child care or transportation. We have found that cancellations and dropouts decrease when services are brought to the client. In-home interventions also increase the likelihood that all family and household members will participate in counseling.

In-home services allow more accurate assessments and more appropriate treatment plans, because therapists directly observe family interactions and routines, children's behavior, and the physical environment. Therapists can observe family members trying out new skills, revise treatment plans as needed based on those observations, and provide support until clients experience success. In-home services also increase a therapist's credibility; clients know the therapist has directly witnessed family difficulties rather than just hearing about them. Generalization of learning is facilitated when services are provided in the natural environment of the client. Finally, family members appreciate in-home services. It is more convenient for them, and many say it helps alleviate their embarrassment at having to receive services.

Intensive Services

Services are intensive, with caseloads averaging two families at a time. Hours of contact with family members are allocated according to their needs. Total time per family usually varies between 16 and 20 hours per week, about half of which is face to face and telephone contact with family members.

This intensity of services allows therapists to serve families who need frequent contact to ensure child safety. High intensity also facilitates rapid change. It allows the time to provide a range of psychoeducational interventions as well as help meet basic needs of the family. With low caseloads, therapists are able to be flexible about the length of client sessions, and can take advantage of times when the family is most open to change.

Time-Limited Services

Services average 4 to 6 weeks, with the option of service extension if the risk of placement remains high and it is likely further service will lower that risk.

Four to 6 weeks seems a short time. It is important to remember that 40 hours of face-to-face and telephone contact are typically delivered in this time. Although therapists, clients, and referring workers sometimes express a wish for a longer intervention, success at averting placement is attainable in this time period. The model does allow for one or two "booster sessions" during the 6 months following service closure.

Twenty-Four Hour Availability to Clients

Therapists ask family members to contact them whenever a crisis occurs, or whenever the therapist could be most helpful. Therapists are available to their clients 24 hours a day, 7 days a week. When a family's therapist is not available, the therapist's supervisor or another Homebuilders therapist responds to the family.

Therapists Operate Within a Supervised Team

Because of the high-risk families served, and the 24/7 nature of the job, Homebuilders requires therapists to work within a team, with a .20 FTE supervisor per therapist. Teams generally consist of three to five therapists and one supervisor. Each family is assigned a single therapist, who uses the supervisor and team as back up. The team meets at least weekly, and all open cases are staffed. In rare circumstances, a supervisor or second therapist may also assist the family. Therapists generally have a master's degree in social work, counseling, or a related field. They are not required to be licensed.

Accountability

The program routinely uses a variety of methods to ensure accountability. Placement prevention and reunification outcomes are tracked. Data are collected on behavior change, goal attainment and fidelity to all aspects of the program model. Clients and referents are asked to provide written feedback about their satisfaction with services.

Training and Quality Assurance

Specialized training and ongoing quality assurance is integral to the model. Training for clinical staff includes at least 5 days initial training, and 6 days of advanced training. Program supervisors receive additional specialized supervisory training. Program replication and quality assurance activities include review of adherence to standards and fidelity measures, direct observation of therapist sessions, consultation with therapist teams, and client record reviews.

Intervention Components

The Homebuilders model has nine intervention components that define the clinical activities that take place within the framework of the structural components. These intervention components guide the work of the clinician. Adherence to these components is tracked and reported as part of ongoing program evaluation and monitoring of model fidelity.

Flexible Scheduling

Therapists work a flexible schedule, with considerable variance in the total hours worked per week. This, combined with the low caseload, allows them to give clients as much time as needed, when they need it. Intake visits may be several hours in duration; therapists stay long enough to be sure clients are calm and safety plans are in place. After the initial visit, appointments are scheduled as often as needed, typically three to five times per week. Sessions are held at times convenient to the families, including evenings and weekends. Sessions are offered on holidays when needed. To take advantage of crises and "teachable moments," visits are often scheduled at times when family problems are most likely to occur.

Individually Tailored Services

In addition to flexibility in scheduling and length of sessions, Homebuilders requires flexibility in service design, individually tailoring the goals and intervention activities to the needs of each family. Clients may need help with a variety of life skills including parenting, communication, emotion control, problem solving, assertiveness, and management of drug or alcohol use. They may request help in meeting such basic needs as food, clothing, or shelter. They may work on building a stronger social support network or interacting with school or social service personnel. Therapists are expected to implement a wide array of research-based treatment strategies and approaches.

In some family preservation models, paraprofessionals rather than therapists are used to help families meet their hard service needs. In Homebuilders, the therapist is responsible for addressing all the needs of the family. We have found that activities such as helping clean an apartment or driving a client to the grocery store are powerful engagement tools. Clients are grateful for the help, and often share critical information when they are involved in doing concrete tasks with their therapist.

Engagement and Motivation

Therapists take responsibility for engaging clients and helping them increase their motivation for change. Therapists use a collaborative approach to treatment. Engagement strategies include reflective listening, Motivational Interviewing (MI), (Miller & Rollnick, 2002), showing respect, acting as a guest in the family's home, meeting individually with family members as well as with the family as a group, and meeting at times and places convenient to the family.

Assessment and Goal Setting

Therapists conduct a client-directed assessment across the family's life domains, including behavioral analyses, safety assessment and safety planning, domestic violence assessment, suicide assessment, and crisis planning. Assessment tools include: NCFAS—North Carolina Family Assessment Scale (Reed-Ashcraft, Kirk, & Fraser, 2001); Your Deal® Assessment Cards developed by the Institute to help clients identify their values, strengths, and goals; and functional behavioral analysis. Behaviorally specific and measurable goals and outcomes are developed and evaluated with the family.

Behavior Change

Perhaps the most critical aspect of the IFPS intervention is the use of cognitive and behavioral evidence-based practices. These practices include: Cognitive Behavior Therapy (CBT) such as Rational Emotive Behavior Therapy (REBT), (Ellis & Dryden, 2007) and behavioral interventions such as skills training, behavioral parent training, coaching, shaping, behavioral rehearsal, reinforcement, positive behavioral support, and relapse prevention and harm reduction strategies.

Skills Development

Therapists teach family members a variety of life skills, including parenting, decision making, mood control and self-management, relapse prevention, resisting peer pressure, interpersonal relations, developing daily routines, and household management. Teaching methods include direct teaching, provision of educational materials, coaching, practice, feedback, and homework.

The Homebuilders model focuses on the goal of using services to help clients become strong instead of dependent. Helping family members learn new life skills empowers them. Even when helping clients meet their basic needs, our goal is to teach them to access what they need for themselves. We might go with clients to a food bank, to support them and model interactions with the agency, but the goal from the beginning is to teach them how to do it on their own.

Personal Scientist Approach

Therapists and family members are taught to think and behave as personal scientists. Scientists gather data, conduct experiments, analyze experimental outcomes, and conduct more experiments. The family and therapist assess family strengths and problems, (gather data), design and implement change strategies (experiment), assess the effectiveness of the change strategies (evaluate outcomes), and modify the intervention (conduct more experiments). We have found there is as much to learn from failures as from successes.

Concrete and Advocacy Services

The IFPS therapist provides and/or helps the family access concrete goods and services that are directly related to achieving the family's goals, while teaching them to advocate and meet these needs on their own. Flexible funds are available for concrete needs.

Community Coordination and Interactions

Client families often experience difficulty interacting with others in the community. Therapists coordinate and advocate with other service and supports including schools, health and mental health providers, juvenile justice, and other social services. Therapists work with the public agency to coordinate services, attend family team meetings, and help identify and access ongoing informal and formal resources and supports.

The Homebuilders Model in Action

Homebuilders is not a highly prescriptive model with required session by session topics or activities. Instead, there are specific components that are delivered within an individualized and tailored approach, using research-based strategies. These components are overlapping and often occur simultaneously. For example, the Homebuilders therapist uses similar strategies (e.g., reflective listening) to engage and motivate family members and also to assess problems and strengths. The primary treatment components and steps are:

➤ Engagement and motivation
➤ Holistic assessment and identification of individual and family strengths
➤ Goal setting and treatment planning
➤ Behavior change
➤ Assessing and maintaining progress

Engagement and Motivation

Engagement and motivation begins with the first family contact, which is typically in the phone call to set up the first home visit. During this call the therapist briefly describes the program, and spends time active listening to the parent's concerns and situation. Therapists also use MI to begin enhancing the family members' motivation to participate in the service. For those families without a phone, either the referent arranges the first face-to-face meeting, or the Homebuilders therapist drops by the family's home with the goal of setting up the first session.

During the first meeting, which typically lasts 2 to 3 hours, a large portion of the time is devoted to active/reflective listening to gather information, engage family members, and de-escalate strong emotions. Therapists show a personal interest in all aspects of the family's life, not just their problems (e.g., chatting about their interests, home, pets). In the first telephone call and face-to-face visit, therapists demonstrate respect by asking permission (e.g., where to sit, who to involve in the sessions), reflecting individual family member's feelings and perceptions of the problems; and addressing the parents by their names, rather than Mom or Dad. Therapists use behaviorally specific language and avoid labels, jargon, and inferences. It is important for therapists to remember that they are guests in the family's home and their goals of the first visit are to begin developing a relationship with family members, begin the assessment process, structure for safety, and be invited back. Although the first session may include all family members, it is also helpful to meet individually with family members in other early sessions to focus on engagement and motivation at the individual, personal level.

Holistic Assessment

Assessment begins with the initial phone calls with the referring worker and client family, and is ongoing throughout the intervention The primary skills and tools for assessment include reflective listening; direct observations; functional behavior analyses; and gathering information from family members, referral sources, schools, other mental health professionals, social service, and health care providers as indicated. Other tools therapists may use include the Your Deal® assessment cards, and parenting inventories and measures (e.g., parenting inventories, social support network maps). Therapists use the NCFAS to summarize their assessment of strengths and problems within the major domains of environment, parental capabilities, family interactions, family safety, and child well-being. For reunification interventions, the scale includes two additional domains; readiness for reunification, and ambivalence. In addition to examining these domains, therapists gather information about individual and family routines, learning styles, culture, and social supports. A written assessment that includes the ratings for each domain and a summary of the strengths and problems identified in each domain is usually completed after the first few home visits with the family. Although the written family assessment is completed early in the intervention and guides goal development, assessment is continuous. Assessment of safety of family members is ongoing, and safety plans are developed and implemented at any time during the intervention should concerns arise.

Goal Setting and Treatment Planning

No later than the end of the first week, at least one goal is set with the family that is directly related to the reasons for referral. Once the written assessment is completed, a treatment plan is developed that includes two to three major goals and specific indicators of goal achievement (i.e., client report, therapist observation, and other measureable indicators). The plan, which is the *road map* to the intervention, includes specific descriptions of what the therapist will do (e.g., MI, skill building, cognitive strategies, teaching methods) to help family members reach the goals. Goal progress is assessed throughout the service, and intervention strategies are revised based on observed progress. Figure 15.1 shows the primary intervention activities and key skills utilized during early sessions with families.

Behavior Change: Cognitive and Behavioral Interventions

As discussed earlier, therapists use a variety of cognitive and behavioral intervention strategies to facilitate behavior change. Treatment plans typically include both a cognitive and behavioral component to address emotional and behavioral concerns. Therapists help family members recognize how their feelings and behavior are influenced by their cognitions, and how to control and change their cognitive distortions. Therapists

Figure 15.1   Primary Activities: Early Sessions

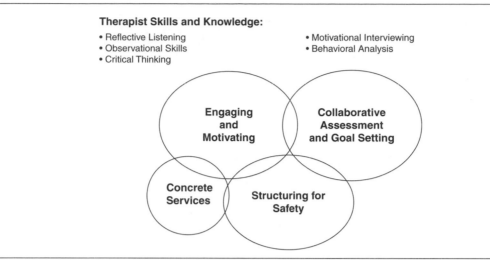

introduce these strategies to young children using stories like "Maxwell's Magnificent Monster" (Water, 2008), and to teens and adults using a variety of methods including exercises, practice, and homework activities. Using a behavioral framework, therapists help family members identify and target problem behaviors, conduct functional behavioral analyses, and implement strategies for reducing problem behaviors and increasing more helpful behaviors.

Behavior Change: Teaching Skills

One of the most important behavioral change strategies is teaching new skills to family members. Therapists teach a wide range of skills from household maintenance and management, baby care and parenting skills, to sophisticated cognitive change skills. Some of the common skills we teach include: establishing daily routines; using effective praise and positive attention; planned ignoring; developing motivation (reinforcement, consequence) systems; tracking and charting behavior, "I" messages; active listening; assertive skills; giving clear requests; problem solving and negotiation; and decision making skills. In addition, we help parents teach their children skills such as: following instructions, accepting no for an answer, asking permission, and resisting peer pressure.

Therapists use a variety of teaching methods and tools, which they tailor to the family members' learning styles, culture, literacy, and specific situations. These methods include direct teaching, coaching, modeling, reinforcing small steps, providing written and audio/visual tools, role-playing and practice, and developing individualized tools such as writing stories to teach CBT concepts and skills, charts, and other visual aids. To facilitate learning, therapists assign homework, which can be as simple as asking the parent to use two praise statements over the next day, or as complex as using a "feeling thermometer," behavior charts, or diaries to track behavior, cognitions, and feelings. The primary activities during the behavior change step are shown in Figure 15.2.

Figure 15.2 Primary Activities: Behavior Change

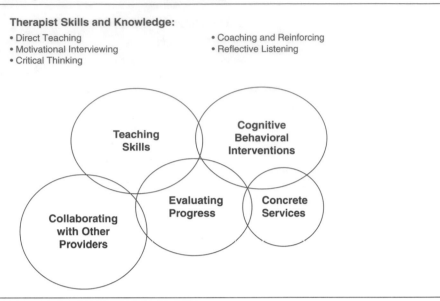

Therapist Skills and Knowledge:

- Direct Teaching
- Motivational Interviewing
- Critical Thinking

- Coaching and Reinforcing
- Reflective Listening

Teaching Skills

Cognitive Behavioral Interventions

Collaborating with Other Providers

Evaluating Progress

Concrete Services

Assessing and Maintaining Progress

Throughout the intervention, therapists assess goal attainment and progress, and make adjustments to the intervention methods as needed. They also identify ongoing supports, services, and resources to help families maintain and continue their changes. During the last week, therapists help families develop a formal progress maintenance plan, which involves family ratings of goal attainment and a written maintenance plan for each intervention goal. These plans often include continued practice and reinforcement of the new skills and routines; relapse prevention strategies; and connections with formal and informal resources. At closure, therapists complete a "post" NCFAS, using the tool to measure changes in the primary domains, and families and referents are asked to complete consumer satisfaction surveys to provide us with feedback on the intervention and goal attainment. Figure 15.3 shows the major activities and therapist skills at service closure.

Case Example: Motivating Clients

The family included a 23-year-old mother, Danielle, and her 3-year-old daughter, Maria (not their actual names). Danielle had just completed 6 months of inpatient drug treatment for an addiction to a prescription pain medication. The residential treatment program allowed Maria to live with her mother throughout the treatment.

Upon leaving treatment, Danielle was given a number of requirements by CPS (child protective services). However, after a month of being home, Danielle had yet to begin any of the required services, and CPS was extremely concerned for Maria's safety. The referent wanted Homebuilders to motivate Danielle to enroll Maria in childcare; have Danielle begin random urine analyses; have Danielle begin an outpatient drug treatment program; and have Danielle end her relationship with Maria's father, who was described as abusive and was considered to be the biggest threat to Danielle's sobriety.

Figure 15.3 Primary Activities: Closure

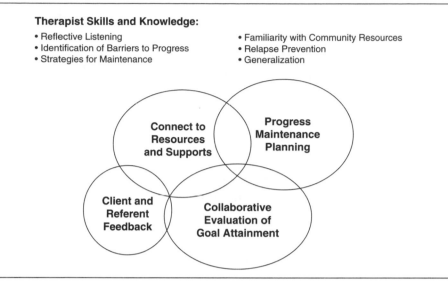

Therapist Skills and Knowledge:
- Reflective Listening
- Identification of Barriers to Progress
- Strategies for Maintenance
- Familiarity with Community Resources
- Relapse Prevention
- Generalization

Connect to Resources and Supports

Progress Maintenance Planning

Client and Referent Feedback

Collaborative Evaluation of Goal Attainment

The therapist used MI strategies from the outset. He began by active listening to Danielle regarding her history, noting her concerns about her relationship and her desire to maintain the relationship. He active listened to the barriers she described to fulfilling CPS requirements, and focused on her statements of desire to be in compliance with CPS and begin an outpatient treatment program. He gave her a great deal of praise and affirmation regarding her successful completion of inpatient treatment, her commitment to Maria, and her desire to build a good home for her daughter.

Danielle and the therapist set small, immediately achievable goals to build momentum and allow Danielle to experience successes. The therapist purchased supplies to help Danielle become organized, as her disorganization was contributing to her lack of follow through. He bought and taught her to use an electronic organizer/calendar/address book. They installed a white board wall calendar near her phone so appointments could be immediately posted. They purchased hanging files and organized all her important paperwork, including medical information, treatment information, bills, rental agreement, daycare information, TANF and medical coupon benefits, and so on. Danielle immediately began using these and maintained the use throughout services, often commenting on how helpful these tools were.

The therapist and Danielle then visited and assessed daycare centers. Danielle selected one based on her comfort level with the provider, the activities offered at the center, and the flexibility of its hours, because her treatment and AA meetings required day and evening access to care.

After these initial successes, Danielle felt ready to begin her outpatient treatment. She set up the intake session and began attending sessions. To support her treatment and begin to challenge her relationship with Maria's father, the therapist used the Homebuilders Your Deal values cards. After Danielle defined her top five values, it was apparent she had not included Maria's father in the "family" or "relationship" values she had identified and defined. The therapist used that as a discrepancy to further explore that relationship and her thoughts and feelings about him. He also used the Your Deal strengths exercise to help Danielle identify her inner strengths that could be drawn upon to support her possible decision.

Early in the intervention the therapist taught Rational Emotive Behavioral Therapy (REBT). Danielle loved it. She related it to the Dialectical Behavioral Therapy (DBT) she had learned in inpatient treatment, and gave examples of how she had used DBT skills in various situations that occurred during her treatment. Given her proficiency at REBT, the therapist was able to use this skill to challenge her unhelpful self-talk regarding relationships in general and with Maria's father.

Danielle's awareness of her strengths and values helped her replace her unhelpful self-talk with more helpful self-talk regarding Maria's father. She was then able to assess her relationship and see it as abusive. Danielle was able to make a decision to end it, even securing a restraining order to prevent all contact from her former partner. Danielle repeatedly drew upon her values and how they reflected what she wanted in her life to strengthen the discrepancy between this man's behavior and the kind of people she wanted in her life.

The therapist also helped Danielle relate her values to her choices regarding treatment, staying sober, and building a future for herself and her daughter. Affirmations of her strengths and past and current successes were given frequently.

Case Example: Goal Setting and Treatment Planning

The following case example illustrates the Homebuilders process for gathering information about the family situation, forming an initial assessment, and working with the client to set attainable service goals and a treatment plan directly related to the risks that led to referral.

Reason for Referral

The Simmons family consisted of 27-year-old Amanda and her two sons, Andrew, age 9 and Joseph, age 7 (not their actual names). The family was referred to Homebuilders after numerous CPS reports from the children's school. They reported the children often came to school dirty and hungry. They also had serious concerns about Joseph's behavior—he frequently left school grounds without permission, was physically and sexually aggressive, used extremely foul language, and cried when it was time to go home. Joseph also told his teacher that he did not eat or sleep well, and when his mother went to bed around 11 P.M., he stayed up and watched adult cartoons all night. His behavior in school was so extreme that if he showed up without his medication the school would give his mother only 30 minutes to bring it before sending him home. Joseph was in a behavior-disordered classroom and sometimes required an adult aid to escort him home on the bus because his behavior was disruptive and dangerous to others. Andrew was diagnosed with developmental delays and received school-based services. The school reported the mother had been uncooperative and did not follow through on their recommendations. The CPS social worker stated she found the home "filthy" and infested with mice. The family had a history of CPS reports, and during the last year had been referred to less intensive in-home services and parenting classes. Both were terminated early due to the mother's lack of participation. The referring social worker stated that without Homebuilders the children would be immediately removed.

Early Sessions and Assessment and Goal Setting

The therapist received the referral at 9 A.M., and called Amanda immediately. They set up the first visit for 2 P.M. that day so they could spend time together before the children returned from school. During the initial session the therapist active listened to elicit Amanda's concerns about the children's behavior, her frustration trying to get assistance with Joseph's behavior at home and school, and her feelings of being overwhelmed with the condition of the apartment. Amanda reported that Joseph struggled with following directions, was sometimes physically aggressive with her, and sometimes aggressive when playing with his brother. She described the difficulties she had getting Joseph to bed, and said she often went to sleep before he did because they had to get up early. She was concerned he was not getting enough sleep and reported his behavior was more problematic when he was tired. Through active listening and open-ended questions, the therapist also learned that the fathers of the boys were not involved with the family—one had a history of domestic violence and substance abuse, and the other lived in another state and had not responded to attempts to contact him. Amanda's mother and sister provided occasional help with child care and transportation.

At 3:30 P.M. the therapist accompanied Amanda to the school bus stop to pick up the children. Over the next hour the therapist had the opportunity to engage and observe the children interacting together and with Amanda. During this time she saw that both boys had a very difficult time following instructions, and had a number of brief verbal disagreements and physical interactions (taking toys away from each other, kicking each other, and whining and crying). Amanda stated she had taken parenting classes and found it difficult to use time-out or consequences with the boys because they would not stay in time-out and did not seem to care about earning stickers or other rewards. The therapist set up an appointment for the next evening, since Amanda suggested it would be a good time to observe her struggles getting Joseph to bed.

During the first week the therapist spent 10 face-to-face hours with the family over four visits. She also obtained releases of information to talk to the school personnel and the previous counselors who had worked with Joseph individually and the family together. At the end of the first week the therapist and mother had established the following goals and treatment plan.

Goal 1: Joseph's Behavior Improves at Home and School

Goal Indicators

1. Teachers report (using a daily school note) a decrease in Joseph's problem behaviors.
2. Amanda reports a decrease in Joseph's arguing and fighting at home.
3. Amanda reports, and Joseph's behavior chart shows an increase in following instructions.
4. Amanda demonstrates a consistent use of behavioral parenting skills (e.g., praise, positive attention, planned ignoring, positive consequences, time-out).

Treatment Plan

➤ Continue to active listen to Amanda about her challenges with managing Joseph's behavior.

➤ Continue to use MI strategies to motivate Amanda to try new parenting strategies.

➤ Observe family interactions and conduct a functional behavioral analysis with Amanda.

➤ Provide rationales and teach Amanda behavior parenting skills including: giving clear instructions, use of praise and positive attention, planned ignoring, time out, and use of consequences.

➤ Develop behavioral tracking system, behavior chart and reinforcers (e.g., "good behavior bucks to exchange for activities and other reinforcers") with family.

➤ Coach, prompt, and reinforce Amanda's use of behavioral parenting skills.

➤ With Amanda, teach Joseph and Andrew the skills of "following instructions," and "accepting no for an answer."

➤ Provide homework, practice assignments, and written materials.

➢ Help Amanda identify her unhelpful "self-talk" and help her implement REBT strategies.

➢ Meet with school personnel and make school observations of Joseph.

➢ Facilitate school meeting with Amanda and help Amanda practice using effective communication skills with the school.

➢ Coordinate with school to implement behavioral plan in the school.

Goal 2: Amanda Implements a Plan for Cleaning and Maintaining the Cleanliness of the Home

Goal Indicators

1. Amanda reports that the chores assigned to the children and her are being accomplished each day.

2. Therapist observes the home to be less dirty and cluttered.

3. Amanda receives assistance from the building management to rid the home of mice and prevent reinfestation.

4. Amanda implements a plan to prevent reinfestation of mice and how to respond if there is a reinfestation.

Treatment Plan

➢ Continue to active listen to Amanda to identify the barriers to maintaining the cleanliness of the home.

➢ Continue to use MI strategies to motivate Amanda to develop and implement a plan to clean and maintain the home.

➢ Develop chore list and resources with family.

➢ With Amanda, teach Joseph and Andrew how to clean their room, make beds, and other chores.

➢ Track chores on the behavior chart and identify realistic reinforcers.

➢ Reinforce Amanda's efforts and successes.

➢ Help family clean the home, sort through the clutter, and help Amanda decide what to keep, give away, recycle, or throw away.

➢ Arrange for a vehicle to take garbage to the dump.

➢ Help Amanda understand her rights as a tenant.

➢ Teach Amanda assertive and communication skills and role-play asking for assistance with extermination services from the building management.

➢ Provide advocacy with the building management, if needed.

➢ Help Amanda and family develop a plan to maintain the cleanliness of the home.

Goal 3: Amanda Implements a Daily Routine for the Family

Goal Indicators

1. Amanda and Joseph report that Joseph goes to bed by 9 P.M. each night.

2. The family establishes and follows a mealtime routine.

3. Amanda reports a decrease in problems during the morning routine.

Treatment Plan

➢ Continue to active listen to Amanda's concerns regarding morning, evening, and bedtime problems, meals, and daily activities of all family members.

➢ Observe morning and evening/bedtime routines to gather more information.

- ➤ Review current schedule and daily activities with Amanda.
- ➤ Identify Amanda's desired changes in the daily activities and routines.
- ➤ Develop new routine with Amanda and the children.
- ➤ Teach Amanda, Joseph, and Andrew "I" messages, and practical problem solving skills; role-play these skills in common family situations.
- ➤ Help the family develop daily routine charts (using pictures and other visuals) to identify and implement consequences for following the routine.

Resources

Many additional case examples and much more detailed descriptions of intervention components can be found in *Keeping Families Together: The HOMEBUILDERS Model* (Kinney, Haapala, & Booth, 1991).

Analysis of the skills most often taught families and therapist activities most often used can be found in *Families In Crisis: The Impact of Intensive Family preservation Services* (Fraser et al., 1991).

Descriptions of the Homebuilders' quality assurance system (QUEST), program standards and fidelity measures, and training and site development services for programs wishing to replicate the model can be found at www.institutefamily.org

The Your Deal cards can be found at www.institutefamily.org

References

Ellis, A., & Dryden, W. (2007). *The practice of rational emotive behavior therapy*. New York, NY: Springer.

Fraser, M., Pecora, P., & Haapala, D. (1991). *Families in crisis: The impact of intensive family preservation services*. New York, NY: Walter de Gruyter.

Kinney, J., Haapala, D., & Booth, C. (1991). *Keeping families together. The Homebuilders model*. New York, NY: Walter de Gruyter.

Kirk, R. S., & Griffith, D. P. (2008). Impact of intensive family preservation services on disproportionality of out-of-home placements of children of color in one state's child welfare system. *Child Welfare*, *87*(5), 87–105.

Miller, M. (2006). *Intensive family preservation programs: Program fidelity influences effectiveness—Revised*. Olympia, WA: Washington State Institute for Public Policy, Document Number 06–02–3901.

Miller, W. R., & Rollnick, S. (2002). *Motivational interviewing: Preparing people for change*. New York, NY: Guilford Press.

Reed-Ashcraft, K. B., Kirk, R. S., & Fraser, M. W. (2001). The reliability and validity of the North Carolina family assessment scale. *Research on Social Work Practice*, *11*(4), 503–520.

Tracy, E., Haapala, D., Kinney, J., & Pecora, P. (1991). *Intensive family preservation services: An instructional sourcebook*. Cleveland, OH: Mandel School of Applied Social Sciences, Case Western Reserve University.

Waters, V. (2008). *Rational stories for children*. New York, NY: Albert Ellis Institute.

Whittaker, J., Kinney, J., Tracy, E., & Booth, C. (1990). *Reaching high-risk families: Intensive family preservation in human services*. New York, NY: Walter de Gruyter.

16
Using *1–2–3 Magic* in Child Welfare

Thomas W. Phelan

Goals of the Program

1–2–3 Magic: Effective Discipline for Children 2–12 is a simple, easy-to-learn, and effective program for parents and other caretakers dealing with young children. The goals of *1–2–3 Magic* include reducing, in a fairly short period of time, children's oppositional and disruptive behavior, improving compliance with adult requests, improving the quality of parent-child relationships, reducing family stress, and increasing marital satisfaction. *1–2–3 Magic* is a powerful tool for preventing future mental health and relationship problems.

In a child welfare setting, *1–2–3 Magic* is used with at-risk families to reduce or eliminate physical and emotional child abuse and, in some cases, neglect. The program can be an essential part of reunification efforts, allowing parents to reengage their children with comfort and confidence. *1–2–3 Magic* directly addresses three protective factors. First, it improves parent-child attachment by defining and encouraging parental nurturing while simultaneously reducing aggravating misbehavior. Second, the program provides parents with a specific how-to-do-it, three-step "job description," which is tailored for use with young children. And third, the program directly addresses the issue of parental resilience as it applies to child discipline; parents are instructed, in other words, exactly how to recover when they slip up.

1–2–3 Magic has also been used with foster parents and adoptive families, with the same goal: warm, friendly, and firm discipline that allows parents to enjoy their kids' company and that also helps prevent future mental health problems.

Who Is the Program For?

At the primary contact level, *1–2–3 Magic* is a discipline instruction program intended for birth parents, foster and adoptive parents, teachers, and other caretakers of young children aged approximately 2 to 12.

At the secondary contact level, *1–2–3 Magic* is used by child welfare workers, mental health professionals, pediatricians, and other professionals to train parents and child caretakers to accomplish the objectives described above.

Certain characteristics of both children and parents can bring about a situation where *1–2–3 Magic* may not work as well as hoped. If children do not have a functional mental age of at least 2, they may not benefit from the program. Also, if children have an untreated mental health problem, such as ADHD or bipolar disorder, they will usually benefit from the program, but not as much as they might if they were also being treated with strategies such as education regarding the disorder (for kids and caretakers) and possibly medication.

Parents and caretakers will have trouble benefiting from *1–2–3 Magic* under the following circumstances. First, if an adult implementing the program has trouble following what we call the *No-Talking* and *No-Emotion* rules, results will be compromised or nonexistent. These rules mean that during discipline efforts, expressions of adult anger and excessive adult chattering must be restrained—a lot! If, in an adult, this condition for success cannot be met due to extreme fatigue, alcohol and drug use, undiagnosed mental health issues, or other problems, success with *1–2–3* will be lessened.

Also, in two-parent households, marital instability or conflict can reduce or even obliterate the effectiveness of the program. If one parent, for example, is attempting to count a child for misbehavior, and the other parent is criticizing this approach or expressing extreme frustration about the child's behavior, success is unlikely.

Keep in mind, however, that *1–2–3 Magic* is for average kids or special needs kids. It has been a wonderful addition to the treatment of many children with disruptive behavior disorders. The strategy has also been a godsend to many marriages, especially where the child discipline issue is the straw that's about to break the marital camel's back. Lots of moms and dads have said, with a sense of profound happiness, "*1–2–3 Magic* saved my marriage!"

History of *1–2–3 Magic*

1–2–3 Magic was the direct product of the personal parenting experience and private practice of a clinical psychologist. On entering private practice, the program's author began receiving many referrals from pediatricians. At about the same time he became a parent. The unique ideas underlying the program were discovered and first tested both at home and with a clinical population during the years 1970–1984. The presenting complaints involved the usual complement of ADHD, anxiety, school problems, and so on, but they also involved minor but typical family issues such as going to bed, sibling rivalry, talking back, not eating, getting up in the middle of the night, and whining.

In dealing with these major and minor problems, the author soon found that for any psychological prescriptions to work, they had to meet two criteria: simplicity and effectiveness. Along with this realization came the surprising but fundamental discovery underlying the whole *1–2–3 Magic* philosophy: Too much talking between parents and children is counterproductive, especially in discipline situations. This is explained more in the next section.

Once the program had been developed in these one-to-one clinical situations, it was then tested, retested, and refined hundreds of times in different families who had young children. Rather than a large study with a big N, in other words, we had a series of small, $N = 1$ studies. In these "studies" it appeared to the author and the participating families that *1–2–3 Magic* was simple, easy to learn, and effective. Behavioral problems were significantly reduced or eliminated, family members enjoyed each other's company to a much greater extent, and marriages were strengthened.

Because of this success, in 1984 the author decided to "take the show on the road" and the first public *1–2–3 Magic* seminar was given. The seminars became quite popular, generating 80 to 90 requests per year from hospitals, schools, mental health practices, day-care centers, and child welfare agencies. The seminars also generated 250 to 300 referrals per year to the office for clinical evaluations, a number that was impossible to fulfill in a one-person practice.

The success of the *1–2–3 Magic* workshops led to the production of a video (VHS at the time) and the first edition of the *1–2–3 Magic* book, which had existed previously as a 60-page pamphlet. The video has since been revised into a two-DVD format and an audio CD was also produced. Up to the present time the *1–2–3 Magic* book has sold more than 1,200,000 copies and has been translated into 20 languages. A *1–2–3 Magic for Teachers* book and DVD are also available.

Orientation to Training

There are several reasons why *1–2–3 Magic* has been successful. Knowledge of these factors provide the foundation for effective training of parents, foster parents, teachers, and other caretakers. First, the program is simple and not intimidating. Second, *1–2–3 Magic* resonates with parental experience and—when the method is presented well—it produces therapeutic results and generates optimism. Third, the plan has an understandable and effective theoretical foundation. And fourth, its rapid and substantial results reinforce adult and child compliance.

Simplicity

1–2–3 Magic explains to parents that they basically have three jobs, and that these three jobs are best accomplished with a warm and demanding parenting style. The three parenting jobs are (1) controlling obnoxious behavior, (2) encouraging good behavior, and (3) strengthening relationships with kids. Moms and dads are told that if they can accomplish these three things they will be pretty good parents.

Parents can wrap their minds around this concept, and each of the steps is understandable—at least to some extent. The simplicity of the job description also generates some hope in adults' minds: "Hey, maybe I can do this." Well-written-but-long parenting books seem to demand of parents that they have IQs over 160 along with saintly, therapist-like dispositions. This is discouraging right from the beginning, and such difficult parenting tomes also often leave caretakers with no clear place to start.

The simplicity of *1–2–3 Magic* has not been easy to maintain over the years. Email, amazon.com comments, workshop questions, and other communications have occasionally pointed out certain important concepts that might have been included in the book, such as the effects of child temperament or the relationship between parenting style and one's family of origin. Though it was extremely difficult to know where to draw the line in terms of adding new material versus maintaining simplicity, draw the line we did and a number of concepts were not explained in great detail.

The reason for doing this was a fundamental rule: *If you don't keep it simple, nobody will do it*. Parents, especially child welfare clients, need something to do in the moment, and a bulging text that frightens people will produce change only in the most intelligent and well-motivated parents. With this in mind, what has not been included in *1–2–3 Magic* is a *thorough* discussion of the following: child temperament, childhood emotional/behavioral disorders, more complex strategies for teaching children problem-solving techniques, more extensive two-way communication skills, parenting styles, cognitive therapy, and the effect of a marriage relationship on the children. In the fourth edition of *1–2–3 Magic* references are provided in a new appendix for people interested in further exploration of these concepts.

Resonates With Parental Experience

A second reason for *1–2–3 Magic*'s success is that the *1–2–3* material resonates with parental experience—especially with the unexpected frustrations of parenting. And when the material is well presented, this resonance is increased and provides a significant boost to parents' motivation to do the program. In addition to being logically organized, *well presented* means using down-to-earth language, humor, and relevant personal experience.

Whether *1–2–3 Magic* is taught in one-on-one clinical sessions or through the medium of DVD, audio CD, book, or group presentations, the presentation of the material should be both entertaining as well as informative. The general population tends to be intimidated by mental health professionals, who are seen as aloof, flawless, and even somewhat arrogant. Shattering this image early in the presentation goes a long way toward helping clients open up to the material, feel willing to change, and also to feel optimistic.

Simple language makes the material understandable. Humor (related to parenting) engages people and helps them identify with the presenter. And personal experience—especially stories about one's parenting mistakes—makes the presenter seem human—not aloof or flawless. Without saying it explicitly (and it is important not to) the message is ''Parenting is unexpectedly hard, we're in this boat together, and we've all made mistakes. But there are solutions.''

The program qualities and presentation attributes just described also make the *1–2–3 Magic* program therapeutic. It is important to recognize where parents who are at risk for emotional and physical abuse have been. In the past, while trying to deal with their children's screaming, whining, teasing, fighting, arguing, and so on, these parents have been trying to simultaneously manage four problems: (1) their children's behavior, (2) their own rage at their kids' behavior, (3) their shock and dismay regarding the intensity of their anger, and (4) their resulting disillusionment and depression regarding the new but permanent redefinition of their life as "Parent."

The therapeutic emotional effect of *1–2–3 Magic* addresses each of these four problems with the following messages: (1) believe it or not, there's a way to manage kids' behavior that works, (2) being very mad at your kids is normal—all parents feel that way from time to time, (3) you won't be nearly as angry once you're running the house, and (4) there's hope—you can actually enjoy being with your own children.

From a cognitive therapy perspective, in other words, *1–2–3 Magic* tears apart, explains and resolves the basic, haunting question that tortures abusive parents: "What's wrong with me or my children that everyone else in the world finds their kids so adorable and I can't stand mine!?"

Effective Theoretical Orientation

The theoretical orientation for *1–2–3 Magic* combines family systems notions, cognitive restructuring and education, and a unique behavior management technology that includes aspects of operant conditioning, reciprocal inhibition, and anxiety reduction theory. The issue of child discipline is seen as a huge factor that impacts many other aspects of family functioning, such as maternal mental health, marital stability, and the prognosis for the kids' futures. To set up an effective discipline intervention, certain cognitive adjustments must first be made in parents' minds, such as the three-part job definition for parenting, the Little Adult Assumption, the No-Talking and No-Emotion Rules, and the Six Kinds of Testing and Manipulation. With this cognitive foundation, the behavioral technology is explained and implemented.

Rapid, Substantial Change

1–2–3 Magic has surprised many people over the years, parents and professionals alike. Not only is it easy to learn, but the results are often rapid and substantial. The change in children's conduct has more than once been compared to the effects of stimulant medication on ADHD behavior. Many parents see changes in the first few hours of using the program. In some families the changes take a few days, and a few folks have to endure what we call "hell week" before making believers out of the youngsters.

This rapid behavioral change confers an immediate benefit on everyone in the family. Relationships improve and people start enjoying one another's company. When problems do arise, they are resolved quickly, instead of people having to endure hour after hour of back-and-forth screaming and the increased likelihood of emotional or physical abuse.

The potency and immediacy of the *1–2–3* program also has another benefit: It gets dads involved. Dads do not like psychology, they like action. *1–2–3 Magic* is action, but no arguing, yelling, or spanking are allowed. Parents in at-risk families do not need to be instructed in patience. They need something *to do right away* to end the child behavior problem and thus eliminate the risk of abuse.

How to Implement *1–2–3 Magic*

The *1-2-3 Magic* program can be taught using several different formats, depending on the needs and preferences of potential trainees. Some folks, for example, like to learn on their own, so the *1-2-3 Magic* book, DVD, or audio CD formats might be useful for them. Some people, especially dads, prefer the anonymity of a one-shot large group presentation to the intimacy of multiple-session, small-group training.

Training Formats

The *1–2–3 Magic* book (4th edition) can be considered the basic manual for the whole program, but the training can also be facilitated by means of a two-DVD set (4 hours) and an audio CD (4-hour soundtrack from DVDs).

Training formats include independent instruction, large group presentations, small groups, and one-on-one training during counseling sessions or home visits. Each has advantages and disadvantages.

Independent Self-Instruction

For people who like to read, the *1–2–3 Magic* book is short, simple, and written for about a fifth- to sixth-grade reading level. The most powerful independent learning experience, of course, will be provided by the two DVDs. The DVDs show a workshop presented by the author to a live audience. Integrated into the presentation are professionally acted scenes illustrating the principles of *1–2–3 Magic*. For adults who prefer to learn on their own or who refuse clinical or small group contacts, the DVDs or audio CDs can be an effective way of getting started. The possible disadvantages here include lack of follow-up and the chance that an individual might misunderstand parts of the program.

Large Group Presentations

1–2–3 Magic can be effectively presented in 2 to 3 hours to larger groups ranging from 25 to several hundred people. This format has several advantages. First of all, it offers the program to folks who are threatened by small group or one-on-one encounters (such as males!). Second, large group presentations offer a sense of hope and direction to more people. After being exposed to *1–2–3 Magic*, many of these people will be more amenable to further counseling. Third, large group presentations are usually more fun and more therapeutic. In an atmosphere of sympathetic humor and serious education, the entire group, in a sense, can agree that parenting is emotionally draining and even the best parents make plenty of mistakes.

Small Group and One-on-One Sessions

Many parents benefit most when they have someone available to hold their hand through the process of learning and applying *1–2–3 Magic*. Small groups and individual sessions allow time for accurate initial learning, careful application of that learning to each client's parenting situation, and follow-up support to reinforce success, correct mistakes, and prevent parents from falling off the wagon. The disadvantages with these smaller-audience formats include the expense of staff time and the fact that—as far as group treatment goes—the more sessions required the fewer parents will show up (especially dads).

Some parents, however, cannot implement the program without this consistent support. Small group *1–2–3 Magic* training, for example, can vary from two to three sessions to six to eight or even more. Parent education home visits by some caseworkers, for example, can sometimes continue for more than a year.

The organization of a 1- to 2-hour small group or clinical session can go like this: First of all, the significance of the section to be discussed is described and any questions answered. Then a new piece of the *1–2–3 Magic* material is presented by means of the DVD or audio CD; sometimes people are asked to watch or listen as part of their between-session homework.

Eliciting the reactions of clients or group members to the new *1–2–3 Magic* section comes next. What did they think of what they heard? Did they agree, disagree, or not understand certain concepts? To help clarify their understanding, the therapist or group leader can ask certain questions that require relating the material to personal experience. Examples are given in each section below.

Once the section's concepts are understood, it is time for parents to decide exactly how they will apply these ideas to their home situations. What child behavior will they target and how? How will they deal with their own attitudes and thoughts in the process? What difficulties do they anticipate from their children, partners, or themselves?

After the first session, future get-togethers can follow this pattern:

1. Review of homework success and homework difficulties.
2. Significance of new *1–2–3 Magic* concepts to be presented.
3. Presentation of new material.
4. Participant reactions to new material.
5. Questions relating new ideas to participants' personal experience.
6. Planning home applications and role-play.
7. Advance troubleshooting.

In clinical situations where time allows, the therapist might not continue on to new sections of *1–2–3 Magic* until a parent has demonstrated mastery of the previous ones. In more limited group settings, the group leader moves ahead with new material, but allows for review of old material at any time.

The Training Content

The *1–2–3 Magic* plan consists of several pieces that follow each other in logical order. Each element of the program has a central unifying concept and each part builds directly on the previous sections. Here are the basic parts of *1–2–3 Magic*:

➤ Thinking Straight
➤ Parenting Job #1: Controlling Obnoxious Behavior
➤ Managing Kids' Testing and Manipulation

➤ Parenting Job #2: Encouraging Good Behavior

➤ Parenting Job #3: Strengthening Relationships With Your Children

➤ Your New Life: Staying on the Wagon

Let us look at how this one-on-one or small-group format would be applied to the different pieces of the *1–2–3 Magic* program.

Thinking Straight

Before beginning the actual *1-2-3 Magic* parenting training, it's important for moms and dads to dispel some of the parenting myths and misconceptions that might be floating around in their brains.

New Material The new concepts in the Thinking Straight section include a description of the universal difficulties involved in parenting, the Warm/Demanding parenting model, an explanation of the three parenting jobs, the notion of the Little Adult Assumption, and the Two Biggest Discipline Mistakes.

Significance The Thinking Straight segment of the program is designed to (a) give parents a basic framework for their job, and (b) correct some faulty but almost universal notions they have about young children. The ideas presented tell parents exactly what their job is—what they need to do, in other words, to be a good parent. The ideas in Part I, especially the Little Adult Assumption, will also explain with eye-opening clarity exactly why these folks have found parenting so difficult in the past. This insight will lay the groundwork for all the strategies that follow, especially counting.

Participant Reactions When you explain to parents that the best underlying philosophy of parenting is what we call the warm/friendly and demanding/firm model, they will usually nod in agreement, as if to say "Fine, okay. That's nice." When you point out that it is the demanding/firm side of the job that causes the trouble, however, they will become more interested. They will appreciate the definition and simplification of their job into three concrete tasks: controlling obnoxious behavior, encouraging good behavior, and strengthening relationships with children. This job description makes the job seem manageable and down-to-earth.

In addition to appreciating their new job description, parents will also appreciate your blunt description of the difficulty of parenting. It is important to try to avoid euphemisms such as *undesirable* or *challenging* to describe kids' problem behavior. *Obnoxious* will do just fine. Emotional and realistic descriptions are especially important to moms and dads who have been emotionally and physically abusive to their children.

Questions Relating to Personal Experience

1. What is the hardest part of the parenting job for you?

2. Describe the difference between "Stop" and "Start" behavior? Which is the hardest for you to deal with?

3. Describe a time when you were guilty of the "Little Adult Assumption." What effect did your words and reasons have on your child's cooperation?

4. What effect does your talking in discipline situations have on your relationship with your children? Describe a time when you got too emotional or upset with a child.

5. What do you think of the "wild animal trainer" idea?

Planning the Home Application of *1–2–3 Magic* Unless you are going to also cover counting obnoxious behavior in your first session, at this point the best homework is for parents to spend a week or so just observing how things are going at their house regarding child discipline. Their homework can include making a list of the behavior they would like their kids to Stop (e.g., whining, teasing, arguing), as well as a list of the behavior they would like their kids to Start (up and out, going to bed, picking up). Parents should also prepare to describe for the therapist or group the nature of their relationship with each of their kids. Finally, moms and dads should observe how much they talk when trying to discipline, as well as how upset they get, how this in turn affects their chattering, and how all this affects their kids' cooperation. Role-playing is not necessary at this point.

Troubleshooting The biggest problem is people remembering to do their observations and not just respond automatically. Encouraging a brief written summary of the main observational insights to bring back is helpful.

Parenting Job #1: Controlling Obnoxious Behavior

The first big parenting job is learning how to deal with obnoxious behavior, or what *1-2-3 Magic* calls "Stop Behavior." This section will be the parents' first introduction to "counting," the surprising, simple-yet-effective technique that really provides the backbone for the whole program.

Homework Review Most parents will be surprised at how much they talk and also at how unproductive their nattering is. Many will be dismayed at how upset they get, at how little the kids seem to care, and at how depressing child discipline as a whole is. Parents will still be frustrated at not knowing what to do.

New Material The brand new concept in this section is the idea of counting obnoxious behavior. Counting is simple, direct, and effective. It is not easy, however, because the No-Talking and No-Emotion rules must be respected for counting to work. The basic how-to of counting is described, including the three scenes of the "Famous Twinkie Example." Also included are the benefits of counting and answers to about two dozen Frequently Asked Questions. The section concludes with what to do in public, how to apply counting to sibling rivalry, tantrums, and pouting, and finally how to do the "Kickoff Conversation" with the kids.

An example of counting will help to clarify the procedure. Counting is a simple warning system that is used most of the time to control obnoxious behavior. Let us say that 5-year-old Max asks his mother for a cookie 20 minutes before dinner. Mom says no, and explains that she does not want her son to spoil his supper. Though the limit has been set and an explanation given, Max pushes the issue, so—rather than engaging in futile explanations—Mom will use counting to deal with her son's badgering:

Max: "Come on, I just want one cookie."
Mom: "That's 1." (Mom says *nothing else.*)
Max: "I promise I'll eat my dinner."
Mom: "That's 2."
Max: "You never give me anything!!"
Mom: "That's 3, take 5."

If Max had stopped badgering at a count of 1 or 2, the whole incident would have been over. But in this instance the little fellow persists till his mother hits 3. Hitting 3 means a consequence for Max, a time-out (1 minute per year of his life) or a time-out alternative (e.g., bedtime 10 minutes earlier). When counting is done calmly and consistently, kids soon learn to stop their obnoxious behavior at a count of 1 or 2.

Counting is deceptively simple. In fact, most parents think they understand it when they really do not. Most folks assume the key to success is the "Three strikes and you're out" methodology. That is not the case. The key to success is the *silence after each count*. When caretakers can explain why that silence is critical, when they have mastered the FAQ section, and after they understand the Six Types of Testing and Manipulation, they are then ready to count. Not before.

Significance Counting is the backbone of the *1–2–3 Magic* program. It is the strategy that made the program famous. Effective parental counting invariably comes as a surprise—and even a shock—to the kids, because when it is done correctly, this tactic lets the kids know who is in charge of the house. Once parents begin counting, they usually experience relief, disbelief that the strategy works so well, and hope for the future of their family. Success with counting contributes immensely to parents' buying in to the *1–2–3 Magic* program, which is especially helpful with involuntary or reluctant participants.

Participant Reactions When parents are first presented with the counting method, they are almost always skeptical. Comments such as "Too simple!" "You don't know my kid!" or "I've already tried that and it didn't work!" are common.

Questions Relating to Personal Experience Here questions are often not applicable, except for those who say they have tried counting and it did not work. Sympathetic questions to these folks will usually reveal violations of the No-Talking and No-Emotion rules or kids' responses to counting that the parents did not know how to handle (such as counting the parents back or ignoring the counts).

1. If you have tried counting before, describe in detail how you did it.
2. How did you manage the No-Talking, No-Emotion rules?
3. How did the children respond?

Planning the Home Application of *1–2–3 Magic* The therapist's job here is to encourage clients to try the program even if they are skeptical about how it will work. Role-playing different counting situations is important so people get a feel for *the silence after each count.* Parents usually also need to be reminded that counting is for Stop (obnoxious) behavior, not for encouraging Start (positive) behavior.

Troubleshooting The biggest problems will involve extra talking and excess emotion. These issues should be discussed before and after the role-plays.

Managing Kids' Testing and Manipulation

Kids won't thank their caretakers for the adults' new commitment to counting obnoxious behavior. On the contrary, about half of the youngsters will protest using one or more of the Six Types of Testing and Manipulation. Preparing parents for this potential sidetrack is critical.

Homework Review Reactions to counting will most often involve pleasant surprises. For families having trouble, the specific situations where difficulties are occurring should be examined closely. Solutions will usually be found by looking at the Two Biggest Discipline Mistakes or the FAQ section.

New Material Kids can react to counting by cooperating or by trying different forms of testing and manipulation. There are six major testing tactics, and if a child has a favorite tactic, that's bad because it's working. *Working* can mean either the child gets his way by means of that tactic or he gets effective revenge. Understanding and managing testing are made clear.

Significance Though testing and manipulation are universal, these behaviors often throw parents for a loop because the adults take them seriously at a superficial, cognitive level. The testing strategies themselves, however, are emotional power plays that have little or nothing to do with logic. Seeing testing for what it is and managing it correctly are critical to the success of *1–2–3 Magic.*

Participant Reactions Clients and group participants often find the testing and manipulation material humorous, which, of course, it is. Though their ability to laugh at the problem is helpful, their laughter does not mean that they grasp the concept and are ready to manage it. Educational and therapeutic work must be done to get them prepared.

Questions Relating to Personal Experience

1. Most kids are naturals when it comes to testing. Which testing behaviors by your children could win an Oscar?
2. Describe a time when you handled your children's testing well.

3. Describe a time when you gave in or got very upset.

4. Which manipulative tactic is the hardest for you to handle?

Planning the Home Application of *1–2–3 Magic* Home application of the testing material should focus on (a) the identification of each child's favorite testing tactics, and (b) decisions about how to manage these. When to count and when to ignore should be clarified.

Troubleshooting The notions of delayed testing, tactic switching, and tactic escalation should also be discussed and role-played.

Parenting Job #2: Encouraging Good Behavior

The next big parenting job is kind of the opposite of the first. Parenting job #2 is encouraging good ("Start") behavior, such as going to bed, doing chores, or getting up and out in the morning. Since Start Behavior requires more motivation from the children, it is also going to require more motivation, as well as expertise, from the adults.

Homework Review Parents will show an improvement in their ability to identify testing and manipulation, but they will still be prone to getting involved in too much talking and in getting too upset. Homework focus here is on identification and management.

New Material The second parenting job involves getting kids to do the good things, or what *1–2–3 Magic* calls Start behavior. The importance of avoiding spontaneous requests and instead establishing positive routines is emphasized. Seven strategies that can assist in this process are described. Then suggestions for handling specific Start behavior situations, such as up and out, suppertime, chores, and bedtime, are illustrated.

Significance Encouraging good behavior is a huge parenting task, and no parent/child relationship will survive well if there are daily battles around getting off to school, picking up after yourself, and going to bed. But the tactics for Start behavior are different than those for Stop behavior. Positive behaviors take longer and therefore require more motivation from kids and parents. Encouraging good behavior is *harder* than counting.

Participant Reactions Parents feel a lot of frustration with their kids' lack of initiative in carrying out positive behaviors. They will describe unpleasant scenes involving nagging and then yelling. The comment, "How many times do I have to ask you?" will be heard often. Though on one hand parents will welcome new solutions, they will be somewhat resistant to the "trouble" involved setting up routines, and they will continue to think "Why can't the children just do what they're told!?"

Questions Relating to Personal Experience

1. Describe the typical bedtime procedure at your house.

2. What is your biggest problem with getting the kids out in the morning?

3. Have you ever tried charting? What was the reaction?

4. What is your personal ratio of positive to negative feedback to your kids?

5. Describe, in your own words, how the Docking System and natural consequences work.

Planning the Home Application of *1–2–3 Magic* Each parent should decide to work on the two or three Start behavior problems that are giving them the most trouble. Then, choosing from the seven Start behavior tactics, they will need to design routines for managing these behaviors. The No-Talking and No-Emotion rules still apply, and parents need to keep the counting strategy in their back pockets should testing or other misbehavior occur in response to the new routines.

Troubleshooting Two things are important to prepare for. The first is praising and rewarding (sometimes with artificial reinforcers) cooperation. The second is what to do and say if noncompliance occurs. Chattering is not permitted!

Parenting Job #3: Strengthening Relationships With Your Children

The final parenting task in *1-2-3 Magic* is for parents to work on bonding with their kids. When parenting jobs #1 and #2 are done correctly, a lot of bonding will have occurred naturally—parents will enjoy their offspring much more than before. However, the connection can be further strengthened by using other strategies, such as shared one-on-one fun and sympathetic listening.

Homework Review Parents will usually report success with their new Start behavior tactics, though the success may not be as dramatic as what they experienced when they began counting. They will need to be reminded that the No-Talking and No-Emotion rules still apply when encouraging positive behavior. Talk can be used as a signal, but nagging and other extended attempts at persuasion are outlawed. Reinforcing children's independence is critical, and counting can be used when necessary to back up Start behavior strategies.

New Material The third parenting job involves deliberately doing things that increase the parent/child bond. The two most powerful attachment builders are sympathetic listening and shared one-on-one fun. Other relationship enhancers include one-on-one problem solving, family negotiations, and constructive involvement with the issue of kids and technology.

Significance Success with the first two parenting jobs will usually increase parent/child bonding automatically. Parents will feel more like spending time with their kids if the children are cooperating with parental requests, and the children, in turn, will like their parents more when parental nagging, arguing, and yelling have disappeared. Success with the third parenting job and improved bonding, on the other hand, will also make dealing with obnoxious behavior and encouraging good behavior easier.

Participant Reactions Parents will often show some hesitation or bewilderment in relating to this new material. For those whose main focus was to "get the kids off their backs," the notion of listening carefully to the children or spending more time with them may seem foreign. But once parents feel they can control the kids' difficult behavior and effectively elicit cooperation, the moms and dads will be more receptive to Job #3. They will also be more open to remembering their own childhoods, and the roles that having fun with and talking to their parents played (or might have played).

Questions Relating to Personal Experience

1. How would your children respond if someone asked, "How much fun are your parents?"
2. What can you do to make whole-family activities more enjoyable for your family?
3. When do you have trouble listening to a particular child?
4. Describe a time when one of your parents really listened sympathetically to you.
5. What are some possible issues in your family that could be addressed in a family meeting?

Planning the Home Application of *1–2–3 Magic* Trying to do all the bonding tactics at once will usually be too much for most parents. A better strategy is to begin with listening and fun. Ask parents to select a time when they might do nothing more than listen to a child with sympathy. This will be especially effective if the child is feeling something strongly. Role-play the possible conversations. Then ask each parent to plan out loud a time for shared one-on-one fun with each child. The shared-fun time and listening time can often go together. One-on-one problem solving times, family meetings, and managing kids and technology can be dealt with later.

Troubleshooting Once they commit to a one-on-one fun time, most parents will not have trouble with the idea. The biggest issue is not canceling due to the emergence of a possible competing commitment (very bad message to the child). The biggest trouble with sympathetic listening is not giving advice or telling the child what to do, as well as the effort involved in asking nonjudgmental questions. Joint problem solving also requires some self-restraint, which can be encouraged and modeled in the role-plays.

Your New Life: Staying on the Wagon

It's a good feeling for parents to both enjoy their own children and also to be in charge of their own homes, especially when this is done in a way that eliminates yelling, arguing, nagging, whining, and physical abuse. The next job is to keep the victory alive by learning how to avoid setbacks and also how to recover from an occasional slip.

Homework Review Parents will usually report positive experiences with shared fun, though some will have difficulty shaking a discipline oriented or critical frame of mind. Sympathetic listening will not come so easily, and it is important to use role-play to help parents communicate their experiences to the therapist. Some parents are just not good historians. A few parents may report success with joint problem solving efforts.

New Material Continued success and resilience involve being able to identify how anger, anxiety, depression, or guilt might cause a parent to fall off the wagon. Role-playing slip-ups is helpful. How to recognize when one is falling back into old, nonproductive patterns and specifically how to recover is described.

Significance Being able to recognize and recover from temporary failure is one of the most important skills in any endeavor. Developing resilience removes hope from the realm of wishful thinking and makes it justified and substantial.

Participant Reactions Parents at this point will usually feel somewhat mixed. On the one hand, they will feel a spark of hope they had not had before. On the other hand, some parents will worry that kids' or spouse/partners' lack of cooperation or outright interference might still disrupt their success.

Questions Relating to Personal Experience

1. How has your family changed since implementing *1–2–3 Magic*?
2. What are some difficulties you anticipate in the future?
3. What particular emotional obstacles might arise in you that would interfere with your success as a warm and demanding parent?
4. How will you elicit cooperation with *1–2–3 Magic* from other significant adults in your life?
5. How are you going to enjoy your children and your free time?

Planning the Home Application of *1–2–3 Magic* Discussion should focus on the good feeling of success and how to maintain that feeling by anticipating when slip-ups might occur and exactly how slip-ups will be handled.

Troubleshooting The focus on emotional obstacles should identify what situations are likely to cause difficulty, what troublesome thoughts would occur in those situations, what feelings would be generated by those thoughts, and finally what ineffective actions would be motivated by those feelings.

Learning More About *1–2–3 Magic*

1–2–3 Magic is available in several formats. The fourth edition is an illustrated 226-page book that is written for about a fifth- or sixth-grade reading level. For those who have difficulty with reading, a two-DVD set probably provides the most powerful experience. The first DVD (blue, 2 hours), *1–2–3 Magic: Managing Difficult Behavior in Children 2–12*, covers parenting Job #1, controlling obnoxious behavior. The blue DVD also covers testing and manipulation, so it covers the material in approximately the first half of the book. The second DVD (purple, 2 hours), *More 1–2–3 Magic: Encouraging Good Behavior, Independence and Self-Esteem*, covers parenting Job #2 and parenting Job #3. The second DVD, therefore, covers the material in approximately the second half of the book. The DVDs have both English and Spanish tracks.

For those who like to learn while driving, an audio CD is available for the whole program. The audio CD is basically the sound track from the two-DVD set.

To help the children get oriented to *1–2–3 Magic*, a short (50 page), four-color, illustrated book, *1–2–3 Magic for Kids,* is available. Parents can read the book to a 4-year-old, while an 8-year-old might be able to read it by herself. Parents and kids can then discuss the *1–2–3* concepts and how they will be applied at home.

For the educational market, the *1–2–3 Magic for Teachers* book applies the *1–2–3* concepts to the school and classroom settings. The teacher program is also available in a 3-hour DVD, which also includes an extensive special features section.

Leader guides are available for both parent and teacher versions of the program, although they are not always required since the books and DVDs are extremely simple and straightforward. ParentMagic, Inc. also occasionally offers Certified *1–2–3 Magic* training.

The *1–2–3 Magic* book can be found at any bookstore in the United States. The book and all the other materials mentioned above can also be found by visiting www.parentmagic.com or by calling (800) 442–4453.

17

SafeCare

Application of an Evidence–Based Program to Prevent Child Maltreatment

Anna Edwards–Gaura, Daniel J. Whitaker, John R. Lutzker, Shannon Self–Brown, and Ericka Lewis

SafeCare is one of the few interventions shown to ameliorate parental skill deficits related to neglect risk factors (Gershater-Molko, Lutzker, & Wesch, 2002, 2003). Of the substantiated child maltreatment (CM) cases in 2008, 71% were neglect (U.S. Department of Health and Human Services, 2009). Analysis of CM trends since the 1990s indicates that, fortunately, rates of child physical abuse and sexual abuse have decreased considerably over time. Unfortunately, the rate of neglect has largely remained the same.

The SafeCare model focuses on children, ages 0 to 5, who are most at risk for CM. SafeCare originated from Project 12-Ways, which utilized a combination of 12 different service modules to address individual parent needs. SafeCare was developed to be a more succinct version of 12-Ways, employing the three most commonly used and replicable 12-Ways intervention modules (child safety, health, and parent-child interaction). Consistent with an ecological framework, SafeCare services are delivered in a family's home and community. The model addresses the health risks for children (related to home safety hazards, filth, and lack of proper health care skills and resources), and the psychosocial risks (poor parent-child interactions and parenting skills) that are associated with maltreatment. Agencies that provide SafeCare across the country utilize service providers with diverse backgrounds, including graduate students, master's level counselors, nurses, and bachelors' level caseworkers.

SafeCare Structure

The SafeCare model provides home-based skill training for parents who are at-risk or have been reported for CM. It consists of three modules: Parent-Child/Parent-Infant

Interactions, Health, and Home Safety. These three modules target deficits in parental skills and the home environment that often lead to CM referrals. Structured problem-solving strategies are a part of skills trained to SafeCare providers.

SafeCare delivery involves a structured approach in each module that includes: (a) an initial assessment, (b) four to five training sessions to teach new skills, and (c) a posttraining assessment. The structure allows SafeCare providers to *see* behavior change and to gauge parental skill acquisition. The modules are typically conducted sequentially, with providers starting on the module that addresses the area of greatest need for a given family.

Assessment

All SafeCare modules involve considerable assessment, including baseline and post-training assessment, and ongoing assessments during training. All assessments are conducted via direct observations of the parent's skill (or the home environment in the case of Safety). Each of the three modules has a specific assessment process, and validated tools for conducting the assessment.

A baseline assessment occurs within each module, before any parent training begins. This assessment allows the provider to gain information about how the parent currently functions in terms of the targeted parenting skills. Parent skills are assessed in several different contexts to best inform the treatment plan. Even once parent training begins, observational assessments continue so that the provider can understand a parent's progress and acquisition of skills. Finally, the post-training assessment for each module occurs after all training sessions are complete, and allows a provider to determine whether a parent has mastered the requisite skills. Again, parents are observed in several contexts to determine if skills have been mastered and generalized.

Training

Training begins after the baseline assessment. SafeCare's training format is based on social learning theory (Bandura, 1977) and evidence from previous research (Latham & Saari, 1979), and uses the following format:

1. *Explain* the desired skills. The provider tells the parent what the targeted skills are, why they are important, and how they might be beneficial to the parent.
2. *Model* each skill. The provider demonstrates what they want the parent to do. For example, in the parent-child interaction module, the provider may show the parent how to play with a young child using positive verbalizations.
3. Parent *practices* the skill(s). Parents are directed to practice the targeted skills in a variety of settings (one at a time). The provider observes the sessions and assesses the parent's use of skills.
4. Provide *feedback*. The provider gives positive and corrective feedback to parents on their use of the targeted skills. As sessions progress, parents will master more of the steps and provider feedback will focus on fewer areas of need.

Figure 17.1   The SafeCare Modules

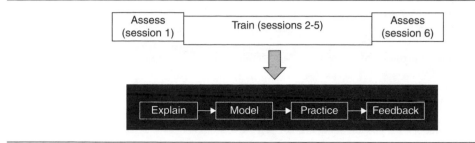

Using this format, parents are trained so that skills are generalized across time, behaviors, and/or settings. Providers work with parents until they meet a set of skill-based criteria that are established for each module. More specifically, the provider continues this Explain-Model-Practice-Feedback loop until the parent demonstrates correct use of skills in three different situations. As illustrated in Figure 17.1, each module is typically implemented with one baseline assessment session and four training sessions and is followed by a post-training assessment to assess mastery of skills and a questionnaire to assess parent satisfaction with training.

Parent–Child Interactions Module (PCI)

Parent-child interactions are paramount in children's development. The most well-adjusted children socially, emotionally, academically, and behaviorally are reared with a parenting style that is both high in expectations and structure, as well as high in warmth and responsiveness (Baumrind, 1991). Recent studies have found that not only is this combination of structure and support critical, but the roles of language and interactions are equally as significant (Hart & Risley, 1995). More specifically, parents who frequently talk to their infants and children, as well as interact with them regularly and frequently in a positive manner, have children with higher academic, social, and cognitive outcomes.

SafeCare's PCI module is informed by developmental research. The PCI module consists of training on parent-child interaction skills for parents with children approximately 1 to 5 years of age. Using the Planned Activities Training Checklist (PAT Checklist), parents learn to structure play and daily living activities and also to increase positive interaction opportunities with their children. The module helps parents to structure their activities to increase parental consistency, and to promote predictable and reliable expectations for the child. A secondary goal of the module is to increase parents' use of language within everyday settings so that children will benefit from incidental teaching.

PCI Assessment

The key tool used for assessments in the PCI module is the Planned Activities Training Checklist (PAT Checklist). The PAT Checklist steps are listed in Table 17.1.

Table 17.1 PAT Checklist Steps

1. Prepare in advance—Have a plan for what you want to do; get supplies ready in advance.
2. Explain the activity—Get the child's attention, be positive and excited, explain the activity so that the child knows what to expect.
3. Explain the rules—Make the rules clear, simple, and easy to follow; tell the child what to do instead of what not to do.
4. Explain the consequences—Tell the child what will happen if she follows the rules, and what will happen if she does not follow the rules.
5. Give choices—Give choices of activities, materials, and what comes first.
6. Talk about what you are doing—Talk and ask questions about what the child is doing; teach simple skills during daily activities; describe what the child is doing.
7. Use good interaction skills—Be on the child's level, pay attention to the child, touch the child affectionately, talk to the child warmly.
8. Ignore minor misbehavior and pay attention to positive behavior—Don't pay attention to minor problems, as the attention will reinforce negative behavior.
9. Give feedback—Praise the child for what he did well; use frequent labeled praise.
10. Provide rewards and consequences—Use natural rewards, praise, favorite activities, and attention as rewards for good behavior.

To gather baseline data during Session 1, the provider begins by asking the parent about her most difficult daily interactions with the child. The provider narrows this down to the two most difficult home activities. For example, a parent might report that mealtime and bedtime are the most difficult activities with her child. Next, the provider conducts observations of the parent interacting with her child during play and the two activities. As much as possible, providers try to match the time of the difficult activity (e.g., hold a session in the morning if breakfast is a problem). If this is not feasible, role-plays can be used.

Following an introduction to help the parent feel comfortable, the provider unobtrusively observes the activities and scores behaviors observed and not observed using the PAT Checklist. The provider scores each of the 10 behaviors with a check for correct use of the skill and a minus for minimal or no use of the skill. By the end of the baseline assessment process, the provider will have completed three PAT Checklists, one for each activity. On each of the three checklists, the 10 PAT Steps will have been scored.

Training Training typically begins in Session 2, during which parents are taught to promote positive interactions with their child and increase structure. This includes teaching of skills on the PAT checklist. The provider uses the three scored PAT Checklists to guide training. Training sessions will be structured so that skills are taught in one setting before moving on to the next. That is, SafeCare providers focus on one activity at a time, and typically begin with a play activity in Session 2.

Session 2 begins with a session overview and rationale for the PAT skills. Following this, the provider begins to explain the 10 PAT steps and engages the parent in discussion about each. Following a discussion of the 10 steps, the provider models the PAT steps for the parent by playing with the child. If the child is not present, the steps can be modeled during a role-play with the parent. After the provider models the steps during play, the parent is prompted to practice, and the provider observes skills the parent is using well, and skills that need improvement.

During and after the activity, the provider offers positive and corrective feedback to the parent. Positive feedback should come before corrective feedback, as this is critical for building and maintaining rapport with the parent. Providers often must make choices about corrective feedback. In some cases, there may be quite a few skills in need of improvement. The provider should not overwhelm the parent with a long list of skill deficits. Rather, feedback should be provided on one or two skills at a time, and the provider works with the parent to improve those before moving on to others.

PCI Sessions 2 to 5 involve teaching skills during play and two routine activities. At the beginning of each training session, the provider first conducts an observation of the parent interacting with the child during the current activity. For example, if the provider focused on training during a play activity in Session 2, they would conduct an observation of a play activity at the beginning of Session 3. This allows the provider to gauge progress, and provides information about skills that need further practice. If a parent masters all the PAT steps in this assessment, the provider should move onto a new activity. Parents who do not master all steps, but show marked skill improvement, can move onto a new activity at the provider's discretion. This decision may be affected by the provider's judgment about the parent's ability to master the steps, the number of sessions allowable under a particular funding stream, and other factors that affect real world implementation of any program. In the final session, usually Session 6, the three activities that were the focus of training are re-assessed to obtain a final confirmation of mastery, skill retention, and skill generalization.

Working With Infants SafeCare has a module designed specifically for newborns to approximately 1 year of age, known as the Parent-Infant Interactions (PII) module. The goals for parents in PII are to increase positive interactions between parents and infants, teach parents to engage infants in activities, enhance responsivity between parents and their infants, and help parents learn how to plan activities. For PII, a variation of the PAT-Checklist is used to assess and teach skills; this is called the PAT-Checklist Infant Version. Although the structure of the assessment and teaching of skills is much like PCI, the specific skills taught during PII are somewhat different. PII skills focus on physical and verbal interactions between the parent and infant. Core skills that are taught for all infants include smiling, touching, looking, and positive verbalizing. Other skills taught, but which may vary across contexts and stages of infant development, include imitating the infant, holding, light bouncing, and rocking.

Health Module

Parents who are reported or at risk for maltreatment often lack the skills needed to provide adequate health care to their children (Cordon, Lutzker, Bigelow, & Doctor, 1998). Thus, they often make ineffective decisions about appropriate medical treatment (e.g., bring their child to the ER for a toothache, fail to bring child to doctor for bronchial infection, or get immunizations). Consequently, their children may become more at risk for health problems. The goals of the health module are to train parents to prevent childhood illnesses, identify symptoms of childhood illnesses and injuries, and provide and seek appropriate treatment for their children. The health module relies heavily on scenarios for role-playing. SafeCare health scenarios consist of 24 health conditions that are common to childhood. In each scenario, the provider describes symptoms of a common condition, and then he or she elicits responses from the parent about the condition (i.e., what it is) and about how the parent would assess and treat the condition. Scenarios include conditions that can be treated at home (e.g., a cold), that require a call or a visit to the physician (e.g., ear infection with fever), or require an emergency room visit (e.g., dog bite with open wound). As they are trained, parents are expected to correctly assess the symptoms and arrive at the correct outcomes (treat at home, call doctor, or go to ER). All parents are provided with a health manual that is used to determine the correct responses and to record the child's symptoms for accurate reporting to a physician.

Health Assessment

As with the PCI module, the same basic assessment process is used: (a) conduct baseline assessment; (b) conduct ongoing assessments during training to assess progress; and, (c) conduct posttraining assessment to determine skill mastery. To assess parents for baseline health-related behaviors and decision-making, three different types of role-play scenarios are administered: Treat at Home (TH), Call the Doctor (CD), and Emergency Treatment (ER). The key tool used to assess and score parent responses during role-play scenarios is the Sick and Injured Child Checklist (SICC). Table 17.2 provides key behaviors assessed on the SICC.

Administering and Scoring Scenarios For Treat at Home (TH), the provider begins by reading the parent a scenario and asking, "Tell me what the problem is" and "Show me what you would do." The parent is then asked additional nonleading questions to determine how she would respond over time, including whether the parent would check a health reference guide, call the doctor, or administer an appropriate treatment. For example, to assess whether she would continue to monitor symptoms and provide

Table 17.2 Key SICC Steps

First Steps in All Scenario Types
1. Parent identifies and states symptoms.
2. Assesses additional symptoms as needed (e.g., takes child's temperature). A Health Manual may be helpful.

Treat at Home Scenarios
1. Looks up symptoms/illness in a reference guide or consults a health professional.
2. Reads instructions on medicines or gets specific instructions about medicine from doctor.
3. Administers appropriate treatments correctly.
4. Checks symptoms again after recommended time.
5. If symptoms still present, continues treatment or calls doctor/nurse for advice.

Call the Doctor Scenarios
1. Calls the doctor's office.
2. Describes symptoms correctly.
3. Asks for or accepts an appointment.

ER Scenarios
1. Goes to the ER or calls 911.

treatment, the provider asks further questions (e.g., "It's three hours later, tell me and show me what you would do now"). If the child is not available to participate in the scenario, a doll may be used. In a Call the Doctor scenario, the provider assesses whether the parent will call the doctor and describe the symptoms appropriately to the doctor. If the parent correctly identifies that she needs to call the doctor, the provider prompts a role-play of calling the doctor's office. Parents are expected to accurately describe the symptoms they have observed and recorded. ER scenarios are fairly straightforward, as the one correct step is to call 911 or take the child to the ER.

For each of these scenarios, as the parent responds, the provider follows along the SICC checklist and scores the items based on the parent's responses (correct, incorrect, or not applicable).

Health Training The training phase of the Health module typically begins in Session 2, during which parents are taught to follow the steps of the SICC. Session 2 begins with a session overview and rationale for the SICC skills. Following this, the provider gives the parent a copy of a Health Manual and the reviews the organization of the manual in the Table of Contents. The provider then begins to explain the SICC steps and engages the parent in discussion about each one.

A collaborative discussion occurs for each of the SICC steps in the Treat at Home column. Following a discussion of the steps, the provider has the parent practice using a scenario. During this practice time, the provider observes skills the parent is using well, and skills that need improvement. Parents are expected to demonstrate the behaviors that would be involved in assessing and treating the condition (e.g., taking a temperature, measuring medication). The provider also helps guide the parent to engage in correct steps and use the Health Manual for reference as needed. During and after the activity, the provider provides positive and corrective feedback based on the SICC checklist.

The decision to move on to a new type of scenario in Sessions 3 to 5 (e.g., move from Treat at Home scenarios to Call the Doctor) is determined by parent mastery of the SICC steps. For example, when a parent can score 100% correct on Treat at Home role-play steps, the provider moves on to a Call the Doctor scenario. The Call the Doctor steps are taught using the same explanation, model, practice, feedback process. Once the parent shows 100% correct steps in a Call the Doctor scenario, training is provided on an ER scenario. The final session, often Session 6, is a re-assessment conducted to confirm mastery of skills during the three different types of role-plays.

While the first part of every health session is spent on role-plays, the second part of every session focuses on education, prevention, and practice of behavioral skills. Sample topics that are taught and practiced during these session segments include:

- Helpful Medical Supplies
- Taking Temperatures
- When to Call 911 or Go to the Emergency Room
- When to Call the Doctor's Office or Nurse Hotline
- Hygiene
- Regular Medical Checkups and Immunizations
- Sleep Safety and Sudden Infant Death Syndrome (SIDS) Prevention

Safety Module

The Safety module seeks to prevent unintentional injuries by helping parents make their homes safe and encouraging supervision. A home with multiple hazards accessible to children or with filth and clutter places children in the home at risk of safety and health hazards, and can lead to a CPS (Child Protective Services) referral for environmental neglect. Children's natural curiosity and poor impulse control can draw their attention to home hazards that can result in injury and sometimes death. Most home accident fatalities involving children between birth and 4 years are caused by accidents involving suffocation, drowning, poisoning, and fire (Centers for Disease Control and Prevention, 2005). SafeCare defines an accessible hazard as one that is both reachable by the child and unsecured, meaning in an unlocked container or space, and without a childproof cap.

As with the other SafeCare modules, a baseline assessment of the home environment to identify hazards precedes the training phase. The training phase focuses on assisting parents in identifying hazards accessible to their child and removing or securing them. Parental supervision is strongly emphasized in the training phase as well.

Safety Assessment The initial safety baseline focuses on three rooms and includes a thorough search for accessible home hazards. The selection of rooms for assessment should be based on where children spend most of their time. The key tool used during the Safety module assessment is the Home Accident Prevention Inventory-Revised (HAPI-R), a validated and reliable assessment checklist designed to help the provider measure the number of hazards accessible to children in a home. The HAPI-R hazard categories are provided in Table 17.3.

Prior to gathering baseline data during Session 1, the provider must obtain written permission from the parent to assess different rooms in the home. The consent form details how the assessment process will be conducted, including that the provider will need to look in such places as cabinets and drawers. The parent is given the opportunity to decline any portion of the assessment, or to specify places where she does not want the provider to look.

Following the consent and an introduction, the provider measures the eye level and reach of the tallest child to determine which items are accessible. A child can climb onto anything that is at or below eye level. The provider begins in one room, and moves around the room in a clockwise fashion to find all hazardous items within reach of the child. It is important that the provider look in all cabinets, drawers, under furniture, and

Table 17.3 HAPI–R Hazard Categories

Solids and Liquids (e.g., medicines, cleaners)	**Organic Matter and Allergens** (e.g., decaying food, animal droppings)
Fire & Electrical (e.g., matches, bare electrical cords)	**Falling & Trip** (e.g., balconies, nongated steps)
Suffocation (e.g., plastics, hanging cords)	**Crush** (e.g., boxes or other heavy objects the child could pull down on him/herself)
Small Objects (e.g., pennies, jellybeans)	**Drowning** (e.g., water in bathtubs, sinks, pools, or buckets)
Sharp Objects (e.g., knives, razors)	**Firearms** (guns)

behind furniture. Accessible hazards are recorded on the HAPI-R. At the end of the assessment of one room, the number of hazards is tallied to yield a total score for the room. A new HAPI-R is used for every room assessed; thus, by the end of the assessment process, the provider will have completed three HAPI-Rs.

Safety Training The training phase of the Safety module typically begins in Session 2, during which the provider gives a session overview and rationale for identifying and removing home safety hazards. Following this, the provider explains the 10 categories of hazards and engages the parent in discussion about each category. The provider then discusses how to determine if hazards are accessible and also how to reduce identified hazards. The provider gives feedback about the HAPI-R scores from the first room and models how to find and remove hazards from Room 1. Hazards are removed by using a childproof latch or lock, or placing the object out of the child's reach. The responsibility of identifying and removing hazards gradually shifts from the provider to the parent. As the parent practices, the provider gives positive and corrective feedback, as well as modeling, when appropriate.

Sessions 3 to 5 begin with a review of the room addressed in the previous session and identification of any remaining hazards. The provider continues to model and give feedback, and only proceeds to the next room once a parent has eliminated all accessible hazards in the current room. Mastery for the safety module is defined as zero hazards in each room. For a variety of reasons (e.g., other adults living in the home, hazards that are beyond the parent's control to remedy) it is often difficult to reach zero hazards. However, drastic reductions in hazards are typically seen, and thus success (marked improvement from baseline) can still be achieved. When all hazards cannot be removed, the importance of parental supervision around the remaining hazards is emphasized. Session 5 involves a discussion of additional measures to ensure the safety of children in the home. Topics covered include burns and scalds, gun safety, carbon monoxide detectors, fire safety, and car seats. Session 6, often the last session in the module, is designed to re-evaluate how well the parent has maintained gains in the three rooms trained. The provider uses the HAPI-R to re-asses the original three rooms. Problem solving for the identification and removal of future hazards also occurs.

Common Challenges in Conducting SafeCare

Implementation of any evidence-based program brings with it inherent challenges. In the following section, some common challenges and special populations are discussed. These include implementation of SafeCare with parents with limited reading abilities, engagement, cultural adaptations, children with special needs, and implementation within community settings.

Parents With Limited Reading Abilities

It is common for SafeCare providers to encounter parents who have intellectual disabilities, suspected intellectual disabilities, or have limited reading abilities. Informal surveys of SafeCare sites have suggested that as many as one-third of parents served by SafeCare may have an intellectual disability. This can create a challenge for providers, as several of the SafeCare materials, particularly the Health materials, rely on reading skills. Parents with intellectual disabilities are especially at risk for child neglect; thus, it is important to reach this critical audience.

Several strategies may be needed to serve families with limited reading abilities. First, the provider should plan for additional sessions beyond the typical six per module. Parents with intellectual disabilities will likely need additional time to learn and process the new information. They also may need an increased number of opportunities for behavioral rehearsal of skills and repetition in order to master the SafeCare skills. Second, providers will need to be creative in utilizing other resources for communicating information. For example, during Health training, instead of relying on the Health Manual as a primary reference, the provider and parent can practice seeking health information by calling a nurse hotline. Third, providers can ask parents if there is family or friends available who might be able to assist with using reading-based reference materials. For example, a helpful neighbor or family member can assist the parent in referencing the Health Manual, if needed. Finally, picture aids should be used whenever possible. Forms such as the PAT Checklist can be supplemented by picture cues to help the parent learn and remember specific steps. Frequent praise and teaching in smaller steps should be employed.

Adaptations are currently underway to address this important issue. Given that the Health module is the most literacy-dependent module, adaptations are being created specifically for parents with intellectual disabilities and limited reading abilities. This adaptation will include a reduced reading level and an increased number of pictures to represent key concepts and behavioral steps.

Engaging Families

Engagement of families can be a challenge, especially if those families are being served as part of child welfare services and may have a history of negative experiences with social service providers (Webster-Stratton & Reid, 2010). Within child welfare, families may fear being reported to CPS systems, having their children removed, and may generally perceive child welfare workers as paternalistic. When delivered as part of child welfare services, parents may meet the SafeCare provider (or a provider of any service) with skepticism and lack of trust, and initial rapport may be difficult to establish. However, in a statewide study of SafeCare in Oklahoma, families receiving SafeCare were more satisfied with services and rated their providers as more culturally competent than families receiving standard family preservation (Silovsky, 2009). Still, engagement will pose a challenge for any service provider working within a child welfare system.

A number of provider behaviors and strategies can be helpful in improving family engagement. Demonstration of empathy and respect are certainly important in the development of rapport with parents; however, research shows that these qualities are most effective when combined with specific behaviors and interactions that take place between a provider and parent. These behaviors and interactions include: providing collaborative services that clients find important and helpful, focusing on specific client skills as opposed to insights, setting mutually acceptable treatment goals, and spending enough time with clients to demonstrate skills and provide concrete resources (Dawson & Berry, 2002). These practices can all help to improve engagement in child welfare services when applied in a collaborative, supportive, and nonblaming way.

One additional research-based intervention method for improving client engagement and motivation is the Motivational Interviewing approach. *Motivational Interviewing (MI) is a directive, client-centered counseling style for eliciting behavior change by helping clients to explore and resolve ambivalence* (Miller & Rollnick, 2002). In comparison to traditional nondirective approaches, MI is goal-oriented. It was originally developed for use with individuals with substance abuse histories, but is quickly emerging as a preferred approach for engagement in many types of intervention services, including child welfare. MI has been implemented with other evidence-based parenting programs (i.e., Parent-Child Interaction Therapy) delivered in a child welfare setting and has effectively increased parent participation and completion of the intervention (Chaffin et al., 2009).

Cultural Adaptations

Given the culturally diverse nature of families involved with child welfare, it is important for providers to be culturally sensitive. In some cases, the need for cultural adaptations can arise. There is a debate in the field about whether adaptations of evidence-based programs are needed for particular cultural groups, or whether programs can successfully be implemented without adaptation. Some argue that cultural adaptations may improve communication between providers and their clients as well as client comfort and engagement, all of which may increase retention in SafeCare services.

In an exploratory study by Self-Brown and colleagues (Self-Brown et al., under review) findings indicated that practitioners perceive SafeCare to work well with culturally diverse populations and do not recommend making systematic adaptations for specific populations. The study participants noted concerns that cultural adaptations for specific populations (e.g., specific adaptations for Hispanic families) could inappropriately stereotype individuals or families based on their membership in a large sociocultural group. Although culturally specific adaptations were not recommended, findings indicated that more general adaptations, used on a case-by-case basis, can be helpful. For instance, many providers recommended being flexible in terms of session scheduling and the inclusion of extended family members or others who serve a caretaking role. Other common adaptations discussed included modifying materials to be more culturally acceptable and using culturally accepted verbiage or language when describing or explaining commonly targeted SafeCare skills. For instance, in one state providers added a health scenario related to fallen fontanelle, a commonly occurring health issue with the Latino families served in that area, to the SafeCare health module. Other providers adapted the way they presented the term *active ignoring*, especially for African-American parents, which is a targeted skill in the parent-child interaction module. Language-based adaptations also included making Spanish translations on written materials more appropriate or revising materials so that the reading level was more appropriate for parents. Importantly, participants did not report reductions in dosage or elimination of critical content from SafeCare when making modifications or adaptations—changes that have been associated with reducing positive outcomes for other evidence based practices (Castro et al., 2004; Kumpfer et al., 2002).

Children With Special Needs

SafeCare teaches a range of skills that are helpful in promoting health, safety, and positive parent-child interactions and preventing some child behavior problems; however, it may be insufficient to address children with special clinical or developmental needs. Examples of such cases include children with developmental disabilities, pervasive developmental disabilities (e.g., autism), and children with severe behavior problems. In these cases, it is important for the provider to identify the extent of the family's needs. In most cases, a referral to an intervention program specially designed for the need is recommended. For example, a child with a developmental disability may need a referral to a program that provides a more customized intervention designed using a functional analysis for problem behavior. Similarly, a child with severe behavior problems may be better served by an evidence-based program that focuses more specifically on teaching parents noncoercive discipline strategies as well as the promotion of positive parent child interactions, such as Parent Child Interaction Therapy (PCIT). As discussed in Chapter 5 of this volume (and in Appendix A), PCIT has been found to be an effective intervention protocol for reducing behavior problems in children with oppositional defiant disorder and conduct disorder (Eyberg et al., 2001).

Implementing Evidenced–Based Practice Within Community Settings

For an effective practice such as SafeCare to have a large impact on child maltreatment, it must be implemented broadly. Any treatment can be broadly disseminated by the distribution of training manuals; however, the dissemination of training manuals usually does not lead to proper implementation (Baumann, Kolko, Collins, & Herschell, 2006). Rather, there is a growing literature that suggests that rigorous training models are needed for implementation with fidelity (Fixsen, Naoom, Blasé, Friedman, & Wallace, 2005), and a very large literature that suggests that implementation with fidelity is related to better family outcomes (Durlak & DuPre, 2008).

Faculty and staff at the National SafeCare Training and Research Center (NSTRC), formed in 2007, have developed a rigorous training model that attempts to ensure the success of SafeCare dissemination and implementation, with an emphasis on program sustainability. The training model involves several steps, including:

> ➤ Addressing site readiness through initial assessments of capacity to conduct SafeCare.

> ➤ Conducting orientation visits prior to workshop training to ensure that all parties are informed of the model and the training procedure.

> Training workshops that involve didactics and trainee demonstration of SafeCare skills through role-play to a mastery criterion.

> Ongoing coaching in the field, which includes fidelity monitoring of sessions, to ensure SafeCare is delivered as designed (this is typically done by locally trained coaches).

> Trainer training (if desired) so that sites can train new staff members in SafeCare without relying on NSTRC.

At the time of this writing, NSTRC has trained several hundred providers across 10 states. NSTRC is working to develop the most rigorous training model possible, by incorporating technology into training to reduce the face-to-face time necessary for training, and by rigorously evaluating the effectiveness and costs of various training components. As data become available on the effectiveness of new training processes, they will be incorporated into NSTRC's dissemination model.

Conclusion

SafeCare has had a number of different studies to support its efficacy as a CM prevention model (Gershater-Molko et al., 2002). It has been rated by families as a model that is culturally sensitive and satisfying as compared to services as usual delivered in the child welfare setting. Further, providers describe the model as easy to implement and learn, and as a model that works for improving parenting skills across diverse groups of families. The dissemination and implementation of SafeCare is increasing, as training for SafeCare providers involves using training manuals, checklists of steps to follow, and practice activities. Further, SafeCare implementation always involves the coaching process, which ensures that providers attain and maintain fidelity to the model. It also utilizes implementation strategies that value the importance of readiness, and provides opportunities for training trainers to promote sustainability at new SafeCare sites.

NSTRC has numerous goals and opportunities that will be explored. First, it is important that we understand more about factors involved with successful implementation. As well, future research needs to assess how technology may facilitate more cost-effective implementation. Staff members at NSTRC also seek to understand more about how to tailor this model to meet family needs. For example, it may be that SafeCare combined with other evidence-based programs, or with added components such as Intimate Partner Violence or substance abuse modules, may increase family outcomes. Thus, much interesting important work will continue to examine SafeCare effectiveness for families, as well as the most viable and efficient processes for leading to widespread implementation.

References

Bandura, A. (1977). *Social learning theory*. Oxford, England: Prentice-Hall.

Baumann, B. L., Kolko, D. J., Collins, K., & Herschell, A. D. (2006). Understanding practitioners' characteristics and perspectives prior to the dissemination of an evidence-based intervention. *Child Abuse & Neglect, 30*(7), 771–787.

Baumrind, D. (1991). The influence of parenting style on adolescent competence and substance use. *The Journal of Early Adolescence, 11*(1), 56–95.

Castro, F. G., Barrera, M., & Martinez, C. R. (2004). The cultural adaptation of prevention implementations: Resolving tensions between fidelity and fit. *Prevention Science, 5*(1), 41–45.

Centers for Disease Control and Prevention, N. C. f. I. P. a. C. (2005). *Web-based injury statistics query and reporting system (WISQARS).* Retrieved August 15, 2010 from http://webappa.cdc.gov/sasweb/ncipc/mortrate10_sy.html

Chaffin, M., Valle, L. A., Funderburk, B., Gurwitch, R., Silovsky, J., Bard, D., McCoy, C., and Kees, M. (2009). A motivational intervention can improve retention in PCIT for low-motivation child welfare clients. *Child Maltreatment, 14*(4), 356–368.

Cordon, I., Lutzker, J., Bigelow, K., & Doctor, R. (1998). Evaluating Spanish protocols for teaching bonding, home safety, and health care skills to a mother reported for child abuse. *Journal of Behavior Therapy and Experimental Psychiatry, 29*(1), 41–54.

Dawson, K., & Berry, M. (2002). Engaging families in child welfare services: An evidence-based approach to best practice. *Child Welfare: Journal of Policy, Practice, and Program, 81*(2), 293–317.

Durlak, J. A., & DuPre, E. P. (2008). Implementation matters: A review of research on the influence of implementation on program outcomes and the factors affecting implementation. *American Journal of Community Psychology, 41*(3), 327–350.

Eyberg, S. M., Funderburk, B. W., Hembree-Kigin, T. L., McNeil, C. B., Querido, J. G., & Hood, K. K. (2001). Parent-child interaction therapy with behavior problem children: One and two year maintenance of treatment effects in the family. *Child and Family Behavior Therapy, 23*(4), 1–20.

Fixsen, D., Naoom, S., Blasé, K., Friedman, R., & Wallace, F. (2005). *Implementation research: A synthesis of the literature.* Tampa: University of South Florida.

Gershater-Molko, R., Lutzker, J., & Wesch, D. (2003). Project SafeCare: Improving health, safety, and parenting skills in families reported for, and at-risk for child maltreatment. *Journal of Family Violence, 18*(6), 377–386.

Gershater-Molko, R. M., Lutzker, J. R., & Wesch, D. (2002). Using recidivism to evaluate project SafeCare: Teaching bonding, safety, and health care skills to parents. *Child Maltreatment, 7*(3), 277–285.

Hart, B., & Risley, T. R. (1995). *Meaningful differences in the everyday experience of young American children.* Baltimore, MD: Brookes.

Kumpfer, K. L., Alvarado, R., Smith, P., & Bellamy, N. (2002). Cultural sensitivity and adaptation in family-based prevention interventions. *Prevention Science, 3*(3), 241–246.

Latham, G. P., & Saari, L. M. (1979). Application of social-learning theory to training supervisors through behavioral modeling. *Journal of Applied Psychology, 64*(3), 239–246.

Miller, W. R., & Rollnick, S. (2002). *Motivational interviewing: Preparing people for change.* New York, NY: Guilford Press.

Self-Brown, S., Frederick, K., Binder, S., Whitaker, D., Lutzker, J., Edwards, A., & Blankenship, J. (Under Review). *Examining the need for cultural adaptations to an evidence-based parent training program targeting the prevention of child maltreatment.*

Silovsky, J. F. (2009, August). *Prevention of child maltreatment in families at high risk.* Paper presented at the University of Oklahoma Health Sciences Center, Oklahoma City, OK.

U.S. Department of Health and Human Services. (2009). *Child Maltreatment 2007.*

Webster-Stratton, C., & Reid, M.J. (2010). Adapting the Incredible Years, an evidence-based parenting program, for families involved in the child welfare system. *Journal of Children's Services, 5*(1), 25–42.

18
Parenting Wisely

Enhancing Wise Practice for Service Providers

Robert E. Pushak and Donald A. Gordon

Parenting Wisely (PW) is a video-based interactive computer training program for parents and families that targets multiple risk and protective factors for behavior problems, youth violence, school dropout, youth substance use, and a host of other negative child outcomes (Gordon, 2003). The program provides skill training in several areas including the use of communications skills, I statements, active listening, contracting, monitoring child behavior, problem-solving skills, assertive discipline, positive reinforcement, speaking respectfully, and contingency management. Parents are also given strategies that target risk factors that go beyond the immediate context of the family, such as managing difficulties at school and dealing with negative peer influences. This training occurs in the context of a family systems perspective, which emphasizes the interdependence of family members' interactions. The program has a cognitive emphasis, and various family members' thoughts are depicted as setting a context that shapes family interactions.

The program can be self-administered by parents or used by practitioners together with their clients, and it can be used for group parent training. The program was designed to be easy to use. Parents who are functionally illiterate or have little computer experience can successfully use the program on their own after a short tutorial on how to use a mouse. Parents can complete the interactive computer portion of the program in 2.5 to 3 hours. Parents are initially presented with 10 family-problem scenarios, including: getting children to cooperate with housework; helping children with school problems; dealing with a child who stays out too late; step-parent/step-child conflict; monitoring school, homework, and friends; loud music and incomplete chores; speaking respectfully and sharing computer time; sibling conflict and aggression; getting children ready for school on time; and peer influences and drug use. Parents can choose a problem scenario by clicking the mouse. These problem scenarios were chosen based on research identifying common family problems that tend to frequently occur in high-risk families.

Voiceovers from the actors communicate parents' and children's thoughts that contribute to the family conflict.

After viewing a problem scenario parents are provided with three choices for responding to that problem and are prompted to choose the response that they are most likely to use. Parents can make their choice by clicking on that response. The parents then watch another video depicting how the parents' chosen response is likely to play out. This is followed by feedback in the form of questions and answers that help the parents consider the pros and cons of their choices and why it is or is not an effective solution. Parents can then make a second, and later if they wish, a third choice on how they might respond to the problem scenario. Parents then watch another video depicting how that choice is likely to play out followed by another review quiz. This helps parents realize that child problem behavior can be greatly increased or reduced depending on how parents respond to that behavior. Text that appears on the bottom of the screen helps parents to identify effective skills portrayed by the actors. Usually two of the solution videos depict parents making a number of mistakes. The remaining solution video depicts a parent using several effective parenting skills and for the most part responding in a more effective way. Sometimes the parent still makes a few mistakes in the video of the effective solution. This lets parents know that use of new skills can still help improve family interactions even if the parent's performance is not always perfect.

During the review quiz parents can click on specific skills such as "Praise" or "I Messages," which are highlighted in bold text. A voice along with written text defines the skill and discusses the advantages of using the skill. Clicking on a "Play examples" button at the bottom of the screen activates examples of the actors using that particular skill. After completing the review questions for the more effective solution, parents can precede to multiple choice questions that test their knowledge of the skills and content covered so far. Both the review questions and the multiple-choice test help parents recognize how internal self-talk sets up family interactions in healthy and not so healthy ways. For each problem scenario parents must view the more effective solution and complete the review questions before the computer allows them to proceed to the next problem scenario.

After completing the computer portion of the program parents are given a *Parenting Wisely Program* workbook. The workbook introduces each skill by describing the purpose of the skill followed by a list of Advantages of how the skill will benefit parents and their families. Next the skill is broken down into numbered How to Use steps followed by several examples of the skill.

The primary home practice assignments in the workbook are point systems, active listening, I messages, problem solving, contracting, and assertive discipline. Other skills covered in the program include attending, planned ignoring, job compliance, setting consequences, contracting, mindfulness, prompting, role modeling, school and home-work monitoring, monitoring peer relationships, cognitive reframes, specific commands, and praise.

The program can be accessed on the Internet either in a family's home or through a community service agency or a public library. The CD-ROM, DVD, and the Internet-based versions of the program automatically track how much of the program has been completed and track the parent's performance on review questions. The online version has recently been revised, with a grant from the National Institute of Drug Abuse. In addition to a new video, the instructional design stimulates more skill practice within the program, and promotes ongoing skill practice and use via email prompts with additional exercises. There is more focus on enhancing the quality of parent-child relationships through mindful parenting practices, which are explained and legitimized using neuroscience.

Relevance to Child Welfare

Parent training based on social learning principles is one of the few interventions that has been shown to reduce recidivism rates for parents who are physically abusive to their children (Chaffin et al., 2004). PW has been shown to reduce rates of family violence, including spouse abuse, in families with child welfare concerns who were previously resistant to intervention efforts (Gordon, Kacir, & Pushak, 2008; Rolland-Stanar, Gordon, Carlston, & Pushak, 2008). There are several aspects to the PW program that enhance its suitability for child protection work. The program can achieve rapid reductions in child behavior problems and make quick improvements in family functioning soon after families have first become involved in child protection services (Segal, Chen, Gordon, Kacir, & Gylys, 2003).

Families involved with child welfare agencies are often difficult to engage and are quick to drop out of intervention services. When service providers try to discuss parenting issues parents feel judged and criticized. A great deal of service provider time is squandered dealing with problems related to resistance. Parents do not feel judged or criticized when using a self-administered computer program. On the computer program parents are able to view common parenting mistakes made by other parents. This allows parents to learn better parenting strategies without reference to their own poor parenting skills. Because PW can achieve rapid gains in family functioning it is easier to maintain families in intervention services since parents are seeing benefits shortly after initial contact. Table 18.1 lists several advantages of self-administered PW compared to therapy or counseling. These advantages likely contribute to the quick gains mentioned earlier.

Practitioner Strategies

We shall consider a number of implementation suggestions for direct service practitioners, many of which are unique to PW.

Contacting Parents

When service providers first contact parents we recommend that they suggest meeting alone with parents for the first appointment rather than meeting both the parents and the child. The parents can be told that if they wish to pass on information about their child's negative behavior it might be better to not do this in front of their child. If both the parent

Table 18.1 Comparison of Therapy and Interactive Computer–Based Intervention

Therapy	Interactive computer program
1. Verbal and sometimes abstract descriptions of parenting skills.	1. Specific and detailed visual and verbal examples of parenting skills.
2. Focus on developing and maintaining therapist-client rapport.	2. Exclusive focus on teaching good parenting.
3. Client often feels judged by therapist.	3. No perception of judgment by computer
4. Client defensiveness main obstacle to progress.	4. Minimal client defensiveness.
5. Therapist confronts client on parenting mistakes.	5. Client recognizes common parenting mistakes made by actors.
6. Client receives infrequent and indirect feedback on parenting errors.	6. Client actively seeks feedback on parenting errors performed by actors.
7. Client rarely asks for repetition of unclear advice.	7. Client can repeat any portion of the program at any time.
8. Pace usually set by therapist.	8. Client sets pace.
9. Infrequent reinforcement of good parenting practices.	9. Very frequent reinforcement of good parenting practices.
10. Possible decreased self-efficacy if benefits of intervention are attributed to suggestions made by therapist.	10. Increased self-efficacy because client attributes benefits to their own choices.
11. Risk of client becoming entrenched in victim role and becoming overly dependent on therapist for emotional support.	11. Risk of becoming overly emotionally dependent on computer program is unlikely.
12. Majority of therapy time devoted to resistance.	12. Virtually no program time devoted to resistance.
13. Difficult to train or improve therapist skills in evidence-based practice.	13. Relatively easy to improve program structure and content as evidence-base continues to develop.
14. Maintaining program integrity is difficult and expensive.	14. Program integrity is automatic.
15. Ongoing costs of intervention are high.	15. Ongoing costs are low.

Adapted from Gordon (2003).

and the child attend the first appointment together there is a danger that if for any reason the clinician fails to engage the child the parent is not likely to attend any further sessions. Without the child present the service provider is free to focus exclusively on engaging the parent into the parent education program.

During the first session the service provider can describe the PW program and let parents know the program can be completed in 3 hours or less, achieve very quick improvements in child behavior, and improve family relationships. Very often an appointment can be set up for the parent to complete the self-administered program before the session where the service provider meets the child. Then if the family does drop out of treatment prematurely they have at least received one dose of a program that significantly reduces child behavior problems (Cefai, Smith, & Pushak, 2010; Gordon et al., 2008; Pushak & Pretty, 2008) and family violence (Rolland-Stanar et al., 2008).

Using Parents' Goals

Engaging parents mandated to receive child welfare services can be daunting. One of the best ways to engage parents is to ask them to identify any goals they may have for their child or for their family. The service provider can then speak to how PW can help the parent to achieve their goals. The most common reason parents seek access to child services is due to problems with child behavior. Many service providers are reluctant to focus on this goal because child behavior problems are often resistant to intervention. This, however, is not a problem for service providers using the PW program. Practitioners can tell parents that this program can significantly reduce behavior problems in many children. After parents have completed the program many children no longer score in the clinically significant range for behavior disorders (Pushak & Pretty, 2008).

For example, a social worker once referred a mother to a practitioner who could provide PW and noted that the mother was hunting for a diagnosis of oppositional defiant disorder (ODD) for her son. The social worker indicated that there was nothing really wrong with the child. She stated that the mother's inept parenting was the real problem and said that the mother had already indicated she would refuse to attend any parent training. This mother was adamant that her son's behavior had nothing to do with her parenting abilities. When the mother was phoned to set up an appointment she repeated that she did not need parent training. During the first appointment with the PW provider the mother indicated that she believed her son had ODD but nobody was willing to diagnose it. After engaging her in a review of the diagnostic criteria for ODD she was told that based on the information she was providing her son did meet criteria for ODD. The mother was very pleased to hear this. She was then asked what kind of service she was looking for, and she responded she wanted treatment for ODD. The practitioner smiled and told her that he had a powerful program for treating ODD, called Parenting Wisely. He had no further trouble engaging the mother in using the program.

Role-Plays and the Neurobiology of Social Learning

Research is beginning to show that when humans observe someone else performing an action this triggers the firing of neurons in the observer's brain that mirror the firing of neurons in the person performing the action (Mukamel, Ekstrom, Kaplan, Iacoboni, & Fried, 2010). This activation of mirror neurons may help to explain why video-based role modeling of parenting skills is an effective way to teach parents better parenting practices. When parents watch someone else demonstrate a new parenting skill this activates neural pathways in the brain for performing this skill. If service providers entice parents into performing this skill in a role-play this activates and strengthens the neural pathway related to these actions. This enhances the learning process and increases the chances parents will use this skill in the future. When practitioners try to teach parenting skills verbally, by explaining and instructing, mirror neurons are not activated because parents are not observing actions. Their ability to remember and reproduce verbally transmitted information is impaired relative to visually transmitted information. The superiority of visual memory to auditory memory may explain why PW, which uses extensive videotaped modeling, achieves such quick and strong results compared to other approaches that rely on verbal instruction.

Practitioners can provide a rationale for role-plays by pointing out that it is a good idea for parents to practice skills before they try them out with their families. The tone used in engaging parents in role-plays needs to be positive and supportive without being condescending. Although some parents may express hesitation about role-plays, if the practitioner acts in a confident, matter-of-fact manner, most parents can be enticed into role-plays with little difficulty. It is often a good idea to use the scenes depicted in the computer program for the role-plays. This will activate mirror neurons in the parent's

Table 18.2 Steps for Role-Plays

1. Watch the skill performed in the computer program.
2. Refer to the workbook and discuss purpose of skills.
3. Discuss advantages of skill listed in the workbook.
4. Discuss steps of skill in workbook.
5. Practitioner demonstrates skill or rewatch skill on computer program.
6. Review steps covered in role-play.
7. Parent has opportunity to ask questions.
8. Parent practices skill in role-play with practitioner providing frequent, enthusiastic praise for each step.
9. Ignore any mistakes or omissions.
10. Prompt parent to do another role-play and make the skill even stronger by adding in any missing component.

brain that correspond to the practice of that skill. The practitioner can play the role of the parent first to demonstrate the skill while the parent plays the role of the child. After modeling the skill the practitioner should review the steps of the skill described in the workbook and demonstrated in the role-play. Next, parents can be given an opportunity to ask questions before it is their turn to practice the skill. Especially in the beginning parents should be given praise for each step in the role-play. Practitioners should not point out any errors or omissions in the parent's performance. Instead, the practitioner should enthusiastically praise each component of the role-play the parent did correctly. Next, the parents can be asked to repeat the role-play and make it even stronger by adding in the missing component. Table 18.2 provides a summary of the steps of the role-plays.

Parents can be asked to complete the exercises in the workbook that are related to that specific skill and bring the completed exercises to the next session so the practitioner can provide feedback. When assigning home practice service providers should provide a rationale for a recommended parenting skill by referring back to the advantages of using a specific skill. It will be easier to engage parents in home practice assignments if practitioners are familiar enough with this material that they can connect practice of these skills to any goals indentified by the parent at first contact. In these discussions care must be taken to not blame the parent for the family's problems. Blaming clients for their problems, even if the problems are largely self-imposed, does not facilitate engagement and has been shown to lead to dropout. Patterson and Chamberlain (1994) have shown that when therapists respond to caregiver resistance with teaching or confrontation parental resistance and rates of dropout increase, but when they respond to a resistant parent with nondirective support, problems with resistance and dropout decrease.

Benchmark Parent Knowledge Test Strategy for Parents Mandated to Receive Service

The program comes with a CD with a number of measures including the Parent Knowledge Test (PKT), which measures parents' knowledge of the skills taught in the PW program. For parents who are resistant to intervention or claim they already know and use the parenting skills taught in the PW program it can be helpful to require the parents to achieve a benchmark score on the PKT as evidence that they have a desirable knowledge level of effective parenting skills. For example, a PW provider received a referral from a middle school for a single father and his son who had been suspended for fighting at school. The school indicated they would not allow the boy to return to school until the family was involved in treatment and until the practitioner made the recommendation for the boy to return to school. The father was angry because the practitioner would not make an immediate recommendation for his son to return to school. The practitioner told the father that if he completed self-administered PW and scored over 80% on the PKT he would write a letter recommending his son's return to school. He indicated that the father could redo the self-administered program as many times as he liked until his test scores were high enough. In the sessions with the practitioner the father was far too hostile for the practitioner to try to do any instruction. Instead, he worked on calming the father down, letting him know that his test scores were improving, and encouraging him to try again. Since the practitioner was not present while the father was completing the computer program his anger toward the practitioner didn't undermine his opportunity to learn from PW. The father completed the self-administered PW four times before he scored more than 80% on the test. In the next session he sat in the practitioner's office with his face down and stated that his relationship with his son and his son's behavior were both improving. He asked if he could continue working with the practitioner because he was worried that he might not be able to maintain these gains on his own. The father attended the next PW group program, where he continued to make gains. Earlier the practitioner chose to not invite the father to attend the group program because at that time his hostility toward the practitioner would have been problematic for the other parents.

Clients Who Talk Too Much

Probably all experienced service providers have encountered clients who are overly talkative and who jump from topic to topic, and this makes it difficult to engage them in productive work. It is easy to waste considerable time in discussions that are either not relevant to the referral problem, or worse, that are actually counterproductive. Self-administered PW is an obvious choice for these types of clients, but these clients are often seeking therapist attention and may not be that interested in a self-administered program. It can be helpful for service providers to use the PW program together with these clients. The discussion generated by the program automatically allows the service provider to shift the conversation away from unproductive discussions such as a parent who rattles on about a litany of complaints about other family members' negative behavior. The content of the PW program automatically focuses on material that is positive, therapeutically relevant, and productive. If the client begins to stray from pertinent conversation it is easy to use a click of the mouse to bring the discussion back to a conversation, which productively addresses the concerns that initially led to the need for service.

Attribution of Change and Program Sustainability

Service providers should be aware of a potential weakness of self-administered use of PW with a subgroup of parents and how this problem can be avoided. We refer here to parents who do not make a conscious effort at changing their behavior but still make subtle changes in their behavior that lead to quick improvements in family functioning.[1] Unfortunately, if parents do not recognize that they have changed their behavior they may be less likely to maintain these changes. When parents use the program they are seeing examples of some of the most common mistakes parents make, such as yelling or using coercion to force children into doing what the parents want. After viewing the program, most parents unintentionally reduce the frequency of making these parenting mistakes. Parents may already use some of the more effective parenting strategies depicted in the program, so use of the program may prompt parents into using these more effective strategies more often—for example, giving encouragement. Parents who are not consciously aware of how use of the program has changed their behavior are less likely to anecdotally report improvements in child behavior or in family functioning to practitioners. This may result in service providers concluding that the self-administered PW is less effective than the research suggests.

There are a number of strategies for helping parents to recognize how their behavior has changed. For example, parents can be asked to complete an objective outcome measure prior to using PW and then repeat use of the measure a few weeks after they have used the program. If there is a discrepancy between the parent's anecdotal report and improvements on the outcome measure, this can be drawn to the parent's attention and they can be asked to reflect on what might have led to the improved child behavior. One common spontaneous improvement is parents tending to yell less frequently at their children following use of PW. If prompted, parents are often more likely to acknowledge they are yelling less frequently. It is also useful to ask parents if they are feeling more confident in their parenting. After reflecting on this, many parents report they are more confident because they now have a greater number of options for dealing with difficult behavior. If parents are more confident in their use of effective discipline, then their children are less likely to test them.

If parents report that they did not learn much that was new from PW but found that the program affirmed many things they already were doing with their children, it is helpful for practitioners to point out that the parents perhaps are using these positive strategies more often. It is important for service providers to empower parents by helping them to become aware of their attitudinal and behavior changes and how these changes are related to the improvement in their child's and family's functioning. Otherwise, these gains may be less likely to endure. Program sustainability has been better at sites that track clinical outcomes on standardized measures (Gordon & Rolland-Stanar, 2003). This may be due to practitioners having more tangible evidence of program effectiveness than agencies that rely solely on anecdotal parent reports.

Another reason the PW program is sustained once implemented is that practitioners experience personal benefits from its use. In a study of 25 practitioners in British Columbia who use the PW program, 87.5% reported a reduction in job stress and

---

[1] This is a problem only with a subgroup of parents. The Cefai study discussed later shows there is another subgroup of parents where parent self-efficacy is increased by self-administered PW.

burnout as a consequence of using PW. All the practitioners reported an increase in job satisfaction, and 87.5% indicated a greater interest in evidence-based approaches (Pushak & Nihie, 2005).

Program Integrity

A word of caution should be made that when service providers use PW together with their clients the program's effectiveness can be undermined by reducing some of the advantages of the self-administered program that were listed in Table 18.1. An evaluation of the Young Child version of PW (Hoskins, McFarlane, & Tattersall, 2002) failed to find significant reductions in child behavior problems when practitioners were present as parents used the program. In that study many of the parents did not complete the PW program because they ended up having discussions with the practitioner. In another study (Cefai et al., 2010), self-administered PW achieved superior outcomes compared to practitioner administered PW in a group setting. The self-administered parents reported a greater sense of self-efficacy compared to practitioner led use of PW. The Cefai et al. study suggests that parents were more likely to attribute the benefits of intervention to themselves because they chose to change their behavior after completing self-administered PW. Parents who change their behavior because a clinician suggested they do so are less likely to see the change as intrinsic or as due to their own choices. This increased self-efficacy may have contributed to the stronger findings for self-administered PW.

When using the PW together with their clients practitioners can reduce the likelihood of inadvertently compromising the program by doing the following:

➤ Monitor discussion time to ensure that there is adequate time to complete the computer portion of the program.

➤ If the client's discussion strays off topic, direct parents back to the program. This is easy to do with a click of the mouse.

➤ Use enthusiastic praise for parents' choices as they complete the program. Enthusiastic praise releases dopamine in the parent's brain, which helps the parent to focus and improves learning.

➤ Avoid statements that the parent might interpret as criticism. Do not confront parents on errors. As parents proceed with the program it will eventually cover the most common mistakes parents make. The positive content of the program will reduce most parents' use of ineffective or harmful parenting approaches. If the service provider confronts parents, this will probably increase resistance and will likely result in dropout.

➤ Look for opportunities to attribute concepts and principles to the parents in ways that reinforce parental self-efficacy. For example, it is better to say to the parent, "Your answer is absolutely right and this ties in with your earlier point about the importance of being consistent" instead of saying, "This ties in with an important principle taught in this program about being consistent."

➤ When parents report improvements with their child or family, attribute these changes to the parents' efforts and the new skills they are using.

Accessing Additional Program Support

Further information that can guide parent/practitioner discussions can be found in the service provider's manual and the group program curriculum that come with the program. Use of the discussion protocols in the group program likely contributed to the stronger outcomes for group use of PW compared to self-administered PW alone in the Pushak and Pretty (2008) evaluation. These protocols were not used in the Cefai et al. evaluation, where self-administered PW achieved stronger outcomes than group use of the program. The group curriculum provides further information on engagement strategies and provides information on role-plays that can help parents practice the skills taught by PW in a way that is supportive to the parent. Since the content for the program is computer-based, there is no need for practitioners to memorize copious materials to use the program. We have found that most service providers do not need more than minimal support to begin using the program. If practitioners require additional support in implementing PW they can contact Family Works at http://familyworksinc.com/. For families with many risk factors who are unlikely to use the self-administered PW or who have failed to use it, we have developed a 6-session *Brief Treatment* manual. The manual provides an approach that involves a combination of practitioner-led sessions with a parent where several of the scenarios are completed together, and self-administered PW is used for several scenarios. Parents are given homework assignments from the workbook, which are to be completed between sessions.

References

Cefai, J., Smith, D., & Pushak, R., (2010). The PW parent training program: An evaluation with an Australian sample. *Journal of Child & Family Behavior Therapy, 32,* 17–33.

Chaffin, M., Silovsky, J. F., Funderburk, B., Valle, L. A., Brestan, E. V., Balachova, T., . . . Bonner, B. L. (2004). Parent-child interaction therapy with physically abusive parents: Efficacy for reducing future abuse. *Journal of Consulting and Clinical Psychology, 72,* 500–510.

Gordon, D. A. (2003). Intervening with families of troubled youth: Functional family therapy and parenting wisely. In J. McGuire (Ed.), *Offender rehabilitation and treatment* (pp. 193–220). Sussex, England: John Wiley & Sons.

Gordon, D. A., Kacir, C. D., & Pushak, R. E., (2008). *Effectiveness of an interactive parent training program for changing adolescent behavior for court-referred parents.* Manuscript submitted to the Substance Abuse Mental Health Service National Registry of Evidence-based Programs and Practices.

Gordon, D. A., & Rolland-Stanar, C. (2003). Lessons learned from the dissemination of parenting wisely: A parent training CD-ROM. *Cognitive and Behavioral Practice, 10,* 312–323.

Hoskins, C., McFarlane, H., & Tattersall, A. (2002). *Greater Manchester pathways project: PW. Technical report to the youth justice board.* Unpublished manuscript.

Mukamel, R., Ekstrom, A., Kaplan, J., Iacoboni, M., & Fried, I., (2010). Single-neuron responses in humans during execution and observation of actions. *Current Biology, 20,* 750–756.

Patterson, G. R., & Chamberlain, P. (1994). A functional analysis of resistance during parent training therapy. *Clinical Psychology: Science and Practice, 1,* 53–70.

Pushak, R., & Nihie, R., (2005). *Assessing community practitioner's use of an evidence-based treatment program: Survey results on evidence-based family interventions.* (Unpublished manuscript).

Pushak, R., & Pretty, J. (2008). *Individual and group use of CD-ROM for parent training*. Manuscript submitted to the Substance Abuse Mental Health Service National Registry of Evidence-based Programs and Practices.

Rolland-Stanar, C., Gordon, D., A., Carlston, D., & Pushak, R., E., (2008). *Family violence prevention via school-based CD-ROM parent training*. Manuscript submitted to the Substance Abuse Mental Health Service National Registry of Evidence-Based Programs and Practices.

Segal, D., Chen, P. Y., Gordon, D. A., Kacir, C. Y., & Gylys, J. (2003). Development and evaluation of a parenting intervention program: Integration of scientific and practical approaches. *International Journal of Human-Computer Interaction, 15*, 453–468.

19

The Nurturing Parenting Programs

Preventing and Treating Child Abuse and Neglect

Stephen J. Bavolek and Rhenda Hotard Hodnett

Introduction

The Nurturing Parenting programs are family-centered, competency-based programs designed to build nurturing parenting skills as an alternative to abusive and neglecting parenting and child-rearing practices. First developed with funding from the National Institute of Mental Health (Bavolek, Comstock, & McLaughlin, 1983), Nurturing programs are empirically supported programs created to prevent recidivism of dysfunction in families receiving social services, lower the rate of multiparent teenage pregnancies, reduce the rate of juvenile delinquency and alcohol abuse, and stop the intergenerational cycle of child abuse by teaching positive parenting behaviors. The Nurturing programs target all families at risk for abuse and neglect from the prenatal stage of development to 18 years of age.

Identification of Abusive and Neglecting Parenting Patterns

The initial work in developing the Nurturing Parenting programs began with the research of Bavolek, Kline, and McLaughlin (1979) in testing the hypothesis whether the parenting beliefs of adolescents with known histories of abuse and neglect were different from the parenting beliefs of adolescents without known histories of maltreatment. To test the intergenerational hypothesis that abusive and neglecting parenting beliefs are passed down from parents to adolescents, the development of a valid and reliable inventory designed to assess abusive and neglecting parenting practices would be the first step. The question to answer was: What are the parenting practices of abusive and neglecting parents? Four distinct parenting patterns were identified and are presented in the form of parenting constructs. A parenting construct is a theoretical and empirical summary of a series of related behaviors that entail observable and consistent parenting practices that play a very significant role in childrearing. The following parenting constructs were identified as the patterns of parenting most likely responsible for child abuse and neglect.

Construct A: Inappropriate Parental Expectations

Beginning very early in the infant's life, abusive parents tend to inaccurately perceive the skills and abilities of their children. Inappropriate expectations of children are generally the result of parents simply not knowing the needs and capabilities of children at various stages of growth and development; feelings of inadequacy as an adult that stem from early childhood experiences of failure, ridicule, and disappointment; and generally lacking empathy that is required to determine what an appropriate expectation is for children at different stages of development.

Construct B: Parental Lack of an Empathic Awareness of Children's Needs

Empathy is the ability of being aware of another person's needs, feelings, and state of being. Empathic parents are sensitive to their children and create an environment that is conducive to promoting children's emotional, intellectual, physical, social, spiritual, and creative growth. Parents lacking sufficient levels of empathy find children's needs and wants as irritating and overwhelming. Everyday normal demands are perceived as unrealistic resulting in increased levels of stress.

Construct C: Strong Belief in the Use of Corporal Punishment

Physical punishment is generally the preferred means of discipline used by abusive parents. The effects of physical abuse are demonstrated in the observed destructive behaviors of children. It is a common tendency for abused children to identify with the aggressive parent in an effort to gain some measure of self-protection and mastery. Abused children often develop a set pattern of discharging aggression against the outside world in order to manage their own insecurities. Children who see and experience recurrent serious expressions of violence in their own family learn that violence is a way to solve problems.

Construct D: Parent–Child Role Reversal

A fourth common parenting behavior among abusive parents is their need to reverse parent-child roles. Children are expected to be sensitive to and responsible for much of the happiness of their parents. Parent-child role reversal is an interchanging of traditional role behaviors between a parent and child, so that the child adopts some of the behaviors traditionally associated with parents. In role reversal, parents act like helpless, needy children looking to their own children for parental care and comfort.

The findings in the study by Bavolek et al. (1979) found that significant differences did exist between the parenting beliefs of abused and nonabused teens in all four of the parenting constructs. The replication of the study with abusive and nonabusive adult parents produced identical findings (Bavolek, 1984). Abusive and neglecting parents expressed significantly more abusive parenting beliefs than nonabusive parents. In renorming the AAPI, Bavolek and Keene (2001) discovered yet a fifth parenting construct that was added to the AAPI-2, as described next.

Construct E: Oppressing Children's Power and Independence

Closely aligned with the value of physical punishment and the lack of an empathic awareness of children's needs is the belief that children's independence and power need to be oppressed. Parents fear that if children are permitted to use their power to explore their environment, or ask questions, or challenge parental authority, they will become "acting-out" and disrespectful. Hence, obedience and complete compliance to parental authority is demanded.

Adult–Adolescent Parenting Inventory (AAPI-2)

The identification and validation of the parenting constructs led to the development of the AAPI-2, a valid and reliable inventory designed to assess the parenting and child rearing beliefs of adult and teen parents and nonparents. Responses to the AAPI-2 provide an index of risk in each of the five parenting constructs. Based on the research validating the AAPI and AAPI-2, work on developing the Nurturing Parenting programs began, using the five parenting constructs of abuse and neglect as the foundation of the lessons.

Philosophy of Nurturing Parenting

The Nurturing programs have two distinct philosophical and educational paths: (1) to help families adopt the beliefs, knowledge, skills, and practices that make up the nurturing philosophy of parenting; and (2) to help parents adopt the philosophy that men and women who nurture themselves by getting their needs met are better equipped in becoming nurturing fathers and mothers.

The word *nurturing* comes from the Latin word *nutritura*, which means to promote, nurse, and nourish life. Strictly viewed as a process, however, the energy of nurturing is nondiscriminatory. That is, both positive and negative nurturing exists. As it applies to parenting, positive nurturing is nourishing the aspects of life we want for ourselves and for our children. Negative nurturing is nourishing the aspects of life we do not want for ourselves and for our children, but get anyway. The critical characteristic of positive nurturing parenting is *empathy*, which comes from the Greek word *empatheia*. Empathy means to project into or identify with another, to enter fully through understanding another's feelings or motives. Education in positive nurturing parenting embraces the concept of nonviolent parenting through building caring, empathic

Table 19.1 Positive Nurturing (Empathy)

	Positive Nurturing (Empathy)				
Frequency	Always	Frequent	Sometimes	Infrequent	Never
Intensity	Very High	High	Average	Low	Not Present
	10	9 8 7	6 5 4	3 2 1	0
	Negative Nurturing (Abuse and Neglect)				
Frequency	Never	Infrequent	Sometimes	Frequent	Always
Intensity	Not Present	Low	Average	High	Very High
	0	1 2 3	4 5 6	7 8 9	10

parent-child attachments. Empathy forms the cornerstone of the Nurturing programs. Negative nurturing parenting is called *abuse* and *neglect*. The word abuse comes from the Latin word *abusus*, which means to mistreat; cruel and harsh punishment. *Neglect* comes from the Latin word *neglegere*. Neg means *not* and legere means *pick up*. Neglectful parenting means not holding or touching children. To this end, positive nurturing and negative nurturing are two parenting styles that exist on a continuum of frequency and intensity from 0 to 10.

A review of Table 19.1 indicates that the presence of positive nurturing parenting as a 10 in frequency and intensity is the complete absence of negative nurturing (0) in both frequency and intensity. As positive nurturing parenting practices decrease, the frequency and intensity of abusive and neglectful parenting practices increase. A 10 in negative nurturing parenting translates to the absence of positive nurturing (0). The absence of any degree of positive nurturing often results in the death of the child. The basic premise of the Nurturing philosophy is that maltreatment to any frequency and intensity are unacceptable parenting practices. Nurturing Parenting embraces the practice of "reparenting." Through program lessons, new patterns of behavior replace old, destructive ones through systematic instruction in positive nurturing. Long-term dysfunctional patterns of parenting require long-term interventions. The goal of education is the ability to incorporate new knowledge, understanding, and skills into the daily lives of all family members.

Session Content

The Nurturing Parenting programs teach age-specific parenting skills as well as the need to nurture oneself as men and women. Each program session is divided into parenting instruction and self-improvement instruction. Lessons are generally designed to build self-awareness, positive concept/self-esteem and levels of empathy; to teach alternatives to hitting and yelling; to enhance family communication and awareness of needs; to replace abusive behaviors with nurturing behaviors to promote healthy physical and emotional development; and to teach appropriate role and developmental expectations of children.

Implementation of Program Formats

The lessons of the Nurturing programs can be delivered in a home-based setting, group-based setting, or combination of home and group settings.

Home-Based Nurturing Programs

In home-based settings, parents and their children enjoy separate and together times to strengthen their time together. Nurturing programs offered in a home-based setting are designed to meet weekly for 90 minutes. Home-based sessions involve parents and their children, as well as other significant family members who have "parental responsibilities" including teens, grandparents, and other extended family members. Each home visit begins with a "Check-In" time, which allows the home visitor and parent to get caught up with the events that went on in the family since the last home visit. The Home Practice Assignment is then reviewed in detail, ensuring that the parents are practicing the skills that are being taught in each session. If the home practice has not been completed, the Home Visitor will use this time to practice the skill with the parent. This time may entail a role-play between the parent and the home-visitor, or, if the child is present, the Home Visitor will monitor the activity and provide feedback. The main lesson follows the Home Practice Time. The lessons include the presentation of the concept or skill on DVD, followed by a discussion if the lesson is about a concept, artwork if the lesson deals with increasing self-awareness, or a role-play if the lesson addresses a skill. Following the lesson, the parent and the child have 30 minutes of interactive play activities designed to build the parent-child attachment. The Home Visitor observes the time and offers comments or direct instruction in teaching the skill. The Home Visit ends with a parent, child, and Home Visitor group hug.

Group-Based Nurturing Programs

In group-based settings, parents and children attend separate classes that meet concurrently. The frequency and length of the program sessions differs for each of the programs. Generally, group-based sessions run 2½ hours to 3 hours once a week. The number of group-based sessions varies from 12 (Parents and Adolescent program) to 27 (Parents and Their Infants, Toddlers and Preschoolers Program). In the group-based programs, Parents and Children attend separate groups that meet concurrently. Activities in the Children's group entail an active Hello Time, which involves song and perhaps a dance. Children then engage in art activities, discussion, puppets, playing games, and having free leisure time that allows them make choices in art, dress-up, blocks, or the reading corner. For teen groups, parents and teens engage in discussion, role-play, complete questionnaires and share responses, and learn to use art to draw themselves, their families, and their feelings. Parents also engage in self-awareness activities that involve art, music, psychodrama, music, meditation, and visualizations, as well as completing questionnaires and sharing responses, watching DVDs and role-playing the skills they are learning in the program.

Group-Based and Home-Based Combination Program Model

In home-based and group-based combination settings, families share the learning environment with other families but also have the one-to-one instruction of a home instructor. In situations of chronic maltreatment, an appropriate design is the combination of a series of group sessions interspersed with home visitations. The functional purpose of the combination of group- and home-based education is to allow parents the opportunity to practice and implement the parenting strategies discussed in the group. In this model, the education is competency-based, meaning that the group sessions may finish, but based on the attainment of the competencies, the home-based visitations continue until competencies have been learned.

Levels of Prevention, Dosage of Lessons, and Nurturing Program Format Descriptions

The Nurturing Parenting programs are designed for the prevention and treatment of child abuse and neglect. To meet the specific needs of families, programs have been identified according to the standard levels of prevention:

Primary Prevention: Education to prevent the initial occurrence of risk factors.

Secondary Prevention or Intervention: Actions taken to stop the further development of the risk factors and begin the process remediation.

Tertiary Prevention or Treatment: Actions taken to replace old, long-standing dysfunctional behavior patterns with newer, healthier ones.

Dosage and Levels of Prevention

Dosage (the number of lessons) is related to the severity of condition. To this end, the dosage is related to the levels of prevention:

Primary Prevention or Education

➢ Short term: 5 to 12 lessons

➢ Competency-based lessons

➢ Open-ended or closed-group delivery

➢ Prepost program assessment or individual session assessment

Secondary Prevention or Intervention

➢ Moderate term: 12 to 15 sessions

➢ Competency-based lessons

➢ Home visit or closed-group delivery

➢ Prepost program assessment with longitudinal follow-up

➢ Family-based when appropriate

Tertiary Prevention or Treatment

➢ Long term: 16 to 26 sessions

➢ Competency-based lessons

➢ Home-based, group-based, or combination home and group-based delivery

➢ Prepost program assessment with longitudinal follow-up

➢ Family-based program

Table 19.2 presents the Nurturing programs as they were designed to be most effective.

Teaching Aids

The program lessons are presented in activities manuals (training manuals) for parents, children, and adolescents. These manuals are program-specific and constitute the curriculum for each of the programs. Adult and teen participants receive handbooks

Table 19.2 Nurturing Parenting Program Reference Table by Levels of Prevention

	Group-Based	Home-Based	# of Sessions	Session Length	Child Care or Children's Program Curriculum
Prevention Programs (Primary Prevention)					
Prenatal Families	X		9	$2\frac{1}{2}$ hours	Child care
Community-Based Education in Nurturing Parenting	X		10	$1\frac{1}{2}$ hours	Parents only
Community-Based Education in Nurturing Parenting – Military Families	X		7	$1\frac{1}{2}$ hours	Parents only
Nurturing Skills for Families	X		12	2 hours	Parents & Children
ABCs for Parents and Their Children 5 to 7 years	X		7	2 hours	(Pre-K and Kindergarten)
Alcohol and Kids Don't Mix	X		5	$1\frac{1}{2}$ hours	Parents only
Alcohol, Anger, and Abuse	X		5	2 hours	Staff Training/Parents only
Nurturing Skills for Latina, Arabic, and Haitian Families	X	X	12	2 hours	Parents & Children
"Nurturing God's Way" Parenting Program for Christian Families	X		12	2 hours	Parents only
Parents and Their Children with Health Challenges	X		8	2 hours	Parents & Children
Intervention Programs (Secondary Prevention)					
Nurturing Skills for Families	X	X	15	1–2 hours	Parents & Children
Nurturing Skills for Teen Parents	X	X	15	1–2 hours	Parents & Children
Nurturing America's Military Families		X	16	1–2 hours	Parents & Children
Nurturing Skills for Latina, Arabic, and Haitian Families	X	X	15	1–2 hours	Parents & Children
Family Nurturing Camp Weekend Experience	X		N/A	N/A	Parents & Children
Families in Substance Abuse Treatment and Recovery	X		15	$1\frac{1}{2}$ hours	Parents & Children
Hmong Parents and Their Adolescents	X		12	3 hours	Parents & Children
Treatment Programs (Tertiary Prevention)					
Parents and Their Infants, Toddlers and Preschoolers	X		27	$2\frac{1}{2}$ hours	Parents & Children
Parents and Their Infants, Toddlers, and Preschoolers		X	55	$1\frac{1}{2}$ hours	Parents & Children
Parents and Their School-Age Children 5 to 11	X		15	$2\frac{1}{2}$ hours	Parents & Children
Parents and Adolescents	X		12	3 hours	Parents & Children
Teen Parents and Their Families	X	X	16	$2\frac{1}{2}$ hours	Parents & Children
Parents and Their Infants, Toddlers, and Preschoolers	X	X	16	$2\frac{1}{2}$ hours	Parents & Children
Nurturing Father's Program	X		13	$2\frac{1}{2}$ hours	Fathers only
Crianza con Cariño (Latina Parents and Children Birth to 12 Years)		X	55	$1\frac{1}{2}$ hours	Parents & Children
Crianza con Carino (Latina Parents and Children Birth to 12 Years)	X		16	$2\frac{1}{2}$ hours	Parents & Children

that present the information of the lesson in an easy-to-understand manner. The implementation manual describes the how-to's of implementing the programs, facilitating groups, gathering pretest and posttest data, recruiting families, and working with children. Parents view instructional DVDs, in which actors present examples of appropriate and inappropriate parenting practices. Parents have an opportunity to take on the role of the instructor and critique the quality of the parent-child interaction displayed in the video. Parents and their children also play instructional board games and card games to help build their nurturing skills and provide an opportunity for them to interact and have fun together.

Home Practice Assignments

Each week families are assigned Home Practice Assignments designed to build mastery and competence in new parenting skills.

Program Assessment and Evaluation

Data and information are gathered three times during the Nurturing Parenting programs.

Pretest and Posttest Data

Pretest and posttest data are collected at the beginning and end of each program with the following two instruments.

Adult-Adolescent Parenting Inventory (AAPI-2) A norm-referenced inventory designed to assess the parenting and child-rearing beliefs of adults and adolescents.

Nurturing Skills Competency Scale (NSCS) An inventory designed to assess six domains: About Me; About My Childhood; About My Spouse/Partner; About My Children and Family; My Knowledge of Nurturing Parenting; My Utilization of Nurturing Parenting Practices.

Process Data

Process data are gathered during the program sessions to ensure parents are learning new knowledge and skills. The following inventories are utilized to gather process data.

Family Nurturing Plan The Family Nurturing Plan (FNP) is a competency-based document that assists the parents and program facilitators in monitoring the acquisition of new knowledge, beliefs, and skills.

Family Nurturing Journal The *Family Nurturing Journal* (FNJ) is a document that encourages parents to keep track of changes that are happening to themselves, their children, and their family.

Session Evaluation Form The Session Evaluation Form is designed for parents to rate how well they learned each competency on a scale of 0 to 3.

Staff to Facilitate Programs

Professionals in parent education, social work, psychology, education, public health, and the general helping fields (medicine, mental health, parent aide programs, and home visitor programs) and paraprofessional home visitors are often facilitators of the parent, adolescent, and children's programs. Generally, two staff members are required to facilitate the parents' groups, and two or more staff members are required to facilitate the children's and adolescents' groups. Professionals who have previously facilitated groups and taught parenting education and who subscribe to teaching nonviolent, nurturing parenting values and practices can successfully facilitate the Nurturing Parenting programs.

Instructor Training

Instructor training workshops are 3 days. Costs vary depending on whether: (1) the workshops are sponsored by an agency seeking to implement the Nurturing Parenting program; or (2) the training is provided by the community, and participants register individually. In the latter case, registration fees generally average $250 per person. More information can be found at the following website: www.nurturingparenting.com

References

Bavolek, S. J. (1984). *Research and validation of the adult adolescent parenting inventory (AAPI-2)*. Park City, UT: Family Development Resources.

Bavolek. S. J., & Comstock, C. C. (1984). Child Resource World Review: Approaches to Child Abuse Prevention. International Child Resource Institute (publishers) Berkeley, CA # 2, 1984.

Bavolek, S. J., Comstock, C. C., & McLaughlin, J. (1983). The nurturing program for parents and children. Final report, NIMH Research Project.

Bavolek, S. J., & Keene, R. G. (2001). *Adult-adolescent parenting inventory (AAPI-2): Re-norming the data*. Asheville, NC: Family Development Resources.

Bavolek, S. J., Kline, D., & McLaughlin, J. (1979). Primary prevention of child abuse: Identification of high risk adolescents. *International Journal of Child Abuse and Neglect*, 3, 1071–1080.

PART VIII
An Evidence-Based Public Health Approach

In the final section and chapter of this book, Matthew Sanders, Ronald Prinz, and Cheri Shapiro describe an empirically supported public health approach to reduce the prevalence of child maltreatment. Their approach, the Triple P-Positive Parenting Program, has been designed to reach large segments of the population. It uses multiple strategies and components, including a media strategy that the Chapter 20 authors say aims to "normalize and de-stigmatize the process of seeking or receiving support for parenting" (Sanders, Prinz, and Shapiro, this volume). The approach also includes low- and high-intensity group interventions to parents at different levels of problems and risk. By describing the lessons learned from their research on implementing their program in various settings, their chapter also provides useful guidance for readers who might want to adopt one of the empirically supported programs described in other chapters of this volume. For example, they discuss the importance of and suggestions for stakeholder engagement, provider training, organizational consulting and technical support, and cultural sensitivity. Their chapter also offers some suggestions for alleviating the dual problem of maximizing fidelity when implementing empirically supported programs and interventions while at the same time being flexible in tailoring those programs and interventions to the unique attributes of local communities or individual clients.

20

Parenting and Child Maltreatment as Public Health Issues

Implications From the Triple P System of Intervention

Matthew R. Sanders, Ronald J. Prinz, and Cheri Shapiro

Child maltreatment and inadequate parenting are major public health issues with serious consequences for children, families, and society. The vast majority of parents caught up in the child welfare system for abuse or neglect struggle with parenting challenges. Parents cited for physical abuse obviously have a need to acquire noncoercive parenting methods to replace coercive and violent actions. The more common child maltreatment category of neglect also involves parenting issues, although this category is heterogeneous. Some parents cited for neglect might have engaged in parenting practices bordering on physical abuse but the caseworker either found it easier to document neglect or was not exposed to the physical abuse problem. In other words, being cited for neglect does not mean an absence of physical abuse. Additionally, many of the parents cited for neglect have serious parenting problems even if these have not risen to the level of physical abuse.

Why Adopt a Public Health Approach?

Child maltreatment and associated parenting problems fall on a continuum that also includes coercive practices not rising to the level of official maltreatment, the everyday difficulties in parenting faced by many parents, all the way to optimal parenting at the other end. Although substantiated child maltreatment is a low-frequency phenomenon, problematic parenting practices are much more common. Consequently, a public health approach is needed to reach large segments of the population. Instead of presenting a program labeled as addressing child abuse, a public health strategy involves the dissemination of parenting and family support presented as a normative, nonstigmatizing opportunity that any parent can use (Prinz, 2009b). A public health approach to parenting further builds on multiple strategies to efficiently serve many parents, including integration of media-based programming (Sanders & Prinz, 2008). A public health perspective has the potential to greatly increase the impact of evidence-based interventions targeting parents and families. However, a reduction in prevalence rates of child problems are unlikely to be achieved unless programmatic efforts are undertaken to increase the reach of efficacious interventions.

Need for Blending Universal and Targeted Interventions

Parenting and family support interventions can contribute to the prevention of child maltreatment and also address the needs of parents already in the child welfare system (Prinz, 2009a; Sanders, Cann, & Markie-Dadds, 2003). The Triple P-Positive Parenting Program (Sanders, 2008) is used as an example to illustrate how a system of parenting interventions can serve these separate goals by blending universal and targeted interventions that share a core set of positive parenting principles and practices. With only modest variation to accommodate setting and circumstance, this blended approach contributes efficiency and continuity while lowering stigma. We discuss the challenges involved in delivering a comprehensive system of parenting support, services, and programs. Policy implications for wider dissemination of parenting interventions and possible future directions for research are identified.

Description of the Triple P System

Triple P is a multilevel system of parenting and family support developed by Sanders and colleagues (Sanders, 2008). The Triple P-Positive Parenting Program began as an individually administered home-based intervention for parents of disruptive preschoolers (Sanders & Gylnn, 1981). It gradually evolved into a comprehensive multi-level population based system of intervention over a 30-year period.

Theoretical Basis

Triple P aims to prevent severe behavioral, emotional, and developmental problems in children and the abuse of children by enhancing the knowledge, skills, and confidence of parents. It incorporates five levels of intervention on a tiered continuum of increasing strength and narrowing population reach (see Figure 20.1) for parents of children and adolescents from birth to age 16. It blends universal and targeted or indicated interventions and seeks to serve all parents in a community.

Figure 20.1 depicts the differing levels of intensity and reach of the Triple P system. Level 1, a universal media and communication strategy, provides all interested parents with access to useful information about parenting through a coordinated print, electronic

Figure 20.1 **The Increasing Intensity and Breadth of Reach of the Triple P System of Intervention**

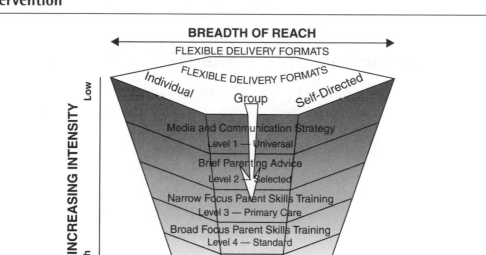

media, and promotional effort. This level of intervention aims to increase community awareness of parenting resources and the receptivity of parents to participating in parenting programs, and to create a sense of optimism by depicting solutions to common behavioral and developmental concerns. Level 2 is a brief, 1- to 2-session primary health-care intervention that provides early anticipatory developmental guidance to parents of children with mild behavioral difficulties. There is also a large group seminar series on positive parenting consisting of 2-hour stand-alone seminars. Level 3, a 4-session intervention, targets children with mild to moderate behavioral and emotional difficulties and includes active skills training for parents. Level 4 is an intensive 8- to 10-session individual or group parent-training program for children with more severe behavioral and emotional difficulties, and Level 5 is an enhanced behavioral family intervention program for families in which parenting difficulties are complicated by other sources of family distress (e.g., marital conflict, child maltreatment, parental depression, or high levels of stress).

The rationale for this tiered multilevel strategy is that there are differing levels of behavioral and emotional disturbance in children, and problematic parenting practices in parents. Parents also have different needs and preferences regarding the type, intensity, and mode of assistance they may require. The multilevel strategy is designed to maximize efficiency of program delivery, contain costs, avoid waste and over-servicing, and ensure that the program has the widest possible reach in the community. Importantly, the multidisciplinary nature of the program encourages the better utilization of the existing professional workforce in the task of promoting competent parenting.

Triple P targets five different developmental periods from infancy to adolescence. Within each developmental period the reach of the intervention can vary from being very broad (targeting an entire population) to quite narrow (targeting only parents of high-risk children). This flexibility enables practitioners to determine the scope of the intervention given their own service priorities, funding, and client needs.

Distinguishing Features of the Triple P System

Triple P shares some features in common with other parenting interventions based on social learning principles (e.g., use of active skills coaching methods, teaching parents positive ways to teach prosocial behavior and effective contingency management routines for dealing with disruptive behavior). Several aspects of the program differentiate it from other currently available evidence-based parenting programs such as the Incredible Years (Webster-Stratton, 1992), Parent-Child Interaction Therapy (Zisser & Eyberg, 2010), Treatment Foster Care (Smith, Chamberlain, & Eddy, 2010), and Helping the Non-Compliant Child (McMahon & Forehand, 2003). These are outlined next.

Triple P—An Integrated System of Interventions

Most parenting programs were designed to target a particular problem (e.g., non-compliance, aggression) in a defined group of children (e.g., disruptive preschool-age/young children). Although some programs have developed versions for other age groups (toddlers, teenagers) they typically use an 8- to 12-session format and are delivered on either a group or individual basis. In contrast, although Triple P began as an intervention delivered in parent's homes for disruptive preschoolers (Sanders & Glynn, 1981), it has evolved into a comprehensive multilevel system comprising a number of specific complementary parenting programs. It covers interventions from the antenatal period (Baby Triple P) through to the parenting of teenagers (Teen Triple P). The multilevel system blends universal and targeted interventions for each age group and has been successfully applied to a diverse range of child and family problems including children with disruptive behavior disorders (Bor, Sanders, & Markie-Dadds, 2002), developmental disabilities (Whittingham, Sofronoff, Sheffield, & Sanders, 2009), feeding disorders, pain syndromes, and obesity (West, Sanders, Cleghorn, & Davies, 2010), to name a few. It has also developed variants for a range of family types and circumstances (e.g., maritally discordant couples, parents going who are separated or divorced, parents with a mental illness, and parents with anger management problems).

A Self-Regulatory System

At all levels of the Triple P system there is an emphasis on the development of the self-regulatory capabilities of children, parents, providers, and organizations through the application of self-change skills. This self-regulation approach is applied through parent-child interactions where parents learn to promote independence and autonomy in children (e.g., providing descriptive praise when child completes task on his or her own). Practitioners' interactions with parents foster independent problem solving and specific techniques to enable parents to generalize the skills they learn across settings (e.g., various home and community situations), siblings, and time. Triple P professional training programs use exercises and activities that apply self-regulation strategies to develop practitioners' consultation skills (personal goal setting, self-monitoring, self-evaluation, and self-reinforcement). A peer supported self-regulatory approach to clinical supervision of trained and accredited professional staff is advocated to promote effective use of the program and to foster appropriate tailoring of interventions to the needs of families. Finally, disseminator-agency interactions promote each agency in developing its own customized application of Triple P tailored to local circumstances and opportunities. This customization might include making local decisions about target age groups or the program variants needed to meet local priorities (e.g., Primary Care Triple P as brief interventions; or group, standard, or enhanced variants as more intensive interventions). The expected consequence of this flexibility is that each Triple P site will be somewhat different from other sites using the same program. The rationale for this approach is that sites that use Triple P vary in the availability of well-developed parenting, prevention, and mental health services for children and youth, and resources to support parenting interventions (e.g., in poor rural communities, well-staffed medium-size cities, and major metropolitan areas).

The same self-regulatory framework used in working with parents and children and consistently applied throughout the Triple P system has been the hallmark of the dissemination efforts to bring Triple P to families in many diverse countries and cultures. The fundamental aim is to create a positive, self-sustaining social environment (in homes and communities) that supports children's development and that promotes competent parenting throughout their children's lives. The concurrent promotion of self-regulatory capacities of children, parents, practitioners, and agencies is the key to the development of such a family- and child-friendly environment.

The emphasis on self-regulation is infused throughout all levels of the program. It includes allowing parents to set goals for themselves, choose which parenting skills they plan to use with their children, which skills they will practice, and what homework tasks are selected, carried out, and reviewed in subsequent sessions. This approach is designed to reduce parental dependency and family resistance and to promote problem ownership and independent problem solving. However, it should not be confused with simply encouraging parents to do what they like with little or no guidance. On the contrary, there are extensive practitioner and program materials, which provide structure and guidance, particularly when the parent has limited self-regulatory capacity. However, this guidance in the form of DVD demonstrations of parenting skills, written and verbal prompts, and feedback from practitioner to parent can be faded progressively over the course of an intervention to avoid prompt-dependent learning. These teaching aids are used to the minimally sufficient degree required to enable a parent or practitioner to competently implement a skill.

Consumer-Informed Evidence-Based Practices

The Triple P system has continued to evolve over a 30-year period. This evolution is in part a response to end-user feedback from consumers—namely parents, practitioners, and organizations encountering the system. Triple P also evolved as a consequence of the decision to create a multilevel public health model of intervention, driven by continually emerging evidence regarding the efficacy of the intervention. Adoption of a consumer focus to program development has led to the increasing inclusion of qualitative data from focus groups (Sanders & Kirby, 2010), household surveys (Sanders, Markie-Dadds, Rinaldis, Firman & Baig, 2007) and web surveys (Sanders, Haslam, Calam, Southwell, & Stallman, in press) of parents to better identify the parenting tasks and family issues parents experience difficulties with or are looking for assistance with. For example, we have undertaken surveys of working parents (Sanders et al., in press) to better understand the parenting experiences of working parents and how they wished to access parenting support. This survey with British working parents showed that although many working parents had problems with their children, few had participated in a parenting program, but the vast majority said they would if delivered as an employee assistance program at work. Consumer input has continued to inform content and process of delivery for new variants of Triple P such as work with parents of multiples (Brown, Morawska, & Sanders, in prep), parents of children with cerebral palsy (Whittingham, Wee, Sanders, & Boyd, in press), parents of premature babies (Whittingham, Boyd, Sanders, & Colditz, in prep) and grandparents (Kirby & Sanders, under review). Consumer input provides useful information that assists programmers in identifying the kind of tailoring that would make parenting programs acceptable and relevant to different consumer groups. We have learned from this process that parents and practitioners can have markedly different views on parents' concerns and priorities and that parents as end users are probably the most valid source of this information about parental preferences. Practitioners should not function as *cultural gatekeepers* for parents' access to parenting programs. The views of practitioners are important in their own right. However, many practitioners have limited access to the population of parents who might benefit from parenting interventions and should not be seen as having the knowledge required to adequately represent parents at large.

Many Providers, Many Delivery Contexts

Although Triple P has its disciplinary origins in learning theory, developmental psychology, applied behavior analysis, and cognitive behavioral therapy methods, the intervention has also been strongly influenced by public health approaches that promote healthy living, including epidemiology, social marketing, communication and media research, and the diffusion of innovation literature. The intervention system works on the assumption that different types of professionals provide counsel and support to parents. Furthermore, the goals of prevalence rate reduction in problems such as child maltreatment and behavioral and emotional problems of children and youth are unlikely to be achieved by a single discipline. Many communities have a distinct shortage of suitably qualified staff to undertake evidence-based interventions. This is particularly the case in communities in rural or remote areas, areas with high concentrations of indigenous peoples or ethnic minorities, and in almost all low-income countries. As a result, the available workforce serving families is given priority to be trained to use evidence-based programs. Not to do so would virtually guarantee that families in many disadvantaged communities cannot access evidence-based programs. Although there is always likely to be debate about the necessary professional standards and qualifications required to deliver evidence-based parenting programs, we have chosen to train the existing workforce who are in an immediate position to implement Triple P. This decision increases the chances that low-income, relatively underserved populations can access Triple P because it does not require a new specially trained workforce to deliver the program.

Applying the Principle of the Minimally Sufficient Intervention

The Triple P system is based on applying the principle of the *minimally sufficient intervention*. This approach to intervention seeks to identify the minimally intrusive and least costly approach to assisting a parent or child or professional to learn a skill or new behavior. It is similar to the concept found in the special education and developmental disabilities literature regarding the least restrictive method of intervention used. This principle allows for considerable flexibility in responding to the needs of families. Some parents require and indeed seek brief low-intensity intervention such as self-help materials (e.g., tipsheets or self-help workbooks), while others may require more intensive intervention, including multiple sessions with practitioners either individually or in a group context.

However, the same principle can also apply to how interventions are delivered within levels (e.g., Selected, Primary Care, Standard, or Enhanced Triple P) or modalities (group, telephone assisted, web delivered). For example, in Standard Triple P where parents receive feedback from a practitioner after direct observation of parent-child interaction, a practitioner uses a self-regulatory approach that involves prompting parents to the minimally sufficient degree required to be able to: (a) self-identify their practice goal (e.g., increase descriptive praise comments); (b) self-identify what they did well during the interaction (e.g., got close); (c) what they need to do differently (e.g., remain calm); and (d) what their goal will be between this and the next session (e.g., remember to use incidental teaching when my child approaches me for help with something). A parent may initially need prompting to complete these tasks, such as: "So how did it go for the goal you set yourself?" or "So what did you do well?" However, once the self-regulatory review format is learned by the parent, the practitioner can be less intrusive and simply say, "Take it away. How did it go?" In this way parents become more active and self-sufficient in guiding their own learning. The practitioner provides scaffolding to enable the parent to reflect and review, to the minimally sufficient degree required. Of course, if the parents struggle or are unable to identify what they did well or not so well the practitioner provides partial feedback, such as, "Well, one thing I thought you did well today was that you got close to him when you asked him to do something," then prompts for further examples such as, "Can you think of anything else you did well or at least better than last time?" The rationale for such an approach is that an intervention is time-limited, while most parenting is done in private without help. Parents benefit from learning how to become more reflective in their parenting and change their own behavior.

Components of the Intervention

The Triple P system comprises five levels of intervention that blend a universal media and communication strategy with both low intensity and high intensity interventions tailored to the needs of parents.

Media and Communication Strategy

The aim of the first level of intervention (Universal Triple P) is to normalize and destigmatize the process of seeking or receiving support for parenting. This is particularly important for parents at risk of harming their children because completing a parenting class or course can be associated with stigma and fear that children may be removed by authorities from their care. This level of intervention can include the Stay Positive communications strategy, which encompasses media and communications strategies that promote positive parenting practices community-wide. Components include the Stay Positive website (see www.staypositive-triplep.net), brochures, posters, flyers, parent newspapers (*Tip* paper), media and communications kits, production of radio spots, a television spot, artwork for newspaper ads, and large and small format outdoor ads. Parents who might benefit from Triple P have a navigation route for identifying the appropriate level of intervention and delivery method to be used or to provide a referral to a provider trained at that level.

It is important to note that we focus on positive media messages about raising happy, healthy children and not on messages about child abuse. Media and communication strategies seek to promote engagement and interest in all parents though positive, aspirational messages focusing on the well-being of children and what parents can do to achieve this goal. These messages do not focus on how parenting programs prevent parents from harming children, or any other prevention message such as avoiding crime, substance use, school failure, or mental health problems.

Low-Intensity Interventions

Interventions at Levels 2 through 5 are typically delivered by a network of local providers from a variety of settings (e.g., home visits, health care, preschools, elementary schools, mental health, social services) who have completed a Triple P professional training course. Low-intensity parenting interventions in Triple P include a positive parenting seminar series (Level 2), brief 15- to 30-minute primary care consultations (Primary Care Triple P), or 2-hour parent discussion groups on specific topics (Primary Care Group Triple P). These interventions are designed to provide "light touch" options for parents to engage with Triple P. Each of these brief, low-intensity delivery options has been evaluated in its own right to ensure that interventions offered are efficacious; however, it is recognized that some families require more intensive services.

High-Intensity Interventions

Families that require more intensive programs can be referred to group Triple P (8 sessions), Standard Triple P (10 sessions), Pathways Triple P (12 sessions), or Enhanced

Triple P (12 to 16 sessions). Parents in the high-intensity category include those with a mental illness such as depression, parents with significant anger management problems, parents with high levels of interparental relationship conflict, and parents with high levels of stress. One such example of a more intensive variant of Triple P is Pathways Triple P. Pathways Triple P (PTP) is an adaptation of Group Triple P (see Sanders, 2008) and consists of four 2-hour group sessions, which specifically address the two risk factors associated with child maltreatment—dysfunctional attributions for parent-child interactions and parents' dysfunctional anger and angry-related behavior. In PTP, parents are taught a variety of skills aimed at challenging and countering their maladaptive attributions for parent-child interactions and to change any negative parenting practices they are currently using in line with these attributions. The attributional retraining strategies focus on teaching parents how to counter their misattributions regarding their child's negative behavior, and their negative parenting behavior toward their child. This involves teaching parents how to challenge their misattributions and generate more benign attributions regarding their child's negative behavior and generate less anger-justifying attributions for their own negative behavior. These sessions teach parents how to counter and alter not only their anger-intensifying attributional style for their child's behavior, but also their anger-justifying attributions for their negative parenting behavior.

Blending of Universal and Targeted Programs

The public health approach to parenting support that we advocate involves the synergistic blending of universal and targeted interventions for vulnerable groups in the same geographical catchment area. When a range of intervention options are available and wide population reach can be achieved, a vastly increased number of parents will participate in parenting programs. This increased reach has the potential to change the cultural context of parenting so that it become a healthy, normal, positive experience to participate in parenting programs, and the level of social isolation, ignorance, and program avoidance is minimized.

Implementation Issues: Lessons Learned From Large-Scale Trials

As indicated in Appendix A of this volume, Triple P is an evidence-based approach that has been put to the test of large-scale trials focused on community-wide effects. These trials have been conducted to focus on prevention of a wide range of adverse outcomes for youth, including behavioral and emotional problems as well as child maltreatment (Prinz, Sanders, Shapiro, Whitaker, & Lutzker, 2009; Sanders et al., 2008). Our discussion here focuses on implementation issues related to our efforts in the child maltreatment prevention arena.

Partnerships and Engagement of Stakeholders

Engagement of stakeholders across multiple human service systems likely represents one of the greatest challenges to implementing evidence-based parenting programs on a large scale. In order for parenting programs to have population-level reach, engagement of the existing provider workforce across traditional and nontraditional service settings is necessary. These service settings include child care, education, health, mental health, social services, and prevention services. However, a significant barrier to such engagement is the lack of a common infrastructure or organization for parenting support. Such duties are typically spread across a variety of organizations. Furthermore, many of these critical agencies and organizations do not share a mandate for provision of parenting support or education, despite their high level of contact with parents on a regular basis. If an organization does have a mandate to serve parents, the reach may be quite limited (e.g., only to parents in poverty or only for parents where child maltreatment has been indicated).

Parents must also be conceptualized as necessary stakeholders in any population-level rollout of a parenting support and intervention program. A major barrier to parent involvement is the lack of universal acceptance of the need for parenting support, coupled with the stigmatization of parenting services that are restricted to high-need parent populations. To change this negative perception, additional stakeholders for population-level interventions include the media and community leaders in a position to broadly promote and disseminate positive messages around parenting and help-seeking.

As noted by Horwitz, Chamberlain, Landsverk, and Mullican (2010), child welfare systems, in particular, may be poorly prepared to adopt innovations such as evidence-based parenting programs because implementation drivers, including development of knowledge and incentives for adopting evidence-based practices, are lacking (p. 32). An additional challenge for large-scale dissemination of evidence-based programs is the relative lack of awareness of such interventions among many child welfare service providers (Horwitz et al., 2010). Our experience with the U.S. Triple P Population Trial (Prinz & Sanders, 2006; Prinz et al., 2009) underscored the role of lack of awareness of Triple P as an initial barrier to organization-level engagement that was addressed through intensive contact by project staff (Shapiro, Prinz, & Sanders, 2010).

Stakeholder engagement is consistent with early stages of preparation for adoption of evidence-based innovations noted in implementation research. These initial stages include exploration or awareness of a need, identification of a program or intervention to fit that need, assessment of existing organizational resources, and the ability to address concerns prior to adoption (Fixsen, Naoom, Blase, Friedman, & Wallace, 2005; Greenhalgh, MacFarlane, Bate, & Kyriakidou, 2004). This initial exploration phase is critical to the process of engagement. Organizations need to be able to assess interventions for compatibility (the fit with agency needs, goals, and resources) prior to making an adoption decision. Such pretraining contact is necessary to examine the "ecological fit" of the intervention and the organizational context in which the program will be delivered (Sanders & Murphy-Brennan, 2010). It is important to note that the greater the level of pretraining contact on an agency level, the more prepared an organization and their staff are to receive the training and the more likely practitioners within those organizations are likely to implement the intervention. As noted by

Sanders, Prinz, and Shapiro (2009), use of Triple P by practitioners trained as part of the U.S. Triple P Population Trial was positively impacted by workplace support and lack of barriers to program use.

Stakeholder engagement can also be influenced by key individuals. Identified in the dissemination literature as opinion leaders or champions, they can impact engagement through social influence (Chrusciel, 2008; Greenhalgh et al., 2004; Zakocs, Tiwari, Vehige, & DeJong, 2008). In our experience, champions might also emerge over time. For example, individuals trained to deliver Triple P services who experience success can become influential in the engagement of both parents and other practitioners.

Another source of support for engagement are the purveyors of the intervention (Fixsen et al., 2005). Purveyors are defined by Fixsen et al. as those representing a program that actively work to support implementation. Triple P meets the Standards of Evidence criteria set forth by the Society for Prevention Research for dissemination (Flay et al., 2005), including technical support that can be accessed in the exploration phase of engagement.

Provider Training

Policy makers, organizations, and providers are increasingly focused on the need to provide evidence-based interventions. Bridging the science to practice gap by bringing evidence-based interventions to real-world settings places demands on both the evidence-based intervention itself, as well as on the provider systems into which the intervention is to be disseminated. Purveyors of the intervention must assure that all program materials and supports are in place, including the ability to train and support large groups of providers (Flay et al., 2005). The Triple P system has well-established manualized professional training courses for levels of the intervention involving direct contact with parents, along with an infrastructure for evaluation of both training staff and courses. Use of such standardized training materials prevents program drift, which is a serious concern with alternative "train the trainer" models of intervention (Sanders & Murphy-Brennan, 2010; Turner & Sanders, 2006).

In addition to high standards for the intervention itself, training providers in evidence-based interventions places specific demands on providers and organizations. Providers need to be able to access relatively intensive training that typically occurs over a period of days. Providers also need to have the time and organizational support necessary to achieve training goals. Triple P training requires attendance at a 1- to 5-day training course and attendance at a 1- or 2-day accreditation process involving competency-based assessments (Sanders & Murphy-Brennan, 2010). Many potential barriers exist to provider participation in training at this level that must be considered. Common barriers include workplace concerns regarding contact hour production or client services, lack of agency time for professional education, and lack of funding for staff training. To successfully launch provider training on a broad scale, these issues need to be resolved prior to scheduling training. Solutions to these dilemmas are influenced by organization-level variables such as type of services provided and organization size (Shapiro et al., 2010).

Posttraining Organizational Consulting and Technical Support

As noted by Sanders and Murphy-Brennan (2010), the posttraining environment represents the most important determinant of program implementation. This environment is multifaceted and includes aspects of the intervention itself, as well as characteristics of the organization such as goals and priorities, structure, and climate. Provider and client characteristics, as well as the larger social and fiscal context in which organizations operate, must also be considered when examining the posttraining environment (Fixsen et al., 2005; Sanders & Murphy-Brennan, 2010). Recent empirical work in this area found that utilization of Triple P was increased when providers received positive client feedback and had consulted with other Triple P providers; program use was less likely for providers who had with lower levels of self-confidence, difficulty integrating Triple P into their work, and where there was less workplace support (Sanders et al., 2009; Turner & Sanders, 2006).

In order to address the multitude of potential barriers to posttraining implementation of evidence-based interventions, Triple P has established a posttraining technical support system (which, we must stress, cannot compensate for inadequate assessment of compatibility between an intervention and agency or service system needs and priorities prior to implementation). As noted by Fixsen et al. (2005), implementation is a process, not an event. During the initial implementation phase, the primary focus of consultation is typically with issues related to assimilation of the intervention into services as usual. This process can be supported by active discussions between the purveyor and the organization. This type of support is critical for Triple P, in part because of the built-in flexibility of the model. A common potential barrier for providers and organizations newly trained in an evidence-based model is rigid adherence to a manualized intervention. As noted by Mazzucchelli and Sanders (2010) rigid adherence is neither desirable nor appropriate when delivering a clinical intervention. Posttraining consultation can help providers and organizations balance the tension between adherence and fidelity in a manner that can lead to positive outcomes for both providers and consumers.

Other unique features of Triple P that have been developed specifically to support posttraining implementation include the promotion of peer support strategies and access to a web-based provider network. Creation of peer support for the purpose of furthering the learning environment beyond initial training involves regular meetings to discuss cases using a self-regulatory framework. Professional growth and development training beyond formal coursework or degree programs rests on self-regulation—self-assessment, choosing professional goals, and engaging in activities to meet those goals (Falender & Shafranske, 2007). Use of a self-regulatory framework to guide provider self-evaluation of program implementation and self-selection of performance goals through peer support strategies promotes post-training implementation.

Another form of posttraining support in Triple P occurs through an online provider network. Use of technology provides ready access to program developments, answers to common implementation questions, and program materials to support implementation. Posttraining support for implementation also rests on engagement of key stakeholder group-parents that are the targets for support and intervention. Triple P uses the web-based provider network to disseminate universal strategies for parent engagement and the Stay Positive system mentioned earlier that includes articles, brochures, and other materials providers can use to promote Triple P services locally. Once accredited, providers can access these services as needed.

Cultural Diversity and Engagement of Parents

For population-level parenting interventions to be effective in reducing rates of child maltreatment, the intervention must be accessible to a wide range of parents of different ages, cultural backgrounds, beliefs, and preferences. For effective parent engagement, interventions must provide a range of options for obtaining parenting information and support. Triple P, as noted previously, consists of multiple levels of support to flexibly provide the amount and type of intervention parents need and desire. Interventions must also be culturally sensitive in order to reach the wide range of parents within targeted regions or populations. Triple P has a growing evidence base demonstrating efficacy, effectiveness, and acceptability of the interventions across diverse cultural and community groups (Heinrichs, 2006; Leung, Sanders, Leung, Mak, & Lau, 2003; Matsumoto, Sofronoff, & Sanders, 2009). Importantly, modifications made to the intervention to increase acceptability among culturally diverse populations have been what Mazzucchelli and Sanders (2010) term *low risk* modifications—that is, changes to intervention delivery procedures or modifications of strategies that do not represent major challenges to fidelity.

Considerations of cultural sensitivity must also include discussion of providers. Providers are gatekeepers for the implementation of evidence-based interventions with clients that they serve. Provider assumptions about whether an intervention is appropriate for a client should be examined carefully to determine the basis for this decision.

Fidelity Versus Flexibility

All evidence-based interventions struggle with the dual problem of promoting adherence to protocols used in clinical trials to establish the efficacy of interventions and the demand from practitioners for some flexibility in tailoring interventions to meet local needs. Mazzucchelli and Sanders (2010) recently argued that rather than seeing tailoring and adaptations by practitioners as a threat to the integrity of a program, developers need to be more explicit regarding the kinds of low-risk variations in both content and process of delivery that would be considered appropriate and legitimate that would not compromise the integrity of the program. Practitioners need to be trained in a manner that promotes their capacity to "generalize" their skills and knowledge to "nontrained" examplars, which may include somewhat different target populations than those used in foundational randomized trials (parents of multiples, parents with a hearing impairment, low-literacy clients). In order to generalize appropriately practitioners need to know how to discriminate when a variation is not appropriate or would seriously weaken an intervention (e.g., making untested assumptions about which Triple P parenting strategies an individual parent will find acceptable). Training of practitioners should treat flexible adaption as the rule rather than the exception. In other words, every application of Triple P needs to be tailored to the parent or group that is participating in the intervention. In many instances minor tailoring is required, such as example selection and emphasis given to certain skills. This training to flexibly generalize may increase the likelihood that practitioners will view interventions such as Triple P as consumer responsive, rather than formulaic, rigid, prescriptive, or nonresponsive to parents needs.

Quality Maintenance Issues

Quality maintenance refers to procedures used in the dissemination process to support the sustained effective use of an intervention over time. The training of a workforce to use Triple P effectively requires organizations to foster work practices that support the continued use of evidence-based programs. Organizations that commission training of staff need to ensure that they have the capacity and mandate to deliver the intervention. Investment in staff training can be wasted if practitioners do not use the program competently. Strategies such as briefings of line managers before staff attend training, the building in of staff time to attend peer support sessions, and, most importantly, of all having jobs that provide an opportunity to use the program as part of core business rather than as a "bolt on" helps to embed the delivery of the intervention in the culture of an organization and its service priorities.

Policy-Level Implications and Conclusions

A population-based approach to improving parenting has growing appeal as an important contributor to the prevention and reduction of child maltreatment (Barth, 2009; Prinz, 2009a; Sanders et al., 2003). Singling out small segments of the population for intervention is insufficient to reduce prevalence rates and has the potential to be off-putting or stigmatizing for parents. Prevention of child maltreatment does not just call for parenting intervention. The community must also address contributing factors such as parental substance abuse, domestic violence, and extreme conditions of poverty. But when parenting intervention is undertaken, it makes sense to adopt a population-level frame.

From a policy perspective, the key to the population approach is to derive other benefits besides prevention of child maltreatment from the same implementation of parenting and family support. A population approach to parenting and family support can play a role in the prevention of children's social, emotional, behavioral, and health problems, the facilitation of school readiness, and the promotion of overall child development. This coalescing of goals makes a cost effective approach (Foster, Prinz, Sanders, & Shapiro, 2008) even more attractive to policy makers.

References

Barth, R. P. (2009). Preventing child abuse and neglect with parent training: Evidence and opportunities. *The Future of Children, 19*, 95–118.

Bor, W., Sanders, M. R., & Markie-Dadds, C. (2002). The effects of the triple p-positive parenting program on preschool children with co-occuring disruptive behavior and attentional/hyperactive difficulties. *Journal of Abnormal Child Psychology, 30*(6), 571–587.

Brown, S., Morawska, A., & Sanders, M. R. (in prep). *Surviving multiples: An evaluation of a group behavioural parenting intervention for parents of twins and triplets.*

Chrusciel, D. (2008). What motivates the significant/strategic change champion(s)? *Journal of Organizational Change Management, 21*(2), 148–160.

Falender, C. A., & Shafranske, E. P. (2007). Competence in competency-based supervision practice: Construct and application. *Professional Psychology: Research and Practice, 38,* 232–240.

Fixsen, D. L., Naoom, S. F., Blase, K. A., Friedman, R. M., & Wallace, F. (2005). *Implementation research: A synthesis of the literature.* Tampa, FL: University of South Florida, Louis de la Parte Florida Mental Health Institute, the National Implementation Research Network (FMHI Publication #231).

Flay, B. R., Biglan, A., Boruch, R. F., Boruch, R. F., Castro, F. G., Gottfredson, D., Kellam, S. et al. (2005). Standards of evidence: Criteria for efficacy, effectiveness, and dissemination. *Prevention Science, 6,* 151–175.

Foster, E. M., Prinz, R. J., Sanders, M. R., & Shapiro, C. J. (2008). The costs of a public health infrastructure for delivering parenting and family support. *Children and Youth Services Review, 30,* 493–501.

Greenhalgh, T., Robert, G., MacFarlane, F., Bate, P., & Kyriakidou, O. (2004). Diffusion of innovations in service organizations: Systematic review and recommendations. *The Milbank Quarterly, 82*(4), 581–629.

Heinrichs, N. (2006). The effects of two different incentives on recruitment rates of families into a prevention program. *Journal of Primary Prevention, 27,* 345–365.

Horwitz, S. M., Chamberlain, P., Landsverk, J., & Mullican, C. (2010). Improving the mental health of children in child welfare through the implementation of evidence-based parenting interventions. *Administration and Policy in Mental Health, 37,* 27–39.

Kirby, J. N., & Sanders, M. R. (under review). Parenting across the lifespan: Consumer involvement in the development of a grandparent program. *Journal of Family Psychology.* Manuscript submitted on November 12, 2010.

Leung, C., Sanders, M. R., Leung, S., Mak, R., & Lau, J. (2003). An outcome evaluation of the implementation of the triple p-positive parenting program in Hong Kong. *Family Process, 42,* 531–544.

Matsumoto, Y., Sofronoff, K., & Sanders, M. R. (2009). The efficacy and acceptability of the triple P-positive parenting program with Japanese parents. *Behavior Change, 24,* 205–218.

Mazzucchelli, T. R., & Sanders, M. R. (2010). Facilitating practitioner flexibility within an empirically supported intervention: Lessons from a system of parenting support. *Clinical Psychology: Science and Practice, 17,* 3, 238–252.

McMahon, R. J., & Forehand, R. (2003). *Helping the noncompliant child: Family-based treatment for oppositional behavior* (2nd ed.). New York, NY: Guilford Press.

Prinz, R. J. (2009a). The dissemination of a multi-level evidence-based system of parenting interventions. *Child Welfare Journal, 88,* 142–147.

Prinz, R. J. (2009b). Towards a population-based paradigm for parenting intervention, prevention of child maltreatment, and promotion of child well-being. In K. Dodge & D. Coleman (Eds.), *Community prevention of child maltreatment.* New York, NY: Guilford Press.

Prinz, R. J., & Sanders, M. R. (2006). Testing effects on parenting at a broad scale: The U.S. triple p system population trial. In N. Heinrichs, K. Hahlweg, & M. Doepfner (Eds.), *Strengthening families: Different evidence based approaches to support child mental health.* Muenster, Germany: Psychotherapie Verlag.

Prinz, R. J., Sanders, M. R., Shapiro, C. J., Whitaker, D. J., & Lutzker, J. R. (2009). Population-based prevention of child maltreatment: The U.S. Triple P System Population Trial. *Prevention Science, 10,* 1–12.

Sanders, M. R. (2008). The triple p-positive parenting program as a public health approach to strengthening parenting. *Journal of Family Psychology, 22*(4), 506–517.

Sanders, M. R., Cann, W., & Markie-Dadds, C. (2003). Why a universal population-based approach to the prevention of child abuse is essential. *Child Abuse Review, 12*, 145–154.

Sanders, M. R., & Glynn, E. L. (1981). Training parents in behavioral self-management: An analysis of generalization and maintenance effects. *Journal of Applied Behavior Analysis, 14*(3), 223–237.

Sanders, M. R., Haslam, D., Calam, R., Southwell, C., & Stallman, H. M. (in press). Enhancing dissemination outcomes through a population-based approach to parenting intervention. *Journal of Children's Services*. Accepted August 31, 2010.

Sanders, M. R. & Kirby, J.N. (2010). Consumer involvement and population based parenting interventions. *Administration, 33*(2), 33–50.

Sanders, M. R., Markie-Dadds, C., Rinaldis, M., Firman, D., & Baig, N. (2007). Using household survey data to inform policy decisions regarding the delivery of evidenced-based parenting interventions. *Child: Care, Health and Development, 33*(6), 768–783.

Sanders, M. R., & Murphy-Brennan, M. (2010). Creating conditions for success beyond the professional training environment. *Clinical Psychology: Science and Practice, 17*, 1, 31–35.

Sanders, M. R., & Prinz, R. J. (2008). Using the mass media as a population level strategy to strengthen parenting skills. *Journal of Clinical Child and Adolescent Psychology, 37*, 609–621.

Sanders, M. R., Prinz, R. J., & Shapiro, C. J. (2009). Predicting uptake and utilization of evidence-based parenting interventions with organizational, service-provider and client variables. *Administration and Policy in Mental Health and Mental Health Services Research, 36*, 133–143.

Sanders, M. R., Ralph, A., Sofronoff, K., Gardiner, P., Thompson, R., Dwyer, S., & Bidwell, K. (2008). Every family: A population approach to reducing behavioral and emotional problems in children making the transition to school. *Journal of Primary Prevention, 29*, 3, 197–222.

Shapiro, C. J., Prinz, R. J., & Sanders, M. R. (2010). Population-based provider engagement in delivery of evidence-based parenting interventions: Challenges and solutions. *Journal of Primary Prevention, 31*, 223–234.

Smith, D., Chamberlain, P., & Eddy, M. (2010). Preliminary support for multidimensional support treatment foster care in reducing substance use in delinquent boys. *Journal of Child & Adolescent Substance Abuse, 19*, 343–358.

Turner, K. T., & Sanders, M. R. (2006). Dissemination of evidence-based parenting and family support strategies: Learning from the triple p-positive parenting program system approach. *Aggression and Violent Behavior, 11*, 176–193.

Webster-Stratton, C. H. (1992). *The incredible years: A trouble-shooting guide for parents of children ages 3–8 years*. Toronto, Canada: Umbrella Press.

West, F., Sanders, M. R., Cleghorn, G. J., & Davies, P. S. W. (2010). Randomised clinical trial of a family-based lifestyle intervention for childhood obesity involving parents as the exclusive agents of change. *Behaviour Research and Therapy*. doi 10.1016/j.brat.2010.08.008

Whittingham, K., Boyd, R., Sanders, M. R., & Colditz, P. (in prep). *Parenting and prematurity: Developing a tailored parenting intervention through a focus group of parents*.

Whittingham, K., Sofronoff, K., Sheffield, J., & Sanders, M. R. (2009). Stepping stones triple P: An RCT of a parenting program with parents of a child diagnosed with an autism spectrum disorder. *Journal of Abnormal Child Psychology, 37*, 469–480.

Whittingham, K., Wee, D., Sanders, M. R., & Boyd, R. (in press). Responding to the challenges of parenting a child with cerebral palsy: A focus group. *Disability and Rehabilitation*. Accepted October 22, 2010.

Zakocs, R. C., Tiwari, R., Vehige, T., & DeJong, W. (2008). Roles of organizers and champions in building campus community prevention partnerships. *Journal of American College Health, 57*, 233–239

Zisser, A., & Eyberg, S. M. (2010). Treating oppositional behavior in children using parent-child interaction therapy. In A. E. Kazdin & J. R. Weisz (Eds.), *Evidence-based psychotherapies for children and adolescents* (2nd ed., pp. 179–193). New York, NY: Guilford Press.

A
Empirical Support for the Programs and Interventions in This Volume

Allen Rubin

This appendix summarizes the key studies providing empirical support for the programs and interventions described in each chapter of this book. As will be seen, some of programs and interventions have more empirical support than others. Some have only modest empirical support. Some have quite a bit. As with all outcome evaluations in child welfare and related human services fields, none of the studies providing the empirical support are flawless. The various programs and interventions described in this volume vary not only in the number of studies supporting them, but in the degree of rigor in those studies.

However, each of the programs and interventions comprising the chapters of this book have been rated by the California Evidence-Based Clearinghouse for Child Welfare (www.cebc4cw.org/scientific-rating/scale) as having *at least* promising research evidence, which requires that there is no empirical evidence or theoretical basis indicating a substantial risk of harm and that at least one controlled study supporting its effectiveness has been published in peer-reviewed literature. Most of the programs and interventions in this book have received higher ratings by the clearinghouse, which deemed them to have much more than promising research evidence.

The rationale for deeming programs or interventions with only promising evidence to be empirically supported is based on the conceptualization of the phases of evidence-based practice (EBP) process. As discussed in various texts on research methods (Rubin, 2008; Rubin & Babbie, 2011) and in original sources describing the EBP process (Sackett, Rosenberg, Gray, Haynes, & Richardson, 1996; Sackett, Straus, Richardson, Rosenberg, & Haynes, 2000), deeming a program or intervention to have empirical support does not necessarily mean that a large number of rigorous experimental outcome studies have supported its effectiveness. That is because an important phase of the EBP process calls for practitioners to integrate the research findings with their knowledge of client attributes, needs, values, and preferences.

The EBP process involves five phases:

Phase 1: Formulate a question.

Phase 2: Search for evidence.

Phase 3: Critically appraise the evidence.

Phase 4: Integrate the evidence with practitioner expertise and knowledge of client circumstances, attributes, and preferences.

Phase 5: Monitor client progress.

The room for practitioners to use their expertise and judgment in the integration phase of the EBP process pertains to the important distinction between defining EBP as a *process* versus defining it as a list of approved interventions. The integration phase might involve recognizing that a program or intervention that has amassed the most or the best scientific evidence might not be a good fit for a particular client or community.

Suppose, for example, that Program A has amassed the most empirical support for its effectiveness, but that all of the studies that have evaluated it had excluded substance-abusing parents from their samples. In contrast, suppose Program B has been supported by only one or two fairly rigorous studies and has far less empirical support than Program A, but the Program B studies included many substance abusing parents in their samples. When selecting an intervention approach for substance-abusing parents, practitioners might be wise to be guided by the approach used in Program B, because it might be a better fit for their clients. Similar examples could be applied to differences in ethnicity, language, and other socioeconomic attributes between programs with a great deal of empirical support and those with much less.

Another way in which the EBP *process* differs from a list of interventions with a great deal of rigorous empirical support is that the EBP process recognizes that to have the *best* available empirical support for effectively intervening with a particular target problem does not necessarily imply having a great deal of rigorous empirical support. If only one or two moderately rigorous studies have ever been done regarding how to intervene effectively with a particular target problem and if they supported a particular intervention, then that intervention has the best empirical support for that particular target problem despite the limitations in that support.

Thus, the integration phase of the EBP process provides room for practitioners to select a program or intervention with only modest empirical support because: (1) that program or intervention might be a better fit for their clients than alternatives with more empirical support; and (2) that degree of empirical support, although modest, might be the only empirical support for intervening effectively for their particular target problem or target population.

In addition, pragmatic constraints might make it impossible to provide the program or intervention with the best empirical support. Some agencies might not be able to afford the program with the best empirical support. Practitioners might lack the training and supervision required to effectively provide the intervention with the best empirical support. They might not be able to afford the cost of such training, and supervisory resources might not be available in their area. And even if they could obtain the requisite training or supervision, that would take time, therefore making the intervention inapplicable for a client who needs help now.

Moreover, being supported by a large number of the most rigorous randomized clinical trials does not mean that an intervention will be effective with every client. There are always some clients who do not benefit from some interventions—including interventions with the best empirical support. Also, not all practitioners are equally skilled in providing interventions with the strongest empirical support. A particular practitioner might be more adept (and thus perhaps more effective) in providing an intervention with only modest empirical support than he or she is in providing an intervention that has stronger empirical support. If a practitioner ascertains—during the fifth phase of the EBP process—that the client is not making progress—he or she might conclude that a different approach is needed, one that has only modest empirical support but with which the practitioner is more skillful or that is a better fit for the client.

Chapter-by-Chapter Empirical Support

The remaining sections of this appendix provide chapter-by-chapter overviews of the empirical support for the programs and interventions that have been described in this book. Readers are advised to keep the above considerations in mind as they examine the following overviews.

Chapter 2

The effectiveness of the Incredible Years Series has been supported in multiple randomized controlled trials (RCTs) by its developer and by independent investigators in different countries, and across diverse high-risk populations. Significant improvements were found in parenting competencies, child social and emotional competence, and child behavior problems. Webster-Stratton and Reid (2010) provided a recent review of these studies, and the actual research articles in that review can be found at www.incredibleyears.com.

Chapter 3

MST-CAN is an adaptation of the Standard MST model. MST was selected as the basis of MST-CAN because the ecological focus and the way services are delivered matches the risk factors and serious clinical needs of families who are experiencing abuse or neglect and due to the strong empirical support for MST. This model is supported by 30 years of clinical trials showing efficacy and effectiveness for reducing youth criminal activity, out-of-home placements, and substance abuse. It is important to note that reviews of MST have been mixed. Littell, Popa, and Forsythe (2005) conducted a meta-analysis and concluded that MST was not significantly more effective that comparison treatments for reducing youth criminal activity and out-of-home placements. These findings have not been replicated in other meta-analyses of MST (Aos, Miller, & Drake, 2008; Curtis, Ronan,

& Borduin, 2004). To the contrary, MST has received favorable reviews by leading researchers in the field (Burns, Hoagwood, & Mrazek, 1999; Eyberg, Nelson, & Boggs, 2008; Farrington & Welsh, 1999; Hoge, Guerra, & Boxer, 2008; Stanton & Shadish, 1997; Waldron & Turner, 2008; Weithorn, 2005). In addition, MST has been viewed favorably by national (U.S.) entities that evaluate research. These include: President's New Freedom Commission on Mental Health (2003); Office of Juvenile Justice and Delinquency Prevention (2007); Center for Substance Abuse Prevention (2001); Center for Substance Abuse Treatment (1998); U.S. Surgeon General (U.S. Department of Health and Human Services, 1999; U.S. Public Health Service, 2001); National Institutes of Health (2006); National Institute on Drug Abuse (1999); National Alliance on Mental Illness (2003, 2008); National Mental Health Association (2004); Substance Abuse and Mental Health Administration's National Registry of Evidence-Based Programs and Practices (2007); Blueprints for Violence Prevention (Elliott, 1998); Institute for Public Policy Research (Margo, 2008); Washington Statue Institute for Public Policy (Aos et al., 2008); and Office of Justice Programs (2005).[1]

Chapter 4

Multidimensional Treatment Foster Care (MTFC) for adolescents has been supported in five RTCs. Three of the RTCs found it to be effective in the treatment of: (1) boys with severe delinquency and conduct disorders (Chamberlain & Reid, 1998); (2) children and adolescents leaving a state mental hospital (Chamberlain & Reid, 1991); and (3) girls with chronic delinquency (Chamberlain, Leve, & DeGarmo, 2007; Leve & Chamberlain, 2007; Leve, Chamberlain, & Reid, 2005). A fourth RTC found an approach based on the MTFC model to be effective in increasing the chances for reunification and in mitigating the chances for placement disruption risks for children age 5 to 12 in the child welfare system (Price et al., 2008). A fifth RTC found that MTFC is effective for preschool children in stabilizing placements and in increasing the likelihood of successful permanent placement outcomes (Fisher, Burraston, & Pears, 2005). Another outcome of this RTC was reported by Fisher and Kim (2007), who found that preschool children who received MTFC demonstrated significant increases in secure attachment and significant decreases in avoidant behaviors as compared to children in the control condition. The MTFC preschool children also had physiological improvements related to stress and dysregulation, and were comparable to children in a community comparison group in that regard, where the preschool children in the control group worsened.

Chapter 5

The effectiveness of parent-child interaction therapy (PCIT) has been supported by many rigorous outcome studies. It has been found to reduce the risk of child abuse (Chaffin et al., 2004; Chaffin, Funderburk, Bard, Valle, & Gurwitch, 2010; Thomas & Zimmer-Gembeck, 2011); improve parenting skills and attitudes (Harwood & Eyberg, 2006; Schuhmann,

---

[1] This summary of the research supporting Chapter 3 was written by Cynthia Cupit Swenson, the lead author of Chapter 3.

Foote, Eyberg, Boggs, & Algina, 1998); improve child behavior (Gallagher, 2003); and decrease child behavior problems and caregiver distress (Bagner & Eyberg, 2011).

Support for the generalization of PCIT has been demonstrated in studies showing improvements in child behavior in the school setting following treatment (McNeil, Eyberg, Eisenstadt, Newcomb, & Funderburk, 1991). Positive changes demonstrated in the behavior of untreated siblings support the generalization of the new parenting skills in the home (Brestan, Eyberg, Boggs, & Algina, 1997). In addition, follow-up studies have indicated that the treatment gains of PCIT are maintained over time, for as long as six years after treatment (Eyberg, et al., 2001; Hood & Eyberg, 2003). A meta-analysis of randomized control evaluations of PCIT found that it had mostly large effect-sizes in improving parenting behavior and reducing negative child behaviors (Thomas & Zimmer-Gembeck, 2007).

The efficacy of PCIT has been documented across cultural groups including Mexican American families (McCabe & Yeh, 2009), Puerto Rican families (Matos, Torres, Santiago, Jurado, & Rodriguez, 2006), Chinese families (Leung, Tsang, Heung, & Yiu, 2009), and Australian families (Phillips, Morgan, Cawthorne, & Barnett, 2008). Recent studies have demonstrated successful implementation in community mental health clinics in the US and abroad (Lyon & Budd, 2010; Phillips, et al., 2008).

Chapter 6

The effectiveness of the Coping Power program has been supported in seven RCTs that are summarized by the California Evidence-Based Clearinghouse for Child Welfare (CEBC, 2006–2007), which (like several other programs described in this volume) gave it the highest rating of "1" or "well-supported by research evidence."

Chapter 7

The interventions used in the Coping Cat program have been tested in five RCTs and were found to have success in helping children overcome anxiety related to generalized worry, separation from caregivers, and social situations (Flannery-Schroeder & Kendall, 2000; Kendall, 1994; Kendall et al., 1997; Kendall et al., 2008; Walkup et al., 2008). In addition, the long-term maintenance of treatment gains were supported in follow-ups of three of the RCTs (Flannery-Schroeder, Choudhury, & Kendall, 2005; Kendall, Safford, Flannery-Schroeder, & Webb, 2004; Kendall & Southam-Gerow, 1996).

Chapter 8

The most rigorous study supporting the effectiveness of Theraplay was an RCT conducted in Hong Kong, which found Theraplay to be effective in decreasing internalizing scores on the Child Behavior Checklist (Siu, 2009). Two other studies, conducted in Germany and Austria, have recently been reported by Wettig, Rand Coleman, and Geider (in press). Both examined improvements over time (before and after Theraplay treatment) among children with a dual diagnosis of social anxiety and language disorder. In the first study, the children made significant improvements on seven of nine symptom measures at posttest. In a 2-year follow-up significant improvements were achieved on eight of the nine measures, and none of the 20 children had relapsed. The second study found significant improvements on every variable at posttest (there was no longer-term follow-up), and for five of the nine symptom measures the treated children's mean posttest scores were not significantly different than the scores of a matched group of children with no history of language, behavioral, or neurological problems.

Chapter 9

In light of the replicated series of RCTs supporting it, trauma-focused cognitive behavioral therapy (TFCBT) is considered to be the gold standard for treating traumatized children and their nonoffending caregivers. Five RCTs have supported its effectiveness with sexually abused children (Cohen, Deblinger, Mannarino, & Steer, 2004; Cohen & Mannarino, 1996, 1996; Cohen, Mannarino, & Knudsen, 2005; Deblinger, Lippmann, & Steer, 1996; Deblinger, Stauffer, & Steer, 2001; King et al., 2000).

Chapter 10

Based on various meta-analyses and many well-controlled outcomes studies, EMDR (along with prolonged exposure therapy) is considered to be one of the two most empirically supported treatments for PTSD (Rubin, 2009). Although most of that research was done with adult participants, RTCs have emerged supporting the effectiveness of EMDR with children. In one RTC, for example, Chemtob, Kakashima, Hamada, and Carlson (2002) found it to be effective in treating children with disaster-related PTSD. Other RTCs have found it to be effective in treating boys with conduct problems, sexually abused girls, and children suffering from PTSD after familial abuse or neglect (Adler-Tapia & Settle, 2009).

Chapter 11

The effectiveness of Project Support has been supported in four studies, including three RCTs. In the earliest RCT, in which all participating children had either oppositional defiant disorder or conduct disorder, Jouriles et al. (2001) found that families in the Project Support condition had better outcomes than their counterparts receiving traditional services on measures of improvement in mothers' child management skills and in children's conduct problems. Those results were replicated in a later RCT (Jouriles et al., 2009), and another study found that the earlier study's results were maintained approximately two years after treatment (McDonald, Jouriles, & Skopp, 2006). In the most recent RCT, Jouriles et al. (2010) found that Project Support was effective in reducing problematic parenting and risk for further maltreatment in CPS-referred families.

Chapter 12

The effectiveness of Child-Parent Psychotherapy (CPP) has been supported in five RTCs. The samples in two of these studies consisted of mother-child dyads with attachment problems (Cicchetti, Rogosch, & Toth, 1999; Lieberman, Weston, & Pawl, 1991). Three of the RTCs involved samples comprised exclusively or primarily of families with a history of child maltreatment or domestic violence. In two of these three studies (Cicchetti,

Rogosch, & Toth, 2006; Toth, Maughan, Manly, Spagnola, & Cicchetti, 2002), the families treated with CPP did significantly better than controls on measures related to attachment problems. In the third study (Lieberman, Van Horn, & Ghosh Ippen, 2005), the CPP children had significantly better declines in trauma symptoms and behavior problems, and their mothers had better outcomes regarding avoidant symptoms. These results were further supported in a 6-month follow-up study (Lieberman, Van Horn, & Ghosh Ippen, 2006).

Chapter 13

The effectiveness of motivational interviewing (MI) for clients who abuse alcohol or drugs has been well supported in numerous controlled trials, as reviewed in a meta-analysis by Hettema, Steele, and Miller (2005). MI is listed on the California Evidence-Based Clearinghouse for Child Welfare (CEBC, 2006–2007) as an intervention to engage parents in substance misuse treatment with the highest rating of "1" or "well-supported by research evidence" (see Carroll, Libby, Sheehan, & Hyland, 2001; Mullins, Suarez, Ondersma, & Page, 2004). Chaffin et al. (2009) found that use of MI improved the engagement and retention of CPS parents in a parenting intervention (Parent-Child Interaction Therapy, as discussed in Chapter 5 of this volume).

Chapter 14

The effectiveness of the Parent-Child Assistance Program (PCAP) was supported in a controlled trial, nonequivalent groups design in which the PCAP mothers scored significantly better than controls at postintervention on a composite summary rating regarding substance use, risk and protective factors, and use of community services (Ernst, Streissguth, & Sampson, 1999). A subsequent study conducted an average of 2.5 years post–PCAP intervention found that the gains made by the PCAP mothers were maintained (Grant, Ernst, Pagaliauan, & Streissguth, 2003). The positive results of the controlled trial were replicated in pretest/posttest findings at two other PCAP replication sites (Grant, Ernst, Streissguth, & Stark, 2005).

Chapter 15

The effectiveness of the Homebuilders program in preventing out-of-home placements was originally supported in a nonequivalent comparison groups quasi-experiment (Wood, Barton, & Schroeder, 1988). Next, a randomized control trial by Fraser, Walton, Lewis, Pecora, and Walton (1996) found it to be effective in reunifying families and keeping them together. In a 6-year follow-up of the Fraser et al. experiment, Walton (1998) found that the families that received the Homebuilders intervention were more likely to remain stabilized than the controls. Later, Kirk and Griffith (2008) conducted a retrospective analysis of North Carolina's data archive on all 30,060 high-risk families during a 10-year period and found that minority children who received the Homebuilders intervention were less likely to be placed out-of-home than their counterparts who received traditional services. Although not every study evaluating the effectiveness of intensive family-preservation services has had results like the ones above, those with less positive results have been criticized for having changed the Homebuilders model or for not verifying fidelity to the model (Blythe & Jayaratne, 1999; Forrester, Copello, Waissbein, & Subhash, 2008). For example, Kirk and Griffith (2004) conducted an event history analysis of a statewide 6-year archival population of children in North Carolina's Child Protective Services and found that services based on the Homebuilders model were more effective than traditional services in reducing out-of-home placements when fidelity to the Homebuilders treatment model was high. Likewise, a meta-analysis of experimental and well-controlled quasi-experimental studies, conducted by the Washington State Institute for Public Policy (2006), found that programs that adhered closely to the Homebuilders model significantly reduced out-of-home placements as well as subsequent neglect and abuse, whereas programs that did not adhere closely to the model produced no significant effect on either outcome.

Chapter 16

Two studies using randomized experimental designs have supported the effectiveness of the 1–2–3 Magic program. The first (Bradley et al., 2003) found that one month after the intervention the 1–2–3 Magic participants scored better than wait-list controls on measures of parenting and child behavior. Most of the intervention group improvements were maintained in a one-year follow-up. Because only white, middle-class families participated in the study, the results might not generalize to families with other socioeconomic attributes. The second (Flaherty & Cooper, 2010) was conducted in a rural and economically disadvantaged area of New South Wales, Australia with parents/caregivers who had been reported for child abuse or neglect. The participants in the 1–2–3 Magic program "reported significant improvements in their mental health and discipline practices, and a significant reduction in child problem behaviour compared to the waitlist control group" (p. 18). The authors caution, however, that the positive results may have been inflated by a social desirability bias in the self-report outcome measurement procedure.

Chapter 17

The main study supporting the effectiveness of SafeCare (Gershater-Molko, Lutzker, & Wesch, 2002) used a quasi-experimental design that compared habitually maltreating families referred to the study by a local child welfare system to a matched control group of families participating in a family preservation program. The SafeCare families had significantly lower rates of recidivism at three years after the intervention. A key limitation in this study was the attrition in the SafeCare group; only families that completed all of the treatment components were included in the analysis, suggesting the empirical support for SafeCare as promising. That said, numerous single-case research design studies bode well for calling SafeCare efficacious. These studies show dramatic behavior change in health, safety, and parent-child interactions in many families. In addition, recent RCTs have found lower attrition rates among SafeCare providers who receive coaching and have also found lower risk scores, better engagement, and longer duration to first report for SafeCare families over control families. Citations for the empirical support for SafeCare can be found at their website at http://chhs.gsu.edu/safecare/2101.html#Empirical_articles_on_the_SafeCare_model

Chapter 18

Three RTCs have supported the effectiveness of Parenting Wisely in reducing behavior problems or increasing parenting skills with participants who were not in the child welfare system (Cefai, Smith, & Pushak, 2008; Kacir & Gordon, 1999; Lagges & Gordon, 1999). In addition, Gordon, Kacir, and Pushak (submitted) evaluated its effectiveness with court-mandated low-income parents of delinquent youths. Compared to a matched control group (with a potential selectivity bias), the Parenting Wisely group had better outcomes on measures of child behavior problems and parenting knowledge.

Chapter 19

The Nurturing Parenting Programs (NPP) have been consistently supported by three pretest/posttest evaluations (Cowen, 2001; Devall, 2004; Hodnett, Faulk, Dellinger, & Maher, 2009) and by a multivariate longitudinal analysis showing that caregivers who attended more NPP sessions were significantly less likely to be reported for child maltreatment at 6 months after participating in the program and significantly less likely to have a substantiated maltreatment incident at 2 years after participating (Maher, Marcynyszyn, Corwin, & Hodnett, 2010). The consistency of these findings provides an empirical basis for considering implementation of NPP where it is a better fit (in light of local circumstances and practitioner judgment) than other programs that have been supported by RCTs or well-controlled quasi-experiments.

Chapter 20

Because the Triple P system of intervention is a public health approach, the authors of the chapter on that system refer to the outcome research on it as providing evidence supporting a public health approach to reducing child maltreatment. For example, they note that in the U.S. Triple P System Population Trial a place randomization study of 18 counties tested the impact of Triple P disseminated population-wide on prevalence rates associated with child maltreatment. After training more than 600 service-delivery staff members from many settings in the implementation of Triple P, 2.5 years of programming resulted in significantly fewer child maltreatment cases, hospital-treated maltreatment injuries, and out-of-home placements (foster care) in the nine intervention counties compared with the nine comparison counties (Prinz & Sanders, 2006; Prinz, Sanders, Shapiro, Whitaker & Lutzker, 2009).

However, they also note that even with community-wide implementation of parenting and family support to reduce child maltreatment, parents in the child welfare system nonetheless need focused intervention services to improve parenting. Therefore, they cite evidence supporting the targeted Pathways Triple P, which is a specific element of the Triple P system that applies to parents who have engaged in child maltreatment or are at high risk to do so. For example, Sanders et al. (2004) examined whether PTP enhances clinical outcomes for either parent or child in families at risk of child maltreatment compared to Group Triple P. Parents participating in both versions of the Triple P behavior family interventions showed significant improvements across a wide range of indices of family functioning, with families receiving the Pathways Triple P intervention showing greater improvements on two key indicators of abuse potential both in the short and long terms (i.e., 6-month follow-up), namely anger-intensifying attributions and child-blame attributions. In further support of the efficacy of PTP, Wiggins, Sofronoff, and Sanders (2009) examined the effects of Pathways Triple P on 60 parents who met the inclusion criteria of borderline to clinically significant relationship disturbance and child emotional and behavioral problems. Participants were randomly allocated into PTP or a wait-list control group. PTP was delivered in a group format for 9 weeks and consisted of parent skills training and cognitive behavior therapy targeting negative attributions for child behavior. Participants in the PTP condition reported significantly higher levels of parent-child relationship quality from pre- to postintervention compared to participants in the control group with benefits maintained at 3-month follow-up. Participants in the PTP condition also reported a significantly greater increase in parent-child attachment, parenting confidence, and involvement than those in the control group, as well as a significantly greater reduction in the use of dysfunctional parenting practices such as laxness, verbosity, and overreactivity.

References

Adler-Tapia, R., & Settle, C. (2009). Evidence of the efficacy of EMDR with children and adolescents in individual psychotherapy: A review of the research published in peer-reviewed journals. *Journal of EMDR Practice and Research, 3*(4), 232–247.

Aos, S., Miller, M., & Drake, E. (2006). *Evidence-based public policy options to reduce future prison construction, criminal justice costs, and crime rates.* Olympia: Washington State Institute for Public Policy.

Bagner, D. M., & Eyberg, S. M. (2007). Parent-child interaction therapy for disruptive behavior in children with mental retardation: A randomized controlled trial. *Journal of Clinical Child & Adolescent Psychology, 36,* 418–429.

Blythe, B. J., & Jayaratne, S. (1999). *Michigan families first effectiveness study.* Report submitted to the State of Michigan Family Independence Agency.

Bradley, S. J., Jadaa, D., Brody, J., Landy, S., Tallett, S. E., Watson, W., . . . Stephens, D. (2003). Brief psychoeducational parenting program: An evaluation and 1-year follow-up. *Journal of the American Academy of Child and Adolescent Psychiatry, 42*(10), 1171–1178.

Brestan, E., Eyberg, S., Boggs, S., & Algina, J. (1997). Parent-child interaction therapy: Parents' perceptions of untreated siblings. *Child and Family Behavior Therapy, 19,* 13–28.

Burns, B. J., Hoagwood, K., & Mrazek, P. J. (1999). Effective treatment for mental disorders in children and adolescents. *Clinical Child and Family Psychology Review, 2,* 199–254.

California Evidence-Based Clearinghouse for Child Welfare. (2006–2007). Retrieved 7/20/2010, 2008, from http://www.cachildwelfareclearinghouse.org/

Carroll, K. M., Libby, B., Sheehan, J., & Hyland, N. (2001). Motivational interviewing to enhance treatment initiation in substance abusers: An effectiveness study. *American Journal on Addictions, 1,* 335–339.

Cefai, J., Smith, D., & Pushak, R., (2008). *The parenting wisely parent training program: An evaluation with an Australian sample*. Manuscript submitted to the Substance Abuse Mental Health Service National Registry of Evidence-based Programs and Practices.

Center for Substance Abuse Prevention (CSAP). (2001). *Strengthening America's families: Model family programs for substance abuse and delinquency prevention*. Salt Lake City: Department of Health Promotion and Education, University of Utah.

Center for Substance Abuse Treatment, Denver Juvenile Justice Integrated Treatment Network (CSAT). (1998). *Strategies for integrating substance abuse treatment and the juvenile justice system: A practice guide*. Denver Juvenile Justice Integrated Treatment Network.

Chaffin, M., Funderburk, B., Bard, D., Valle, L., & Gurwitch, R. (2010). A combined motivation and parent-child interaction therapy package reduces child welfare recidivism in a randomized dismantling field trial. *Journal of Consulting and Clinical Psychology*. Advance online publication. doi: 10.1037/a0021227

Chaffin, M., Silovsky, J. F., Funderburk, B., Valle, L. A., Brestan, E. V., Balachova, T., . . . Bonner, B. L. (2004). Parent-child interaction therapy with physically abusive parents: Efficacy for reducing future abuse. *Journal of Consulting and Clinical Psychology, 72*, 500–510.

Chaffin, M., Valle, L. A., Funderburk, B., Gurwitch, R., Silovsky, J., Bard, D., . . . Kees, M. (2009). A motivational intervention can improve retention in PCIT for low-motivation child welfare clients. *Child Maltreatment, 14*(4), 356–368.

Chamberlain, P., Leve, L. D., & DeGarmo, D. S. (2007). Multidimensional treatment foster care for girls in the juvenile justice system: 2-year follow-up of a randomized clinical trial. *Journal of Consulting and Clinical Psychology, 75*, 187–193.

Chamberlain, P., & Reid, J. B. (1991). Using a specialized foster care community treatment model for children and adolescents leaving a state mental hospital. *Journal of Community Psychology, 19*, 226–276.

Chamberlain, P., & Reid, J. B. (1998). Comparison of two community alternatives to incarceration for chronic juvenile offenders. *Journal of Consulting and Clinical Psychology, 66*(4), 624–633.

Chemtob, C. M., Nakashima, J., Hamada, R. S., & Carlson, J. G. (2002). Brief treatment for elementary school children with disaster-related posttraumatic stress disorder: A field study. *Journal of Clinical Psychology, 58*, 99–112.

Cicchetti, D., Rogosh, F. A., & Toth, S. L. (2006). Fostering secure attachment in infants in maltreating families through preventive interventions. *Development and Psychopathology, 18*, 623–649.

Cicchetti, D., Toth, S. L., & Rogosch, F. A. (1999). The efficacy of toddler-parent psychotherapy to increase attachment security in offspring of depressed mothers. *Attachment & Human Development, 1*(1), 34–66.

Cohen, J. A., Deblinger, E., Mannarino, A. P., & Steer, R. A. (2004). A multisite, randomized controlled trial for children with sexual abuse-related PTSD symptoms. *Journal of the American Academy of Child and Adolescent Psychiatry, 43*(4), 393–402.

Cohen, J. A., & Mannarino, A. P. (1996). A treatment outcome study for sexually abused preschool children: Initial findings. *Journal of the American Academy of Child and Adolescent Psychiatry, 35*(1), 42–50.

Cohen, J. A., & Mannarino, A. P. (1997). A treatment study for sexually abused preschool children: Outcome during a one-year follow-up. *Journal of the American Academy of Child and Adolescent Psychiatry, 36*(9), 1228–1235.

Cohen, J. A., Mannarino, A. P., & Knudsen K. (2005). Treating sexually abused children: One year follow-up of a randomized controlled trial. *Child Abuse & Neglect, 29*, 135–146.

Cowen, P. S. (2001). Effectiveness of a parent education intervention for at risk families. *Journal of the Society for Pediatric Nursing, 6*(2), 73–82.

Curtis, N. M., Ronan, K. R., & Borduin, C. M. (2004). Multisystemic treatment: A meta-analysis of outcome studies. *Journal of Family Psychology, 18*, 411–419.

Deblinger, E., Lippmann, J., & Steer, R. (1996). Sexually abused children suffering posttraumatic stress symptoms: Initial treatment outcome findings. *Child Maltreatment, 1*(4), 310–321.

Deblinger, E., Stauffer, L. B., & Steer, R. A. (2001). Comparitive efficacies of supportive and cognitive behavioral group therapies for young children who have been sexually abused and their non-offending mothers. *Child Maltreatment, 6*(4), 332–343.

Devall, E. (2004). Positive parenting for high-risk families. *Journal for Family and Consumer Sciences, 96*(4), 22–28.

Elliott, D. S. (1998). *Blueprints for violence prevention* (Series Ed.). University of Colorado, Center for the Study and Prevention of Violence. Boulder, CO: Blueprints.

Ernst, C. C., Grant, T. M., Streissguth, A. P., & Sampson, P. D. (1999) Intervention with high-risk alcohol and drug-abusing mothers: II. 3-year findings from the Seattle Model of Paraprofessional Advocacy. *Journal of Community Psychology, 27*(1), 19–38.

Eyberg, S. M., Funderburk, B. W., Hembree-Kigin, T. L., McNeil, C. B., Querido, J. G., & Hood, K. (2001). Parent-child interaction therapy with behavior problem children: One and two year maintenance of treatment effects in the family. *Child & Family Behavior Therapy, 23*, 1–20.

Eyberg, S. M., Nelson, M. M., & Boggs, S. R. (2008). Evidence-based psychosocial treatments for children and adolescents with disruptive behavior. *Journal of Clinical Child & Adolescent Psychology, 37*, 215–237.

Farrington, D. P., & Welsh, B. C. (1999). Delinquency prevention using family-based interventions. *Children & Society, 13*, 287–303.

Fisher, P. A., Burraston, B., & Pears, K. (2005). The early intervention foster care program: Permanent placement outcomes from a randomized trial. *Child Maltreatment, 10*(1), 61–71.

Fisher, P. A., & Kim, H. K. (2007). Intervention effects on foster preschoolers' attachment-related behaviors from a randomized trial. *Prevention Science, 8*(2), 161–170.

Flaherty, R., & Cooper, R. (2010). Piloting a parenting skills program in an Australian rural child protection setting. *Children Australia, 35*(3), 18–24.

Flannery-Schroeder, E., Choudhury, M. Y., & Kendall, P. C. (2005). Group and individual cognitive-behavioral treatments for youth with anxiety disorders: 1-year follow-up. *Cognitive Therapy and Research, 29*(2), 253–259.

Flannery-Schroeder, E. C., & Kendall, P. C. (2000). Group and individual cognitive-behavioral treatments for youth with anxiety disorders: A randomized clinical trial. *Cognitive Therapy and Research, 24*(3), 251–278.

Forrester, D., Copello, A., Waissbein, C., & Subhash, P. (2008, November-December). Evaluation of an intensive family preservation service for families affected by parental substance misuse. *Child Abuse Review, 17*(6), 410–426.

Fraser, M. W., Walton, E., Lewis, R. E., Pecora, P. J., & Walton, W. K. (1996). An experiment in family reunification: Correlates of outcomes at one-year follow-up. *Children and Youth Services Review, 18*(4/5), 335–361.

Gallagher, N. (2003). Effects of parent-child interaction therapy on young children with disruptive behavior disorders. *Bridges: Practice-Based Research Synthesis, 1*, 1–17.

Gershater-Molko, R. M., Lutzker, J. R., & Wesch, D. (2002). Using recidivism to evaluate project SafeCare: Teaching bonding, safety, and health care skills to parents. *Child Maltreatment, 7*(3), 277–285.

Gordon, D. A., Kacir, C. D., & Pushak, R. E. (submitted manuscript). *Effectiveness of an interactive parent training program for changing adolescent behaviour for court-referred parents.*

Grant, T., Ernst, C. C., Pagalilauan G., & Streissguth, A. P. (2003). Post-program follow-up effects of paraprofessional intervention with high-risk women who abused alcohol and drugs during pregnancy. *Journal of Community Psychology, 31*(3), 211–222.

Grant, T., Ernst, C., Streissguth, A., & Stark, K. (2005). Preventing alcohol and drug exposed births in Washington state: Intervention findings from three parent-child assistance program sites. *American Journal of Drug and Alcohol Abuse, 31*(3), 471–490.

Harwood, M.D., & Eyberg, S.M. (2006). Child-directed interaction: Prediction of change in impaired mother-child functioning. *Journal of Abnormal Child Psychology, 34,* 335–347

Hettema, J., Steele, J., & Miller, W. R. (2005). Motivational interviewing. *Annual Review of Clinical Psychology, 1,* 91–111.

Hodnett, R., Faulk, K., Dellinger, A., & Maher, E. (2009). *Evaluation of the statewide implementation of a parent education program in Louisiana's child welfare agency: The nurturing parenting program for infants, toddlers, and pre-school children.* Seattle, WA: Casey Family Programs.

Hoge, R. D., Guerra, N. G., & Boxer, P. (Eds.). (2008). *Treating the juvenile offender.* New York, NY: Guilford Press.

Hood, K., & Eyberg, S. M. (2003). Outcomes of parent-child interaction therapy: Mothers' reports on maintenance three to six years after treatment. *Journal of Clinical Child and Adolescent Psychology, 32,* 419–429.

Jouriles, E. N., McDonald, R., Rosenfield, D., Norwood, W. D., Spiller, L. C., Stephens, N., . . . Ehrensaft, M. (2010). Improving parenting in families referred for child maltreatment: A randomized controlled trial examining effects of Project Support. *Journal of Family Psychology, 24,* 328–338.

Jouriles, E. N., McDonald, R., Rosenfield, D., Stephens, N., Corbitt-Shindler, D., Miller, P. C. (2009). Reducing conduct problems among children exposed to intimate partner violence: A randomized clinical trial examining effects of project support. *Journal of Consulting and Clinical Psychology, 77,* 705–717. doi: 10.1037/a0015994

Jouriles, E. N., McDonald, R., Spiller, L., Norwood, W. D., Swank, P. R., Stephens, N., . . . Buzy, W. (2001). Reducing conduct problems among children of battered women. *Journal of Consulting and Clinical Psychology, 69,* 774–785.

Kacir, C. D., & Gordon, D. A. (1999). Parenting adolescents wisely: The effectiveness of an interactive videodisk parent training program in Appalachia. *Child and Family Behavior Therapy, 21*(4), 1–22.

Kendall, P. C. (1994). Treating anxiety disorders in children: Results of a randomized clinical trial. *Journal of Consulting and Clinical Psychology, 62*(1), 100–110.

Kendall, P. C., Flannery-Schroeder, E., Panichelli-Mindell, S. M., Southam-Gerow, M., Henin, A., & Warman, M. (1997). Therapy for youths with anxiety disorders: A second randomized clinical trial. *Journal of Consulting and Clinical Psychology, 65*(3), 366–380.

Kendall, P. C., Hudson, J. L., Gosch, E., Flannery-Schroeder, E., & Suveg, C. (2008). Cognitive-behavioral therapy for anxiety disordered youth: A randomized clinical trial evaluating child and family modalities. *Journal of Consulting and Clinical Psychology, 76*(2), 282–297.

Kendall, P. C., Safford, S., Flannery-Schroeder, E., & Webb, A. (2004). Child anxiety treatment: Outcomes in adolescence and impact on substance abuse and depression at 7.4 year follow-up. *Journal of Consulting and Clinical Psychology, 72*(2), 276–287.

Kendall, P. C., & Southam-Gerow, M. A. (1996). Long-term follow-up of a cognitive-behavioral therapy for anxiety-disordered youth. *Journal of Consulting and Clinical Psychology, 64*(4), 724–730.

King, N. J., Tonge, B. J., Mullen, P., Myerson, N., Heyne, D., Rollings, S., . . . Ollendick, T. H. (2000). Treating sexually abused children with posttraumatic stress symptoms: A randomized clinical trial. *Journal of the American Academy of Child and Adolescent Psychiatry, 39*(11), 1347–1355.

Kirk, R. S., & Griffith, D. P. (2004, March). Intensive family preservation services: Demonstrating placement prevention using event history analysis. *Social Work Research, 28*(1), 5–18.

Kirk, R. S., & Griffith, D. P. (2008). Impact of intensive family preservation services on disproportionality of out-of-home placements of children of color in one state's child welfare system. *Child Welfare, 87*(5), 87–105.

Lagges, A. M., & Gordon, G. A. (1999). Use of an interactive laserdisc parent training program with teenage parents. *Child and Family Behavior Therapy, 21*(1), 19–37.

Leung, C., Tsang, S., Heung, K., Yiu, I. (2009). Effectiveness of parent-child interaction therapy among Chinese families. *Research on Social Work Practice, 19*, 304–313.

Leve, L. D., & Chamberlain, P. (2007). A randomized evaluation of multidimensional treatment foster care: Effects on school attendance and homework completion in juvenile justice girls. *Research on Social Work Practice, 17*(6), 657–663.

Leve, L. D., Chamberlain, P., & Reid, J. B. (2005). Intervention outcomes for girls referred from juvenile justice: Effects on delinquency. *Journal of Consulting and Clinical Psychology, 73*, 1181–1185.

Lieberman, A. F., Van Horn, P., & Ghosh Ippen, C. (2005). Toward evidence-based treatment: Child-parent psychotherapy with preschoolers exposed to marital violence. *Journal of the American Academy of Child and Adolescent Psychiatry, 44*(12), 1241–1448.

Lieberman, A. F., Ghosh Ippen, C., & Van Horn, P. (2006). Child-parent psychotherapy: 6-month follow-up of a randomized controlled trial. *Journal of the American Academy of Child and Adolescent Psychiatry, 45*(8), 913–918.

Lieberman, A. F., Weston, D. R., & Pawl, J. H. (1991). Preventive interaction and outcome with anxiously attached dyads. *Child Development, 62*, 199–209.

Littell, J. H., Popa, M., & Forsythe, B. (2005). *Multisystemic therapy for social, emotional, and behavioral problems in youth aged 10–17* (Cochrane Review). In: *The Cochrane Database of Systematic Reviews, 4, 2005*. Chichester, UK: John Wiley & Sons, Inc.

Lyon, A., & Budd, K. (2010). A community mental health implementation of Parent-Child Interaction Therapy (PCIT). *Journal of Child and Family Studies, Vol 19*, 654–668. doi: 10.1007/s10826-010-9353-z

Maher, E. J., Marcynyszyn, L. A., Corwin, T. W., & Hodnett, R. (2010). *Dosage matters: The relationship between participation in the nurturing parenting program and subsequent child maltreatment*. Unpublished manuscript under review.

Margo, J. (2008). *Make me a criminal: Preventing youth crime*. London, England: Institute for Public Policy Research.

Matos, M., Torres, R., Santiago, R., Jurado, M., & Rodríguez, I. (2006). Adaptation of parent-child interaction therapy for Puerto Rican Families: A preliminary study. *Family Process, 45*, 205–222.

McCabe, K., & Yeh, M. (2009). Parent-child interaction therapy for Mexican Americans: A randomized clinical trial. *Journal of Clinical Child and Adolescent Psychology, 38*, 753–759.

McDonald, R., Jouriles, E. N., & Skopp, N. A. (2006). Reducing conduct problems among children brought to women's shelters: Intervention effects 24 months following termination of services. *Journal of Family Psychology, 20*, 127–36. doi:10.1037/0893-3200. 20.1.27

McNeil, C.B., Eyberg, S., Eisenstadt, T.H., Newcomb, K., & Funderburk, B. (1991). Parent-child interaction therapy with behavior problem children: Generalization of treatment effects to the school setting. *Journal of Clinical Child Psychology, 20*, 140–151.

Mullins, S. M., Suarez, M., Ondersma, S. J., & Page, M. C. (2004). The impact of motivational interviewing on substance abuse treatment retention: A randomized control trial of women involved with child welfare. *Journal of Substance Abuse Treatment, 27*, 51–58.

National Alliance on Mental Illness. (2003, Fall). *NAMI beginnings*. Arlington, VA: Author.

National Alliance on Mental Illness. (2008, Winter). Medicaid coverage of multisystemic therapy. *NAMI beginnings*. Arlington, VA: Author.

National Institute on Drug Abuse. (1999). *Principles of drug addiction treatment: A research-based guide*. NIH Publication No. 99–4180.

National Institutes of Health. (2006). National Institutes of Health state-of-the-science conferences statement: Preventing violence and related health-risking, social behaviors in adolescent, October 13–15, 2004. *Journal of Abnormal Child Psychology, 34*, 457–470.

National Mental Health Association. (2004). *Mental health treatment for youth in the juvenile justice system: A compendium of promising practices*. Alexandria, VA: Author.

Office of Justice Programs. (2005). *The OJP what works repository: Working group of the federal collaboration on what works*. Washington, DC: Author.

Office of Juvenile Justice and Delinquency Prevention. (2007). *The office of juvenile justice and delinquency prevention's model programs guide (MPG)*. Available from www.dsgonline.com/mpg2.5// TitleV_MPG_Table_Ind_Rec.asp?id=363

Phillips, J., Morgan, S., Cawthorne, K., & Barnett, B. (2008). Pilot evaluation of parent-child interaction therapy delivered in an Australian community early childhood clinic setting. *Australian and New Zealand Journal of Psychiatry, 42*, 712–719.

President's New Freedom Commission on Mental Health. (2003). *Achieving the promise: Transforming mental health care in America—Final report*. Rockville, MD: DHHS.

Price, J. M., Chamberlain, P., Landsverk, J., Reid, J., Leve, L., & Laurent, H. (2008). Effects of a foster parent training intervention on placement changes of children in foster care. *Child Maltreatment, 13*, 64–75.

Prinz, R. J., & Sanders, M. R. (2006). Testing effects on parenting at a broad scale: The U.S. triple p system population trial. In N. Heinrichs, K. Hahlweg, & M. Doepfner (Eds.), *Strengthening families: Different evidence-based approaches to support child mental health*. Muenster, Germany: Psychotherapie Verlag.

Prinz, R. J., Sanders, M. R., Shapiro, C. J., Whitaker, D. J., & Lutzker, J. R. (2009). Population-based prevention of child maltreatment: The U.S. triple p system population trial. *Prevention Science, 10*, 1–12.

Rubin, A. (2008). *Practitioner's guide to using research for evidence-based practice*. Hoboken, NJ: John Wiley & Sons.

Rubin, A. (2009). Research providing the evidence base for the interventions in this volume. In A. Rubin & D. W. Springer (Eds.), *Treatment of traumatized adults and children* (pp. 423–429). Hoboken, NJ: John Wiley & Sons.

Rubin, A., & Babbie, E. (2011). *Research methods for social work* (6th ed.). Belmont, CA: Thomson Brooks/Cole.

Sackett, D. L., Rosenberg, W.M.C., Gray, J.A.M., Haynes, R. B., & Richardson, W. S. (1996). Evidence based medicine: What it is and what it isn't. *British Medical Journal, 312*, 71–72.

Sackett, D. L., Straus, S. E., Richardson, W. S., Rosenberg, W.M.C., & Haynes, R. B. (2000). Evidence-based medicine: How to practice and teach EBM (2nd ed.). New York, NY: Churchill Livingstone.

Sanders, M. R., Pidgeon, A. M., Gravestock, F., Connors, M. D., Brown, S., & Young, R. (2004). Does parental attributional retraining and anger management enhance the effects of the triple p-positive parenting program with parents at risk of child maltreatment? *Behaviour Therapy, 35*, 513–535.

Schuhmann, E., Foote, R., Eyberg, S.M., Boggs, S., & Algina, J. (1998). Efficacy of parent-child interaction therapy: Interim report of a randomized trial with short-term maintenance. *Journal of Clinical Child Psychology, 27*, 34–45.

Siu, A.F.Y. (2009). Theraplay in the Chinese world: An intervention program for Hong Kong children with internalizing problems. *International Journal of Play Therapy, 18*(1), 1–12.

Stanton, M. D., & Shadish, W. R. (1997). Outcome, attrition, and family-couples treatment for drug abuse: A meta-analysis and review of the controlled, comparative studies. *Psychological Bulletin, 122,* 170–191.

Substance Abuse and Mental Health Services Administration (SAMHSA). (2007). National registry of evidence-based programs and practices. Available from www.nrepp.samhsa.gov/programfull details.asp?PROGRAM_lD=102

Thomas, R., & Zimmer-Gembeck, M. J. (2007). Behavioral outcomes of parent-child interaction therapy and Triple P—Positive Parenting Program: A review and meta-analysis. *Journal of Abnormal Child Psychology, 35,* 475–495.

Thomas, R., & Zimmer-Gembeck, M. J. (2011). Accumulating evidence for parent-child interaction therapy in the prevention of child maltreatment. *Child Development, 82,* 177–192. doi: 10.1111/j. 1467-8624. 2010.01548.x

Toth, S. L., Maughan, A., Manly, J. T., Spagnola, M., & Cicchetti, D. (2002). The relative efficacy of two interventions in altering maltreated preschool children's representational models: Implications for attachment theory. *Development and Psychopathology, 14,* 877–908.

U.S. Department of Health and Human Services. (1999). *Mental health: A report of the surgeon general.* Rockville, MD: U.S. Department of Health and Human Services, National Institutes of Health, National Institute of Mental Health.

U.S. Public Health Service. (2001). *Youth violence: A report of the surgeon general.* Washington, DC: Author.

Waldron, H. B., & Turner, C. W. (2008). Evidence-based psychosocial treatments for adolescent substance abuse. *Journal of Clinical Child and Adolescent Psychology, 37,* 238–261.

Walkup, J., Albano, A. M., Piacentini, J., Birmaher, B., Compton, S. N., Sherrill, J. T., . . . Kendall, P. C. (2008). Cognitive behavioral therapy, sertraline, or a combination in childhood anxiety. *New England Journal of Medicine, 359*(26), 2753–2766.

Walton, E. (1998). In-home family focused reunification: A six-year follow-up of a successful experiment. *Social Work Research, 22*(4), 205–214.

Washington State Institute for Public Policy. (2006). *Intensive family preservation programs: Program fidelity influences effectiveness.* Olympia, WA: Washington State Institute for Public Policy.

Webster-Stratton, C., & Reid, M. J. (2010). The incredible years parents, teachers and children training series: A multifaceted treatment approach for young children with conduct problems. In J. Weisz & A. Kazdin (Eds.), *Evidence-based psychotherapies for children and adolescents,* (2nd ed., pp. 194–210). New York, NY: Guilford Press.

Weithorn, L. A. (2005, Summer). Envisioning second-order change in America's responses to troubled and troublesome youth. *Hofstra Law Review, 33*(4), 1305–1506.

Wettig, H. G., Rand Coleman, A., & Geider, F. J. (2011). Evaluating the effectiveness of Theraplay in treating shy, socially withdrawn children. *International Journal of Play Therapy. 20*(1), 26–37.

Wiggins, T. L., Sofronoff, K., & Sanders, M. R. (2009). Pathways triple p-positive parenting program: Effects on parent-child relationships and child behaviour problems. *Family Process. 48*(4), 517–530.

Wood, S., Barton, K., & Schroeder, C. (1988). In-home treatment of abusive families: Cost and placement at one year. *Psychotherapy, 25*(3), 409–414.

APPENDIX B

The Evidence–Based Practice Process

Allen Rubin

As mentioned in this volume's introduction, in its original and most prominent definition, evidence-based practice is a five-step process for making practice decisions. The term *evidence-based practice* (EBP) sprang from the term *evidence-based medicine* (EBM), which was coined in the 1980s and was ultimately defined as "the integration of best research evidence with clinical expertise and patient values" (Sackett, Straus, Richardson, Rosenberg, & Haynes, 2000, p. 1). By including clinical expertise and patient values in the definition, EBM was distinguished from the notion that it was an unchanging list of approved interventions that physicians should implement even if they seemed to be contraindicated in light of the physician's knowledge about the patient. Nevertheless, as the concept of EBM spread to the nonmedical helping professions with the label EBP, some critics disregarded its integration component and misconstrued it as recommending that practitioners mechanistically implement scientifically approved interventions regardless of their clinical expertise and knowledge about client attributes, values, and preferences.

Pointing out the integration component of the EBP process is not meant to diminish the importance of the role of empirically supported interventions in EBP. The best research evidence is a key component of the EBP process. Indeed, this entire volume has aimed to facilitate your ability to find and implement interventions that have the best research evidence regarding their effectiveness with maltreated children and families at risk. In fact, the ultimate priority of the EBP process is to maximize the chances that practice decisions will yield desired outcomes in light of the best scientific evidence. Thus, the integration component of EBP is not meant to give practitioners so much wiggle room that they can disregard or diminish the importance of the best scientific evidence in making practice decisions. It just recognizes the need to blend that evidence with clinical expertise and client attributes.

There are various practical obstacles to the feasibility of the EBP process often encountered by clinicians. Key among those obstacles are the time, expertise, and other resources required to find relevant research evidence, to critically appraise various studies and sort through their bewildering array of inconsistent findings to ascertain which interventions are supported by the *best* evidence, and ultimately to learn how to implement one or more of those interventions. This volume has been geared to practitioners for whom those daunting obstacles make implementing the entire EBP process infeasible. However, if you would like to try to implement that process, the remainder of this appendix can guide you in a step-by-step fashion.

Step 1. Formulate a Question

The first step in the EBP process involves formulating a question based on a practice decision that you need to make. The question could pertain to any level of practice, including questions bearing on administrative or policy decisions. Here are four common types of EBP questions (Rubin, 2008):

1. What intervention, program, or policy is most effective?
2. What factors best predict desirable or undesirable outcomes?
3. What's it like to have had my client's experiences?
4. What assessment tool should be used?

At the clinical level, you are most likely to formulate the first type of question above—one geared to choosing the intervention that has the best chance to be effective for your client. This volume has been geared to that type of question.

In order to make the next step in the EBP process both expedient and productive, you will need to add as much specificity to your question as possible—without making it so specific that you will find no evidence bearing on it. To illustrate questions that are too broadly worded, I once went online to the *PsycINFO* literature database and requested that it show each published work that included all of the following three search terms somewhere in its text: *effective, treatment, trauma.* My implicit question was, "What intervention is most effective for treating trauma?" More than 1,000 published works came up. Too many!

My question was too broad. After all, there are many different types of trauma. So I redid my search, substituting *PTSD* for *trauma.* My implicit question was, "What intervention is most effective for treating PTSD?" That reduced the listed results to 677 publications. Still a lot. Assuming that my client was a victim of sexual abuse, I added the term *sexual abuse* to the search, with the implicit EBP question, "What intervention is most effective for treating PTSD among victims of sexual abuse?" That reduced the list to 51 published works—much more manageable and relevant to my hypothetical client.

To illustrate adding more specificity, I repeated my search by adding the term *African American* to the search, with the implicit EBP question, "What intervention is most effective for treating PTSD among African American victims of sexual abuse?" However, no works were found when I added that search term. The same happened when I substituted *Hispanic* for *African American.*

In formulating your EBP questions, it is usually best to go in the opposite direction, formulating a specific question, and then broadening it in your search if necessary. That way, you can skip the search term tries that give you too many publications that are irrelevant or tangential to your specific practice decision or client, and add (broadening) terms only as needed.

Not all EBP questions about effectiveness are open-ended, without specifying one or more specific interventions in advance. For example, perhaps you know that both EMDR and exposure therapy are accepted as the most effective treatments for PTSD and are wondering which has the best evidence. Your EBP question therefore might be, "Is EMDR or exposure therapy more effective in treating PTSD?" When I asked PsycINFO to find all publications that contained all of the following search terms—*EMDR, exposure therapy*, and *PTSD*—it listed 23 results.

Step 2. Search for Evidence

As a busy practitioner, the least time-consuming way to search for evidence is to use Internet search engines and electronic literature databases. *PsycINFO*, as discussed above, is one useful option. Using it requires a subscription, but there are ways to get around that cost if your work setting does not have such a subscription. One way is to see if you can get free access through any university faculty members or internship students with whom you are affiliated (especially if you serve as an adjunct faculty member or a field internship instructor). Another way is through your local library. Many local libraries provide free access to databases like *PsycINFO* for residents with a library card. You probably will not have to go to the library to use its computers; you should be able to do it all online from your own computer. There are many alternative electronic literature databases, including Google Scholar and MedLine. The nice thing about MedLine is that the National Library of Medicine offers free access to it at www.nlm.nih.gov

Although different professional literature databases typically require the entering of search terms to retrieve studies, they differ in their search rules and procedures. You will need to scan their search guidelines before proceeding so that you can expedite your search. For some databases, you can connect the various parts of your search term with words like AND, OR, and NOT. Using AND limits the number of studies that come up to only those that contain all of the keywords in your search term. For example, if you want to find studies that compare EMDR to exposure therapy, you could enter "EMDR AND exposure therapy." Using OR will expand the number of studies that come up. Thus, if you enter "EMDR OR exposure therapy," studies that come up will include those that look only at EMDR, only at exposure therapy, and at both (whereas using AND would include only those studies that look at both). If you enter "EMDR AND exposure therapy NOT pilot study," the list of references that come up will include those that address *both* EMDR *and* exposure therapy, but will exclude pilot studies. For some databases, such as *PsycINFO*, you will not have to enter the connecting words like AND, OR, and NOT. Instead, you can enter the keywords in different boxes that are prefaced with the connecting words.

So far I have been discussing the search for evidence in terms of looking for individual studies. Implicit in this approach is the need to critically appraise (in the next step of the EBP process) the quality of the evidence in each of the relevant studies that you find. A more expedient alternative would be to look first for systematic reviews of the studies already completed by others. This would also include meta-analyses, which are systematic reviews that pool the statistical results of the reviewed studies. Systematic reviews are expedient in several ways. First, they save you the time of searching for and reading individual studies. Second, they spare you the difficulty of critically appraising the research methodology of each study, which can be a daunting task for clinicians with limited expertise in research design, methods, and statistics. Third, even those studies that are methodologically rigorous and that supply the best evidence often report findings that are inconsistent from one study to another, and for some EBP questions, that inconsistency can be bewildering. A good systematic review will synthesize the various findings and provide you with a bottom line as to which interventions have the best evidence, for what types of clients and problems, and under what conditions.

Of course, an even more expedient way for busy practitioners to engage in EBP is to rely on volumes like the one you are reading. If you read Appendix A, you saw a synopsis of the ample empirical support—including systematic reviews and meta-analyses—for the interventions selected for this volume. However, if your EBP question is one for which no systematic reviews or books like this have been published, you may have no alternative to searching for and appraising individual studies. When you start your search, you will not know in advance what you will find. Assuming that time and other practical constraints make searching for individual studies an undesirable option from the standpoint of feasibility, I recommend that you begin looking for systematic reviews and volumes like this and then look for individual studies only as a last resort. That said, however, you need to be careful that the authors of systematic reviews or books like this do not have a vested interested in the interventions that they depict as having the best evidence. If I, for example, had developed or run workshops on the interventions described in this volume, then the credibility of the previous appendix on the supportive research would be highly suspect, and the value of this book's chapters therefore would suffer. In case you are wondering, I have no vested interest in any of the interventions described in this book.

You should also bear in mind that for some problem areas, different systematic reviews might produce different conclusions regarding which interventions have the best evidence supporting their effectiveness with that problem. For example, some authors with well-established reputations in EMDR have conducted reviews that concluded that EMDR is more effective than exposure therapy, while other authors have conducted reviews that reached the opposite conclusion, while still others conducted reviews that concluded that both interventions appear to be equally effective. Systematic reviews should be transparent about the presence or lack of vested interests by the authors of the review. Reviews that lack that transparency should be viewed with suspicion, as should reviews that admit to a vested interest, while reviews in which the authors have no vested interests probably should have the most credibility (all other criteria being equal, as will be discussed below).

Two highly regarded sources for unbiased and methodologically sophisticated systematic reviews are the Cochrane Collaboration and the Campbell Collaboration. Both are international nonprofit organizations that recruit into review teams researchers, practitioners, and consumers without vested interests in the subjects of their reviews. Each of their sites can be accessed on line. If you can find a review bearing on your EBP question in the onsite library at either of those sites, you can probably rely on it to answer your question and thus save you the trouble of searching for and appraising other sources of evidence. Moreover, their libraries also contain comments and criticisms of their own reviews as well as abstracts of other reviews, bibliographies of studies, reviews regarding methodology, and links that can help you conduct your own review. The Cochrane Collaboration focuses on reviews in the areas of health and mental health and can be accessed at www.cochrane.org. Its sibling organization, the Campbell Collaboration, focuses on reviews in social welfare, education, and criminal justice. You can access its website at www.campbellcollaboration.org.

Step 3. Critically Appraise the Evidence

The next step of the EBP process involves critically appraising the evidence found in the previous step. Being published is no guarantee that study's evidence is sound. Some studies are better than others, and some have fatal flaws that severely undermine their utility for guiding practice decisions. All studies have at least one or two minor flaws. Your prime task is not looking for the holy grail of a perfectly flawless study, but rather looking for one or more studies (or systematic reviews) whose strengths and relevance to your practice decision far outweigh their minor flaws.

The criteria to use in critically appraising any study depend on the nature of your EBP question. For questions such as, "What's it like to have had my client's experiences?" studies that employ qualitative research methods are likely to provide better evidence than quantitative studies such as experiments or surveys. For questions like, "What factors best predict desirable or undesirable outcomes?" studies that employ multivariate correlation analyses along with survey designs, case-control designs, or longitudinal designs may be your best bet. For questions like, "What assessment tool should be used?" you'll need to examine studies that administer assessment tools to large samples of people and calculate the tools' reliability, validity, and sensitivity.

As mentioned earlier, however, the most commonly asked EBP question asks something like, "What intervention, program, or policy is most effective?" For questions about effectiveness, the evidentiary hierarchy table in Table B.1 should guide your appraisal of the evidence.

It is beyond the scope of this appendix to explain everything in Table B.1. If you have had one or more good courses on research methods, perhaps you already have sufficient familiarity with the terminology and standards of research rigor to guide your appraisal. To brush up on that material, you might want to examine my book, *Practitioner's Guide to*

Table B.1 Evidentiary Hierarchy for Questions About Effectiveness (Best Evidence at the Top)*

Level 1	Systematic reviews and meta-analyses
Level 2	Multisite replications of randomized experiments
Level 3	Randomized experiments
Level 4	Quasi-experiments
Level 5	Single-case experiments
Level 6	Correlational studies
Level 7	Other:

➢ Anecdotal case reports

➢ Pretest–posttest studies without control groups

➢ Qualitative descriptions of client experiences during or after treatment

➢ Surveys of clients as to what they think helped them

➢ Surveys of practitioners as to what they think is effective

*This hierarchy assumes that each type of study is well designed. If not well designed, then a particular study would merit a lower level on the hierarchy. For example, a randomized experiment with egregiously biased measurement would not deserve to be at Level 3 and perhaps would be so fatally flawed as to merit dropping to the lowest level. The same applies to a quasi-experiment with a severe vulnerability to a selectivity bias.

Using Research for Evidence-Based Practice (Rubin, 2008). In the meantime, five criteria to keep in mind when appraising individual studies are:

1. Was a control group used?

2. Was random assignment used to avoid a selectivity bias that would make one group more likely to have a successful outcome than the other?

3. If random assignment was not used (i.e., in a quasi-experiment), do the authors provide solid evidence and a persuasive case for considering a selectivity bias to be unlikely?

4. Was outcome measured in an unbiased manner?

5. Were the attrition rates in both groups roughly equivalent?

Although the above list does not exhaust all the criteria to consider, if the answers to Questions 1, 4, and 5 are all *yes*, coupled with an affirmative answer to *either* Question 2 or 3, then chances are the study is supplying some relatively strong evidence regarding whether a policy, program, or intervention is effective.

When appraising systematic reviews (including meta-analyses), you should ask whether the reviewed studies were appraised in connection to the above types of evidentiary standards. Reviews can do so in two ways. One way is for the authors of the review to take the strengths and weaknesses of the reviewed studies into account when deriving their conclusions and guidelines for practice. The other way is to exclude from the review any studies that fail to meet certain evidentiary standards, such as the ones listed above.

As mentioned earlier, another important consideration when appraising a systematic review is whether the authors have vested interests in any of the policies, programs, or interventions addressed in the review and whether they are transparent about such vested interests. They also should identify the inclusion and exclusion criteria they used in selecting studies for their review and describe how comprehensively they searched for studies. For example, if they excluded studies of clients with substance abuse comorbidity from their review of treatment for PTSD, and your client has such comorbidity, then their review might have less value to you than one that included such studies. As to comprehensiveness, a key issue is whether the authors searched well for unpublished studies to include in their review, based on the notion that if only published studies are included, the deck might be stacked toward studies with findings supporting the effectiveness of interventions, since studies with null findings often are not submitted for publication.

Step 4. Integration, Selection, and Implementation

As mentioned earlier, the EBP process is not merely a mechanistic, cookbook approach in which practice decisions are made and implemented based solely on the best evidence regardless of clinician expertise and knowledge of client attributes and preferences. Consequently, after appraising the evidence, the next step of the EBP process involves selecting an intervention and implementing it only after integrating the critical appraisal of the evidence with your clinical expertise and knowledge of client circumstances and preferences. You might, for example, opt to implement an intervention that has the second or third best evidence because the studies done on that intervention involved clients like yours, where the studies done on the interventions with the best evidence involved only clients very unlike yours in ways that you deem to be very important. Likewise, your client might refuse to participate in an intervention supported by the best evidence, such as when some parents cannot be persuaded (through psychoeducation) to permit their child to undergo EMDR or exposure therapy because they fear such treatment would retraumatize their child.

Feasibility issues also must be considered. What if you lack training in the intervention supported by the best evidence? Is it possible to get the needed training? Can you afford the time and money that will be required? Can you get it soon enough? If you cannot get it, can you refer the client to another service provider who has the expertise to provide the desired intervention? If the answers to these questions are negative, the client might be better off if you provide an intervention that has the second or third best evidence but is one that you have the expertise to provide competently. If the preferred intervention is one covered in this volume, perhaps reading the pertinent chapter will suffice to get you started.

Step 5. Monitor/Evaluate Outcome

In the final step of the EBP process, you monitor or evaluate the outcome of the intervention (or other practice decision that is implemented in Step 4). You might wonder why this final step is needed. After all, haven't you implemented the option that has already been evaluated and found to have the best evidence supporting its effectiveness? There are several answers to these questions. One reason is that even in studies providing the best evidence some of the participants do not benefit from the empirically supported interventions. A related reason is that those studies might not have included participants with some of your client's key attributes. A third reason is that in Step 4 you may have opted for an intervention that does not have the best evidence.

Moreover, you might complete all four preceding steps and find no empirically supported intervention that fits your client. You may therefore have to proceed according to theory or clinical judgment, alone, thus implementing an intervention that lacks empirical support. Keep in mind that doing so does not mean you have violated the EBP process. The fact that you completed the preceding steps means you have implemented the EBP process even if your search is fruitless. But if that is so, then it is all the more important to complete the final step of the process; that is, to evaluate whether the intervention you have chosen attains the desired outcome.

A final reason for the final step of the EBP process is the possibility that you might not implement the selected intervention in a sufficiently competent manner. Remember, even the best evidence is only probabilistic. Rather than assure treatment success, it merely means that the chosen intervention has the best *likelihood* of success.

Now that you see the rationale for this final step, you might wonder how to do it. Your options are many, and some might be a lot more feasible for you than you think. The most feasible options pertain to situations where you have implemented an intervention that has already been supported by strong studies. In such situations, you should not feel the need to employ a sophisticated evaluation design aimed at producing causal inferences about whether the chosen intervention is really the cause of any client outcomes. Instead, all you need to do is monitor client outcomes. That is, you just need to see if the client achieves his or her desired outcome, regardless of the cause. That is because previous studies have already produced probabilistic causal evidence about the intervention, and your task as a practitioner (and not as a researcher), therefore, is merely to see if your client gets where he or she wants to go after receiving that intervention and whether (assuming a desired outcome is not attained) a different intervention may need to be introduced.

For a comprehensive guide to monitoring client progress, you can examine Chapter 12 of the book I mentioned earlier (Rubin, 2008). For example, if you are monitoring a client's PTSD symptoms, the client could self-monitor one or more symptoms (including perhaps just one overall rating of the day's symptoms) by completing an individualized self-rating scale each day, such as the one shown in Figure B.1 from Rubin (2008, p. 259).

You could graph the daily ratings chronologically, as appears in Figure B.2, to see if the desired level of progress is being achieved. The graph in Figure B.2 (from Rubin, 2008, p. 257) would indicate a successful outcome was being achieved in reducing an undesirable symptom (or overall rating of PTSD symptoms in general).

In contrast, the graph in Figure B.3 (from Rubin, 2008, p. 257) illustrates an outcome in which progress was not being made with the selected intervention (Intervention A), but then after an alternative intervention (Intervention B) was introduced the desired progress was being achieved in reducing an undesirable symptom (or overall rating of PTSD symptoms in general).

Figure B.1 An Individualized Daily Rating Scale for Depressed Mood*

Instructions: At the end of each day, enter the day's date and then circle a number to approximate how depressed you felt on average for that day.

DATE	Average Level of Depression** for the Day							
	Not at all	→		Moderate	→			Severe
____	0	1	2	3	4	5	6	7
____	0	1	2	3	4	5	6	7
____	0	1	2	3	4	5	6	7
____	0	1	2	3	4	5	6	7
____	0	1	2	3	4	5	6	7
____	0	1	2	3	4	5	6	7
____	0	1	2	3	4	5	6	7

*The development of this scale was inspired by ideas in Bloom, Fischer, and Orme (2006).
**This scale can be adapted for other target problems or goals by substituting those problems (anxiety, anger, etc.) or goals (self-confidence, assertiveness, etc.) for depressed or depression.

Figure B.2 Illustration of a Successful Outcome in Reducing an Undesirable Symptom

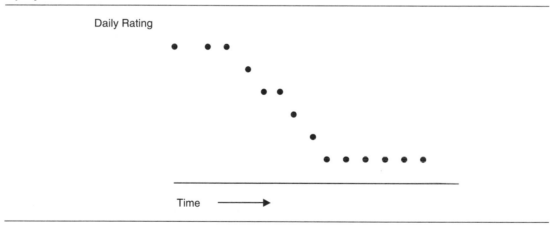

Figure B.3 Illustration of an Unsuccessful Outcome for Intervention A Followed by a Successful Outcome for Intervention B

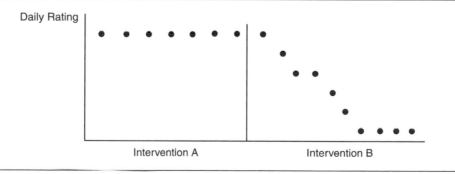

If you have implemented an intervention that lacks adequate prior empirical support, you might want to employ a more sophisticated evaluation design that aims to produce causal inferences (assuming, of course, that such a design is feasible for you). Such designs include experiments, quasi-experiments, time-series designs, and single-case experiments.

The above examples were discussed in the context of clinical practice with a specific client. However, they can be adapted to a macro level of practice in which you want to monitor or evaluate outcomes with a large number of clients or with an entire community. For example, if you want to see whether a new crisis intervention modality is more effective than previous efforts to prevent PTSD among victims of natural disasters, you could compare the incidence of PTSD among its recipients to the incidence among victims who received alternative or no crisis intervention modalities. To learn more about such macro evaluations, you can read Rubin and Babbie (2011).

The main thing to keep in mind about this phase of the EBP process, however, is to implement it in whatever way that is feasible for you. As a practitioner, you should not feel immobilized just because a rigorous research evaluation design is beyond your reach. Remember, all practitioners routinely have to make judgments as to whether what they are doing is working and whether they need to try something different. The same applies regardless of what you find and implement in the previous steps of the EBP process. The ideas presented here and in the suggested reference volumes can help you make your monitoring or evaluation efforts more systematic and doable. Just do the best you can, and good luck!

References

Bloom, M., Fischer, J., & Orme, J. G. (2006). *Evaluating practice: Guidelines for the accountable professional* (5th ed.). Boston, MA: Allyn & Bacon.

Rubin, A. (2008). *Practitioner's guide to using research for evidence-based practice*. Hoboken, NJ: John Wiley & Sons.

Rubin, A., & Babbie, E. (2011). *Research methods for social work* (6th ed.). Belmont, CA: Thomson Brooks/ Cole.

Sackett, D. L., Straus, S. E., Richardson, W. S., Rosenberg, W.M.C., & Haynes, R. B. (2000). *Evidence-based medicine: How to practice and teach EBM* (2nd ed.). New York, NY: Churchill Livingstone.

Author Index

Subject Index